"SEEING RED"

BLACKS IN THE DIASPORA

*Darlene Clark Hine, John McCluskey, Jr., and
David Barry Gaspar, General Editors*

"SEEING RED"

FEDERAL CAMPAIGNS

AGAINST BLACK

MILITANCY,

1919-1925

THEODORE KORNWEIBEL, JR.

Indiana
University
Press

BLOOMINGTON AND INDIANAPOLIS

This book is a publication of

Indiana University Press
601 North Morton Street
Bloomington, IN 47404-3797 USA

http://www.indiana.edu/~iupress

Telephone orders 800-842-6796
Fax orders 812-855-7931
Orders by e-mail iuporder@indiana.edu

The paper used in this publication meets the minimum requirements of
American National Standard for Information Sciences—Permanence of Paper for
Printed Library Materials, ANSI Z39.48-1984.

Manufactured in the United States of America

Library of Congress Cataloging-in-Publication Data

Kornweibel, Theodore.
  Seeing red : federal campaigns against Black militancy,
1919–1925 / Theodore Kornweibel, Jr.
     p.   cm. — (Blacks in the diaspora)
  Includes bibliographical references and index.
  ISBN 0–253–33337–7 (cloth)
  1. Black Power—United States—History—20th century.
2. Afro-Americans—Civil Rights—History—20th century.
3. Afro-American communists—History. 4. United States—
Race relations. 5. Intelligence service—United States—
History—20th century. 6. Anti-communist movements—
United States—History—20th century. 7. United States.
Federal Bureau of Investigation—History. I. Title. II.
Series.
E185.61.K59 1998
323.1'196073'00945—dc21   97–10294

ISBN 0-253-21354-1 (paper)

2 3 4 5 6 04 03 02 01 00 99

For Catherine

CONTENTS

ACKNOWLEDGMENTS

This book could never have been completed without the help and encouragement of numerous archivists and librarians, colleagues and students, friends and family members. When I began research on this topic in the National Archives, more than fifteen years ago, the staff of half a dozen branches—now combined into the Civil Reference and Military Reference branches— proved extremely knowledgeable and helpful. Especially valuable was the assistance of Susan Rosenfeld and Mike McReynolds in the old Judicial and Fiscal Branch. Later, staff at National Archives branches in Suitland, Maryland; Bayonne, New Jersey; East Point, Georgia; Chicago; Kansas City; Fort Worth; and Laguna Niguel, California, gave me additional help. Prying case files out of the FBI through the Freedom of Information Act was an arduous process, but at key roadblocks I was greatly assisted by Susan Rosenfeld, who left the Archives to become the FBI's official historian. The FBI stonewalled on some important FOI requests, however, and I regret that it proceeded to destroy personnel files of all but a few of its early agents, records which would have proven enormously useful to me and any other scholars working on the Bureau of Investigation's history.

Librarians and archivists at the following institutions also proved helpful as I used their manuscript collections: the Library of Congress Manuscript Division; New York Public Library; Ohio Historical Society; Hoover Institution; Howard University; Yale University; SUNY Buffalo; University of Texas; and East Carolina University. Financial support for travel and research expenses, granted by San Diego State University, the National Endowment for the Humanities, and the American Philosophical Society, is gratefully acknowledged.

I could not have achieved complete coverage of the National Archives' Bureau of Investigation case files without the Howard University students who laboriously combed the microfilm index reels for the names of black individuals, organizations, and publications. I also owe a great debt to my research assistants Kathy Weakley, Margaret Grimshaw, Sharon Odegaard, and T. J. Roman, who abstracted thousands of pages of case files. Randy Boehm, of University Publications of America, applied his broad knowledge of federal archives to help search for documents to include in my 25-reel microfilm collection, *Federal Surveillance of Afro-Americans (1917–1925): The First World War, the Red Scare, and the Garvey Movement* (1986). Many of the documents cited in the present volume, and in a book-in-progress on the World War I years, can be found in these microfilms. Special thanks go to Gerald E. Sullivan, whose computer programming made working with such a large number of documents almost easy.

The suggestions and criticisms of colleagues and conference commentators helped me sharpen my focus and avoid numerous mistakes. Whatever errors remain are my responsibility, not theirs. Susan Rosenfeld, now an independent scholar, applied her vast knowledge of the FBI and the Justice Department to the entire manuscript, and she has my special thanks. Colleagues Francis Stites and Richard Steele also read the full manuscript, and I profited greatly from their comments. Sharon Odegaard applied her editorial skills as the final draft took shape. Portions of my research were presented at professional meetings over the last decade, and the following commentators and co-panelists offered helpful suggestions: Ernest Allen, Jr., Jay Beaman, Michael Casey, Murray W. Dempster, Vincent Fort, David J. Garrow, Charles H. Martin, Kenneth O'Reilly, Judith Stein, Roy Talbert, Jr., Athan Theoharis, Emory Tolbert, and Patrick S. Washburn.

I am especially grateful to the many friends who had confidence in this project for so long, and who never gave up on me when I couldn't answer their question, "When is your book going to come out?" I am saddened that my mother and younger brother did not live to see this publication, because they, too, looked forward to its completion. My sons Daniel and James spent many weeks of early childhood with their father away from home, doing research in Washington. The burden for keeping the family together fell to my precious wife Catherine, to whom I owe more thanks than I can put in words. Rarely complaining about my absences, prodding me forward when I became stalled, she always believed I could and should write this book. It could only be dedicated to her. Above all I thank God for the opportunity to make this contribution to scholarship.

PROLOGUE

"Radicalism and Sedition among the Negroes"

Three revolver shots reverberated through the crowded tenement on New York's Lower East Side. Residents raised their windows and, screaming for help, attracted two policemen walking their beat on the street below. By the time they summoned a doctor in the Bellevue Hospital ambulance, nothing could be done for the mortally wounded pair. Bullets had pierced the Russian Jewish woman's heart and abdomen. Over the body keened her mother and two teenage children. The black man beside her was an even more gruesome sight, the right side of his face blown off by a single shot. His coat sported a badge proclaiming membership in the notorious Industrial Workers of the World; in his hand was clutched the fatal weapon. The newspaper account the next day only hinted at the tragedy which played out its final act that night in 1919. Seemingly, nothing extraordinary had transpired: two members of the teeming underclass had succumbed to the commonplace interpersonal violence of the slums. Most such incidents did not even merit newspaper coverage or the headline "IWW Agent Kills Woman and Dies by His Own Hand."[1]

Theresa Klein and Joseph J. Jones were both "Wobblies," members of the Industrial Workers of the World. His story illustrates many of the themes in this volume. He was a "red," a potential leader, and black. Federal agents and local police in New York and Boston had been trying to halt his radical activities for months and knew of his connections to militant black socialists who were top targets for suppression by the Justice Department. The IWW was an interracial proletarian movement which opposed corporate capitalism, the existing political party system, and white supremacy. Most whites, had they heard of Jones, would have agreed with the government that his actions were dangerous and intolerable. Certainly the Justice Department was relieved to learn of his death. But many more—socialists, "Bolshevists," and nationalists—remained. "Radicalism and sedition among the Negroes"[2] seemed rampant, and the federal government determined to crush it. Although federal officials did not entirely succeed, they played an important role in aborting the most militant period of African American history prior to the modern civil rights era.

This book also explores a neglected chapter in the history of American political intelligence, which came of age during World War I and the postwar Red Scare. Federal agents monitored the activities of thousands of left-wing suspects, as well as others who defied conventional liberal-conservative labels. Many of them were black, and the federal government's crusade to suppress their militancy has never been told in its entirety. From 1918 into the early twenties, any African Americans who spoke out forcefully for the race—editors, union organizers, civil rights advocates, radical political activists, and Pan-Africanists—were likely to be investigated by a network of federal intelligence agencies. The "crime" which justified such surveillance was almost always the ideas they expressed. Agents of the federal government watched these individuals, tapped their phones, rifled their offices, opened their mail, infiltrated their organizations, intimidated their audiences, and caused them to suffer the prospect of prosecution, all because their beliefs were anathema. These abuses were only compounded by the fact that most federal investigators were "ill-equipped to discern between reform and revolution, defined discontent as subversion and filled their files with a miscellaneous melange of truth, half-truth, and trivia."[3]

The federal government's political intelligence system which took shape during and after the war became a permanent establishment. Despite the fact that the Bureau of Investigation (renamed the FBI in 1935) was ordered by Attorney General Harlan Fiske Stone to cease political spying in 1924, it never did so. Nor did the army or State Department halt their intelligence activities during the interwar years. World War II added new urgency and additional targets to the domestic intelligence system, which then moved unchecked into the Cold War era.

From the perspective of African American history, the same continuity can be charted. Black suspects were an important target during the first Red Scare. "Radicals" continued to be monitored in the twenties and thirties. During World War II outspoken African Americans narrowly avoided federal repression. The most significant continuity from 1919 to modern times was the twin fear that black militancy was communist-inspired, and that it was particularly directed toward achieving "social equality," even intermarriage, with whites.

J. Edgar Hoover's role in this process cannot be overestimated. In spearheading the Bureau of Investigation's anti-radical crusade in 1919, he fixated on the belief that racial militants were seeking to break down social barriers separating blacks from whites, and that they were inspired by communists or were the pawns of communists. These notions became imbedded in the FBI and its director. Hoover's hostility toward Dr. Martin Luther King, Jr., and the civil rights movement of the 1960s was shaped by the fears which Hoover conjured up in 1919 and which he helped cement into the Bureau's institutional memory.

This is also the story of some of the inner workings of American political intelligence and domestic spying. The Bureau's first black agents emerge in this narrative, a handful of pioneers obscured by the subsequent decades during which Hoover, as director of the FBI, refused to employ blacks as fully professional agents. The first black agents were hardly dishonoring themselves in seeking a government career theretofore denied to members of their race. True, they were initially hired only to investigate black suspects. But given the restricted opportunities of their times, they do not deserve to be harshly judged.

A related theme involves the Bureau's extensive use of black undercover informants and infiltrators, a practice necessitated by the inability of white agents to penetrate racial organizations and gain the confidence of black militants. In today's popular mind, informants are either base villains or brave heroes. The following accounts of the Bureau's first black agents and informants describe their accomplishments and failures but resist moral judgment on their activities because the African American population was then, as it is now, large and diverse, with a multiplicity of political viewpoints. Marcus Garvey is today widely honored, but in the 1920s his sizeable following was counterbalanced by many who sincerely believed he was dangerously misleading the race.

This book does not aspire to add to the J. Edgar Hoover demonology. Three lengthy biographies of the FBI's long-time director have appeared since I began my research in 1980, and all analyze Hoover's early life and the effect of family and social milieu on his personality and political views. Hoover figures prominently in this narrative because he organized and directed the Bureau of Investigation's first systematic anti-radical efforts, a task which began his remarkably swift upward path in the organization. I have chosen to let his memoranda and directives speak for themselves. If the picture is unflattering, it is because his own words and actions create such a portrait.

The sources for a study of federal intelligence operations are rich. I have relied overwhelmingly on roughly 25,000 pages of federal government documents housed in the National Archives or obtained from the FBI through the Freedom of Information Act. Many of them have been subsequently published on microfilm.[4] A considerable number of pages have never before been seen or utilized by historians. Documents relating to Marcus Garvey are also available in a superbly annotated series edited by Robert A. Hill which is a model of meticulous scholarship. It is particularly gratifying that Hill's research team and I independently identified the key black informants profiled in these pages, although their names were never used on the reports they filed.[5] Like the accounts of the early informants, most of the stories and events chronicled here have not been told in depth. Indeed, the histories of several other early twentieth-century movements have not been fully explored because the full extent of federal pressure on them has not been charted. New studies of the World War I–era peace, civil liberties, anarchist, labor, and women's movements need to mine the Bureau of Investigation files preserved in 955 reels of National Archives microfilm.[6]

My interest in the federal pursuit of black militants has been sustained by discovering new and exciting documents and seeing the picture emerge as individual pieces of the puzzle were found and assembled. The historian-as-detective process holds great satisfactions. There is undoubtedly pleasure in completing a more thorough or nuanced biography than has previously been written on a subject, but I happily leave revisionist history to others. My fulfillment comes from exploring virgin territory. African American history still has many topics that have not once been fully documented. It remains an exciting field because there are still so many "first" books to be written. But all first attempts at a topic, this one included, are imperfect. There are undoubtedly documents that other scholars will discover, which will add more insight to what is related here. I look forward to their additions. But if future historians regard this volume, and my forthcoming book on federal surveillance activities during World War I, as a good foundation, I will be more than satisfied.

Finally, a word about the title. When Attorney General A. Mitchell Palmer, in late 1919, submitted to the Senate a lengthy report on the *Investigation Activities of the Department of Justice,* he warned that America stood at Armageddon: Bolshevists, anarchists, and seditionists were besieging the nation. As part of their diabolical plans, "practically all of the radical organizations in this country have looked upon the Negroes as particularly fertile ground for the spreading of their doctrines. These radical organizations have endeavored to enlist Negroes on their side, and in many respects have been successful." As a consequence, "the Negro is 'seeing red.'"

Palmer's phrase carried a double meaning. As he (and Hoover and other intelligence bureaucrats) saw it, black rage had been unleashed, and not only in the previous summer's riots: "Defiance and insolently race-centered condemnation of the white race is to be met with in every issue of the more radical publications." But in fact militant blacks weren't anti-white; they were either expressing a Pan-Africanism which celebrated blackness, or expressing their hatred of lynching and mob violence. Palmer and others in like position lost touch with reality on this score. The second meaning implied even greater danger: there was said to exist "a well-concerted movement among a certain class of Negro leaders of thought and action to constitute themselves a determined and persistent source of radical opposition to the Government, and to the established rule of law and order," who proclaimed "an outspoken advocacy of the Bolsheviki or Soviet doctrines."[7] What the federal intelligence establishment had done was use the "red" label to delegitimize blacks' desires for peace, security, and liberation from the racial status quo. The Bolshevik revolution was scarcely two years old, and guardians of every American orthodoxy—racial, political, economic—had already learned the power and usefulness of red baiting.

There is a great irony here: Palmer, Hoover, and their peers, like bulls facing a toreador, were also "seeing red". *They* raged against a black militancy whose main weapon was rhetoric; *they* conjured up a communist bogeyman to avoid acknowledging that blacks had genuine grievances against the racial status quo; *they* claimed that blacks would be happy and contented if not for the evil machinations of aliens and their subversive doctrines. On matters of race, the federal intelligence agencies served their country poorly.

"SEEING RED"

ONE

❧

"UNREST AND RADICALISM ARE RIFE"

The Flowering of Modern Political Intelligence

Modern America's political intelligence system—surveillance, investigation, and spying on individuals because of fear or dislike of their beliefs, resulting in harassment, intimidation, or prosecution—came of age during World War I and the Red Scare of 1919 to 1921, and it would thenceforth justify its existence by identifying a never-ending series of national security threats. The innocence of 1914 was lost forever.[1]

A network of agencies was created to conduct wartime counter-espionage and counter-propaganda among civilians, which continued to function long after the armistice. Militants' activities were monitored, interrupted, and suppressed. The results went even further: Dissidents engaged in self-censorship out of fear of becoming government targets. The Justice Department and its Bureau of Investigation, the intelligence branches of the army and navy, and like-minded bureaucrats in the Post Office and State departments jointly pursued those whom they defined as politically suspect. State and local police, civilian patriotic (vigilante) groups, and large corporations also contributed information and manpower to such efforts. During the war they focused on Germans and other "enemy aliens," pacifists, socialists, draft opponents, labor radicals, and outspoken or disaffected African Americans. After the war major targets included socialists, "Bolshevists," anarchists, Irish and Indian nationalists, and a variety of black militants. Among the latter were those engaged in aggressive civil rights advocacy, some promoting communist or socialist solutions for the problems suffered by blacks, and others pursuing a Pan-Africanist nationalism.

The practice of political intelligence in America developed slowly. The use of political spies was anathema to the Founding Fathers of the Republic, who knew well the abuses of the government of George III. But domestic intelligence received a significant boost during the Civil War when the War Department utilized the Pinkerton Detective Agency for military espionage. Throughout the remainder of the nineteenth century private detectives were hired by employers to smash unions and undermine strikes, infiltrating labor and dissident political groups for the purposes of disruption and gathering intelligence.[2]

Big-city police forces entered the same battles in the late nineteenth century. Political detective units ("bomb squads") arose in response to militant labor activities and the anarchist movement, "specializing in the continued surveillance of agitators and troublemakers." Thus, "by the outbreak of World War I a network of police and private detective agencies girdled urban America, joined together in a unique collaboration, sharing the same objectives and surveillance methods."[3]

The modern federal political intelligence system and federally initiated political repression likewise have roots in the post–Civil War era of labor militancy, corporate anti-radicalism, and nativism. The 1877 national railroad strike convinced many in government and business that the labor movement was violent and subversive, justifying suppression "by the massive use of federal and state troops along with local volunteer 'citizens militia' groups." The long-term impact of these events was to implant a fear of foreign radicals and communism into American politics.[4]

A communist-anarchist-labor scare, climaxing in the 1886 Haymarket bombing, sent another wave of hysteria through the country and helped foster the stereotype of the bearded, bomb-throwing anarchist. Government officials frequently harbored strong nativist stereotypes but an even stronger motivation was their determination to root out radicalism, whether by citizens or noncitizens.[5]

Another but more prolonged anarchist-labor scare lasted from 1892 to 1896. The federal government took an active role in suppressing militant unionism and political dissent. Management successfully persuaded the Justice Department to break the Pullman Strike. Dozens of labor leaders, including Eugene V. Debs, were arrested. The Supreme Court upheld Debs's conviction for violating a strike injunction, reassuring the nation that unions unwilling to accept capitalism, and labor's subordinate position in the economy, would not be tolerated.[6] The federal government was becoming well practiced in the suppression of unpopular political and economic advocacy.

Early twentieth-century Progressivism brought the enlargement of government power, ironically directed toward both much-needed social reforms and new authority to punish unpopular ideas and membership in "dangerous" organizations. Although anarchists and radical labor unionists were the immediate targets, the foundation for more wide-reaching investigation and suppression of political dissent during and after World War I was being laid. Old fears of radicalism as well as anti-immigrant stereotypes were rekindled with the assassination of President William McKinley in 1901, resulting in yet another anarchist scare. For the first time since the 1790s Alien and Sedition acts, federal law targeted individual opinion, advocacy, and membership in organizations, without the actual commission of a crime; immigrants could be barred from the United States for belief in political assassination or in the overthrow of the government by force and violence, and for a philosophical opposition to all government. Proceedings were summary and nonjudicial. Even though there were very few exclusions and deportations under this law prior to World War I, it initiated a trend in which the federal government took the lead in political repression, surpassing state and local governments and business. Previous victims of government intelligence activities and suppression had usually been labor activists; now, increasingly, targets were selected simply because they held bad beliefs and were members of despised (although legal) organizations such as the Socialist Party. Guilt by association was institutionalized for the first time in American history. The federal government had declared its hostility to "subversive" ideas.[7]

The pre-war peak of federal political intelligence and persecution occurred in response to a new working-class movement, the Industrial Workers of the World, founded in 1905, which announced that "the working class and the employing class have nothing in common" and that "between these two classes a struggle must go on until the workers of the world organize as a class, take possession of the earth and the machinery of production, and abolish the wage system."[8] Not surprisingly, the Wobblies engaged in sabotage as well as strikes.

The "IWW threat" was coupled to nativist demands for more swift immigrant exclusion and deportation. But deeper than nativism was the desire among many in the federal government to crush all radicals, whether alien or citizen. The stage was set for a dramatic expansion of political surveillance during World War I, and the establishment of America's modern political intelligence system, when any radical dissent would be labeled pro-German and a threat to national security.[9] German, British, and French agents carried on extensive propaganda and espionage in the United States during 1915 and 1916. The Secret Service, founded in 1865 and the oldest federal investigative arm, appeared dramatically successful in apprehending alleged enemies, while the Justice Department's fledgling Bureau of Investigation was perceived by the public as inept.[10] Then, once the United States embarked on war, additional players entered domestic espionage and increased interagency conflicts as both the army and the navy began to create modern intelligence branches. The Post Office Department was assigned responsibility for censorship and registration of enemy aliens. And the State Department remained anxious about German and Austrian residents even though many were interned or expelled.

Interagency squabbling, especially between the Secret Service and the Bureau of Investigation, impaired efficiency. What was needed was cooperation in allocating responsibilities and avoiding duplication of effort. The one person powerful enough to impose such efficiency, President Woodrow Wilson, failed to provide the necessary leadership. In that vacuum, Treasury Secretary William Gibbs McAdoo, anxious to preserve a major role for his department's Secret Service, urged creation of a central "Bureau of Intelligence." But jealousy between Justice and Treasury plus President Wilson's opposition to a "unified counterespionage agency" doomed the proposal.[11] Meanwhile, the Bureau of Investigation was recruiting a hundred new agents in the first two months of the war while also creating a civilian auxiliary, the American Protective League (APL), whose volunteers wore badges identifying them as "secret service" men, to the chagrin of McAdoo.[12]

Coordination between agencies—and modern America's political intelligence framework—finally emerged in the summer of 1917. The Secret Service was largely excluded from domestic counter-espionage as officials from the State and Justice departments began to meet weekly with the intelligence chiefs of the army and navy. The APL expanded rapidly, and its volunteers assisted army and navy intelligence as well as the Bureau. The addition of the Post Office Department completed the cast of major players dedicated to spy catching, union busting, radical hunting, press, mail, cable, and telegraph censoring, and, in general, enforcing 100 percent conformity and 110 percent patriotism.[13] Modern American political intelligence had come of age.

This system drew authority from draconian wartime legislation and presidential orders. The Espionage Act of 1917 and its amendment the following year, popularly known as the Sedition Act, plus the Trading-with-the-Enemy Act (1917) granted broad power to the federal government to punish any appearance of disloyalty or interference with the draft; muzzle the dissenting press and censor other forms of communication; and, most ominously, punish writing or speech that *might* harm the country's war efforts, promote the cause of Germany, or discredit the American government, Constitution, or flag. Presidential orders allowed summary arrest and internment of "enemy aliens" and dismissal of "disloyal" civil servants, while encouraging "voluntary" press censorship. As the war progressed preoccupation with German enemies was gradually supplanted by fear of anarchists and communists. The Alien Act, passed only four weeks before the armistice, streamlined procedures for deporting those with "un-American" political beliefs. This act was a bridge to the Red Scare, enshrining guilt by association in immigration proceedings.[14]

The legislative edifice erected during the war caused more than erosion of civil liberties; it removed important "legal guarantees traditionally enjoyed by Americans against the arbitrary actions of hysterical or irresponsible government officials." Even though Congress intended the Espionage and Sedition acts as wartime measures, the official end to hostilities did not come until 1921, giving the Justice Department, under new Attorney General A. Mitchell Palmer, powerful weapons against enemies of the state: anarchists, socialists, and communists, including blacks in all three categories. Army and navy intelligence operatives continued to spy on civilians, while the State Department monitored the foreign travel of those holding unpopular beliefs. The Post Office Department also maintained censorship long after the war emergency. President Wilson allowed civil liberties abuses to continue to the end of his term of office in 1921. And as political intelligence reached maturity, its fixation on the Left had become irrevocable.[15]

The Red Scare obsessions of the Bureau of Investigation were linked to an anti-radical frenzy whipped up by Attorney General Palmer in his efforts to capture the presidential nomination in 1920. Initially, unknown radicals gave him ammunition. Thirty-eight prominent government officials and industrialists were sent mail bombs shortly before May Day 1919. Although all but one was discovered before it could explode, it was clear that prominent opponents of radicalism were marked for death. On June 2, the front porch of Attorney General Palmer's house was demolished by a bomb-carrying assailant, while simultaneous blasts went off in seven other cities. Anarchist literature was found at several bomb sites, and the press and public assumed the attacks were the work of Reds.

Quickly getting a half million dollars from Congress, Palmer hired William J. Flynn, former chief of the Secret Service, as director of the Bureau of Investigation. His assistant director and chief, overseeing day-to-day Bureau operations, was Frank Burke, who had worked under Flynn. Their task was to establish an anti-radical General Intelligence Division and track down the bombers. A young Justice Department attorney, J. Edgar Hoover, was appointed to spearhead the Bureau's anti-radical efforts as head of the GID. He soon convinced himself and his superiors that a worldwide communist conspiracy to subvert all governments had more than a foothold in the United States.[16]

Flynn ordered the GID to investigate every manifestation of radicalism and focus on alien agitators who could be deported without the necessity of lengthy legal procedures. Thousands were rounded up in dragnets. But despite Hoover's diligence only a small number were deported and no bombers were convicted. Although this lackluster record did not reflect well on the Justice Department (and the left-wing press was unanimous in condemning the "Palmer raids"), it did keep the public on edge and willing to tolerate flagrant violations of due process.

Since the war had not formally ended, the Justice Department first tried to prosecute alleged anarchists using the Espionage Act, but this tack proved unproductive. What did work, however, was the Alien Act, passed shortly before the end of the war, which provided that

> any alien who, at any time after entering the United States, is found to have been at the time of entry, or to have become thereafter, a member of any one of the classes of aliens [advocating violent overthrow of the government] shall . . . be taken into custody and deported.[17]

Such summary procedures, based often on guilt by association, were obviously preferred by those in the Justice Department who saw constitutional guarantees as obstacles, not protections.

Across the country, Bureau agents and local police raided meetings and rounded up suspected alien enemies. Informers infiltrated radical and nationalist groups—including several black organizations—and volunteered themselves onto the staffs of militant publications; again, black periodicals were targeted. Homes and meeting halls were invaded without search warrants. Government raiders carried out "black bag" jobs (warrantless break-ins) and stole, scattered, or demolished the contents of radicals' offices. Suspects were arrested by Bureau agents, who possessed no statutory authority to take them into custody, but the presence of local police officers lent legitimacy to such apprehensions. Prisoners were denied access to counsel and held without warrants. Agents were accused of assaults, forgery, and perjury in their zeal to ensure convictions.

Critics correctly noted that many of the Bureau's targets were guilty only of holding unpopular opinions, not plotting sabotage or overthrow of the government. Despite the fact that Bureau infiltrators discovered little more than "the borderland of conspiratorial secrecy about revolutionary ideas" the Justice Department clamored for a new federal sedition act that would permit suppression of suspects simply on the basis of their opinions, thus perpetuating wartime abridgments of speech, assembly, and association. Black publications had good reason to fear such legislation, knowing it could be used to stifle protests against lynching or disfranchisement. When Congress sanely refused to pass such a law, Attorney General Palmer's minions funneled evidence and advice to state officials who prosecuted alleged radicals using new state sedition laws that were hastily passed during the anti-communist hysteria. The practices of political intelligence and subversion of due process and civil liberties had become hallmarks of the Bureau of Investigation.[18]

Of all the World War I–era domestic intelligence agencies, the Bureau of Investigation emerged as the strongest and most durable, laying the foundation for the FBI's preeminence to this day. It did not begin auspiciously, however. Formed in 1908, the Bureau's initial jurisdiction was quite limited, and it employed only about 300 agents by early 1917. But the war brought a tremendous increase in responsibilities and growth in personnel. Led by Chief A. Bruce Bielaski, by the end of the war 1,500 agents watched enemy aliens, domestic enemies, war dissenters, and pacifists, helped prepare Espionage and Sedition act prosecutions, and enforced selective service regulations.[19]

Many Americans expected that the Bureau would shrink in size and scope once the war ended, but that did not occur. The Attorney General reported in mid-1919 that "the signing of the armistice did not end the war activities of the bureau." Fifty thousand draft delinquency cases still awaited indictments, and enemy alien cases continued to be pursued more than six months after quiet descended on the western front. And although the number of agents decreased after January 1919, the Bureau began to grow again in July.[20]

During the second half of 1919 Hoover, a bureaucrat's bureaucrat dedicated to thoroughness and efficiency, instituted a requirement that every Bureau field office submit weekly reports on local radical activities. To ensure that agents did not miss anything he ordered that they comment on Bolshevik, anarchist, and socialist activities, labor unions and strikes, and militant activities of Japanese, Mexicans, Sinn Feiners (anti-British, working for Irish independence), and Hindus, plus "Negro Activities" and the "Negro Press." Agents were expected to report on the prescribed topics even if they could only write that there was "no radical activity" for the preceding week. (For decades after Hoover became head of the FBI, agents feared being caught with no information about a subject on which Hoover showed interest.) The reasons for this elaborate system were several: to keep Hoover and the Bureau leadership up-to-date on threats of radicalism throughout the country; to train agents to keep watch over the full spectrum of dangerous activity; and to provide data for the Bureau's weekly digest of radical activities—which had a category for "Negro Activities"—which was shared with the State Department, army intelligence, and important members of Congress and the administration. This latter function was key to justifying the Bureau's mission and budget.

An efficient file system was established in the General Intelligence Division with index cards for every person, organization, and publication mentioned in agents' reports. By September cards were being added at the rate of 3,000 per week, and a month later nearly 55,000 cards were in index. New categories—strikes, bomb plots, and "the negro[21] agitation movement"— were added. Geographical cards permitted tracking of radicalism in each state. Names and nationalities of militant editors were recorded along with circulation figures and the general contents of their publications.

Hoover found that state prosecution was often more expedient than federal action, with California, Michigan, New York, Ohio, Pennsylvania, Washington, and West Virginia having particularly efficacious anti-syndicalist and anti-anarchist laws. Admitting that not a few statutes "may go too far in abridging free speech," he nonetheless supported state action whenever possible. The GID would prepare summaries of its evidence and encourage Bureau agents to submit such data to local authorities.

A special office of the GID monitored the radical press in New York City, where many militant groups had their headquarters. But so long as publications were not sent through the mails there was no federal law to prevent their circulation. Radicals were aware of this and frequently used express companies for distribution. Hoover urged new legislation not only to interdict materials sent by such means but actually to prevent the printing and sale of objectionable literature.

Finally, as part of his bureaucratization of the GID, Hoover required that key field offices submit a weekly report on radical activities in their regions. Eventually Chicago, New York, Boston, Pittsburgh, Philadelphia, Baltimore, Detroit, St. Louis, New Orleans, San Francisco, Los Angeles, Seattle, Omaha, and San Antonio filed weekly digests plus a separate monthly report on radical publications.

The GID came under the authority of two assistant attorneys general, Robert P. Stewart, who headed all criminal prosecutions and thus oversaw Hoover's efforts, and Francis P. Garvan, who had overall supervision of the Bureau of Investigation. Garvan requested Hoover to prepare a brief of all evidence on the radical black press for presentation to state or local authorities when federal prosecutions did not pan out.[22]

How important was this evolution of the Bureau? Narrow in task and small in staff prior to 1917, the Bureau had gained preeminence in domestic security matters by the war's end. Dedicated to preserving the nation against internal threats, its agents became guardians of the American way of life which sanctified capitalism, damned socialism and communism, and narrowly proscribed the legitimacy of working-class and racial-minority aspirations. Anti-war, Bolshevist, anarchist, and other "subversive" activities and the passage of legislation to meet such perceived threats led into investigations of political belief and activism. As the Bolshevik Revolution spread its influence over Europe and across the Atlantic, it was widely feared that communism would infect labor movements and ethnic minorities while further radicalizing already established militant movements. The Bureau and its companion intelligence agencies skipped nary a beat in making a transition from dread of German subversion and radicals to the Red Scare.

Testifying before a Senate subcommittee investigating "Brewing and Liquor Interests and German and Bolshevist Propaganda" in January 1919, in his last appearance before Congress, Chief Bielaski warned of the march of radicalism. But the alleged link between the past and present was made even more explicit by a former Bureau and military intelligence agent, Archibald E. Stevenson: "German socialism . . . is the father of the Bolsheviki movement in Russia." The new radicalism, he added, was "the gravest menace to the country today." Thus enlightened, the senators went into secret session and decided to focus on investigating radical movements.[23] The Red Scare was being born. One of its victims would be the African American population. Aggressive advocacy of a civil rights agenda and demands for fundamental changes in the racial status quo would be defined as Bolshevik-inspired. A new, threatening era for black militancy had begun.

In the fall of 1919, Attorney General Palmer gave Congress a special report on *Investigation Activities of the Department of Justice,* warning that "from the date of the signing of the armistice, a wave of radicalism appears to have swept over the country." Danger did not stem from the isolated, uncoordinated actions of a few malcontents; rather, there was "a well-concerted movement among a certain class of Negro leaders of thought and action to constitute themselves a determined and persistent course of a radical opposition to the Government, and to the established rule of law and order." Typical publications were imbued with "race consciousness" and were "always antagonistic to the white race, and openly defiantly assertive of its own equality and even superiority." Pride in fighting back against white rioters was also a common theme. "Defiance and insolently race-centered condemnation of the white race is to be met with in every issue of the more radical publications."[24]

Intense investigation of black publications and organizations continued for the next year and a half. But by the beginning of the Harding administration in 1921, the Red Scare was rapidly waning, with the Justice Department, including the Bureau, in disrepute. Federal attorneys had not succeeded in prosecuting alleged communists, only in driving them underground. The public was tired of "Red raiding." Yet aside from critics in Congress and the liberal press, there was no outcry to clean up or curb the Bureau. In fact it continued to hound suspected radicals, black as well as white, seeking deportation of those it deemed undesirable, like the Pan-Africanist Marcus Garvey. The intelligence partnerships born in World War I remained intact, ensuring cooperation in nailing Garvey and pursuing communists and fellow travelers. Bonds forged in the campaign against German suspects and wrought on the anvil of the Red Scare proved durable.

The army entered World War I ill prepared for a domestic security role, but it quickly developed a significant counter-espionage capability. In theory all counter-intelligence—monitoring, infiltrating, and disrupting allegedly dangerous civilian groups—should have ended with the armistice in late 1918. But the Military Intelligence Division (MID), like the Bureau of Investigation, made a transition late in the war from combating domestic subversion by "enemy aliens" to attacking economic and political radicalism.

When the United States declared war on Germany in April 1917, army intelligence consisted of two officers, two clerks, and a handful of national guard officers being trained in the rudiments of the craft. The ranking officer was Maj. Ralph H. Van Deman, known today as the "father of military intelligence." A zealot for his profession, he almost single-handedly began to fashion a corps and a mission in the face of skepticism from the chief of staff and Secretary of War Newton D. Baker who initially saw no need for an independent intelligence branch.[25]

Military intelligence grew dramatically. By the end of the war 272 officers and over 1,000 civilian clerks worked in Washington, while other intelligence officers (IOs) were attached to every important army command, port of embarkation, and camp. An organizational model and terminology were borrowed from the British. The Negative Branch focused on blunting enemy activities on the home front while the Positive Branch studied economic, social, political, and military conditions abroad. The most important sections of the Negative Branch were MI3, Counter Espionage in the Military Service, and MI4, Counter Espionage among the Civilian Population. The Negative Branch also shared censorship responsibilities with the Navy and Post Office departments and helped the State Department determine who would be granted passports.[26]

Since domestic counter-espionage represented a dramatic enlargement of the army's traditional responsibilities, it was necessary to justify interference in civilian affairs. Brig. Gen. Marlborough Churchill, who succeeded Van Deman as head of military intelligence in 1918, later explained the mission:

> Germany unquestionably expected to be able to thwart our military effort by causing sedition and disloyalty in our troops, by fostering the natural grievances of the enemy aliens included in the draft, and by sabotage and destruction in our munitions works, at our docks and on our transports. Neither the Department of Justice nor the Secret Service of the Treasury was adequate to do all the investigation required in the United States during the war.[27]

The army's domestic intelligence efforts focused on radical labor unionists in the IWW; Japanese, Hindu, and Mexican agitators; Germans; "negro subversion and political demagoguery"; foreign "racial" (i.e., ethnic) groups; and enemy aliens. These emphases evolved into MID's postwar intelligence priorities: anarchism and communism (identified with European ethnics); black militancy; the IWW; and Japanese influence on various disaffected groups, including African Americans. Investigations of blacks' loyalties was the specialty of MI4E, a subsection briefly headed by Maj. Joel E. Spingarn, the white chairman of the board of the NAACP.[28]

By mid-1918, MID began to perceive Bolshevism and socialism supplanting German subversion as the major obstacle to winning the war and preserving the status quo.[29] In fact, the armistice did not bring peace to a weary nation, because radical and racial ferment did not cease. The Negative Branch continued counter-espionage among the civilian population, supplementing its own data with reports from the Bureau of Investigation, postal censors, naval intelligence, the State Department, and the intelligence services of Britain and France.[30]

Gen. Churchill, however, wanted to end spying on civilians, fearing that zealous intelligence officers would create "a scandal and a menace to our form of government" by investigating the political beliefs of persons outside the military. Hence he ordered that all unfinished cases be turned over to the Bureau and no new inquiries started. When Gen. Churchill was dispatched to France, however, IOs across the country ignored his order and revived undercover operations. The acting head of MID, convinced by excited intelligence officers in Chicago and New York that the nation was in imminent danger from Bolshevism, overlooked Gen. Churchill's prohibition on civilian counter-espionage.[31]

But when in early 1919 the national press revealed the existence of an MID list of "radicals," including prominent liberals and academicians such as settlement house pioneer Jane Addams and the chancellor of Stanford University, the War Department suffered great embarrassment, prompting Secretary of War Baker to reaffirm Gen. Churchill's order: "The Military Intelligence Division may not properly conduct espionage among the civilian population even to inquire into the political or economic beliefs or activities of individuals or groups of individuals whether they be Anarchists, Socialists, IWWs, Bolshevists, or members of some special ethnic group." But paranoia had become a "way of life" for the Negative Branch. MID offices continued to spy on civilians by using former APL volunteers on an unofficial basis. Returning from France in April 1919, and now convinced that radicals were attacking the nation, Gen. Churchill disregarded Baker's order and put MID back on a wartime footing.[32]

When the Justice Department accelerated its own anti-radical crusade following the mid-1919 bomb attempts, Gen. Churchill determined that military intelligence must be included in such efforts. Needing funds to continue civilian counter-intelligence, he lied to Congress in claiming that "investigation of disloyal persons by the military authorities has been discontinued since the armistice." Congress bought his story and appropriated $400,000 for MID to prepare for the expected revolution. Secretary Baker, although not believing that revolution was imminent, failed to control the rejuvenated MID, which in the meantime had convinced the army hierarchy to place troops on the alert in anticipation of a nationwide general strike on July 4.[33]

The Military Intelligence Division, like the Justice Department, was active both in fostering the Red Scare and suppressing those who were its targets. MID weekly bulletins—intended for the president, cabinet secretaries, the army command structure, and intelligence executives in other departments—were by the second half of 1919 "unusually hysterical about the Bolsheviks, the IWW, the Rand School, strikers, pacifists, Negro subversion," and other targets. Across the country army recruiters served as intelligence eyes and ears; hundreds of retired IOs were secretly encouraged to supply information on radicalism; members of the Officers Reserve Corps conducted free-lance investigations; veterans in the anti-Left American Legion offered tips; and numerous ex-APL members eagerly ferreted out suspect groups.[34]

The postwar alliance between the War and Justice departments was formalized in late 1920 when an agreement was signed between MI4 and the General Intelligence Division. Regular conferences to discuss cases of mutual interest were reinstated. Hoover promised to supply each army corps area with copies of the weekly "General Intelligence Bulletin," a digest of important radical developments, including black militancy. MID officers were also granted access to Bureau field reports. For its part MID furnished copies of its "Weekly Situation Survey" to the Bureau's division superintendents in charge of the nine continental regions. Hoover emphasized that "I am particularly desirous of establishing a thorough cooperation between our two services."

One document supplied to MID was the Bureau's estimate of the number of radical organizations. MID multiplied Hoover's already inflated figures, using a "secret formula," to arrive at a total of 1.5 million domestic enemies (i.e., 1.5 percent of the population!) who were poised to overthrow the government, including 50,000 "unorganized negroes." In keeping with this hysterical estimate, MID sought to keep the army free of infection by compiling a list of over 500 publications, including black periodicals, to be barred from military camps.[35]

But public opinion proved unwilling to tolerate continued military spying on civilians, and MID's domestic counter-intelligence efforts dwindled in the twenties. By that time, however, cooperation between federal agencies had been cemented through both formal arrangements and informal contacts. The partnership established during World War I was strengthened during the Red Scare because MID and Hoover's GID needed one another. Shared antipathy to Bolsheviks—and their alleged influence on blacks—forged a strong link in the chain of American political intelligence. By 1920 both agencies were convinced that communism posed a genuine threat to the nation. Historian Roy Talbert notes that even while "the army's spying empire" declined in the 1920s, its "loathing for the American left persisted." Although a War Department directive in 1924 eliminated the Negative Branch and forbade domestic intelligence, the anti-radical bias was not purged and would be revived again in the early 1930s.[36]

MID operated in the shadow of the Justice Department during the Red Scare, the public not readily associating it with egregious acts like those of Hoover's Red raiders. Secretary of War Baker was ambivalent about peacetime domestic espionage and wanted as low a profile as possible. But MID was just as intent on remaining "at the forefront in the battle against radicalism," energized by the "deeply conservative and suspicious mentality" common to the officer corps. That was the legacy of Van Deman, who steered army sleuths first into civilian espionage and then to pursuit of the Left, a path that would be followed for the next fifty years.[37]

Of all the agencies involved in the political intelligence system during and after World War I, the Post Office Department was the only one with a preexistent nationwide structure that needed no fundamental alterations to meet the national emergency. It efficiently handled "many thousands of communications of confidential character" for its partners in domestic counter-espionage, registered enemy aliens, and censored the mail. A staff of dollar-a-year volunteers, known variously as the Translation Bureau or Bureau M-1, monitored militant black, socialist, and anti-war publications as well as nearly 300 foreign-language newspapers, the latter task done by a translation force of over 400 college professors. President Wilson urged Postmaster General Albert Sidney Burleson to "act with the utmost caution and liberality" in placing restrictions on printed matter, but Burleson took advantage of the president's laissez-faire leadership and cracked down hard on the dissenting and foreign-language press. Many offenders lost their second-class mailing permits—forcing them to pay much higher first-class postage rates—or went out of business rather than knuckle under to government pressure. By the end of the war communist publications were also being interdicted.

The Post Office was most strongly linked to the Justice Department during the war. Postmaster General Burleson was a Texan, like his fishing companion, Attorney General Thomas Watt Gregory, and even less of a civil libertarian. Serving under Burleson was Postal Solicitor William H. Lamar, simultaneously his department's chief legal officer and also an assistant attorney general, maintaining liaison between the two departments, since it was up to Justice to prosecute offending publications.

Close cooperation continued during the postwar Red Scare. Hoover determined that all periodicals suspected of a radical bent be carefully scrutinized for possible prosecution. His staff's own evaluations were supplemented by the meticulous commentaries done by postal analysts. Bureau of Investigation agents and watchdogs in the Translation Bureau shared the same preoccupations and fears at the end of World War I, both making a quick transition from the threat of German intrigue to the even greater menace of international communism. After the war the Translation Bureau dissected each issue of the "New Crowd Negro" magazines and newspapers and frequently pleaded for their suppression. The key player in the Post Office's anti-radical activities continued to be Solicitor Lamar. Well versed in alleged dangers to national security from his wartime work, he was a natural confederate to Hoover's GID.[38]

How did the Post Office Department continue enforcement of the Espionage and Trading-with-the-Enemy acts after the war? According to Burleson:

> The character of the disloyal and seditious matter found in the mails since the signing of the armistice has differed materially from that which the department dealt with during the prosecution of the war. It is now of a radical, revolutionary type, having for its object the solidification of the revolutionary elements in this country and the overturning of our present form of government by force.

The postmaster general's solution, according to historian Harry N. Scheiber, was "a flagrant attempt to stretch the law and thereby meet an alleged emergency."[39] The nation was still technically at war, since America was not a signatory to the Treaty of Versailles. Thus wartime restraints on the press remained in effect.

Burleson's views paralleled those of Hoover: revolutionary movements around the world were consolidating into an unparalleled threat; only the most vigilant and vigorous governmental response would keep the Vandals from sacking Rome. Hence the Bureau and the Post Office tried mightily, although without success, to find grounds to prosecute the editors of militant journals like the black socialist *Messenger* and the white leftist *Liberator.* When that failed, denial of the second-class mail rate became nothing less than executive punishment levied on those who had been convicted of no offense.

The instigators of this federal injustice also joined the State Department and the intelligence services of the army and navy in drafting the nation's first comprehensive passport legislation. They shared responsibility for investigating applicants, the State Department having final authority over who would be issued such documents. This resulted in the diplomatic branch's first major interference in African American politics, preventing militant blacks from traveling to the Versailles peace conference to lobby for independence for Germany's African colonies. The State Department also made it difficult for delegates to attend a Pan-African conference in Paris convened by W. E. B. DuBois to run concurrently with the peace negotiations. It later denied having a formal policy of barring black travelers, but a number were blocked by deliberate bureaucratic delays. Those who managed to reach France, such as outspoken journalist William Monroe Trotter, who traveled as a ship's cook, had to employ a subterfuge and go without passports.[40]

The State Department's link to the domestic intelligence network was the Office of the Counselor, which was redefined as the Office of the Undersecretary in mid-1920. The counselor (undersecretary) was the secretary of state's top advisor. He also spearheaded the department's efforts to monitor and blunt the worldwide spread of communism and shared responsibility for internal security matters as well.[41]

Cooperation with other intelligence agencies begun during the war continued throughout the Red Scare. When black militancy mushroomed in the postwar months, two assistants to the counselor, L. Lanier Winslow and William H. Hurley, became the State Department's "experts" on such matters and worked closely with MID and the GID in efforts to curb Garvey while simultaneously tracking the movements of black Bolsheviks and fellow travelers who visited Russia and aligned with the Communist Third International.[42]

The final major political intelligence partner was the Office of Naval Intelligence, which grew from modest beginnings at the start of the war to a bureaucracy rivaling MID's size by 1919. According to naval historian Jeffery Dorwart, World War I "catapulted ONI into the complicated and murky work of secrecy, international espionage and counter-espionage, code breaking, deception, surreptitious entry, eavesdropping, and domestic surveillance" as it joined the other intelligence agencies in a wide range of investigations from 1917 onward. Focusing initially on alleged German threats to naval facilities and production, ONI began to perceive new dangers by the waning of the war. Like MID and the State, Justice, and Post Office departments, it identified the IWW, black militants, and Bolsheviks as major domestic threats. "Spying, surveillance, and secret operations" persisted in the Red Scare years. The State Department urged ONI (as well as MID) to cooperate in gathering political intelligence on "suspected subversives, radicals, and undesirable aliens" whose names were added to burgeoning government lists. ONI's main interest in black militancy focused on alleged Japanese influence on Marcus Garvey.[43]

By 1919 a full-blown political intelligence system was operating in America. Wartime statutes which had proven so useful in muzzling the press, punishing dissidents, and frightening countless others into prudent silence, were still in effect. The Justice and Post Office departments in particular were eager to use these laws to pursue, convict, and where possible deport a new crop of domestic enemies: anarchists, Bolshevists, socialists, and nationalists, some of whom were black.

None of the key figures in the postwar intelligence agencies was capable of sympathetically understanding the aspirations of a race that had served disproportionally and often unwillingly in World War I and expected improvements in its social and political status in return.[44] Instead, soldiers returned from a Jim Crow army to find that the nation would not reward their patriotic sacrifice with elementary civil rights. Lynching increased after the war, and mid-1919 witnessed the most intense racial rioting up to that time. Most whites blinded themselves to the reasons behind the new mood sweeping through black America, a "New Crowd Negro" spirit, representing the hopes, frustrations, and bitterness of southern migrants who streamed into growing northern ghettos. Whites embraced the easy explanation that subversives were inciting an otherwise passive race to demand unthinkable social readjustments. New heights of black militancy were reached when it became clear that the white majority would not voluntarily accept fundamental changes in the racial status quo. Consciously or not, those leading the postwar political intelligence system were committed to preventing racial improvements simply because such changes were inconceivable to them.

Typical of white males who staffed the upper ranks of the intelligence bureaucracies was young J. Edgar Hoover. To such individuals, the existing class and racial structures seemed essentially reasonable and deserving of protection from alien ideologies and proponents of radical change. Men like Hoover most commonly encountered blacks in superior-inferior relationships; he, like other middle-class white Washingtonians, knew best those African Americans who worked as servants in their households.[45]

Modest numbers of blacks could be found in the federal bureaucracy, but apart from postal clerks—who labored in segregated work areas—most were janitors, maids, or messengers.[46] A handful had more important roles, but were still "invisible men." The State Department employed several black messengers who performed the delicate function of escorting visiting envoys around the premises. One such individual, "schooled in the diplomatic tradition," was Edward Augustine Savoy, who served twenty-one secretaries of state from 1869 to 1933. As "diplomatic" as any Ivy League–bred foreign service officer, in the months before America formally entered the war Savoy was responsible for preventing representatives of warring powers from the embarrassment of encountering each other as they entered and left the State Department.[47] But he received neither the pay nor the status of the professional diplomat he had become. Most other blacks laboring in obscure federal jobs did so without even elementary respect.

Political intelligence executives in the Bureau of Investigation, ONI, MID, the Office of the Counselor, and the postal solicitor's office were unlikely to understand sympathetically the aspirations of African Americans because they had neither direct exposure to accurate information about racial issues nor personal relationships with blacks as social equals. Hoover did embark on an ambitious crash course in radicalism, reading reams of militant literature that was collected by the GID. But his intent was not to gain sensitivity to the grievances of foreign-born sweatshop workers, southern sharecroppers, copper miners in Bisbee and Butte, or unemployed ex-doughboys in Harlem. Rectification of social injustices was not on the personal or professional agenda of the intelligence bureaucrats.

The president and some of his cabinet officers, at least, had better sources of information, but this failed to produce enlightened policies. President Wilson received correspondence from George Foster Peabody, a white liberal dedicated to black education and uplift, and from Robert Russa Moton, Booker T. Washington's successor at Tuskegee Institute. Moton warned that many southern blacks were angry and alienated by the increase in lynching when America was fighting a war to preserve democracy elsewhere. But when President Wilson finally issued a moderately worded denunciation of lynching in mid-1918, he ordered no steps to suppress the barbarous practice. President Wilson's racial views were rooted in the Reconstruction, not the Progressive era.[48]

Secretary of War Baker was probably the most well informed of the cabinet secretaries on matters of race, but only rarely did he bring such issues to President Wilson's attention. Other cabinet members' views paralleled those of the president. Neither Postmaster General Burleson nor Attorney General Gregory had discernible sympathy for the plight or aspirations of black Americans. Like many other southern whites, Burleson and the president occasionally told "darky" jokes and used racially offensive language.[49] Gregory's successor, A. Mitchell Palmer, a Pennsylvania Quaker who once turned down the position of secretary of war because of religious scruples, appears to have had no enlightened racial understanding either. Intelligence bureaucrats and subordinates might have gained more accurate understandings from their investigators' reports had they worn different ideological lenses. But by war's end they were preoccupied with threats, real or imagined, from the Left. Neither the products of Harvard Yard (Van Deman and Churchill) nor George Washington University law school (Hoover) were educated to understand America's racial complexity from other than a WASP perspective. So it is understandable that the new political intelligence bureaucracies, when confronted with militant black demands for change in the racial status quo during and after World War I, responded with fear and loathing.

TWO

❦

"DANGEROUS INFLUENCES AT WORK UPON THE NEGRO"

Fears of Communism during and after the Red Scare

During World War I many socialists, IWWs, and anarchists embraced the Bolshevik revolution and condemned the efforts of the Allies to open a "second front" in Russia aimed as much at the communists as it was at the Germans. But despite their shared enthusiasm for the Russian revolution, American radicals split during the Red Scare over whether a similar upheaval could or should take place in the United States. During the war the Socialist Party's left wing—composed mostly of its foreign-language federations—was much more enthusiastic about a domestic revolution, but the right wing controlled party machinery and opposed the use of Bolshevik methods in the United States. In the summer of 1919 the left wing split when English-speaking members (only about 10 percent of its number) feared that the foreign-language federations wielded too much power within their faction. Meanwhile, the Socialist Party, led by its right wing, expelled the left wing on August 30. That same day native-born left-wing leaders formed the Communist Labor Party. Two days later the alien-dominated foreign-language federations formed their own Communist Party. The IWW, already seriously crippled by wartime raids, lost members to both new parties but continued as a separate organization of those who remained skeptical that Russian revolutionary methods should be exactly duplicated in the United States.[1]

As individual radicals found their niches in this realignment, government officials struggled to identify them properly. One person might be labeled a socialist but also a Bolshevik, or a Wobbly but also a Bolshevik. Worried federal agents tended to lump all radicals into a general category of undesirables, expending little effort to distinguish nuances of ideology. Such subtleties seemed irrelevant anyway: "Radicals" were dangerous because they espoused "alien" doctrines and sought extreme changes in the political landscape.

No word conveyed more fear in the months following the war than "Bolshevik." That term inspired images of assassination, bomb throwing, violent revolution, and anarchy; the destruction of cherished forms of government and the triumph of totalitarianism; the end of rule by those of good breeding and social class and their replacement by the ignorant, mean-spirited rabble; and the overturning of social norms and class relationships. These terrors took root in both the public imagination and government at all levels. Fear of communism was the driving force in molding the postwar federal intelligence establishment. The Red Scare cemented attitudes and responses to radicalism and social change that would dictate government practice for decades. The real potency of communism in America was its symbolic power; the parties themselves never attained significant influence, leverage, or membership. But as the bogeyman of politics, communism wielded greater influence than any other third party in history.

As white Americans, and many blacks as well, contemplated the announced intention of the Bolshevik movement to mobilize peoples of color worldwide into revolutionary action, and as it became apparent that party leadership in Russia saw America as a fertile field for creating revolutionary cadres out of disaffected minorities, the fear of black radicalism mushroomed. Blacks were damned as Wobblies, socialists, Bolsheviks, or anarchists simply for agreeing with ideas that went beyond political orthodoxy. Even black nationalist (and anti-communist) Marcus Garvey received the communist label because he rejected the subordinate "place" assigned to African Americans. Some blacks, like Chandler Owen and A. Philip Randolph, editors of the socialist *Messenger,* who coined the term "New Crowd Negroes" to describe the new generation of militants, were genuine supporters of social and economic revolution but rejected communist affiliation. Others, like members of the African Blood Brotherhood, embraced the Communist Party. But the federal government and wider public were disinclined to distinguish degrees of adherence or advocacy. Any African American who dissented from Democratic or Republican politics and the socio-economic system of American capitalism was likely to be excommunicated as a "Bolshevist."

As the federal intelligence network monitored the growing New Crowd Negro temper, the *Messenger* and its editors seemed its most dangerous proponents. Four days before the Armistice, Randolph was a featured guest at a socialist gathering to celebrate the first anniversary of the Soviet Republic. His speech, recorded by a Bureau of Investigation stenographer, expressed hope for a socialist republic in America. But if world governments were not socialized, and the lust of capitalism not abolished, war between the white and darker races would result. The proposed League of Nations, according to Randolph, was simply a capitalist tool and would be helpless to prevent such events. It is no wonder, then, that the Bureau seriously began to watch Randolph, Owen, and their magazine for promoting "Bolsheviki activities among Negroes," even though Randolph and Owen remained committed to the Socialist Party and rejected formal affiliation with the new communist parties.[2]

Why did the *Messenger* so alarm the federal intelligence agencies? Attorney General Palmer believed it was the most dangerous of all black publications for its emphasis on six unacceptable themes: pride that blacks fought back against white rioters; the right of blacks to arm for self-defense against lynchers and rioters and, if necessary, retaliate in kind; a demand for total social equality, including racial intermarriage; support for the IWW; advocacy of Bolshevik doctrines; and hostility toward the South, the Wilson administration, the peace treaty, and the League of Nations. Again and again investigative reports would charge the *Messenger,* its editors, and other militant voices with "race hatred." Bureau agents, the attorney general, and much of the white public were unable to distinguish between blacks' loathing of Jim Crow, disfranchisement, and lynching, on the one hand, and genuine racism toward whites. Any attack on the racial status quo was an assault on the well-being of society, according to prevailing Social Darwinist thinking. Black self-defense and sexual equality between the races were unthinkable. And behind these nightmares lay the specter of Bolshevik agitators, Bolshevik ideas, Bolshevik money.[3]

Throughout 1919 most manifestations of black militancy were attributed to communist influences. The Bureau's case file on Joseph J. Jones, the Wobbly activist who murdered his would-be lover and then committed suicide, called him an "alleged Bolshevik." William Monroe Trotter, militant editor of the Boston *Guardian,* was said to be an advocate of Bolshevism. Black nationalist Garvey was similarly labeled even though he believed that white communists would always follow their own racial loyalties. The State Department, alerted to the circulation of Garvey's *Negro World* in the Caribbean basin, suspected that it was supported by German or Bolshevik funds. And as the Bureau began to take note of that newspaper, early reports were captioned "probable Bolshevik propaganda."[4] Bolshevism proved to be the simplest explanation for the various new black militancies. If the New Crowd Negro could be attributed to subversive agitation, then its legitimacy could be dismissed.

The Justice Department made strenuous efforts to propagandize the American public and delegitimize radicalism. Attorney General Palmer described the ranks of native-born communists as "criminals, mistaken idealists, social bigots, and many unfortunate men and women suffering from various forms of hyperesthesia." Another Justice Department description claimed that while American-born radicals were "less bloodthirsty and less given to violence than the foreigners . . . many of them border on insanity; many others are women with minds gone slightly awry, morbid, restless, and seeking the sensational, craving for something they know not what." The Justice Department's propaganda machine offered the press "news" stories about radicalism, already engraved on plates and ready for printing. Government documents were leaked to influential, large-circulation magazines with Attorney General Palmer's personal suggestion that they use them to expose the Bolshevik menace. Press releases, with information attributed to "government officials" or "federal sources," warned of Bolshevik and IWW efforts to subvert the black population, particularly through the pages of the *Messenger*.[5]

By the middle of the "Red Summer" of 1919 the government's propaganda had taken on a life of its own. With riots occurring in Washington and Chicago in July, the Bureau sought to prove that Bolshevik propaganda had incited the violence, ignoring the fact that white mobs initiated events in both cities. And even though city officials and Bureau agents investigating the riots concluded that local frictions and issues had caused the outbreaks, Attorney General Palmer's office chose to believe otherwise.[6] Such conclusions were undoubtedly influenced by the analysis of "Radicalism and Sedition among the Negroes as Reflected in their Publications," written by the Post Office Translation Bureau's Robert Adger Bowen. Among the new breed of militant black editors, "the ablest of them all [Randolph] advocates Bolshevism among the negroes and the establishment in this country of Bolshevik rule."[7]

The Bureau found what it considered black Bolshevik activity all across the nation in mid-1919. The May-June issue of the *Messenger* featured editorials entitled "The March of Soviet Government" and "We Want More Bolshevik Patriotism," spurring attention to the magazine from agents in several cities. The riots were probed for possible Bolshevik influence. Newspaper revelations that wealthy white female "parlor Bolsheviks" were spreading anarchism among blacks led J. Edgar Hoover to begin investigating this problem. A report on a tour through the South by white NAACP official Herbert Seligman was filed under "Bolshevik Activities amongst Negroes." All of Dixie was infected, according to Texas governor W. P. Hobby, who urged Attorney General Palmer to investigate "race trouble":

> It is my judgment that the Bolshevik influence, which is manifest in this country to some extent, is seeking to array the negroes against the constituted authorities, both State and Federal. . . . I think it worth while to find out the source of this propaganda, because the publication of negro newspapers in the South, and throughout the country, the circulation and delivery of them free, together with the propaganda carried on by negro speakers, I believe, is financed and prompted by some sinister source.

Bureau investigation in Texas found no "tangible" Bolshevik propaganda although "it is certain that the negroes are being urged to defend their rights."[8]

But sinister influences were perceived elsewhere in mid-1919. The Bureau claimed that blacks in St. Louis were arming themselves with the encouragement of "radical elements such as the IWW and Bolsheviks." When a new black monthly, the *Crusader,* appeared in numerous cities, it was quickly judged "entirely radical" and sympathetic to Bolshevism. So too, it was claimed, was Garvey's *Negro World,* which carried an editorial urging blacks to join Russia, China, India, Egypt, and Ireland to achieve the freedom of all subject peoples. The Military Intelligence Division likewise saw the influence of communism behind black militancy, concluding that the NAACP was a "menace" because it was "dominated" by the Bolsheviki and IWW and promoting racial antagonism. The Office of Naval Intelligence too was convinced that "systematic" propaganda by the IWW and "Socialist sources" (meaning the new communist parties) had promoted the summer's riots.[9]

When J. Edgar Hoover assumed responsibility for the Bureau's anti-radical crusade in August, he quickly identified the "principal phases of the Negro movement into which inquiry should be made." First on his list was the *Messenger* which "is stated to be the Russian organ of the Bolsheviki in the United States and to be the headquarters of revolutionary thought." The second target was Garvey and his Universal Negro Improvement Association. It took nothing more than a reading of the *Messenger's* flamboyant rhetoric to convince Hoover of its revolutionary sympathies, and he was likewise certain that "Soviet Russian Rule is upheld and there is open advocation [*sic*] of Bolshevism" in Garvey's *Negro World.* In short, by mid-1919 the Justice Department had linked the two most frightening voices of the New Crowd Negro spirit with Bolshevism.[10]

Individuals were frequently labeled "Bolshevists" and watched by federal agents because of their ideas, especially admiration for the Russian revolution.

Most such black targets, like Ross D. Brown, were not members of either of the two new communist parties. Known as "the famous colored socialist orator of Muncie" (Indiana), Brown was an itinerant organizer among both blacks and whites, who helped form a socialist local for black mine and mill workers in Fayette County, West Virginia, in 1914. Active in party activities for many years, he was its candidate for Indiana state geologist and statistician in 1914 and 1916. During the war Brown was arrested in Cleveland on three successive nights for telling street-corner crowds that the conflict was antithetical to the interests of the working class.[11]

Brown's allegiance remained with the Socialist Party and its leader, Eugene V. Debs, with whom he sometimes shared the same podium, but he also admired the new Russian government and supported its overall aims. In August 1919 he addressed a Detroit crowd of 2,000 which was protesting the deportation of alien radicals, denouncing the "oppressive" American government and praising Bolshevism as the only system giving workers a fair chance. From there he traveled through Ohio and Indiana, speaking primarily to black audiences. When the special agent in charge of the Indianapolis field office urged that Brown be questioned so that "he might throw some light on the alleged effort of the Bolsheviki element to spread propaganda among the colored citizens," Chief William J. Burns ordered agents in several cities to chart Brown's activities as he crisscrossed the Midwest.[12]

By 1920 Brown was traveling both the communist and socialist circuits to lecture on "Capitalism, the Curse of the World, Socialism the Solution." In addition to speaking fees and collections, he derived income from sale of his slim volume of poems entitled *Rhymes of Reason*. Indianapolis agents purchased the book, placed an informant in local radical circles, and instructed the police to keep Brown "under close surveillance," a task that could not have been easy given his constant travels. In May he went to New York, meeting Randolph and the communist circle led by Cyril Briggs and Wilfred A. Domingo. During the following months agents observed him promoting the socialist ticket in Chicago and St. Louis. But when Brown tried to address a street-corner rally in Buffalo, a hostile crowd ordered him to leave or be hung from a telegraph pole. October found him back in New York, telling a Harlem crowd that the only hope for black and white workers was to hasten the collapse of capitalism. One of the Bureau's black informants described that speech as "the worst that I have ever heard, in openly advocating Bolshevism."[13]

Brown continued to proselytize through 1921, with Bureau agents dutifully monitoring his speeches to socialist "mass meetings" in St. Louis, Detroit, Chicago, Buffalo, and Pittsburgh.[14] The "famous colored socialist orator of

Muncie" disappeared from Bureau reports after 1921, however, as the radical movements faded. Writing more than forty years later, black communist Richard B. Moore recalled the legion of gifted outdoor speakers, debaters, and writers who challenged the racial status quo and earned the scrutiny of Hoover's anti-radical General Intelligence Division. Among that fraternity was the "militant socialist" Brown.[15] Never a communist himself, he was nonetheless labeled a Bolshevik by federal agents who took few pains to make ideological distinctions during the Red Scare.

After 1919 the federal intelligence establishment focused its scrutiny of Black America primarily on four targets: the *Messenger's* admiration for Bolshevism and promotion of socialist electoral politics; the *Crusader's* communist advocacy and sponsorship of the African Blood Brotherhood; African Americans who actively participated in communist activities or traveled to Russia for party training and meetings; and the Garvey movement. The Bureau and the Military Intelligence Division remained convinced that black communist activities posed a serious threat.

MID was especially prone to exaggerate the danger. Its weekly reports in 1920 included a section entitled "Negro Subversion" which was based on data supplied by intelligence officers around the nation as well as material gleaned from Bureau reports. The year began with the army warning that both communist parties were mobilizing blacks to overthrow the existing economic and political systems. MID's propensity to take a propaganda pronouncement and elevate it into imminent danger is illustrated in its alarmed report that Soviet "ambassador" Ludwig Martens was fostering uprisings by blacks in the United States, Kanakas in Hawaii, and the native populations of other colonies.

MID's officer corps imbibed much of American culture's nativist anti-Semitism, and weekly reports also dwelt on the alleged dissemination of radical propaganda among blacks by Russian Jews. "Evidence" that black soldiers were interested in Bolshevism likewise alarmed MID, with the IWW, the *Messenger,* and the short-lived *Emancipator* blamed for much "radical propaganda" among blacks. MID had not learned to distinguish rhetoric from action and took alarm at Garvey's statement that Africans across the world must gain allies—even Trotsky and Lenin—in their quest for liberation. Army analysts remained convinced that the Bolsheviks had a systematic plan for propagandizing all the colored peoples of the world, with money and personnel for agitation being funneled into the United States from Mexico. It is true that Party congresses in Moscow emphasized the need to reach the nonwhite populations, but the amount of concrete assistance provided for such work was much less than MID or the Justice Department supposed.[16]

The Bureau had many more agents in the field and, not surprisingly, it discovered even more "evidence" of communist influence among African Americans than did MID.

By 1920 all the intelligence agencies agreed that the greatest danger existed in northern cities where radical periodicals were published and sold in large quantities, mass meetings were easily held, and street-corner orators abounded. But whenever southern blacks seemed restive, met in "secret," received publications from the North, or were addressed by unfamiliar whites, the hidden hand of communism or the IWW was also perceived. A report of hundreds of blacks attending a secret midnight gathering provoked a Bureau investigation in Fort Bend County, Texas, but undercover informants supplied by the local sheriff failed to substantiate the presence of white communists or Wobblies.[17] This was just one of numerous instances where southern whites, fearing loss of the control they exercised over the black population as well as the interference of "outside agitators," magnified innocuous events into, literally, federal cases.

In urban centers, the Bureau greatly expanded its use of black informants to penetrate radical circles in 1920. Informant Albert Farley covered speeches by Randolph and Owen in Washington. In New York, William A. Bailey infiltrated "radical Negro activities" and found the *Crusader* circle particularly interested in possible support for African independence from German, Russian, and Japanese revolutionaries.[18]

During 1920 and 1921 Jamaican-born informant Herbert S. Boulin provided much of the Bureau's information on alleged Bolshevik activities in New York. Many of his reports described the black Bolsheviks and Wobblies who congregated almost daily at Martin Luther Campbell's tailoring shop on 135th Street in Harlem. Boulin alleged, falsely, that the local Socialist Party branch was really a communist cell; "proof" lay in the fact that a socialist soapbox orator on Lenox Avenue regarded a socialist vote as a vote for Bolshevism. Boulin also alleged that the regulars at Campbell's shop rarely worked and instead spent most of their time discussing Russia, Bolshevism, and other radical topics. This was not true of at least two of them: E. A. Potter was a postal employee, and Grace Campbell was a municipal social worker. Boulin often noted with undisguised disgust that the radicals harped on the rottenness of the capitalist system and the beauty of Soviet rule which, they believed, would bring full equality for blacks in America if duplicated.[19]

Boulin consistently exaggerated the danger of revolutionary activities in Harlem in 1920. The two communist parties had only insignificant numbers and influence with the working masses. Yet he warned that the radicals were hoping that "something is going to happen soon" and that Domingo, especially, would blindly follow any dictate of Lenin or Trotsky; Domingo was, in fact, a paid party propagandist. But the presidential election came and went with no dramatic incidents or results. For all their rhetoric and debate, the tailor shop habitués were not plotting insurrection, merely sponsoring weekly People's Educational Forums where black and white radicals expounded their doctrines. With the return of pleasant weather in the spring of 1921 they added street meetings where denunciations of capitalism and praise for the Russian soviet system were de rigueur. Boulin faithfully reported each event, but he and the Bureau were losing interest in this radical cell which made little permanent impact on Harlem's population. Instead, Boulin began to devote more time to infiltrating the African Blood Brotherhood–*Crusader* circle.[20]

Boulin was an important eye and ear for the Bureau of Investigation, monitoring the radical pulse of Black America's capital. Along with its own agents, the Bureau had the pro-Bolshevik radicals well covered. It should have been clear, however, that their numbers were not increasing and their overall influence was not widespread. But a common failing of the federal intelligence agencies was their inability to see that radical rhetoric did not invariably translate into radical action, much less threats to national security.

Hundreds of thousands of investigation reports from agents and informants flooded into Bureau headquarters during the Red Scare. In addition, Hoover's required weekly summaries of radical trends—including "Bolshevik activities"—were filed by each Bureau field office, plus monthly surveys of the radical press (again covering "Bolshevik publications") from selected cities. Boulin's almost daily reports were regarded as trustworthy by the Bureau agents in New York who composed the weekly summaries, and his words were often repeated verbatim. Hence these digests—read by those in the Bureau hierarchy as well as MID analysts—depicted events and personalities as Boulin saw them, whether accurate or not. For example, readers of New York's weekly report were informed that Marcus Garvey intended to "seek an alliance with Trotzky and Lenine." This was at best a half-truth; Garvey only said that the African liberation movement should seek allies who were anti-imperialist and anti-colonialist. New York agents likewise accepted as truth, and included in a weekly summary, Boulin's alarmed assumption that socialist, IWW, and Bolshevik propaganda in Harlem was spreading rapidly in the second half of 1920.[21]

The other major hub of radical activity was Chicago, center of a great amount of labor militancy. Visible evidence of black radicalism was not as great as in New York, but the Windy City had a strong UNIA membership, a large circulation for the *Messenger,* and its own outspoken newspapers, the *Defender* and the *Whip.* Chicago, like New York, had a Bureau division office, overseeing a number of field offices, and its anti-radical squad was particularly experienced in Wobbly probes. For much of 1920 it focused on labor organizer R. T. Sims, the "ultra radical negro Bolsheviki propagandist and IWW," plus alleged efforts by local communists to foster a "spirit of revolt" among blacks. Unlike New York, however, no black informants or infiltrators worked for long periods in Chicago; its agents had to rely on their own investigative skills.[22]

The same was true for other cities where white informants and Bureau agents, some working undercover, found communists and socialists trying to recruit blacks in 1920 and 1921. But how successful were such radical efforts? Although the Communist Party outlined a "Negro Program" to support blacks in their struggle against "hellish conditions" and encouraged members to support any movement that encouraged a "spirit of revolt"—taking care to avoid racial wars, as solidarity with white workers had to be maintained—relatively few blacks embraced any form of radicalism. Even in New York only tiny numbers could be counted as communists or sympathizers. Elsewhere, evidence was even more scant. Although agents in Springfield, Massachusetts, made much of the fact that many local UNIA members attended a Russian Club picnic and "sang the Internationale as lustily as did the Ruskys," there was no conversion of blacks to Bolshevism.[23]

The Communist Party's most widespread effort to reach the black population came after Tulsa was engulfed by racial violence on May 31 and June 1, 1921. Widespread arson in the black district made impossible an accurate count of the dead, but as many as 270 persons may have lost their lives. Over a thousand black dwellings and businesses were destroyed. Local authorities accused the ABB of starting the riot, although in fact local conditions were the cause.[24]

Seizing the opportunity, the Communist Party printed hundreds of thousands of copies of a pamphlet entitled "The Tulsa Massacre," sending it into every city where members could distribute it in black neighborhoods. Charting its distribution was one of the Bureau's major preoccupations in the summer of 1921. Agents in Pittsburgh described the offensive "dodger" as blaming all blacks' troubles on the government and private enterprise; urging "organized force" against bloodthirsty capitalists and the Ku Klux Klan; and encouraging both black and white workers to establish a soviet republic in America. This one-page, two-sided leaflet, which advised blacks "to resist the armed assaults upon their homes, their women and children" was, in the admission of the head of the Bureau's Pittsburgh office, "cleverly written."[25]

To agents who had spent the previous three years combating Bolshevik attempts to penetrate black America, real and imagined, "The Tulsa Massacre" was "the worst radical type" of propaganda. And the quantities that were circulated were astounding. Distribution occurred countrywide in July. Hoover warned the Chicago field office that one ton of the circulars would be delivered to that city. Delegates to the NAACP's annual convention in Detroit received copies. Agents in Pittsburgh discovered that 24,000 copies were to be distributed there and in seven nearby mill towns. Philadelphia and New York were also major targets. Agents reported its distribution in at least fourteen other cities. The Secret Service and MID also complained of the flyer's circulation.

Was "The Tulsa Massacre" an illegal publication? Bureau agents seeking to interdict the alleged ton of circulars destined for Chicago were advised by Assistant United States Attorney R. A. Milroy that it did not violate any federal statute. But wishing its suppression as much as did the Bureau, Milroy suggested that agents persuade the Illinois state attorney to prosecute the circular's author under the state syndicalist law. Local police were obliging, but there is no record of anyone being apprehended. Pittsburgh was a different matter. When he recognized that federal prosecution was not possible, Bureau division superintendent Robert B. Spencer ordered agents to initiate action under the Flynn Act, a state sedition law. Both the state police and Pittsburgh officers agreed to arrest anyone distributing "The Tulsa Massacre." Warning of such consequences must have reached local radicals, for Bureau agents reported with pride that no distribution took place. Even greater satisfaction was gained by Hartford agents when three individuals, including the local Communist Party leader, were convicted under Connecticut's sedition law and sentenced to five months in the county jail for distributing the circular.[26]

The improbability that even modest numbers of blacks would turn to Bolshevism by the summer of 1921 made dissemination of "The Tulsa Massacre" an act of futility. Pittsburgh agent H. J. Lenon, commenting on extensive coverage of the riot in the black press, noted that "the chief slogan to be heard here [in black neighborhoods] is 'where can I get a job?' In spite of newspaper publications about race riots and disturbing propaganda of all sorts, there would be no way of arousing even the slightest enthusiasm until after the people get work to do."[27] Lenon (and Marx) were right: populations struggling for mere survival are not likely revolutionary material.

Even after the Red Scare ended and Attorney General Palmer departed office along with the rest of the Wilson administration, the Bureau of Investigation remained convinced that communism posed a serious threat to America. Hoover's "General Intelligence Bulletin," copies of which went to the Bureau's intelligence partners and key figures in the new administration, claimed in the spring of 1921 that a new radical organization was born every day and that all radical movements were convinced, now that the sedition section of the Espionage Act was repealed, that the federal government was unable to prosecute them. Not surprisingly, then, when a new (and short-lived) organization called the "Iron Ring" was founded by *Washington Eagle* publisher J. Finley Wilson to disseminate racial news, monitor legislation, and fight the KKK, the GID accepted at face value an informant's wild story that it would receive financial assistance from Japan and Russia![28] The Bureau's capacity to believe its own nightmares was impressive. In fact, the only noteworthy black Bolsheviks during the Harding years were the handful who traveled to Russia to participate in Comintern activities, plus some members of the ABB. Among the ABB's dwindling numbers, Bureau agents and informants focused primarily on its founder, Cyril V. Briggs, and its most dynamic public speaker, Richard B. Moore.

The Bureau of Investigation began what Moore's daughter and biographer terms "lifetime surveillance" of Moore in early 1920. Barbados-born, he arrived in New York as a teenager, a decade before the Red Scare. Like other Afro-Caribbean migrants, he was unprepared for the ferocity of American racism and found antidotes in racial nationalism and socio-economic radicalism as espoused by soapbox speakers like Hubert H. Harrison, Randolph, and Owen. Joining Harlem's 21st Assembly District Socialist Club, Moore studied Marx and Engels in company with Wilfred A. Domingo, Otto Huiswoud, and Grace Campbell while helping organize the People's Educational Forum. Moore soon graduated to street oratory, sometimes declaiming "straight socialism," sometimes "Negro-ology." Then the ABB captured his allegiance, offering an international perspective on the plight of peoples of African descent. Briggs espoused Lenin's idea that oppressed peoples had a right to national self-determination, and Moore, too, adopted this concept. At the same time he and other radicals became alienated from the Socialist Party because of its failure to construct a specific program to address black issues. By the early twenties Moore and others in the ABB were gravitating toward communism.[29]

The Bureau opened a case file on Richard B. Moore in March 1920 when undercover informant Bailey met him in Harlem, working with Domingo on the short-lived *Emancipator*. That magazine's inaugural issue alarmed the federal intelligence community: its editorials were anti-capitalist, pro-IWW, and viewed Bolshevism as the proper antidote to imperialism. Soon Bailey attended the radicals' weekly public program, known as the People's Educational Forum, and heard Moore denounce Bureau agents in attendance as "skunks," causing them so much discomfort that they left the meeting. Soon

MID, alerted by the Bureau, began to include Moore's activities in the category of "Negro subversion."[30] Bailey's replacement, undercover informant P-135, was inducted into the local socialist cell by Moore and Briggs. At one meeting Moore proclaimed that "the embittered and desperate souls of the minority would reach forth from the most daring agitators of Bolshevism." A successful revolution would not require the support of the majority.[31]

When Boulin was installed as the Bureau's Harlem infiltrator in mid-1920, he easily made Moore's acquaintance by frequenting Campbell's Tailor Shop, finding him busily promoting the candidacies of black socialists. Following the election, Boulin reported that the People's Educational Forum was "the greatest school and the most effective spot for the spreading of and the teaching of Bolshevism among Negroes in general." Moore and Domingo selected its speakers, and nearly all the radicals associated with it carried the "Bolshevik red card" and paid monthly dues to Grace Campbell. Moore had clearly progressed beyond socialism, stressing that Bolshevism was the only solution for the "race problem."[32]

When Oklahoma authorities accused the ABB of fomenting the Tulsa riot, the organization's new notoriety greatly encouraged Briggs, Moore, and other members who were described by New York agents as "pronounced radicals and anti-whites." The ABB organized mass meetings in several cities to explain its purposes and reveal the facts about the Tulsa attack. Moore was the featured speaker at one such gathering in New York and, in Boulin's words, "I have never heard anyone who spoke so defiantly and disrespectfully of the U.S.A. and the flag." Moore praised the ABB for teaching "self defence by negroes and preparation to fight back" at lynchers and rioters. Boulin concluded that he was "the most pronounced Communist" and had become "the most outspoken, daring and radical among all the other negro 'Reds' in Harlem." No wonder, then, that Bureau agents in New York kept close tabs on Moore and meticulously recorded his views.[33]

Boulin next reported that the radicals—two of whom were full party members—were slipping communist pamphlets under the doors of Harlem residences. This was of great interest to Boulin's Bureau handlers who were eager to establish the black activists' communist connections. Several of Boulin's reports detailed how the ABB had become a virtual branch of the Communist Party, which was subsidizing the *Crusader*. Convinced that the ABB was inciting racial hatred and retaliation, Boulin urged the government to deport Briggs, Domingo, and Moore, none of whom were American citizens. This, of course, was the tack the Justice Department was pursuing against Garvey, but deportation could occur only after conviction of a felony, and that had not yet occurred. Prosecuting Moore or his associates was an even more remote possibility, despite the alleged perniciousness of their statements and the ABB's purposes.[34]

For almost a year, Boulin provided a near daily record of the activities of Moore and other Harlem militants. But after August 1921, while the Bureau maintained watch on the *Crusader* and ABB, it lost interest in Moore. Not until mid-1922, when Harlem radicals denounced Garvey's meeting with a Ku Klux Klan official, did Moore's name again surface in Bureau reports. Black "special employee" Andrew M. Battle, operating undercover, found his views had not moderated; he was still urging blacks to prepare for the coming revolution.[35] Infiltration of the ABB passed in mid-1923 to Earl E. Titus, one of the Bureau's first black agents. He quickly rose to leadership and met the same inner circle that Bailey and Boulin identified three years previously. Moore, Briggs, Domingo, and Grace Campbell were still members of the Supreme Executive Council. But the organization had fallen on hard times, even to the point of engaging a well-known moderate speaker, NAACP executive secretary James Weldon Johnson, to draw a crowd in hopes of reviving the membership. Finding a suitable location for the event proved difficult, as local police were quick to close down meetings or threaten participants with arrest. The ABB's weakness was apparent in its unwillingness to challenge such obstacles.[36]

Moore hesitated to join the Communist Party. His friend Huiswoud had no qualms and was in fact one of its founding members in 1919. Other black socialists, like Lovett Fort-Whiteman, Grace Campbell, and Cyril Briggs, joined in the early twenties. Moore was excited about the apparent success of the Soviet experiment, hoped for revolutionary change in the United States, but remained skeptical that white American communists had rid themselves of racism and that the party was sincerely willing to address the "Negro problem." Overcoming his reservations, he finally joined the (communist) Workers Party in mid-1922, assuming a leadership position in its West Side Harlem Branch. The Justice Department would maintain a case file on Moore to his death in 1978, even though he was expelled from the Party in 1942 and thereafter devoted himself to anti-colonialism and Pan-Caribbean militancy. These ties to international radical movements also ensured that the State Department would long maintain a file on him.[37]

Both the State and Justice departments monitored communists and communist sympathizers, and each needed the other's cooperation. No other agency had the Bureau of Investigation's capability for domestic counter-espionage, and State relied heavily on Hoover's GID after 1919. But the State Department's international contacts were unsurpassed. Thus numerous consular reports and other documents found their way into Bureau case files. Both departments kept extensive card lists of suspicious individuals, with at least three separate files in Justice alone. State frequently sought the assistance of both the Bureau and MID in passport matters. And all three maintained lists of suspect publications, State having the best resources for monitoring those which originated abroad.[38]

In matters having international implications, the State Department was the unofficial clearinghouse for reports. Such cases were routed to L. Lanier Winslow, an assistant to the Counselor, who decided what information to send to the Bureau. Following Winslow's posting to the embassy in London, incoming reports on radicalism went to assistant undersecretary William L. Hurley. Both men became conversant on Bolshevism and black radicalism.[39]

Fears of radicalism and subversion prompted the growth of each agency in the federal intelligence partnership. Efficiency required cooperation. But there was external pressure as well. The British government also wanted to see an efficient American domestic intelligence operation, hoping for a free flow of information across the Atlantic. Cooperation between the two nations had been formalized during the war as their military intelligence services exchanged liaison officers. By 1919, the British were gravely concerned about the growth of racial radicalism in their West Indian colonies. Links between ferment in the islands, American black militancy, and international communism were suspected. Hence the British encouraged American intelligence agencies to monitor Garvey's UNIA and the activities of black socialists and communists. Their military mission in New York also conducted its own investigations of racial militancy in the United States, using Welsh-born undercover operative R. D. Jonas, who was simultaneously an informer for MID. His extensive analyses of black radicalism were shared with American agencies, an exchange of data which was particularly encouraged by the American embassy in London.[40]

Anglo-American intelligence cooperation enhanced the investigation of the Communist Third International's efforts to enlist and train blacks for leadership and subversion among their race. The conviction that racial unrest was communist-inspired was fed not only by the Red Scare and British colonial fears but also by American consular dispatches from Riga, Latvia, which described the activities of the Second Congress of the Third International, meeting in Russia in 1920. Particularly noteworthy was a speech by American journalist John Reed urging communist propaganda among blacks. Similar advocacy by the American party leadership heightened the government's sense of urgency.[41]

By 1921 the State Department believed that Jamaican-born poet Claude McKay was the key link between black communists and Party leadership in Moscow. He was no stranger to the Bureau, which was well aware that his defiant poem, "If We Must Die," published in militant periodicals like the *Messenger,* had made him a celebrity in both black and white radical circles. Various undercover informants found McKay transparent about his editorial work for the *Liberator,* interest in the IWW, and friendship with radicals and the Greenwich Village literary crowd.[42] In late 1922 interest in McKay intensified when he attended the Fourth Congress of the Third International. Much of the information gathered by the State Department—not all of which was accurate—came from the American consul at Riga. McKay was mistakenly believed to be an official American delegate, although he went on his own and was only accredited as a special representative after arriving in Moscow. It was further reported that McKay would remain in Russia to head a Negro Section of the Third International, but he was an artist, not a political activist, and had no thirst for such a role.[43]

One of the official delegates was listed as J. Billings, the Party name for Otto Huiswoud, a close friend of Briggs and member of the ABB. Bureau agents in New York already knew much about his political and business activities. Another delegate used the party name "Sasha" to disguise her true identity. The legation in Riga finally obtained a photograph printed in *Pravda* and concluded sarcastically that "it looks from the picture as though she might be classed as a 'ginger bread brown,' but it may only be dirt." The diplomats' smugness was shattered two weeks later when American journalists returning from Russia revealed that "Sasha" was the notorious white communist and feminist, Rose Pastor Stokes, who was also well known to the Bureau as a supporter of the ABB.[44]

American officials also suspected that black delegates were returning to the United States with instructions and money from Leon Trotsky to set up a "colored Soviet." McKay was said to have graduated from the Bolshevik "propaganda school," although he was in fact uninterested in such a responsibility. Bureau director Burns ordered agents at all ports of entry to work with customs and immigration officials to ensure that the suspects were intercepted and interrogated upon their return. (Since they might arrive at a Canadian port, Bureau agents in Chicago and other inland cities were also told to be vigilant.) Informants within the Communist Party were also instructed to ascertain their travel plans. And because the delegates did not possess passports, their names were put on the State Department's passport refusal list should they apply for such documents in Europe. In the case of McKay, such precautions proved fruitless; he departed Russia not for the United States, but Paris.[45]

The American intelligence network's frequently unreliable information was supplemented with data supplied by the British, on the understanding that such cooperation would be reciprocated. In fact, many European countries were anxiously watching the Bolshevik situation. Latvian secret police, astride a well-traveled route between Russia and the West, were particularly zealous in intercepting suspected subversives such as Sen Katayama, a prominent Japanese communist (and friend of McKay's) whose photographs and papers they stole. Among Katayama's possessions was a manifesto to "oppressed negro peoples of the world" and designation of New York as the most fruitful location for communist recruitment of blacks. This intelligence was hardly comforting to American authorities.[46]

The Bolsheviks failed to convert more than a handful of blacks to communism in the 1920s. But imperfectly gauging the weakness of the domestic communist movement, the State Department and Bureau continued to monitor McKay and other suspects. A Pan-American communist congress in Mexico did not materialize, and the communist-aligned ABB achieved only a modest membership and was disbanded in 1925 upon its absorption into the American Negro Labor Congress, a communist front organization. McKay settled in France in 1923 for an extended literary exile, drifting far from politics and doctrinaire communism. British authorities kept closest watch on his subsequent movements, on one occasion purloining a letter to an English friend and copying it for the State Department.[47] But from an objective standpoint, the poet and novelist was no longer a subject worthy of political intelligence.

The outcome of these events, however, was far greater than the surveillance of individual "Bolsheviks" or members of communist-leaning organizations like the ABB. The fear of communism was now embedded in American political intelligence. Communism would henceforth be seen as the engine that propelled nearly every militant movement on the Left. Varieties of black militancy, if not communist-led, would be perceived as communist-inspired. In short, communism had become the bogeyman of American politics. And it had likewise become a weapon with which to damn and delegitimize opponents of the status quo. Black militants—genuine Bolsheviks, socialists, but also nondoctrinaire militants—discovered this in the first Red Scare, and their descendants would continue to feel such pressure for the next half century.

THREE

❦

"THEY ARE VICIOUSLY EDITED WITH A VIEW OF CREATING RACIAL HATRED"

Investigation and Intimidation of the
Chicago Defender *and Other*
Black Newspapers

On January 9, 1919, two months after the Armistice, Attorney General Thomas W. Gregory submitted his resignation to President Woodrow Wilson. Thanking the president for the privilege of serving the country, he confidently predicted that "the Department of Justice will have substantially brought its war activities to a close and be working under normal conditions" by March 4, the day on which he intended to leave federal service.[1] But "normal conditions" would not prevail in March, and in one respect would never return: America's modern political intelligence system was in place.

Nearly everyone wanted a resumption of "normal conditions." But knotty problems stood in the way. Liberals urged repeal of the Espionage Act, fearing that continuous prosecutions would turn the working class toward Bolshevism, and likewise wanted government at all levels to again respect freedom of speech and public assembly. Postal censorship and suppression of periodicals also should be halted, they believed, if the country were to return to calm. President Wilson ordered the Post Office Department to cease censorship, but he was thwarted by Postmaster General Albert Sidney Burleson, who later wrote on the bottom of the president's instructions, "Continued to suppress and Courts sustained me every time." Liberals also wanted amnesty for political prisoners, but the Justice Department steadfastly insisted that everyone convicted under the Espionage Act was guilty of actual obstruction of the war, agreeing only that some sentences were disproportionate to the crime. Prosecutions continued into 1919, encouraged by the Supreme Court's validation of the Espionage Act in the *Schenck* case. And "normal" conditions would be impossible in the Justice Department after the appointment of A. Mitchell Palmer as the new Attorney General, over the objections of Gregory.[2]

Overarching all other issues, in the months following the Armistice, was the fear that communism would spread across Europe and then invade the shores of America. As President Wilson sailed for Europe in March for a second round of peace negotiations, Germany was rocked by a general strike as part of an unsuccessful Bolshevik revolt. Commenting to his private physician on board the *U.S.S. George Washington,* President Wilson confided the fear that black soldiers returning from Europe would be "our greatest medium in conveying bolshevism to America."[3] His apprehension was not unique. During the war many whites had believed that African Americans were less than wholeheartedly patriotic and were particular targets of enemy subversion, easily duped into acts of disloyalty. After 1918 these images evolved into fears that "the Negro is seeing Red." Federal intelligence targeted radicalism and militancy among blacks at the same time as native whites and foreigners suffered the same sort of attacks. Especially singled out were black periodicals.

A vibrant tradition of militant racial journalism was well established by World War I. William Monroe Trotter's *Boston Guardian,* founded in 1901, challenged the conservative strategies of Booker T. Washington. Robert Abbott's *Chicago Defender,* from its birth in 1905, excelled in condemning lynching and other examples of racism and, after 1915, exhorted blacks to leave the hated South for new freedoms and economic opportunities in northern cities. The National Association for the Advancement of Colored People, established in 1909, quickly found a militant voice in the *Crisis,* begun and edited by the well-known scholar and anti-Bookerite W. E. B. DuBois. An even more militant "New Crowd Negro journalism" was born during the war, beginning with the socialist and anti-war *Messenger* in 1917, edited by transplanted southerners A. Philip Randolph and Chandler Owen. The following year witnessed the birth of Marcus Garvey's nationalist weekly *Negro World* and three monthlies: Cyril Briggs's *Crusader;* William Bridges's *Challenge;* and Hubert Harrison's *Negro Voice.* By the end of the war it was clear to observers of black journalism that African Americans, in many northern and some southern cities, were more insistent on change than ever before. The new militancy could neither be missed nor ignored.

Racial leadership, too, had evolved and matured in the two decades since Booker T. Washington's ascendancy to national influence. DuBois's short-

lived Niagara Movement helped crystalize opposition to Washington's advocacy of accommodation and conciliation toward white southerners. Its intention to revive the voice of protest against injustice and to fight for civil rights
was adopted by the new NAACP. With Washington's death in 1915, new
leadership styles and approaches to racial issues could more easily be tried. As
hundreds of thousands of African Americans streamed out of the South to find
wartime jobs in booming northern urban centers, would-be leaders like
Garvey, Randolph, Owen, and Harrison mounted street-corner soapboxes to
proclaim militant messages and promote socialism, black nationalism, and
other novel "isms." The New Crowd Negro was born, intent on arousing the
silent masses and challenging the ways whites had defined civil rights and race
relations for half a century. The democratic idealism of Woodrow Wilson's
wartime rhetoric only increased the sense of urgency and demand. By the end
of the war America's white majority would be confronted with demands for
change as far reaching as those voiced during the civil rights era two
generations later.[4]

The first black periodical that federal officials tried to silence after World
War I was the militant *Chicago Defender.* Begun with a capitalization of 25
cents on Abbott's kitchen table in 1905, the weekly had grown to 67,000
copies circulating nationwide by early 1917. A pioneer in the black press in
adopting a "yellow journalism" format, Abbott excoriated lynching, riots, and
other wrongs against the race. The *Defender* also urged southern blacks to
exchange sharecropping, peonage, and disfranchisement for industrial jobs
and greater freedom in the North. The paper's fearless racial defense and
attacks on white racism were bound to excite the opposition of whites who felt
that any dissent or questioning of government policies during wartime was
tantamount to offering aid and comfort to the enemy. Immediately upon
American entry into World War I frightened southern whites informed the
Bureau of Investigation that the *Defender* was being used by German interests
to incite blacks against whites and encourage unrest and even self-defense.
Worried whites also believed the northbound exodus was the work of German
subversion, which reinforced their belief that the Chicago weekly was the tool
of enemy interests. And the *Defender's* militant condemnation of the East St.
Louis riot in mid-1917 added further apprehension to those who feared its
growing influence. By that time circulation had climbed to over 90,000
copies.[5]

The Bureau of Investigation, postal authorities, and army intelligence
officers probed and harassed the *Chicago Defender* throughout the war months.
Bureau chief A. Bruce Bielaski was particularly concerned that the newspaper
was promoting opposition to the government and the war effort, three times
ordering new investigations, although no concrete evidence was found and
editor Abbott stoutly defended his patriotism.[6]

The most serious threat to the *Defender* came from the army's intelligence service. Receiving copies of the Bureau's reports on the newspaper and accepting at face value every allegation made against it, military intelligence assigned its best black operative, Maj. Walter H. Loving, to muzzle Abbott in May 1918. Loving believed the *Defender* to be "the most dangerous of all Negro journals" and warned Abbott that he would be held accountable for any article that displeased the government. The chastened editor promised to print nothing offensive. Soon thereafter the War Department sponsored a conference for black editors which stressed the need to win the war, not pursue the race's own agenda. Abbott's attendance amounted to a public profession of loyalty.[7]

Both during and after the war, postal officials had a direct weapon to use against the *Defender*: authority to ban it from the mail. Warning of this consequence was delivered to Abbott in mid-1918 after he printed an article on lynching which officials believed would discourage black patriotism. Each subsequent week's edition was closely scrutinized, with postal censors convinced that the paper promoted racial hatred and put misguided racial goals ahead of winning the war.[8] However, in the pantheon of "offensive negro papers," the *Defender* was, in the opinion of Postal Solicitor William H. Lamar, neither the most nor the least offensive of the lot. Some of the pressure to curb Abbott's weekly originated not from Washington but in southern communities where private citizens or postmasters continued to take alarm at the newspaper's local circulation. Regulations required postmasters to be vigilant, as Solicitor Lamar reminded one in Louisiana who sought authority to withhold delivery of the *Defender*: "The postmaster shall not give opinions to the public and when in doubt as to the mailability of any matter . . . he shall withhold the same from dispatch or delivery, as the case may be, and submit the question with samples of the matter to the Solicitor for the Post Office Department for instruction."[9]

By the fall of 1918 the federal intelligence network had achieved its goal. Editor Abbott, having endured threatening visits by federal agents, delays in the delivery of the *Defender,* and even more blatant intimidation from the War Department, exercised editorial caution for the duration of the war. Although he continued to urge migration out of the South and condemn lynching and racist policies by the government, professions of patriotism were also prominently featured. Outright suppression had not been needed to gain such compliance, and surveillance slackened in the waning months of the war.[10]

But this respite was short-lived. The Military Intelligence Division renewed its opposition to the *Chicago Defender* when it took offense to the March 1, 1919, issue whose lead headline proclaimed "365th Infantry Lands at New York; White Officers Junk Regimental Flag; Soldiers Ashamed to Parade." Circulation was now at 140,000 copies weekly, including sales to black soldiers at home and abroad. Lacking statutory authority to directly attack the *Defender,* MID urged the Bureau of Investigation to act, reminding it of Maj. Loving's "reprimand" the previous spring and editor Abbott's "promise" to refrain from printing anything that might "stir up strife between the white and colored races." Abbott was back to old habits, reported MID, inciting "trouble." But what could the Bureau do? Yet another investigation of the newspaper seemed fruitless, so acting chief William Elby Allen sought the opinion of the United States attorney in Chicago as to whether the March 1 issue violated the Espionage Act.[11]

If the war had officially ended, investigation of the *Defender* would have been beyond MID's jurisdiction, but as no peace treaty was yet formalized, the country was still technically on a wartime footing. This provided all the justification needed for intelligence officers in Chicago to conduct a thorough probe in the spring of 1919, sending offensive copies to Washington. Abbott was subjected to another "interview" during which he claimed to have purchased two regimental flags, promoted enlistment, and pledged $50,000 in Liberty Bonds during the war. Attempting to deflect charges of radicalism, he called attention instead to the activities of one of Chicago's most prominent black radicals, Industrial Workers of the World activist R. T. Sims.[12]

Abbott was probably unaware of how intrusive MID's investigation would become. Chicago intelligence officers identified his political associates, including former assistant state's attorney Ferdinand L. Barnett (husband of racial militant Ida B. Wells) and several prominent politicians linked to the Republican machine in Chicago. But their coup was to secretly obtain the *Defender's* sixty-four-page subscription and distribution list from the printer. This revealed the newspaper's influence in the South, where, for example, 1,700 newsstand copies were sold every week in Norfolk, 2,000 in Newport News, 2,650 in Richmond, and 2,300 in New Orleans. The greatest newsstand sales outside Chicago were the 10,000 copies weekly in New York City.[13] How MID secured this list and what it did with the information therein is unknown. The most logical beneficiaries of this heist would be the Bureau of Investigation and the Post Office solicitor's office, neither of which appears to have seen it.

The Office of Naval Intelligence was also nervously watching the *Defender* and other militant black publications in the spring of 1919. ONI director Rear Admiral A. P. Niblack sent the Bureau a lengthy report on radical agitation among blacks which labeled the *Defender* "a very red negro paper." The document focused on a link allegedly being forged between black activists and the enemies of Anglo-American hegemony: Irish Sinn Feiners, "Hindu" and Egyptian nationalists; Japanese; and Mexicans. Admiral Niblack believed that blacks were a very "emotional race" whose sinister "advisors" knew that continuous emphasis on wrongs committed against them would incite blacks to militancy and disorder.[14] Linkages between Garvey's UNIA and Indian and Japanese nationalists continued to worry ONI for months to come.

As the Red Scare flowered in the spring of 1919 the *Defender* was monitored by four intelligence agencies, which were receiving frequent pleas for action from alarmed whites. Residents of Wabbeseka, Arkansas, where blacks constituted two-thirds of the population, complained to the Bureau that the *Defender* and Garvey's *Negro World* were stirring up ill feelings between the races. Agent E. J. Kerwin interviewed one of the "best citizens" who reported there was "no danger immediate or otherwise from our old time darkey[,] but from the present younger crowd." Given this threat, the local resident urged that both publications be banned.[15]

The summer's riots brought the *Defender* far greater surveillance and suspicion. When racial violence began in Longview, Texas, members of both races were killed; blacks' determination to resist attacks was plainly evident. Enraged southern whites blamed a *Defender* article containing "disgraceful references" to a white woman for provoking the disorder in the east Texas city where a third of the 5,000 residents were black. On the urging of a constituent, Representative W. D. Upshaw of Georgia visited postal headquarters with copies of the *Defender* and declared that its alleged stimulation of racial tensions was a crime. Acknowledging that it would be hard to prosecute Abbott under existing law, Upshaw suggested a well-tried tactic: "It may be that a remonstrance from the Government might 'slow up' the devilment a little." Senator J. E. Ransdell of Louisiana urged similar action against the weekly. The postal solicitor conferred with Justice Department attorneys to see what options were available. Soon a similar plea came from the sheriff of Caddo Parish (Shreveport), 60 miles east of Longview, where uneasy whites, composing only 55 percent of the population, blamed the *Defender* for misrepresenting southern racial conditions and urged its suppression.[16]

The postmaster of nearby Marshall, Texas, also detailed whites' belief that the *Defender* had started the Longview riot and that it would continue to cause trouble by inciting animosity toward whites. But they would not tolerate blasphemies against their womenfolk. Most blacks were contented in Marshall, he claimed, grateful for white contributions to Bishop and Wiley colleges, both black institutions. Yet despite warnings from the sheriff, the local agent for the *Defender* continued to distribute the "inflammatory" paper while other copies arrived by mail. White attitudes such as those in Marshall were common by the beginning of the summer of 1919, in the view of the special agent in charge of the Bureau's Memphis field office: Criticism of the *Defender* was widespread in the South.[17] And when even more bloody riots occurred in northern cities, condemnation of the newspaper became nation-wide.

Naturally the *Defender* gave extensive coverage to these upheavals. And not surprisingly, when copies surfaced in the South, rural postmasters sounded the alarm, prompting new pleas that the newspaper be banned from the mails. The postmaster of Baldwin, Louisiana, fearing that a local black might be lynched if whites knew he had been mailed thirty copies of the issue devoted to the Washington riot, decided to withhold delivery of the bundle of newspapers. He may also have been motivated by the paper's satisfaction that blacks had battled white servicemen and police for several days in the nation's capital. Meanwhile the postmaster of Marks, Mississippi, relayed local whites' fears that the *Defender* would cause trouble if allowed to circulate, adding that hundreds of copies were mailed to Quitman County, where blacks outnumbered whites three to one. Solicitor Lamar's staff urged that this July 29 issue be declared objectionable and thus nonmailable, and that a permanent revocation of the paper's second-class mailing permit be considered. This recommendation was not implemented, however; Lamar's cooler judgment prevailed.[18] It appears that publisher Abbott knew nothing of these deliberations.

The most destructive racial clash occurred in Chicago in late July 1919, prompting Bureau of Investigation chief Frank Burke to order a thorough probe to determine if subversive influences caused the violence. Three agents began work while the riot was still in progress but soon reported that "investigation of this subject has failed to establish any connecting link between radical propaganda and the race riots." Local government, business, labor, and black community leaders agreed that neither the IWW nor Bolsheviks were behind the upheaval; instead, its causes lay in the racial tensions sown during the war when upwards of 100,000 southern blacks migrated to the city seeking better jobs, "social equality," and housing in formerly all-white neighborhoods.

Despite this generally accurate analysis, the Bureau's investigative team also agreed with Chicago police that the *Defender* and other black publications helped provoke the riot by their "decidedly rabid" attitude toward whites:

> Examination of the editorial contents . . . show that they are viciously edited with a view of creating racial hatred. The editorials are calculated to bring on riots and race wars, and if the readers of these papers shared their editorial beliefs it is strange how long the recent rioters constrained themselves from this week's throatcutting business. . . . All of the . . . publications have heaped fuel

on the sullen fires of racial hatred, which until recently leaders of the two races
have been able to keep down.

These allegations ignored entirely the roles of white gangs and blockbusting
realtors in poisoning racial relations for months before the riot. But at least one
Bureau agent saw matters in a broader context; while agreeing that the
Defender was "very radical in some of its articles," he found it contained
"nothing comparable to the inflammatory articles" in newer and less cautious
black periodicals like the Chicago *Whip* and *Broad-Ax*.[19]

Ripples from Chicago spread to many parts of the nation, in some instances
stimulating other riots, elsewhere spawning white panic that blacks whom
they had assumed were compliant or passive were now openly restive and
militant. The *Defender* was frequently blamed for creating such New Crowd
Negroes. In Mobile alarmed whites at least had the good sense to consult with
"responsible" blacks before violent repression occurred. White leaders were
convinced that the *Defender*, which enjoyed a large circulation, was the main
source of an evident new militancy although the *Mobile Forum* was also
charged with encouraging blacks to "think thoughts which are not good for
[them]." Bureau agent C. Calvin Outlaw asked headquarters whether he could
halt the *Defender's* circulation given the "ticklish situation all through the
South, as regards probable clashes in a riot"; the Chicago paper, he charged,
was keeping blacks "stirred up to the boiling point." Outlaw's answer came
from J. Edgar Hoover, who was just beginning to coordinate the Bureau's anti-
radical crusade. He advised that it was up to the postal solicitor to ban the
Defender and suggested that Outlaw encourage Mobile's postmaster to press
such a case. He also ordered Outlaw to obtain the names of all persons
receiving publications "of a radical nature such as the 'Chicago Defender'
appears to be" and "any articles of an exceedingly radical nature."[20]

Reports on the *Chicago Defender* which swelled the Bureau's files in the Red
Summer of 1919, were hardly reassuring. A lengthy analysis by the Texas
Rangers of the "Negro situation" in Marshall, Dallas, Fort Worth, and Waco
recounted widespread fears that blacks were meeting in secret and purchasing
arms. When the sheriff in Marshall banned the sale of all "radical" black
papers, the *Defender* continued to arrive through mail subscriptions, so the
postmaster agreed to halt mail deliveries until individual issues were checked
for troublesome content. Local police in Dallas and Fort Worth were monitoring the sale of black periodicals, while Waco police ordered a black druggist,
Dr. J. W. Fridia, to halt sales of the *Defender*.[21]

The Bureau entered this case a few days later when Dr. Fridia announced
his determination to keep selling the *Defender* and sought the mayor's

protection. But when that official read "some rather radical articles" in the paper, he and the police chief warned the druggist that any agitation would be summarily punished. Fridia again promised to halt distribution. Apprised of these developments, the Bureau checked his mail but unearthed no evidence that he was "spreading negro propaganda." In addition, R. D. Evans, "a [black] lawyer of good reputation," was also investigated, although no incriminating evidence was found. Why he was monitored in the first place, if his reputation was satisfactory, was not explained.[22]

In contrast to the politically radical *Messenger,* the *Defender* was moderate, but it was still deemed dangerous by many whites who feared it was stirring up local racial conflicts. Indeed, when violence flared in Phillips County, Arkansas, in October 1919, the Chicago weekly was again blamed for inciting matters.

What Arkansas whites described as a "Negro uprising" to massacre whites and take over the government was in reality the violent suppression of a sharecroppers' union in peonage-plagued eastern Arkansas. In the days that followed, angry and fearful whites demanded that the *Defender,* which had a considerable circulation, be banned from the state. Gov. Charles H. Brough blamed its allegedly false and malicious contents for poisoning blacks against whites and encouraging the "conspiracy." The NAACP's *Crisis* was also condemned. Writing directly to Postmaster General Burleson, who was the owner of extensive Texas plantation acreage using convict labor, Gov. Brough demanded suppression of both publications, undoubtedly confident that Burleson would agree that "it is highly imperative that both the races live in harmony but it can never be disputed that all idea of complete equality must be permanently dismissed and that the white race must ever be supreme." Gov. Brough also disputed the *Defender's* view that the maintenance of peonage was the motivation for attacking the black union, claiming instead that blacks were well treated and that debt servitude did not exist in Arkansas. Again he urged the post office department to "suppress this incendiary publication."[23]

Once more the solicitor pondered action against the *Defender.* Review of the files revealed that no copies had previously been ruled nonmailable. Even if a mail ban were instituted now, the newspaper would likely be distributed by express or the railroads. Only the Justice Department could halt such shipments. The Espionage and Trading with the Enemy acts were still in force, but Lamar's office was under no illusion they could be employed to prosecute the *Defender* at this time. In fact there was no legal action that the Post Office Department could take against the weekly. The solicitor could only reply to Gov. Brough and other complainants that their requests would receive careful consideration. Once again Abbott's crusading newspaper escaped government suppression.[24]

By the fall of 1919 the Justice and Post Office departments were stymied, but this was not reason to cease monitoring the *Defender's* content and circulation. The Red Scare was still at fever pitch, and circumstances could quickly change. The newspaper might drop its circumspection. The "Bolshevik menace" within Black America could worsen. Furthermore, the *Defender* continued to attack southern racism. Neither the Bureau nor postal officials could afford to be without evidence should forceful action become justified. So the solicitor continued to register demands from the South that Abbott's militant weekly be banned from the mails. Hoover's GID also continued to collect information on the *Defender* and a dozen other black periodicals. And MID maintained its own belief that the newspaper was dangerous.

Southern whites continued to fear and loathe the *Defender* during the first half of 1920. Virginians, complaining that blacks would no longer compliantly work for whites, blamed the change on the Chicago weekly and Garvey's *Negro World.* The Mississippi legislature passed a law, aimed at the *Crisis* as well as the *Defender,* to punish the publication or circulation of matter advocating "social equality." Elsewhere whites took matters into their own hands. A jurist in Pine Bluff, Arkansas, issued an injunction restraining the *Defender's* circulation on the request of the mayor, who objected to the paper's account of the killing of a local black. Not satisfied, the chamber of commerce sought to ban four black weeklies, including Abbott's publication, from mail delivery. Meanwhile, 500 white Atlantans signed a petition condemning Abbott and Benjamin J. Davis, editor of the *Atlanta Independent* for encouraging "bad attitudes" toward whites and demanded the exclusion of their publications from the mails. In Baldwin, Louisiana, the postmaster again requested permission to halt delivery of the *Defender* because its subscribers might be lynched. And in Muskogee, Oklahoma, blacks charged that local mailmen deliberately delayed delivery of the Chicago newspaper. Solicitor Lamar's office replied to such protests with noncommittal promises to carefully consider the facts as alleged. He knew there were no grounds for a postal ban but nonetheless advised inquiring postmasters to withhold individual issues from delivery if they found them questionable, leaving final determination to Washington.[25]

At the same time, the Bureau was still diligently keeping watch on the newspaper. According to the GID's first weekly radicalism synthesis, issued in January 1920, "conditions among the negroes throughout the country are said to be rather quiet" although the *Defender* "continues its attempts to stir up anti-race feeling through its editorial and news columns. Recently they have been giving prominence to the alleged lynching of nine returned soldiers during 1919."[26] The weekly's sin, according to the GID, was its emphasis on atrocities committed against the race which, it was believed, would encourage blacks' bitterness or even retaliation toward whites. Handicapped by their own racial blindness, Bureau employees could not admit the political significance in lynching of black veterans, nor acknowledge the responsibility of white Americans for poisoned racial relations. But, after all, lynching was not a federal crime, and thus of no official concern to the Bureau.

Collection and analysis of "radical" black publications was a major responsibility of Bureau field offices in 1920 and 1921, nurtured by the belief that numerous periodicals were increasing their "propaganda."[27] The Chicago field office was responsible for detailed coverage of papers published in that city. Weekly radical reports written by agent August H. Loula, who headed Chicago's radical squad, focused on the *Defender* and its younger rival, the *Chicago Whip*. He frequently found articles "tending to create race hatred" in the "radical" *Defender.* By mid-1921 each geographical division of the Bureau (encompassing several cities where agents were posted) had to file a separate "Monthly Report on Radical Publications," which typically contained similar accusations. And the annual report of the Chicago radical squad considered the *Defender* one of the four "ultraradical" local black periodicals. That term was applied very broadly and often reflected more on an agent's prejudices than reality.[28]

How publisher Abbott reacted to all these investigations between 1919 and 1921 is not known. It was no secret the government viewed his paper with suspicion and sometimes alarm, but he was probably unaware of how long and extensively the surveillance continued. Ironically, Abbott cooperated with those who viewed him with such distrust when the government began to close in on Marcus Garvey. The *Defender* was one of the black nationalist's most persistent critics, and Garvey reciprocated the animosity. Several lawsuits were filed by each against the other. It is not surprising, then, that when the Bureau's Chicago field office was ordered to "cover" Garvey's activities it sought Abbott's assistance. The publisher had already hired a black private detective, S. A. Brusseaux, to gather evidence of illegalities in Garvey's sale of Black Star Line stock. Brusseaux shared his leads with the Bureau while Abbott supplied information on Garvey's speaking engagements. *Defender* clippings hostile to Garvey were added to the Bureau's files. Chicago agents now regarded Abbott as one "who has been ever ready to cooperate with this office on all investigations pertaining to Negro radical activities." His ultimate "cooperation" was his signature, along with seven other well-known blacks, on a letter to Attorney General Harry M. Daugherty in early 1923 urging swift federal prosecution of Garvey. And a short time later, after the murder of UNIA defector Rev. J. W. H. Eason, the *Defender's* editorial staff furnished evidence implicating two of Garvey's followers in the killing.[29]

MID also maintained an anxious watch on the *Defender* well into the new decade. Its weekly summary for December 10, 1919, quoted intelligence officers in Chicago as believing that it was promoting racial unrest which would soon erupt in another riot. (Their racial allegiance was more plainly revealed in censuring the *Messenger* for "vicious" attacks on the Ku Klux Klan, which, after all, was merely trying to prevent "the encroachment of the negroes in those neighborhoods populated by white people.") In subsequent weeks MID condemned the *Defender's* promotion of a day of prayer for victims of lynching; its endorsement of Ida B. Wells-Barnett's legal challenges to racism; and its allegedly overall "anti-white" tenor. Particularly offensive was the feature story on nine black veterans who were lynched in 1919. The outrage at the *Defender's* article but not the disgraceful treatment of black soldiers illustrates the racism which permeated the army. MID routinely condemned the newspaper for fanning "flames of racial hate" and "magnifying" alleged instances of mistreatment, making it "one of the most notorious offenders" among the black press. And even after the anarchist attacks predicted by Attorney General Palmer failed to occur on May Day 1920, MID still insisted that the *Defender* posed a radical threat. Particularly egregious were its condemnation of the American military occupation of Haiti and its prediction that blacks would defend themselves if whites renewed racial rioting.[30]

MID's systematic scrutiny of the "radical" press lasted until the middle of 1921. Even after that date it compiled information for its own future use and for the State Department's Division of Passport Control, whose examiners consulted a variety of indices before granting passports to journalists. State also maintained its own index of suspect periodicals and in March 1922, invited MID to submit names for inclusion. It responded with a list of "Red and Pink Publications in the United States." While the *Crisis, Negro World,* and *Crusader* were listed without description, several weekly newspapers—the *Atlanta Independent, Indianapolis Freeman, Nashville Globe, New York Age, Pittsburgh Courier,* and *Washington Eagle*—were deemed "semi-radical." MID analysts accepted the *Messenger's* own claim to being a "journal of scientific radicalism." The *Emancipator* and *Challenge* had "radical tendencies." The worst of the weekly newspapers were the *Baltimore Afro-American, Richmond Planet, Chicago Whip,* and the *Defender.*[31]

Despite the efforts of three intelligence agencies, the federal government found itself powerless to suppress the *Chicago Defender* in the postwar Red

Scare. Hoover's General Intelligence Division, which cooperated closely with
United States attorneys, recognized after abortive efforts to prosecute the
Messenger that there was no possibility of silencing a less militant publication.
But the *Defender* continued to worry the Bureau and the Post Office Department, primarily because of its influence in the South. Much more than the
socialist or communist magazines or even Garvey's *Negro World,* it circulated
among oppressed southern blacks, encouraging their flight to northern cities
while exposing the atrocities they suffered. For daring to challenge the status
quo, the *Defender* incurred the wrath of many southern whites and their
representatives in Congress, who found a sympathetic ear in the federal
intelligence network. Postmaster General Burleson was a Texan; his solicitor,
William H. Lamar, was from Maryland. J. Edgar Hoover was born and bred in
"southern" Washington, D.C. All three would have justified suppression of
the outspoken newspaper simply because it challenged white supremacy.
MID more often objected to the *Defender* on political grounds, identifying it
as a promoter of "radicalism."

Robert S. Abbott's biography offers no hint of how he was affected by these
efforts at intimidation and suppression.[32] Certainly he was forced to trim his
editorial sails during World War I. Whether he, or any other editor or
publisher, knew the full extent of federal surveillance efforts after the war is
doubtful. What could not be mistaken, however, was the climate of oppres-
sion that emerged during the war and peaked in 1919. Each successive
"interview" by a Bureau agent or military intelligence officer must have given
Abbott cause to consider the editorial content of his newspaper. The *Defender*
did not cave in and accept the status quo; had it done so, it would not have
grown so dramatically during the war and Red Scare years. Just as certainly,
they were dangerous times for the most influential "race newspaper" of the
era. Yet Abbott's outspoken weekly managed to operate within the law, if not
within the norms of white permissibility.

The *Defender* was not alone among black newspapers in facing the hostile
scrutiny of federal investigators; other publications endured similar, if less
intense, pressure. Some first encountered problems during the war when their
expression of racial grievances was perceived as disloyalty or impeding
conscription. Following the war, any strong-voiced weekly risked censure for
promoting "anti-white" attitudes.

Chicago was home to two other outspoken black newspapers. The *Whip*
and the *Broad-Ax* had much smaller circulations than the *Defender,* but during
the Red Scare their more militant editorials brought the scrutiny of the
Bureau, starting in mid-1919. Acting on an initial assumption—shared by
local whites, Bureau agents, and GID headquarters—that radicals instigated

the Chicago riot, all black newspapers were searched for evidence of their role. Agent Loula found the *Defender* "very radical in some of its articles" but tame by comparison to the others. The *Whip* was accused of stirring up antagonism toward whites by printing excessive and provocative details about lynching. It was so dangerous that the militia commander in the riot area ordered his troops to purchase all copies from newsstands so that it would not further inflame blacks. Another Chicago agent damned the *Broad-Ax* for waging an anti-white campaign. In fact neither paper was guilty of that charge, but whites were often incapable of distinguishing between "promoting race hatred" and what the papers excelled in, militant advocacy of self-defense and full civil rights.[33]

For the rest of 1919 agents in Chicago were preoccupied with foreign-born anarchists and Bolshevists, following Hoover's policy of targeting those whose lack of American citizenship made them vulnerable to expulsion without complicated legal proceedings. MID, however, was more focused on black newspapers. Its intelligence officer in Chicago, Maj. T. B. Crockett, continued to submit offensive copies to Washington where analysts concluded that the agenda of these publications was to "fan flames of racial hate."[34] And by early 1920 Bureau agents were again surveying the contents of the *Whip* on a weekly basis.

The *Whip*'s sin, in the eyes of the Bureau, was its belief that blacks should raise their racial consciousness, become more dissatisfied with their subordinate position, and "rise up" against any conditions that stood in the way of their progress. The duty of the black press, said the newspaper, was to "awaken the Negro to his economic and political power." For such sentiments the *Whip* was consistently labeled a "radical" periodical. The New Crowd Negro spirit was frightening to many whites, including Agent Loula, who summarized with disgust an article headlined "Started by white hoodlums, finished by tough Negroes" which described a riot in Jersey City in which three whites were badly beaten. Particularly offensive was the statement that "Negroes in the North and South know how to cut and shoot as well as white toughs, and are ready to prove it when badgered or assaulted." On the basis of such hostile reports from Chicago and elsewhere, the GID concluded in the spring of 1920 that "considerable agitation and unrest among the negroes" was being fueled by radical publications and propaganda, including the *Whip*.[35]

During the second half of 1920, as Attorney General Palmer's prediction of further "Red" violence proved to be the figment of his political ambitions, the *Whip* continued to publish statements that aroused the ire of Justice Department personnel. Anarchists were not to blame for the Wall Street bomb blast which killed over thirty whites, claimed the militant paper, but rather the American habit of lawlessness which excused lynching and mob attacks against blacks. Bureau agents were also offended by its comment that white marines did not believe in social equality in the United States but, while occupying the republic of Haiti, showed no aversion to liaisons with black women. Just as bad was an "exceptionally radical editorial" which claimed that whites knew they were not the superior race and in fact were afraid of losing power to the "rising tide of color." The unhealthy result of such articles, reported Agent Loula, was their capacity to "sow discontent" among the black population.[36]

With the election of President Warren G. Harding and the departure of Attorney General Palmer, many Bureau agents no longer found radical black activity to report. Following Hoover's instructions, however, Loula continued to mail copies of Chicago's black newspapers to headquarters, marking items which were, in reality, innocuous. He still insisted that the *Whip* and *Defender* contained "articles tending to create race hatred." Political radicalism was no longer the issue; rather, the right to self-defense, self-determination, or emigration from the South were deemed to be "anti-white." Hence the *Whip* remained, in the view of the Bureau, "ultraradical," a "Negro propaganda publication" which promoted "race radicalism." But even this tired horse had been flogged too often. The Chicago field office ceased reporting on the black press after September 1921.[37]

In addition to Garvey's *Negro World*, three influential weekly "race papers" were published in New York City during the Red Scare: the *New York Age, New York News,* and *New York Amsterdam News.* All had been monitored by federal intelligence agencies during World War I. Zealous bureaucrats in the New York post office's Translation Bureau read every issue of the *New York Age* and *New York News* through most of 1918, repeatedly faulting their allegedly vicious anti-white prejudices. The papers were not in fact antagonistic to Caucasians but simply outspoken in criticizing lynching, discrimination, and other racial indignities. Solicitor Lamar withheld at least one issue of the *News* from the mail. Military intelligence personnel were also convinced that both papers were subversive, given their (entirely justified) criticism of the army's racist policies. The Bureau likewise condemned the *Age* during the war months. But despite numerous pleas from the Translation Bureau, neither Lamar nor the United States attorney in New York found sufficient evidence to ban either newspaper from the mails or prosecute them for violating the Espionage Act.[38] The weeklies complained loudly about practices that mocked the aim of making the world safe for democracy, but it was another thing to prove that such statements actually interfered with the prosecution of the war.

Soon after the armistice, Translation Bureau head Robert A. Bowen perceived a new threat from periodicals like the *New York News*: "I think their editorials are bad, and with their covert threat of violence when the negro soldiers return, are deserving of censure if not of suppression. When Judge Lamar was once in the office he spoke with me about these negro papers. I know that they are very influential among their readers, and I wish there might be found some way in which their entirely wrong attitude could be rectified." Precisely what were such "wrong" attitudes? Two months later, Bowen flagged editorials in the *News* and *Amsterdam News* which opposed the League of Nations: "Although not any more misleading and untruthful than similar outbursts in certain New York daily [white] newspapers," he found the editorials "objectionable at the present time, when efforts are being made to inflame the imagination of the negroes, and to create race discontent." White papers, then, would be permitted to criticize the Wilson administration and the League of Nations, but the black press should be denied that right, as its expression might encourage blacks to seek alteration in the racial status quo.[39]

New York's black weeklies did not avoid condemnation, but they escaped interdiction after the war because genuinely militant periodicals like the *Messenger* and the invigorated *Crisis* absorbed the solicitor's attention. Yet Bowen remained convinced that the entire black press was dangerous, and his report on "Radicalism and Sedition among the Negroes as Reflected in their Publications" was an attempt to persuade both Lamar and, more importantly, the Department of Justice, of his views.[40]

Bowen influenced the Bureau in another way. Ordered by Hoover to survey the spectrum of racial papers, New York agents got all the evidence they needed from Bowen, who provided a list—which included the three local weeklies—of those periodicals he regarded as radical. (Ironically, Bowen had just written to Lamar that their current issues were not objectionable!) The result was that Bowen's much-exaggerated inventory of offending publications became part of the Bureau's own radical index. Thereafter it did not matter whether they lived up to that depiction or not; they had been damned and would remain suspect for months to come.[41]

Bureau agents assigned to New York's radical squad, required to file weekly reports, also combed the black newspapers for offensive articles. But were the publications really radical? *New York News* editorials suggested the impeachment of President Wilson, charged lynching with driving blacks to radicalism, and condemned the misconduct of United States marines in Haiti. The *Amsterdam News* discussed miscegenation and blamed white racism for breeding black radicalism. Clearly no credible case could be made that the newspapers were dangerous. Black informant Herbert S. Boulin finally set the record straight, advising his superiors that the "leading" black papers—the *Amsterdam News, New York Age, New York News,* and *Chicago Defender*—in fact frequently criticized the socialist and communist radicals while also opposing anything likely to increase racial friction. That sealed the matter in New York; Bureau agents finally dropped mention of the erstwhile "radical" newspapers by the end of 1920.[42]

Whether or not a black periodical was considered "radical" or dangerous by federal intelligence agencies depended more on the fears, stereotypes, and prejudices of agents and bureaucrats than its actual editorial content. Local events, rumors, and tensions increased the probability that a paper would be investigated and censured. New York was the fountainhead of black radical- ism and any racial paper published there was certain to be scrutinized. The same was true for Chicago. Other influential black weeklies, like the *Richmond Planet, Baltimore Afro-American,* and *St. Louis Argus* endured pressure during World War I but were spared federal investigations during the Red Scare. The *Pittsburgh Courier, Indianapolis Freeman,* and *Cleveland Advocate* suffered no major scrutiny during either period. And the *Boston Guardian* escaped serious review although federal agents focused on its editor, William Monroe Trotter, one of the leading opponents of Booker T. Washington earlier in the century. Trotter was dubbed a "red radical," Bolshevik, and IWW agitator in 1919 for his militant stance on civil rights, his friendship with A. Philip Randolph and Chandler Owen, and his efforts to bring black issues before the Paris Peace Conference. The Office of Naval Intelligence, Bureau of Investigation, and British military intelligence all monitored his activities during the first year of the Red Scare. But Trotter never embraced socialism or communism, the *Guardian* had only a modest circulation, and the Justice Department rapidly lost interest in them by 1920.[43]

Black newspapers suffered less severe pressure than the monthly maga- zines during the Red Scare. While weekly "race papers" argued for the rights and privileges that were due African Americans, they were business ventures and not primarily vehicles for protest. Without advertising and subscriptions their precarious financial situation would become hopeless. Economic sur- vival demanded editorial positions in the mainstream. None of the papers' publishers embraced Bolshevism or socialism because they themselves were capitalists and businessmen. But as black businessmen they did not shy away from criticizing the government and white society for mistreating African Americans. So the newspapers' "sin" was their alleged cultivation of "race hatred." But in fact they hated only white racism, not white people. And none of the weeklies, with the exception of Garvey's *Negro World,* was a nationalistic publication. The newspapers simply carried on a venerable journalistic tradition, harking back to Frederick Douglass's *North Star*, by providing a predominantly black readership with a mixture of racial news, racial defense, and racial advocacy.

The monthly magazines fared much worse at the hands of the federal intelligence establishment. The *Crisis* was persecuted because it was the voice of the NAACP, which advocated what to many whites in and out of government were unthinkable alterations in the racial status quo: black and white equality in matters social as well as legal. The *Messenger* suffered the most intense pressure from the federal government because it embraced Bolshevism, championed the right to armed self-defense, and advocated full social, even sexual, equality at a time when the country was convulsed with fears that a Russian-style revolution would take place in the United States. And the *Crusader* earned nearly as much hostility for its embrace of communism and the right to fight back against lynchers and rioters. Had these three militant monthlies not existed, the weekly black press might well have faced much stronger efforts to muzzle or suppress it. The monthlies set the "standard" for militant rhetoric and advocacy; without them, the more moderated tone of the weekly newspapers would have seemed just as unacceptable.

Of the militant publications that were born during or immediately after World War I, few survived by 1924. The *Messenger*, shorn of its Bolshevik advocacy and much of its socialist enthusiasm, was no longer viewed as a serious threat by the Department of Justice, Military Intelligence Division, or Post Office Department. The *Crusader* had expired in early 1922. Garvey's weekly *Negro World*, which had been labeled militantly pro-black and "anti-white" during the Red Scare, was now innocuous. The NAACP's membership and influence waned after 1920, as did circulation of the *Crisis*, which was never again as outspokenly critical of the federal government as it had been in 1919. However, the *Chicago Defender* continued to criticize and outrage the white South, though its impact seemed far less dangerous in the "normalcy" of the twenties.

FOUR

❧

"THE EXISTENCE OF
THIS ORGANIZATION MAY BE
FOR NO GOOD PURPOSE"

The NAACP and the Crisis *Avoid
Federal Suppression*

The *Crisis,* official publication of the National Association for the Advancement of Colored People, was accustomed to suspicion and government
intimidation. During World War I military officials, alleging that the interracial civil rights organization's outspoken magazine was under enemy influence and encouraging disaffection among black troops, sought to ban it from
military posts. The army's fears infected other agencies in the growing political
intelligence network; soon the Justice and Post Office departments were also
monitoring the influential monthly, with some officials eager to ban it from the
mails. Such drastic action was forestalled in mid-1918 when the NAACP's
white board chairman, Maj. Joel E. Spingarn, who served during the war as a
military intelligence officer, tightened the association's control of the *Crisis.* At
the same time editor W. E. B. DuBois[1] trimmed his editorial sails, culminating
in the controversial "Close Ranks" admonition to African Americans to
wholeheartedly support the war effort. Although DuBois was motivated in
part by a desire to receive an army commission and serve in a proposed black
military intelligence unit, he recognized that only editorial circumspection
would abort outright government suppression. Once it became evident that

the *Crisis* was muting criticism of the war and urging patriotic participation by blacks, the federal intelligence agencies lost interest in the magazine for the remainder of the war.[2]

But in the postwar months, as Bolshevism, subversion, and disloyalty seemed to escalate within Black America, suspicions became widespread that the NAACP and the *Crisis,* as well as more militant organizations and publications, were threatening the racial status quo. It made no difference that the NAACP's leadership included a number of well-known white liberals. As the transition from wartime began, and the army's Military Intelligence Division and the Justice Department's Bureau of Investigation strengthened their vigilance against black activism, the *Crisis* and its editor would know little peace.

The most immediate concern of federal officials was protecting the Paris peace conference from unwanted interference or pressure. DuBois sailed to France on a dual mission, to shepherd a Pan-African Congress in Paris, which he was largely responsible for organizing, and to investigate charges of army discrimination against black soldiers in France. The Bureau agent who spearheaded investigations of blacks in Washington, D.C., warned that DuBois should be kept under close surveillance as he was a "rock-the-boat type" whose "associations have been along German lines. He is further alleged to be a rank Socialist and all his associations are the same. He may attempt to introduce socialist tendencies at the Peace Conference."[3] The belief that DuBois and the NAACP were allied or in sympathy with radical movements was also shared by MID. Both agencies were convinced, for example, that the Association was linked to Roger Baldwin's National Civil Liberties Bureau (forerunner of the ACLU). And MID erroneously concluded that the NAACP was giving counsel to A. Philip Randolph and Chandler Owen, editors of the militant black socialist *Messenger* magazine.[4]

MID's main allegation against the *Crisis* in the immediate postwar months, however, was the charge that it was radicalizing black troops. Indeed, many veterans displayed a heightened racial consciousness. A white YMCA official serving in France reported black soldiers' assumption that fighting to make the world safe for democracy had earned them the right to enjoy the same at home. He, like other whites, failed to understand that the Jim Crow army had increased blacks' impatience with the status quo. Instead, he blamed DuBois's editorials demanding full rights for the race, and predicted that returning troops would make trouble upon their demobilization.[5]

But black soldiers did not need any stimulus to experience disillusionment and bitterness; the treatment they received from many white officers was sufficient to accomplish that. DuBois made certain that African Americans knew the story, publishing official army documents which revealed the virulent prejudices of many of those who commanded black troops. It is not difficult to corroborate the *Crisis* accounts. Col. Allen J. Greer, chief of staff of the 92nd Division, systematically and unfairly attacked the courage, compe- tence, and character of the troops, particularly their black junior officers. DuBois's exposé was reviewed by MID's two racial "experts." Maj. Walter H. Loving, even though he was regarded as a dependable "white man's Negro" by his white peers in MID, was appalled at the slanderous postwar attacks on the battlefield record of black soldiers. He substantiated Col. Greer's prejudices, which DuBois revealed in the May 1919 *Crisis,* and in uncharacteristically blunt language recommended that Greer be court-martialed for destroying the effectiveness of the 92nd Division. Its white commanding officers, not the black troops, had failed. Loving also urged that black regiments in the still- segregated postwar army be staffed exclusively by officers of their own race, to be drawn from the many capable high school and university graduates who should be given opportunity to attend West Point or stand for competitive examinations.

MID's second specialist in racial affairs was Capt. J. E. Cutler, a Yale graduate, professor of sociology at the University of Michigan, author of a pioneering book on lynching, and an advisor on black troop morale during the war. Cutler endorsed Loving's recommendation that blacks be guaranteed full opportunity to officer their own units and advance to regimental com- mand with the rank of colonel, also agreeing that racial discrimination was both authorized and practiced by high officials in the War Department. Brig. Gen. Marlborough Churchill, Director of Military Intelligence in the early postwar months, personally submitted both memos to the Chief of Staff, noting that Loving was "as impartial and tolerant as a man of his race can be in the treatment of this subject" and that Cutler was "a very well-informed and entirely tolerant and impartial student of the race question." Gen. Churchill himself admitted the seriousness of the issues. Secretary of War Newton D. Baker eventually read all the communications, but took no meaningful action to alter the army's racist policies. DuBois's efforts to unmask army discrimina- tion brought little fruit. And even had Churchill been willing to pursue the issue, the Military Intelligence Division was the weakest of the five general staff divisions and lacked sufficient clout to compel basic changes in army policies and folkways.[6]

The most severe restriction on the *Crisis* in the postwar period resulted from its criticism of the War Department, printed in the May 1919, issue. DuBois's "Essay toward a History of the Black Man in the Great War" included official army memoranda which revealed its racist practices and the prejudice of individual white officers. Even more alarming to the federal intelligence agencies, however, was an editorial entitled "Returning Soldiers." In a complete reversal of the wartime "Close Ranks" editorial, DuBois thundered that "we are cowards and jackasses if now that the war is over, we do not marshal every ounce of our brain and brawn to fight a sterner, longer, more unbending battle against the forces of hell in our own land. *We return. We return from fighting. We return fighting.*"[7]

Even though combat had ceased in western Europe, the Translation Bureau of the Post Office, located in New York City and run by Robert A. Bowen, still exercised authority to deny mailing privileges by utilizing a portion of the wartime Espionage Act interdicting publications that encouraged "treason, insurrection, or forcible resistance to any law."[8] The task of monitoring all suspect literature was enormous, but Bowen nonetheless gave his personal attention to black periodicals. Ten of them were deemed "radical": the *New York Independent, New York News, New York Age, New York Amsterdam News, Veteran, Messenger, Negro World, Crusader, Challenge,* and *Crisis*. Reading the last, Bowen turned apoplectic: "I am not going to let the outrageous editorial ["Returning Soldiers"] go through without the Solicitor's ruling upon it. It is seditious, insolently abusive of the country, and contains its not too veiled threat." The New York postmaster agreed to withhold all 100,000 copies until a decision was rendered.

Obviously this *was* a matter for postal solicitor William H. Lamar to decide. In the end he took his own staff's counsel and rejected Bowen's entreaty. While agreeing that the language of "Returning Soldiers" was "unquestionably violent" and "extremely likely to excite a considerable amount of racial prejudice (if that has not already reached its maximum amongst the Negroes)," the solicitor's staff recognized that "the fight which the writer proposes to wage is against disagreeable and deplorable conditions, and not against the constitutional authority of the United States government. It, therefore, does not violate the provisions of the Espionage Act, and is acceptable for mailing." After the delay of six days Lamar ordered the magazine dispatched to its subscribers.[9]

In the meantime the NAACP had mobilized its membership to protest. Over 150 telegrams flooded the Postmaster General's office, a third from NAACP chapters, many located in the South. Black masonic groups, church denominations and conventions, women's clubs, social and uplift organizations, business leagues, educational associations, newspapers, even the (white) Illinois State Bar Association registered objections. Four members of Congress inquired why the magazine was delayed. Whether these communications influenced Lamar's decision is unknown, but they reveal a remarkable ability of the NAACP to mobilize its constituency.[10]

Before the Post Office decided to release the May *Crisis* the Translation Bureau notified MID of its alarm. Gen. Churchill replied that indeed the issue was of "special interest" although there were no grounds on which the military could independently bar its circulation. Following its release Bowen kept up pressure on the magazine, carefully examining subsequent issues. Writing again to Churchill regarding the June issue, he underscored the magazine's "harsh criticism of the alleged treatment of the negro soldiers in France by army officers." The contents of the July issue were similarly brought to Churchill's attention.[11]

The Bureau of Translation justified its surveillance of the black press in a widely circulated memorandum entitled "Radicalism and Sedition among the Negroes as Reflected in their Publications." Bowen was blunt:

> The negro editors and writers—and some of them are not without a marked ability—are fully alive to the influence they possess over their readers as well as to the fact that in their hands the negro masses may be made to assume a very dangerous power. Some of the ablest of these writers have gone beyond the point where advocacy of moderation and temperate counsel any longer contents them. They preach violence and "direct action."

Continuing, Bowen charged that many periodicals advocated Bolshevik rule and urged retaliation for lynching:

> It is not putting it too strongly to state that the cumulative effect of the various negro publications is to foster a sense of resentment and race antagonism, in which effort, ever since the entry of this country into the recent war, there has been increasingly employed the tone of menace and the threat of violent resistance.

Among the periodicals quoted, DuBois's "Returning Soldiers" editorial was highlighted.

Bowen concluded that the black masses were being exploited by a press which saturated them with dangerous racial views. Editors like DuBois were not interested in alleviating wrongs in a "wholesome" manner but instead encouraged defiance and destructive political approaches. Their publications should not be dismissed as the product of childish minds, "however ill-reasoned and absurd they may often be." The militant press exercised a dangerous influence: Race and class consciousness was growing mightily. Black public opinion was "increasingly more insolently scornful. It is not," wrote Bowen, "an attitude that the government can safely ignore."[12]

For all its fulminations, the Post Office had insufficient grounds for permanently excluding any black publications from the mail. In the midst of its own efforts to suppress the *Crisis* and the *Messenger* the Bureau of Investigation sought Solicitor Lamar's views on the same issue. As the Post Office's top legal officer, while also holding the rank of assistant attorney general, his opinion was definitive. After conferring with Postmaster General Albert Sidney Burleson, he informed Bureau chief Frank Burke that "under the present state of the law there is nothing that can be done to exclude this matter from the mails." Lamar regarded this limitation as extremely unfortunate, for the effect of the *Crisis* was "to fire the colored people" to "join the IWW and engage in the practice of sabotage to bring about the reforms advocated by [the NAACP]."[13] Like other government officials, his racial paranoia magnified the NAACP into a proponent of syndicalist civil disorder. Still, the Post Office could do nothing to stop the *Crisis* in the fall of 1919.

Meanwhile, MID continued to worry about the NAACP's influence on black troops. The intelligence officer at a quartermaster depot in Indiana alerted Washington to handbills proclaiming "The Huns of America— Lynching, Jim Crow, Discrimination—Wipe Them Out . . . Join the NAACP." Gen. Churchill, aware that the NAACP was "beginning an aggressive campaign to organize branches," requested information on the manner in which it was recruiting supporters within the army. At the same time Capt. Cutler directed the intelligence officer at Camp Dix, New Jersey, to investigate the attitudes and grievances of men of the 92nd Division to discover any NAACP influence. And the commander of Camp Jackson, South Carolina, warned that the *Crisis* and *Messenger* were circulating widely in the South and provoking much antagonism toward whites.[14]

MID was now closely watching both magazines as the "Red Summer" of 1919 erupted in over three dozen racial clashes, many involving servicemen of both races. Lynching of African Americans increased dramatically, with several veterans murdered simply for wearing their uniforms in public. Many blacks were angrily impatient, demanding fulfillment of the promises implicit in President Wilson's wartime rhetoric. Many whites were equally adamant that the racial status quo remain unchanged. Thus it is little wonder that the spirit of militancy spread widely among black soldiers, including those stationed overseas. As late as December 1920, army intelligence in the Philippines found NAACP publications among members of the 9th cavalry and urged that such "propaganda" be banned from the mails.[15]

At the Office of Naval Intelligence, Rear Adm. A. P. Niblack wrote to the Bureau of Investigation to damn the *Crisis* for tending "to inflame the negro race." This warning reinvigorated the Bureau's interest in DuBois and his publication in mid-1919, although its files already included many issues of the *Crisis* and "voluminous reports upon the activities of its editor." The New York field office was instructed to forward copies to Washington and detail an agent to keep close watch and "report when it contains any article of a doubtful character."[16] The criteria for such judgments were not spelled out.

Niblack was sufficiently worried about threats to the racial status quo to submit a second, more detailed report to the Bureau in June. According to ONI, recent articles in the *Crisis* and *Messenger* made clear that blacks' efforts to gain social and political equality were well organized, based on revolutionary methods and a soviet form of government, and linked to Irish, Japanese, Mexican, Indian, and Egyptian revolutionary movements. The NAACP, though not as radical as others, was guilty by association, occupying the same building with the Civil Liberties Bureau. This ONI report concluded with the warning that the black race, allegedly emotional and lacking in self-control, could easily be incited to disorder by white subversives. Such fears and stereotypes captured other white observers; nearly identical conclusions were contained in a lengthy document from MID's New York office a few weeks earlier.[17]

Both naval intelligence reports soon reached J. Edgar Hoover. Echoing the fears of his intelligence partners in MID and ONI, Hoover ordered that "all connections financially and otherwise of this Association with the radical element and the IWW should be fully inquired into."[18] This mirrored the widespread perception among worried whites that black militancy could be inspired only by renegade whites—particularly communists and anarchists—not by domestic social, economic, or political conditions.

Hoover's timetable for silencing militant black periodicals and organizations was accelerated by Democratic congressman James F. Byrnes's alarms about the *Crisis* and the *Messenger*. Addressing the House in mid-1919, with racial riots in high season, the South Carolinian blamed black leaders and publications for the meteoric rise in conflict, charging them with deliberately planning a "campaign of violence." Heretofore moderate spokesmen—particularly W. E. B. DuBois—had suddenly turned radical. An apostle of white supremacy, Byrnes assumed the federal government should protect the racial status quo: "This is a white man's country, and will always remain a white man's country. So much for political equality. . . . As to social equality, God Almighty never intended [it]."[19]

Hoover shared the congressman's racial fears, agreeing that "the purpose of the editors [DuBois and A. Philip Randolph and Chandler Owen of the *Messenger*] is to create unrest among the negro element." But since he was preoccupied with deporting alien anarchists, and the editorial staff of the *Crisis* was American-born, Hoover had given it no specific attention.

Assistant Attorney General Frank K. Nebeker assigned responsibility for building a case against the two magazines to United States Attorney Francis G. Caffey in New York. Quoting from the "Returning Soldiers" editorial and alleging that the following three issues also contained inflammatory statements, Nebeker instructed Caffey to propose a course of action against the *Crisis*. The critical issues were: Had DuBois violated the Espionage Act; and, if so, was successful prosecution likely? Caffey approached his task with thoroughness, closely reading copies of the *Messenger* and *Crisis* supplied by the Bureau.[20]

Referring to both magazines, Caffey was convinced that "the articles are so written as to make it very difficult to base criminal prosecutions upon them." He concluded that "while the articles in each [magazine] are offensive and their circulation cannot but foster racial hatred, it seems to me that the subjects discussed and that the purpose stated in the publications as to their object, are lawful." Although Caffey instructed the Bureau's office in New York to keep close watch on the two magazines, formal efforts to silence the *Crisis* through federal prosecution had ended.[21]

During these futile attempts to initiate prosecution of the *Crisis* in the fall of 1919 the Bureau was not lax in monitoring the magazine and its parent association. Recognizing the difficulty white agents encountered in black investigations, it brought to New York its first officially employed black undercover informant, Dr. Arthur Ulysses Craig. A member of the race's educated and advantaged "Talented Tenth," he was the nation's first black graduate electrical engineer and a distinguished teacher. Craig had most recently served as a "dollar-a-year" man heading the Food Administration's Negro Press Section during World War I. In late 1918 he was recruited for undercover work in Washington, reporting on the Liberty League and other new organizations seeking change in the racial status quo and the de-colonization of Africa. Released when the tide of militancy receded in the nation's capital, Craig was recalled during the Red Summer of 1919 to infiltrate socialist and nationalist groups in Harlem. His written reports were signed "C-C" to disguise his identity.[22]

Craig spent most of September filing daily reports on conversations with militants like Randolph, Owen, and Marcus Garvey as well as with moderates who should have been of no interest to the government whatever. Cataloguing the sources of "radical propaganda," he listed the *Crisis* along with the pro-Bolshevik *Messenger* and *Crusader.* Jessie Fauset, literary editor of the *Crisis,* gave him a tour of the magazine's office which led to a subsequent interview with DuBois, who requested that Craig write an article for his new children's magazine. Craig also attended NAACP meetings and secured back issues of the *Crisis* for Justice Department's files. But at the end of the month the Bureau again ended Craig's service. Surveying too many suspects and groups, he was unable to probe deeply into any one of them and the intelligence he gathered was too general to serve prosecutorial purposes.[23]

The Bureau must have been disappointed that Craig was unable to find evidence of criminal activity by the NAACP, since agents in Newark had just reported that gun parts allegedly stolen by black employees of Governor's Island arsenal and the Remington Arms Company in Bridgeport, Connecticut, were secretly stored in the NAACP's headquarters on Fifth Avenue in New York! Craig had no leads on the matter. An agent in Hartford met with Remington's security chief and learned that nine of their thirteen black employees had access to sealed rooms where gun parts were kept. Company police agreed to watch them closely and check their lockers twice daily, but after twelve days' surveillance plant security agents observed nothing suspicious. With the case already dead, New York agents made a clumsy investigation of NAACP headquarters, learning only that the organization did not subscribe to Bolshevik principles.[24]

The New York field office received unexpected assistance in closing this case later in October when Walter White, the NAACP's young assistant secretary, volunteered information to the Bureau. The NAACP was worried about rumors of a massive protest planned for Harlem in December, allegedly being promoted by a white agitator—perhaps the quixotic R. D. Jonas. Division Superintendent George F. Lamb and "radical squad" head Charles J. Scully seized the occasion to question White concerning the NAACP's objectives. Although Lamb became convinced it had legitimate purposes, given the moral and financial backing it enjoyed from citizens like Supreme Court Justice Charles Evans Hughes and Attorney General A. Mitchell Palmer, Scully pressed White on the matter of stolen weapons. White knew the rumors— New York police had already investigated them—but insisted that the organization possessed no firearms. The NAACP's goal was simply to secure justice for blacks, and it was not interested in "social equality." Learning that White had an appointment with the Justice Department in Washington, Lamb encouraged him to brief Hoover on the current racial situation.[25]

There is no record that White accepted this invitation to become a Bureau informant, although given that the interview with Lamb and Scully was at White's initiative, it is clear he was willing to use the Bureau to protect the NAACP from guilt by association with more militant groups or individuals. And White was obviously aware that any hint of promoting "social equality" would guarantee a hostile government stance toward the NAACP.

Undercover informant Craig was succeeded in New York, from January through March 1920, by thirty-five-year-old William A. Bailey, identified in

Bureau reports as "WW." His main task was to infiltrate the pro-communist faction, which was easily accomplished by volunteering to work for Cyril Briggs's *Crusader.* Bailey's reports occasionally mentioned the NAACP and included the *Crisis* in a list of fourteen militant black periodicals sold in Harlem, but investigating the NAACP and its magazine was not a major assignment. The same was true for his successor, Brooklyn-born William E. Lucas (informant "P-135"), who worked undercover from April through June of the same year.[26]

The most sustained undercover operation in Harlem during the Red Scare was the work of "P-138," Herbert S. Boulin. While his primary goals were infiltration of Garvey's movement and Briggs's communist circle, he also filed many reports on the NAACP. Aware that DuBois was passé to Harlem's younger militants, Boulin nonetheless thought it important to watch him and employed a ruse—the offer of a lucrative business deal—to learn his views on racial matters and foreign affairs, a goal that could have been more simply accomplished by reading the *Crisis.* According to Boulin, DuBois believed times were propitious for the darker races to unite and strike for supremacy while the white race was preoccupied with settling war issues. It is doubtful, however, that DuBois actually voiced such sentiments.

Boulin also filed a long report on a speech by White, again distorting matters by labeling him an advocate of "social revolution." According to Boulin's account White agreed with the theories of Bolshevism and urged blacks to organize like the Russians just prior to overthrowing the Czar. From a reading of White's autobiography it is clear that Boulin's assessment was erroneous. It should be noted that in other reports Boulin often told his Bureau handlers what they might want to hear, regardless of the facts. Boulin also detailed NAACP black executive secretary James Weldon Johnson's organization of protest demonstrations against the racist movie *Birth of a Nation* in New York City.[27]

In the end, Bureau undercover informants in New York, where the *Crisis* was published, supplied no more confirmation of alleged subversive activities by the NAACP than had its agents. Despite the priority placed by Hoover on curbing the civil rights organization, the Justice Department was stymied. Federal attorneys did not possess enough evidence or statutory authority to prosecute much more radical editors or activists. But as in many other cases, a failure to bring legal action did not stop efforts to monitor, harass, and suppress the outspoken monthly and its parent organization, especially in localities far distant from its headquarters.

Dislike for both was widespread among whites in 1919 and 1920. The NAACP was well established, having made significant strides since its founding in 1909. Day-to-day executive leadership was in the capable hands of James Weldon Johnson. Most branches—many of which were formed during World War I, with significant growth especially in the South—were also black led. The NAACP was a militant advocate of black civil rights, by no means seen by whites or most blacks as conservative or even moderate. In its first ten years it had gained two powerful legal victories. One was persuading the Supreme Court to strike down the notorious "grandfather clause," which exempted illiterate southern whites from having to pass the literacy tests which were used routinely to keep blacks from voting. The other barred enforced residential segregation, preventing the growth of a formal system of apartheid in America.[28]

The NAACP forced whites in the North grudgingly to recognize a "Negro problem" which they would have preferred to define solely as a southern issue. To southern whites the NAACP was a subversive organization pure and simple, bent on eroding the hallowed racial hierarchy. Its northern leaders were seen as outside agitators who would dictate, if they could, the destruction of the white southern way of life. It is no wonder, then, that both the NAACP and the *Crisis* faced hostility during the Red Scare; many whites believed that subversives were encouraging blacks to reject their "place" in the social order and seek unacceptable familiarity with Caucasians. Furthermore, editor DuBois was lumped into the category of "race radicals" even though the younger generation of New Crowd Negroes regarded him as a passé contemporary of Booker T. Washington. Nothing more than DuBois's "Returning Soldiers" editorial was needed to convince most whites that he, too, was a subverter of the racial status quo.[29]

Scrutiny of the NAACP and the *Crisis* occurred in many northern and border-state cities during the Red Scare. The Bureau's Washington field office, investigating distribution of allegedly radical propaganda among blacks there, noted the availability of the *Crisis*. But local NAACP meetings were more likely to be covered by military intelligence under an agreement with the Bureau which assigned MID primary responsibility for watching black activities in the nation's capital.

Elsewhere, insignificant incidents sparked the Bureau's alarm. The head of the Pennsylvania Railroad police reported a black trespasser in the Louisville yards wearing an NAACP button on his coat. Many blacks around the city displayed the same emblem, and NAACP placards adorned shop windows. A Bureau agent urged that the association be investigated as it "may be for no good purpose." A larger-than-average NAACP meeting could also stir apprehension. An agent in Toledo covered a lecture by DuBois attended by over 500 blacks and more than 100 whites, "mostly radicals," and warned that "Dr.

DuBois is in favor of the IWW." Also in Ohio, a white statewide NAACP leader became a Bureau informant, charging that other state NAACP officials were socialists or radicals. And in Boston an agent convinced himself that DuBois's editorials, particularly "Returning Soldiers," were inspiring William Monroe Trotter, the outspoken editor of the *Guardian,* to do "his utmost to incite riots and cause bloodshed," another outrageously exaggerated charge.[30]

Whites linked to the NAACP were as likely to be suspect. When Hoover ordered the General Intelligence Division to probe settlement house pioneer Jane Addams's allegedly subversive activities, her membership in the "radical" NAACP was noted. When a woman in Boston who corresponded with imprisoned radicals at Leavenworth federal penitentiary was investigated, the fact that she possessed NAACP pamphlets further damned her. More tragic was the case of Charlotte Anita Whitney, a prominent white women's club member in San Francisco who joined the Communist Labor Party and was convicted on state criminal syndicalism charges in February 1920. Her mail was rifled with court approval, and when NAACP literature was discovered, the Bureau's San Francisco field office urged that such publications be barred from the mail "in view of the prevalent suspicion that the IWW organization is active in spreading its propaganda among the colored race, and the danger incident to the stirring up of race strife." United States Attorney Annette A. Adams found the pamphlets insufficiently objectionable to warrant their suppression but agreed to submit them to Washington for definitive review.[31]

In the midst of the "Red Summer" of 1919, rumors arose in Houston of subversive organizing and arms stockpiling by blacks. The fact that the Bureau did not pursue these rumors was due in part to Houston agents' level-headedness and to the knowledge that local authorities were alert, but also to intelligence gained from a highly placed informant, an officer in the Austin branch of the NAACP. What prompted insurance and real estate agent P. A. Williams to become an informant for the Texas attorney general is unknown. Williams supplied the names of every local branch officer along with informa-tion about "influential" white members. He also revealed that the priority of Texas branches was to gain equal accommodations on railroad trains while not directly challenging the principle of segregation.[32] Assuming that the information supplied by Williams was analyzed dispassionately, it may have allayed fears that the civil rights organization was plotting racial warfare. Perhaps the Texas NAACP was saved from further persecution by the "be-trayal" of one of its officers.

Elsewhere in the South, Red Scare fears prompted Bureau agents to seek suppression of the NAACP. In Mobile, Alabama, whose 24,000 black residents constituted one-third of the population, agent G. C. Outlaw agreed with local whites that blacks were harboring "thoughts which are not good" for them. The *Crisis, Chicago Defender,* and the local black weekly *Mobile Forum,* were accused of pernicious agitation. Outlaw urged their suppression.

"Race trouble" received greater attention in Nashville when the Bureau recruited William A. Bailey to go undercover in search of radicalism. During December 1919 he uncovered "some unrest" which he attributed to the *Crisis,* but by January the only danger was said to be increased friction on streetcars prompted by the NAACP and the black ministerial alliance, which were pressing the electric railway to end segregation. Bailey left Nashville for Birmingham later that month where he reported rumors that blacks were stockpiling weapons for use in case of a riot. No outbreak occurred, probably because the city's 70,000 blacks, composing a third of the population, only survived by acquiescing to the naked racial domination of whites. While there, Bailey bought copies of the *Crisis* and marked articles likely to interest the Bureau. Returning to Nashville, he found that the local NAACP was urging blacks to pay poll taxes and register to vote. Some blacks were armed, but Bailey's informant stressed that the guns were for defensive purposes only.[33] If the Bureau hoped Bailey would uncover convincing evidence that the NAACP or the *Crisis* was fomenting serious unrest, it was sorely disappointed.

The Bureau's investigation of the *Crisis* and the NAACP waned in the South after 1919, but this did not signal a disinterest in "Negro Radical Activity." The belief that black militancy posed a serious threat to the racial status quo and that socialists, communists, and anarchists were eager to subvert the race had become embedded in Hoover's thinking and the anti-radical crusade.

Under the necessity to comply with his orders to submit weekly reports on anarchist activities, agents often inflated the significance of individuals and groups that hardly merited government suspicion in the first place. Such vague allegations illustrate the degree to which almost any organized black effort could be construed as "radical." Even moderates must have been inhibited by the fact that the Bureau had no tolerance for civil rights advocacy. Examination of this large volume of weekly radical reports shows that the NAACP and the *Crisis* were widely perceived as a significant threat to white supremacy.

The most systematic weekly reports came from northern cities where thousands of migrants from the South settled into black ghettoes. No city equaled New York in the size of its black population or the numbers of outspoken black publications, radical activists, and racial organizations. New York also housed a greater proportion of West Indian blacks, whose desire for upward mobility often reflected itself in militant expression. Bureau agents staffing the New York radical squad, particularly Charles J. Scully, T. M. Reddy,

Mortimer J. Davis, and Joseph G. Tucker, diligently monitored black activities and placed trust in their black informants. The agents' reports provide an invaluable picture of the day-to-day ebb and flow of militancy in Black America's capital.

New York weekly reports generally followed a formula of identifying allegedly radical statements appearing in black publications or made on behalf of particular organizations. Agents kept close watch on the *Messenger*; the *Crusader* and its parent organization, the communist African Blood Brotherhood; Garvey's Universal Negro Improvement Association; and the NAACP and *Crisis*. Agents considered DuBois a "strong radical" for having criticized the Justice Department's efforts to obtain peacetime anti-sedition legislation. An editorial suggesting that blacks, foreigners, and socialists form a united voting bloc was also read with disapproval. But they admitted that by comparison to other black periodicals the *Crisis* was tame.[34]

Concerns about the NAACP's influence increased in mid-1920, however, even though the Red Scare was fading. The country could still be convulsed with fears of Bolshevism and anarchism and the New York office erroneously reported that the NAACP was urging blacks to join the feared IWW. The Bureau did not miss the fact that the NAACP now had nearly 350 branches and a membership of 100,000. But most of its attention in the second half of the year focused on James Weldon Johnson as the association's new executive secretary. Johnson could be as outspoken as DuBois, and his criticism of the American occupation of Haiti, segregationist policies of the American Legion, disfranchisement, and Ku Klux Klan terrorism in the South were duly noted.[35]

New York agents continued to scrutinize the NAACP through 1921 but found little evidence of genuine radicalism. What remained to be reported were meetings and membership drives; a campaign for pardons for the imprisoned Houston mutineers; opposition to the KKK in New York City; DuBois's involvement in a Pan-African conference in Europe; Walter White's alleged Bolshevik sympathies; and aid for victims of the Tulsa and Elaine, Arkansas, racial riots. Struggling to understand the ebb and flow of black militancy, agents concluded that the NAACP had lost favor with the masses. Yet they read a September 1921 *Crisis* editorial on the worldwide march of socialism and insisted that the magazine was still a "radical Negro monthly."[36]

Although the Red Scare dramatically declined after 1920, Hoover's GID continued to demand field reports on subversive activities, undoubtedly to justify its existence and Hoover's (and the Bureau's) preeminence in the suppression of radicalism. The New York office dutifully monitored the NAACP and *Crisis* in 1922 but the diminishing number of reports mentioning them noted little more than conferences, anti-Garvey activities, and the observation that the monthly magazine was no longer radical.[37] But Hoover did not give up his determination to monitor radical publications, whether they existed or not, and in September 1923 he again ordered the New York office to submit reports. Agent Tucker's reply described accurately the decline of militancy. The *Crusader* was out of business. The *Messenger* and *Crisis* had slipped badly from their postwar peaks, the latter now issuing only 38,000 copies each month. Garvey's *Negro World* had a weekly press run of 60,000 copies yet this, too, was much below previous levels.[38] Many blacks weighed the cost of a periodical against the economic pinch of the postwar depression. And the Red Scare had convinced many others that it was futile, imprudent, or even dangerous to support overt radicalism.

Even though the NAACP and its magazine were no longer of interest to agents in New York, Hoover still refused to abandon this quarry entirely. GID surveys of the "radical press" were compiled as late as mid-1925, one from early 1924 highlighting articles in the *Crisis* on blacks and Russia written by poet and communist fellow traveler Claude McKay. To Hoover's staff, the appearance of these articles proved the existence of a "spirit of revolt slumbering in the *Crisis*."[39] DuBois might have enjoyed this backhanded compliment, but the Bureau was far off the mark; the *Crisis* had never counseled anything resembling "revolt" even at the peak of its militancy in 1919, much less in the Coolidge years.

The Military Intelligence Division also monitored allegedly radical periodicals as it continued surveillance of civilian activities long past the Armistice. For several years each issue of the *Crisis* was carefully read and egregious passages marked with blue pencil. After November 1919 the assistant chief of staff for military intelligence in each of the eight army departments located in the continental United States was required to forward copies of all radical publications circulating in his district to Washington. From that date until early 1921 all manner of allegedly dangerous material flooded MID headquarters. Intelligence officers in New York and Chicago were particularly zealous, supplying multiple copies of the *Crisis, Messenger, Challenge, Crusader,* and *Negro World*. Degrees of militancy escaped MID; not only were avowedly socialist and communist periodicals (in English as well as various foreign languages) deemed offensive but also liberal white magazines such as the *Nation, Dial,* and *World Tomorrow*.[40]

The War Department began publishing weekly intelligence summaries in 1917, at first intended only for its staff, but by the end of the war copies were being sent to the President and the Justice and State departments. MID head Gen. Churchill believed these should transcend reporting of mere military events and analyze political, social, economic, even psychological data so as to keep the army prepared for any contingency. Weekly summaries continued through 1921, after which they were issued biweekly through the remainder of the decade. Were Hoover's weekly GID radicalism reports inspired by MID's example? Given his penchant for orderly process, efficient reporting, and attentiveness to bureaucratic detail, he was undoubtedly impressed by MID's system as he sought to make his own mark in anti-radical work.[41]

Black activism was addressed in MID surveys under the heading "Negro Subversion," implying that agitators were the source of much unrest. Not only was the NAACP frequently damned, it was assigned a much exaggerated role in allegedly fomenting radicalism. Whites in and out of the military commonly believed, following the race riots in mid-1919, that "race war" was about to erupt countrywide. MID's summary for the week ending August 23 noted ominously that

> IWW and other radical organizations, both white and black, have played their part in inciting the negroes to the recent outbreaks both in Chicago and Washington. It is stated that agitators have played upon the feelings of resentment against injustices or fancied injustices suffered by the negro soldiers during the War. The National Association for the Advancement of Colored People had an important part in this, and a negro woman representing this organization is said to have exhorted negro men at a meeting held several months ago in Washington "to go with shot guns in hand and demand what you want."[42]

This example shows the disproportionate influence MID attributed to the NAACP, as well as its unsympathetic attitude toward black grievances.

In late August 1919, John R. Shillady, the white executive secretary of the NAACP, was brutally beaten in Austin, Texas, by a mob led by a county judge. MID weekly surveys commented on this incident with sarcasm, racism, derision, and the assertion that Shillady had gotten what he deserved. Since blacks "were holding meetings at a time when there were constant rumors that the negroes were arming themselves," whites were justified in taking stern action.[43]

The Elaine (Phillips County), Arkansas, "riot" was the worst racial violence in the Red Scare period. Again, MID proved incapable of accurately perceiving the facts. When long-exploited black sharecroppers attempted to organize a "Progressive Farmers and Household Union," whites attacked in October 1919, bringing death to over two hundred blacks, including women and children. On the pretext that a white man had also been killed, authorities railroaded twelve black defendants to murder convictions and death sentences, with sixty-seven others also condemned to long prison terms. After prolonged efforts, the NAACP finally gained the freedom of all the defendants.[44]

The army was keenly interested in the events at Elaine because members of the 57th Infantry were dispatched to restore order. MID analysts accepted the viewpoint of Arkansas whites without question and, referring to NAACP efforts to prevent the executions, wrote that "various negro organizations are making frantic attempts to defeat the ends of justice." Another MID summary reported that the murder convictions were "being used by various radical negro organizations"—particularly the NAACP—"for propaganda purposes." And when blacks in neighboring Desha County mobilized to prevent the arrest of a neighbor on hog-stealing charges, the intelligence officer of that military district charged the *Crisis* with inciting another "negro outbreak." MID saw justice only through the eyes of white southerners. Not only did it lack appreciation for blacks' first and sixth amendment freedoms, but even for their right to dignity, criticizing the NAACP for trying to gain "the 'right' of negroes to eat with white people" in the lunchroom at the Library of Congress.[45] (At the same time, the Justice Department saw no reason to intervene in Phillips County; Attorney General Palmer believed it was strictly a state matter and outside of federal jurisdiction "unless it should clearly appear that there has been a palpable disregard of individual rights." Apparently the Bill of Rights need not be included in that equation.)[46]

The fear of communist subversion often lay behind MID's response to the NAACP in 1919 and 1920. Reporting on the NAACP's eleventh annual meeting, MID noted the participation of "a notorious parlor bolshevist" who advocated solving the "negro problem" through economic solutions. In other cases, MID simply opposed the rhetoric of black militancy; DuBois was labeled "a negro radical" for comparing peonage in Mississippi to Belgian atrocities in the Congo. It also reacted negatively to NAACP criticism of the government, as in its opposition to the proposed Graham-Sterling sedition bill, which would have excluded from the mails any publication using "an appeal to racial prejudice"; obviously such a law could easily have been distorted to harass even moderate black publications.[47]

MID criticism of the NAACP reached a new low in March 1920, charging that "this organization has been particularly offensive throughout the country in its teachings of social equality for the negro, and in attempting to stay the hand of justice in numerous cases where negroes have been accused of crime."[48] The issue of social equality, which to the NAACP simply meant an end to segregation in public facilities, was the racial nightmare for many whites who believed blacks intended to force themselves into the bosom of white society, even in marriage. The peacetime army, its officer corps steeped in southern white traditions, responded to the social equality issue by determining to keep blacks in segregated units and shielding white officers from contact with their black counterparts. As for the "hand of justice," this referred to the NAACP's efforts to prevent lynching, which practice most southern whites regarded as a necessary evil, if evil at all.

The army's intelligence branch also allowed itself to be panicked by Attorney General Palmer's predictions of new May Day bomb attacks in 1920. MID announced a serious increase in radical black activities across the country, including the aggressive circulation of the *Crisis* in Louisiana! The interracial NAACP was also accused of increasing its demands for social, political, and economic equality so as to foment racial hatred, although MID was reassured to learn that "respectable" blacks were shunning such agitation.[49]

After a peaceful May Day the public's willingness to believe the apocalyptic prophecies of Palmer and the Justice Department rapidly waned. Yet MID summaries continued to feature "Negro Subversion," including the fact that the NAACP held its annual (interracial) conference in Atlanta, the first time it braved meeting openly in the South. The organization's protests against the American military occupation of Haiti were also noted. Truth suffered, as in the MID commentary which labeled DuBois "the Karl Marx of Negroes" whose "writings have been used to exploit racial hatred."[50] (Marx, of course, would have disapproved of such hatred.)

Federal intelligence officials seeking to inhibit or suppress black militancy were motivated not only by their own anxieties but by those of Great Britain as well, which conducted counter-espionage in friendly countries as part of its effort to prevent the spread of radicalism to its Caribbean colonies. Communists, socialists, and racial nationalists based in America seemed likely to infect the islands' black majorities and spur unrest or even demands for independence.[51] At first the British made little effort to hide their intelligence operations in the United States and sought to avoid friction by offering copies of its own summaries, expecting the United States to reciprocate. Although they were most fearful of Garvey's nationalist movement, the British also worried about the NAACP. In the spring of 1919 they proposed that the two governments formally cooperate in combating Bolshevism. The American embassy in London strongly endorsed the idea and suggested that the head of British Intelligence in the United States be given direct access to officials in MID and the Justice and Labor departments. Soon, a covert British military intelligence office was established in New York City.[52]

The British compiled about a dozen extensive reports on "negro agitation" in the United States. Copies, supplied to the State Department through the embassy in London, were distributed to the Justice, Labor, and Post Office departments. The main foci were Garvey, black communists and socialists, and radical groups suspected of fomenting sedition among blacks, like the IWW. While the NAACP received less coverage it was not immune from the kind of wild allegations found in the British documents. A report on the beating of Shillady in Texas made the absurd claim that the attack "was planned by DuBois's organization to start trouble for use as propaganda." It is doubtful the judge who thrashed Shillady would have appreciated the idea that the NAACP manipulated him into that act. Another British report focused on the rapid postwar growth of the NAACP and its team of well-known white attorneys preparing to defend black rioters.[53]

Special Report No. 10 on "Unrest among the Negroes" was actually penned by MID's Maj. Walter Loving, given to British intelligence officials in the United States, transmitted to the cabinet in London, then passed on to the American embassy and sent back across the Atlantic. Loving explained the rise in black militancy as due in part to mistreatment of black soldiers by their white officers in France. DuBois's revelations in the Crisis were said to have "aroused the bitter resentment of Negroes throughout the country." The Report stressed, however, that the NAACP utilized only lawful means in opposing injustice and that DuBois, once an important agitator, was now considered behind the times by "younger and more violent leaders" like Randolph, Owen, and Garvey.[54]

British intelligence efforts in America, including interest in the NAACP,[55] persisted into 1920. But when its "spying" was discovered by the pro-Irish press, which played up this violation of American sovereignty, the British agreed to close their office in New York. The State Department knew this would not end covert operations; its agents, anxious to monitor Sinn Fein sympathizers in the United States, would simply act more circumspectly. Anglophiles in the State Department had no objection to British counter-espionage and simply hoped to avoid adverse publicity. This was not easily done as Hearst newspapers continued to dramatize the issue. Meanwhile the State Department was still forwarding information on black militancy to the British as late as the fall of 1920.[56]

As the Red Scare faded, and with it any possibility that radicals would convert large numbers of blacks, federal intelligence interest in the NAACP diminished but did not disappear. One reason had nothing to do with that organization (or any other group). The agencies most preoccupied with radicalism now had budgets, careers, and bureaucratic empires to protect. The Military Intelligence Division was the least influential of the five general staff divisions and struggled to preserve its share of shrinking War Depart-

ment resources. J. Edgar Hoover's General Intelligence Division could justify
its existence only by uncovering threats to domestic security. The State
Department had the least difficulty rationalizing its interest in radicalism
because, while communism stalled in the United States, the Third International was expansionist in other parts of the world.

Although the NAACP and the *Crisis* were never even remote threats to
national security, the issues on which they focused ensured federal surveillance even after the Red Scare. One long-standing campaign was the effort to
make lynching a federal crime, and, when mob violence increased alarmingly
in the postwar months, the NAACP redoubled its efforts. One novel approach
was to send photographs and details of lynch murders to Latin American
newspapers in hopes they might rally international condemnation of the
United States, and then point out to the secretary of state that such atrocities
damaged America's image abroad. The State Department vainly urged Hoover
to suppress the NAACP's "propaganda," but he knew there were no legal
grounds for such a step.[57]

By 1922 the Justice Department's main black target was Marcus Garvey. As
prosecution of the Jamaican Pan-Africanist for mail fraud drew near, in an
ironic twist the Bureau of Investigation gained the help of several of its former
targets. Assisting its efforts to obtain evidence against Garvey were several
NAACP officials who feared he would provoke violent conflict between West
Indians and American-born blacks. Walter White kept in touch with UNIA
dissidents, while William Pickens supplied black agent James E. Amos with
the names of disgruntled stockholders in the UNIA's ill-fated steamship line
who might testify against Garvey. In January 1923, *Messenger* co-editor Chandler Owen, plus Pickens, NAACP official Robert W. Bagnall, and five other well-known blacks sent a letter to the attorney general pleading for swift prosecution of Garvey; NAACP lawyers assisted those who drafted the letter, although
officially they acted as private individuals. Owen and Bagnall also gathered
information regarding the murder of Rev. J. W. H. Eason, a former UNIA
leader. And later in 1923, when the Bureau needed an infiltrator to attend a
UNIA meeting, the NAACP supplied that individual.[58]

By the early 1920s DuBois, the *Crisis,* and the NAACP were incapable of
seriously eroding white Americans' racial hegemony. Efforts to secure an anti-lynching law foundered. Membership (and subscriptions) declined rapidly
from the postwar peak. Militancy was fading all over the country, due to red
baiting, the Red Scare, and overt government suppression. In a larger sense,
the Progressive era, which had actually brought no meaningful racial improvement, was waning. The conservative return to "normalcy" would block
gains for dispossessed or disinherited groups. And yet the NAACP would

continue to be viewed with suspicion by the federal government's guardians of white supremacy. MID included the NAACP on its lists of "Red and Pink Publications" while the Bureau and the Post Office persevered in monitoring the *Crisis*.[59]

This belief that the NAACP had seditious intents was cemented into political intelligence thinking during the Red Scare. In 1925, a white officer in the black 25th Infantry stationed at Nogales sought guidance on whether the NAACP should be allowed to "work" the regiment for members. As this question traveled up the chain of command, the Eighth Army corps area IO repeated the canard that the NAACP was "fostered by the so-called 'Bolshevist' outfit." Then MID headquarters found "evidence" on which to damn the civil rights organization when it dug up two memoranda written during World War I which condemned its alleged radicalism, racism, pacifism, and pro-Germanism. Even in 1925, NAACP board members (including prominent whites) were said to espouse dangerous ideas and the *Crisis* to publish seditious articles in order to incite interracial conflict. "It is obvious that the aims and activities of this organization are not in harmony with the interests of the Army."[60] Needless to say, NAACP membership was to be discouraged among black troopers.

Two decades later, during World War II, army intelligence and the FBI would again allege that the black press was disloyal. Capping a lengthy investigation, Hoover's staff compiled a 714-page "Survey of Racial Conditions in the United States" charging that some publications, including the *Crisis*, were pro-Japanese or otherwise detrimental to the war effort. As in World War I, those who criticized government racial policies or racism in general were easily branded as unpatriotic or worse. Once again, legitimate black dissent was distorted by unsympathetic whites and misconstrued as subversion.[61]

In the final analysis one point stands out: Federal suspicion of black individuals and organizations was not limited to the genuinely radical voices during the Red Scare. It is understandable that the *Messenger*, which advocated "Bolshevik" solutions for American racism, would be the target of suppression. One can also comprehend why Marcus Garvey, who boldly denied that blacks could achieve even a modest version of the American dream, was so strongly opposed by guardians of that myth. But the interracial NAACP neither promoted radical political or economic changes nor rejected the nation's cherished ethos. It was a reformist, not a revolutionary organization, relying on the legal process, not extralegal methods. Yet its strong protests against lynching and discrimination and exposure of racism in the military command structure were sufficient to earn hostile responses from those in power. There was no genuine freedom to dissent during wartime, and precious little during the postwar reaction. Lacking our modern definition of the scope of First Amendment freedoms, the Bill of Rights contained only conditional guarantees to those who found it difficult to embrace "one hundred percent Americanism" in those years. Neither DuBois nor his colleagues in the NAACP could have doubted their cause was unpopular, no more tolerated because others spoke with greater militancy. Only conformity to the nation's racial and cultural shibboleths would have brought them peace, immunity, or acceptance.

FIVE

❦

"THE MOST DANGEROUS OF ALL THE NEGRO PUBLICATIONS"

Federal Efforts to Suppress the Messenger and Black Socialist Activism

Of the numerous radical periodicals born between 1917 and 1921, the *Messenger* was the most feared black publication, a notoriety proudly embraced by its young editors, A. Philip Randolph and Chandler Owen. Begun in the fall of 1917 and lasting to 1928, the *Messenger* was the finest example of "New Negro" or "New Crowd Negro" journalism. Its southern-born editors were both twenty-eight years old at the magazine's birth, each having migrated to New York City where, liberated from the worst restrictions of Jim Crow life, they plunged eagerly into new intellectual and political currents. Before long they were converts to the Socialist Party and rising stars in its efforts to reach the growing black population in Harlem. Because they were campaigning for the Socialist ticket and speaking out against the war wherever they could cadge an audience, a publication of their own was essential. From its premier issue, the *Messenger* was artfully written, boldly iconoclastic, and a blast of raw air compared to the conventional black press. The *Messenger* in its ten-year life would oppose World War I; espouse socialism and, for a time, Bolshevism; challenge Marcus Garvey's Pan-Africanism; shepherd the Harlem Renaissance; and define new black leadership strategies and goals. Its counsel was not always heeded, but rarely was its voice unheard. NAACP executive James Weldon Johnson considered it to be the best edited and most influential radical black periodical of its time. And for more than half a decade it was the object of systematic government investigation and attempted suppression. The white press and government, during the peak of the magazine's militancy, saw it as the most serious black threat to the racial status quo, and Randolph himself was branded "the most dangerous Negro in America."[1]

Randolph and Owen published their inaugural issue in November 1917, praising a variety of pacifist and anti-war groups, railing against war profiteers, urging that America, too, be made safe for democracy, and promoting the socialist mayoral candidacy of Morris Hillquit in New York City. Copies were first sold from Harlem street corners. The next issue, appearing in January 1918, pioneered the idea that blacks should have representation in whatever peace negotiations were conducted at the end of the war. This edition also welcomed the advance of Bolshevism in Russia, supported free speech for dissidents in America, and, referring to lynching and other racial atrocities, proclaimed "Prussianism" to be worse in the South than in Germany. Surprisingly, these first two issues did not catch the attention of the Justice or Post Office departments, nor did the fact that Randolph and his wife, Lucille, ran for secretary of state and the state legislature on the Socialist ticket in 1917. Exactly when the Bureau of Investigation first took alarm at the *Messenger* is unclear.[2]

What ultimately triggered federal action was the editors' midwestern speaking tour in the summer of 1918, coinciding with publication of the magazine's third issue. When they arrived in Cleveland on August 4, two Bureau agents mingled with the large crowd gathered to hear them and white socialist speakers. The agents purchased a copy of the *Messenger* for 15 cents, confiscated the remaining 100 copies, and took Randolph, Owen, and one of the white speakers into custody for interrogation. (This was technically not an arrest; Bureau agents would not be granted that authority until 1934.)[3]

Two matters especially concerned the federal officers. The editors were sponsored, promoted, and paid by the Socialist Party, which was widely believed to be subversive even though the bulk of its leadership supported the war. Second, the contents of the *Messenger,* especially two editorials, seemed outright disloyal. One, entitled "Conscription," advocated a confiscatory tax on all war profits so as to remove any economic incentive for war. The second editorial was to be often cited by federal authorities as a definitive example of the new radical black journalism. "Pro-Germanism among Negroes" commented on widespread fears that black discontent was the result of enemy subversion. The article agreed that the race was seriously disaffected, but on account of "peonage, disfranchisement, Jim-Crowism, segregation, rank civil discrimination, injustice of legislatures, courts and administrators." Naturally blacks put their own interpretation on the government's crusade "to make the world safe for democracy" while they were "denied economic, political, educational and civil democracy" at home. Tweaking the ears of hostile readers, Randolph and Owen suggested that "the Negro may be choosing between being burnt by Tennessee, Georgia or Texas mobs or being shot by Germans in Belgium. We don't know about this pro-Germanism among Negroes. It may be only their anti-Americanism—meaning anti-lynching." Whatever the editors meant in this editorial, two years later Randolph wrote that "with the characteristic stupidity of the Department of Justice, they did not understand that the article was satirical and sarcastic."[4]

An assistant United States attorney authorized the arrest of Randolph, Owen, and two white socialists under Section 3, Title 1 of the Espionage Act. That broad clause allowed up to twenty years in prison for anyone convicted of interfering with the efficiency of the military forces, obstructing enlistments, or inciting disloyalty. The two young radicals were neither the first nor the last to be apprehended under such nebulous proscriptions on political advocacy. Pleading not guilty but unable to raise $1,000 bail apiece, Owen and Randolph were released only when well-known socialist attorney Seymour Stedman arrived from Chicago to handle their defense. The trial judge refused to believe the twenty-nine-year-old "boys" were capable of writing the inflammatory editorials submitted as evidence and assumed others had unscrupulously used their names. "Showing both judicial and racial paternalism, the judge dismissed the charges and, so he thought, sent the two home to their parents." Randolph and Owen instead entrained for Chicago and their next speaking engagement, incarceration in Cleveland having made them minor celebrities in the anti-war movement. Street meetings in a variety of cities garnered sizeable audiences and triggered warnings from Bureau agents to cease criticizing the war and President Wilson. No cowards, they proceeded to repeat their charges to crowds in Washington, too.[5]

Not only did the government hope to suppress the *Messenger's* uncomfortably pointed rhetoric. The black *New York Age,* having complained that Randolph and Owen "for months have stood on the street corners in Harlem and vilified those with whom they differed politically," now applauded their arrest and Owen's induction into military service. It is conceivable that the Justice Department "encouraged" his local board to call him to duty quickly. (Randolph was deferred from the draft because he was married.) The Post Office Department, reacting to "Pro-Germanism among Negroes," ensured that the magazine would be hamstrung by revoking its second-class permit. Forced to pay first-class mail rates, and with Owen in the army, the *Messenger* did not appear again until March 1919. But Randolph continued to speak widely.[6]

The Bureau routinely sent stenographers to radical gatherings, guaranteeing federal surveillance of Randolph's political activities. Just days before the Armistice in November 1918, the Socialist Party held campaign meetings at four locations around New York on the same night, with fifteen speakers rotating from one event to the other. A shorthand reporter accompanied by police was detailed to Brooklyn where he recorded Randolph's celebration of the worldwide working-class movement. The young radical was introduced as one of the finest exponents of socialism among American blacks, praise designed to promote his candidacy for the state assembly. The next day he polled 8 percent of the 13,000 votes cast, while Owen garnered only half as many in a neighboring district, due at least in part to the fact he was in the army and unable to campaign. Two days later, New York agent R. W. Finch summarized the Bureau's fears: "More agitation among the negroes by the Socialists may be looked for, as the Socialist Party considers this the psychological moment to strongly agitate among all classes." Equally ominous was the movement to demand racial improvement and a voice in peace negotiations as rewards for wartime service. Jamaican-born nationalist Marcus Garvey, an early exponent of black representation in the peace talks, organized a mass meeting on December 1 where Randolph, militant journalist Ida B. Wells-Barnett, and Haitian immigrant and merchant Eliezer Cadet were selected to go to France. New York agents took this gathering seriously, believing that black interference in the diplomatic process posed a real threat.[7]

The Bureau's fear of a unified racial militancy was shared by the Military Intelligence Division at the end of 1918. During the war, MID's dependably conservative black investigator, Maj. Walter H. Loving, described a growing "spirit of unrest among Negroes." All over the country the black press was asking how the race would be rewarded for helping win the war. Several organizations had picked delegates to attend the Paris peace talks and present the world leadership with Black America's grievances. Loving suggested careful screening of all passport applicants, and in fact the State Department prevented all but a few blacks from getting to France. When the lynching of five blacks—including a soldier in uniform—stirred the race to outrage, Loving sent undercover operatives to as many indignation meetings as possible, while also making an anguished plea for punishment of the guilty parties. He warned MID that blacks would be satisfied only by meaningful protection of their basic rights. Although not mentioning Randolph by name, Loving was aware of the young socialist's influence. From now on MID would monitor his activities and share its information with the Bureau.[8]

Military surveillance of civilians should have ceased with the end of hostilities, but MID was as alarmed by the rapid growth of radicalism as other agencies and had no intention of relinquishing domestic intelligence. Maj.

Loving's services were continued for several months after the war. He utilized contacts in various northern cities to gather information on a wide variety of individuals and movements. An early report on the *Messenger* editors noted their participation in the International League of Darker Peoples founded by the quixotic Welshman R. D. Jonas. The League was said to be similar to Garvey's movement but to include all the colored races of the world. During the war it had been feared that disaffected blacks would form a hostile alliance with Japan and Mexico. Now, Japanese imperialism and demands for military parity with the European powers and the United States led to planning for possible war. Because several members of the *Messenger* circle were linked to Jonas's organization, both MID and the Bureau maintained surveillance of its meetings and collected its publications.[9]

Jonas was working both sides of the street, and had been for some time. During the war he was an informant on "Negro subversion" for MID and in late 1918 it pawned him off on the British military intelligence office in New York, which was fearful that radical blacks from the United States would infect the black majorities in Caribbean and African colonies. The British paid Jonas to investigate Owen, Randolph, and Japanese contact with blacks. Until the British intelligence mission was closed in April 1920, copies of Jonas's reports were sent to MID and then to the Justice Department.[10]

Jonas also bid for paid employment as an informer for the Bureau of Investigation, visiting the New York office in early 1919 to disclose the hidden purposes behind his League of Darker Peoples. He claimed to be recruiting black, Japanese, Hindu, and Chinese socialists and Bolshevists to learn their plans and then secretly mobilize conservative black churchmen against them. But Jonas was no patriot: He hoped to sell his findings to the Department of Justice, and to whet its appetite he supplied information on the *Messenger's* first postwar issue, printed in March. Bureau agent Finch was immediately alarmed, warning headquarters that "this periodical is one of the most brazen pieces of Bolsheviki propaganda we have seen for some time" with articles criticizing "everything American" and calculated to arouse "the negroes against the white race in general." He promised that New York agents would employ Jonas to attend meetings where Randolph and Owen spoke, monitor the press runs of the magazine, and analyze its "inflammatory" articles.[11]

The Bureau also began to intercept Randolph's mail. The only authority for opening first-class (sealed) letters was granted during the war for international mail to or from countries which had no censorship or where enemy activity was likely. Randolph's tampered mail was strictly domestic in origin. Photographic copies of the most significant items were made before envelopes were re-sealed and delivered. One was a letter to Socialist Party official Adolph

Germer in which Randolph inquired whether the post office was delivering Germer's mail, as "it is common for your letters to be opened and marked." The Bureau also passed copies of purloined letters to MID.[12]

Federal agents gained access to other private communications. When Jonas visited Randolph's office he stole a look at a telegram from Roger Baldwin, the jailed head of the National Civil Liberties Bureau, warning of a spy in the black socialist ranks. More detail on the magazine's editors was gained by Chicago agent August H. Loula who interviewed William Harvey Tibbs, regional organizer for the *Messenger*-advocated National Association for the Promotion of Labor Unionism among Negroes, and managed to read a letter from Owen, now out of the army and again promoting radicalism.[13]

MID also engaged in more systematic investigation of the magazine in early 1919, its efforts now spearheaded by New York–based Capt. John B. Trevor, who became one of MID's most diligent students of black militancy in the postwar period. The March 1919 issue appeared "frankly revolutionary." Relying heavily on information from Jonas and British intelligence, Trevor compiled a ten-page memorandum on "Negro Agitation," the opening paragraph of which established the gravity of the current situation. Black radicalism

> goes far beyond the redress of the alleged grievances of our negro population. It aims at Pan-Negroism and a combination of the other colored races of the world. As a colored movement it looks to Japan for leadership; as a radical movement it follows Bolshevism and has intimate relations with various socialistic groups throughout the United States. With this latter connection it naturally sympathizes with and has relations with the Irish, the Jews and Hindus.[14]

Trevor (and Jonas) clearly exaggerated foreign influences. Although the *Messenger* supported the nationalistic aspirations of the groups Trevor listed, it had no formal ties with them.

But this memorandum did identify a significant change occurring in Black America. The Bookerite generation of accommodationist leaders backed by white philanthropy was being supplanted by those who rejected gradualism. The *Messenger* was one of the most prominent new radical voices, its writers allegedly heaping "abuse on the white man" while identifying with the socialist movement. Trevor failed to see the contradiction in his (or Jonas's) conclusion, as the socialist camp was itself overwhelmingly white.[15]

The attention paid to Randolph and Owen up to the spring of 1919 was due more to their political activities than to their editorship. Only four issues of the *Messenger* had been printed in seventeen months. But regular publication was established in mid-year, simultaneous with the flowering of the Red

Scare. By then, four intelligence branches of the federal government were anxiously watching the magazine and its editors. The pressure would only worsen.

Censorship of objectionable publications continued after the war, based on the unrevoked Espionage and Sedition acts, and was exercised by denying second-class mailing permits to offenders. Final decision on such matters rested with postal solicitor William H. Lamar, who, while no particular defender of First Amendment freedoms, was not as rabid toward the radical press as the Post Office's Translation Bureau, led by Robert Adger Bowen. The first of his many complaints against the "negro radical monthly" reached Lamar shortly after the appearance of the May-June *Messenger.* Bowen was especially exercised at its hope for a Bolshevik triumph in America. Continuing the wartime practice of sharing intelligence among federal agencies, he sent a copy to MID, highlighting criticism of the army's "alleged mistreatment" of black soldiers. (MID intelligence officers around the country also submitted this issue to headquarters.) The Bureau likewise reviewed this edition while Rear Adm. A. P. Niblack, director of the Office of Naval Intelligence, sent a copy of the "negro radical publication" to the Bureau.[16] No wonder the *Messenger's* circulation rose in 1919!

Certainly no intelligence agency could risk apathy at this time, with bombs being thrown at the homes of cabinet secretaries and the country seemingly awash in revolutionary threats. The press regaled the nation with sensational reports based on Justice Department copy supplied to newspapers, engraved and ready for printing. Typical was an article entitled "Enrolling American Negroes under Banners of Bolshevism." Focusing on the *Messenger,* it warned of "a well-planned, well-executed and well-financed propaganda among the Negroes of this country to-day for an absolute overthrow of the present form of government and the substitution of governmental ideas as carried out by Trotsky and Lenin in Russia."[17]

June brought intense scrutiny of the *Messenger* and its editors. Maj. Loving arranged for a stenographic record of their speeches in Washington. The same meetings were covered by a second MID operative, the right hand apparently unaware of what the left was up to. Loving also collected copies of the magazine for headquarters and supplied data on its finances. Maintaining intelligence reciprocity, MID sent portions of this information to the Bureau, whose personnel were tracing the *Messenger's* connections to other radical groups in various cities. Agents in New York grudgingly acknowledged that "the magazine is remarkably well gotten up from a printing standpoint." Certainly the Bureau missed nothing, for it received another long report from

ONI detailing Randolph and Owen's advocacy of "soviet" remedies for blacks' problems.[18]

As the July *Messenger* was brought to the post office for mailing, a copy was transmitted to the Translation Bureau. Bowen saw red: The magazine was "full of significance as to the growing spirit of disloyalty among the negroes." He quoted the lead editorial, "The Hun in America," which minced no words about lynching:

> America, the chief ally in the fight for democracy, stands before the world with her garments dripping with blood and covered with shame, as the land of the most criminal HUNS in Christendom. . . . The Huns of Germany pale into utter insignificance beside the nameless and indescribable fiendishness of the American HUNS.

Bowen also took umbrage at an editorial, "Lynching a Domestic Question," which anticipated Malcolm X's strategy forty years later in proposing that American racism be exposed before the bar of world opinion. Another piece praised the IWW while "Propaganda and the American Negro Soldier" stated that "no intelligent American Negro is willing to lay down his life for the U.S. as it now exists." The Translation Bureau made certain that MID read this last article.[19]

Bowen pressed for denying the *Messenger* all mailing privileges, so the New York post office held all copies on July 1 pending a ruling by Solicitor Lamar. Randolph and Owen urged subscribers to protest this action. The editors gave their version of events in an interview with the *Harlem Home News,* denying any formal connections with the communist movement and blaming the Lusk Committee, a New York state legislative body engaged in a witch-hunt against radicals, for misrepresenting them. The newspaper refused to take sides but added that Harlem was watching the conflict with interest.[20]

The solicitor's staff examined the July issue in detail but concluded that the offending editorials were not "sufficiently grave to warrant the exclusion of this issue from the mails. The principle grievances which the publishers are nursing arise from the fact that the negro is discriminated against in the South, and in the various other parts of the country he is not receiving the attention he is entitled to." On July 3, Lamar ordered the magazine released for mailing, with the warning that, although this issue could pass, similar content in the future could justify prosecution. The New York office did not actually free the magazine until five days later, a punitive delay which likely reflected Bowen's pique. He was plainly disgusted: "The first issue of the *Messenger* read in this office came out flatly, explicitly . . . for Bolshevik rule in this country."[21] Of all the radical publications, the *Messenger* displayed "the fullest flower of negro sedition and flagrant disloyalty" and was "ably edited." Bowen's conclusion was ominous:

> The negro is rapidly being made strongly race conscious and class conscious, and that to him his way of salvation is felt to lie not in conformity to the law but in defiance and antagonism to it. . . . It is not, in my opinion, an attitude that the government can safely ignore.[22]

Despite the solicitor's decision not to impose a postal ban, efforts to suppress the *Messenger* intensified. While the Red Scare inflamed the nation with predictions of more bombs and plots, circulation of radical publications mushroomed. The *Messenger's* readership jumped 50 percent in three months; 15,000 copies of the May-June issue were printed, and by the fall circulation peaked at 21,000 to 33,000 copies.[23]

During the summer of 1919, while postal zealots took aim at the *Messenger*,[24] the Bureau of Investigation intensified its scrutiny of Randolph and Owen, for a time mistakenly believing they were allied with Marcus Garvey because they occasionally shared the same platform, both advocated retaliation against white rioters, and Garvey's *Negro World* promoted a rally condemning postal efforts to suppress black publications. Speakers included Randolph, Owen, and white IWW activist Elizabeth Gurley Flynn. Her presence was sufficient to "prove" sponsorship of black militancy by white radicals.[25]

Bureau personnel in New York conducted the most sustained scrutiny of the *Messenger* and its editors by any field office in the summer of 1919. Agent Finch headed the "radical squad" until he left to work for the Lusk Committee; his new position probably benefited both state and federal investigators since each had information on radical activities that the other desired. J. Edgar Hoover granted the committee's request for Bureau files on Randolph, including evidence gathered by an undercover informant at the Rand School, a "workers university," that a large number of white "Bolsheviki" purchased the *Messenger* there. Agent Mortimer J. Davis visited the magazine's office posing as a reporter and noted portraits of Lenin, Trotsky, and local socialist heroes Scott Nearing and Morris Hillquit on the walls.[26]

Hoover increased pressure on the *Messenger* and its editors as July ended with the most destructive racial violence of the Red Scare period. Although the Justice Department finally admitted that there was no evidence of communist instigation of the worst riot, in Chicago, speculation ran wild. The *New York Times* screamed "Reds Try to Stir Negroes to Revolt," while the *New York Tribune* headlined "Reds Accused of Stirring Up Negro Rioters; IWW and Other Agitators Charged with Spreading Propaganda Aimed to Breed Race

Hatred; Financed from Russia." "Evidence" for these allegations was found in several *Messenger* articles lauding the Soviet form of government. The Bureau's Chicago field office made extensive efforts to discover if the riot was attributable to radical propaganda or whether any federal laws had been violated. Neither charge could be proven, although agents believed that the "incendiary" *Messenger* was partially responsible for the violence. They placed no blame, however, on businesses which imported more black workers than they could employ, realtors whose blockbusting aroused the hatreds of whites, or white prejudice in general.[27]

On August 12, Hoover sent a memorandum to Bureau Chief Frank Burke describing the principal black targets of his anti-radical General Intelligence Division. Foremost among them was the *Messenger* which, Hoover wrote with abandon, "is stated to be the Russian organ of the Bolsheviki in the United States and to be the headquarters of revolutionary thought." Reflecting the Bureau's emphasis on deporting alien subversives, Hoover ordered agents to determine the citizenship of all persons on the staff. Associates of anyone connected with the *Messenger* were to be investigated. "Particular attention should be given to ascertaining whether any of these persons are in any way connected with [socialist editor] Max Eastman, agents of the Bolsheviki in the United States, or the IWW. Income from subscriptions and advertisements, plus any private sources of funds, should also be determined."[28]

From mid-August to September 1919, the Bureau's first regular black undercover informant, Dr. Arthur Ulysses Craig, utilized his considerable personal connections to penetrate the burgeoning black militancy which not only absorbed Harlem, but spilled downtown and joined the rivers of radicalism from immigrant neighborhoods to Greenwich Village. Hoover intended that Craig focus on the *Messenger* and Marcus Garvey's UNIA. This was to be no casual inquiry. Chief Burke personally briefed Craig on his new assignment. And upon arrival in New York on August 22 he met with the head of the anti-radical squad and examined files on Garvey, Randolph, and Owen.[29]

Craig easily met the *Messenger*'s staff and arranged to write for it. Yet he never published anything, and in fact developed no useful new information, primarily because New York agents, desperate for intelligence on the ever-growing array of militant black movements, assigned Craig to investigate too many different groups and individuals. Hoover's purpose in employing Craig was thus subverted, and at the end of the summer his services were terminated. He had found no solid evidence on which to prosecute Randolph and Owen. But this was not his fault; Bureau agents in several cities were vainly seeking the same thing.[30]

White agents in New York continued to gather information on the *Messenger* while Craig was engaged in the same task. Their files were supplemented by another lengthy British Intelligence report, again based on the investigations of Jonas. Particularly significant was the magazine's support for Irish nationalism and its circulation in Britain's Caribbean colonies.[31]

The fear that black radicalism was promoting "social equality" lay at the heart of white nightmares in the summer of 1919. The voice that most clearly articulated this anxiety, and which galvanized the Justice Department into its most intense efforts to suppress the *Messenger,* was that of Rep. James F. Byrnes of South Carolina, writing to the Justice Department on August 25 to demand that the *Crisis* and especially the *Messenger* be banned. Less than a month after riots in Chicago, Washington, Harlem, Norfolk, Longview, Texas, and Bisbee, Arizona, Byrnes blamed deteriorating racial relations on new black leaders and the black press, both allegedly stirring their race to acts of retaliatory violence. The worst influence was the *Messenger,* which he believed to be an organ of the IWW. He was equally alarmed at its call for armed self-defense: "We can all believe in a free press, but we can recognize the distinction between a free press and a revolutionary and anarchistic press." No changes in the racial status quo would be countenanced.[32]

The GID's own agenda coincided with Byrnes's demand for action. Hoover believed that "something should be done to the editors of these publications [the *Crisis* and the *Messenger*] as they are beyond doubt exciting the negro elements of this country to riot and to the committing of outrages of all sorts." United States Attorney Francis G. Caffey in New York, instructed to determine whether prosecution could be sustained against the *Messenger* and its editors, knew that the only likely means was the Sedition Act. Assistant Attorney General Robert P. Stewart, however, recognized that this was not the ideal vehicle and that failure to win a conviction might do more harm than good.[33]

Extensive correspondence ensued in which Caffey repeatedly maintained that conviction was unlikely. An indictment of the *Messenger* based on the Sedition Act would probably be demurrable. That act punished espionage, weakening of the nation's military efforts, "disloyal abuse" of the government, provoking resistance to authority, and supporting the cause of the enemy, all at such times "when the United States is at war." Almost certainly, Caffey believed, the courts would limit its application to cases falling within its intended scope. Even if a technical case were stated he doubted that a conviction would be achieved given popular sentiment in the New York district. After all, in the popular mind, the war was over, even though final termination of hostilities would not be achieved until July 2, 1921. A failed prosecution would only aid the IWWs who, Caffey added, were "persistently endeavoring to induce the Government to start court proceedings against them, for the sake of the advertisement they would get, and also to lend color to their claims of persecution." Pity the poor federal prosecutors, harassed by the Wobblies. At any rate, clearly Caffey was reasoning politically as well as legally.[34]

The attorney general's office agreed with Caffey but the *Messenger* itself forced further consideration by printing a sarcastic reply to Rep. Byrnes, demanding that blacks be allowed to enjoy the same sexual privileges with whites as that race had traditionally exercised over blacks. Hoover, whose southern white sensibilities were as outraged as Byrnes's, directed the New York field office to summarize its investigation "so that in the event the United States Attorney did not see his way clear to take up the prosecution in Federal Court, the information collected by this office would be submitted upon instructions from the Chief of the Bureau, to the office of the [New York] County District Attorney." Exploring every avenue for suppression, Hoover next suggested prosecution under the New York Sedition Act. The attorney general's office also proposed that Section 6 of the Criminal Code, which defined seditious conspiracy, might be used.[35]

Again Caffey recommended against futile prosecution. The *Messenger*, to his reading, had two major goals: to encourage blacks to band together to stop lynching; and to get them to join the IWW. Caffey reminded the attorney general that it was legal for blacks to arm themselves to prevent lynching, as it was to organize for the purpose of striking. "I do not see upon reading the *Messenger* any direct evidence of a conspiracy to overcome by force the Government of the United States or to oppose by force the authority of the United States or to delay the execution of the law of the United States."

The only way to use the criminal code was to convince a jury that the magazine's statements didn't mean simply what they purported to mean, but in fact were designed to encourage blacks to join a revolutionary movement. "If this intent can be established by evidence outside of the publication itself," wrote Caffey, "a conspiracy in violation of Section 6 might be established." He doubted that the *Messenger* had pure motives. "There can be no excuse for its publication." Articles which constantly reminded blacks of lynching and social inequality "cannot but inflame their minds" and would create "an intense hostility toward the forces of law and order." Having refrained from recommending that blacks' distrust of law and order be mitigated by effective measures against lynching and social inequality, Caffey could only suggest that Bureau agents keep close watch on the magazine for evidence of conspiratorial intent.[36]

The Justice Department faced the reality, by late 1919, that its hands were tied legally in trying to suppress the *Messenger*. But Hoover could not admit defeat. He instructed Caffey to prepare a memorandum on the impotence of

*laws
blamed)*

current law. A similar statement requested from the New York district attorney should detail the shortcomings of that state's criminal anarchy statute. "Our purpose in desiring this information is to be able to point out to Congress the fact that the present existing laws, both federal and state are not sufficiently broad to reach the pernicious activities of the *Messenger.*" No reply from state authorities has been found, but Caffey reiterated that the Sedition Act and Section 6 of the Criminal Code were inapplicable. He still believed that the *Messenger's* anti-lynching rhetoric was merely "a cloak to shield it from prosecution and to enable them [the editors] to foster disorder and discontent among the negroes and to encourage them to organize and to arm." Caffey concluded that "if the existence of such ulterior motive on the part of the publishers can be established, there is no question in my mind but that the editors of the *Messenger* are engaged in a conspiracy to overthrow by force the government of the United States." But the Bureau of Investigation never found such definitive evidence, because there was none, and Congress never provided a broader legal basis for suppressing such publications.[37]

Assistant Attorney General Stewart, who oversaw all federal criminal prosecutions, replied to Rep. Byrnes in November 1919, quoting Caffey's opinions and concluding that the *Messenger* was engaged in lawful activity. Stewart reassured Byrnes that the intention to prosecute the magazine's editors had not been abandoned: "It is believed that further developments will enable the Department to present a proper case." Stewart had already urged the Post Office to ban the magazine from the mails. And Hoover's GID was not ready to admit defeat despite its failure to halt socialist, communist, and nationalist advocacy by the black press.[38]

Meanwhile, the Post Office Department maintained pressure on the *Messenger* in the fall of 1919, having already done considerable damage. Its second-class permit, allowing reduced mailing rates, had been revoked in mid-1918 and would not be permanently returned until 1921. The magazine had to depend upon subsidies and contributions from radical and liberal groups for both normal publishing costs and additional postage.[39] Solicitor Lamar instructed Bowen's Translation Bureau to keep him apprised of all "transgressions or mischief-breeding influences" in the black press. The Division of Classification also sent copies of the *Messenger* to Lamar to determine their mailability.[40]

The *Messenger's* militancy—support for Bolshevism abroad and the IWW at home, armed resistance to lynchers and rioters, and total equality between the races—peaked in the summer and fall of 1919. Its editors knew they were courting danger. Denial of the second-class mail rate was only partial punishment; the magazine might be banned from the mails entirely. Randolph and

Owen recognized that the strongest opposition came from the Translation Bureau. Attempting to circumvent Bowen and avoid lengthy delays as had occurred with the July issue, business manager Victor Daly sent an advance copy of the October number directly to Lamar, asking him to notify the New York post office of its mailability.

But within two days of Daly's stratagem Bowen saw a copy and wrote an alarmed personal letter to the solicitor, sputtering that he could hardly find proper words to describe the *Messenger*'s contents, especially its attack on Rep. Byrnes. Randolph and Owen had written that "as for social equality, there are about five million mulattoes in the United States. This is the product of semi-social equality. It shows that social equality galore exists after dark, and we warn you that we expect to have social equality in the day as well as after dark." Bowen's shock was unmistakable: "This is the first time I have seen a negro publication come out openly as advocating or demanding social equality." His outrage revealed fears that the racial status quo was in danger of being breached, plus the realization that the Justice Department had failed to muzzle the magazine.[41]

Bowen was so apoplectic that he forgot to condemn the October *Messenger*'s support for Bolshevism and the IWW, necessitating a second letter to the solicitor that same day in which he urged a final halt to the publication:

> The more I read this issue the more I wish that I might feel you would sanction me in holding it from the mails for your decisive action. I do not so hold it since I feel that sterner measures may be adopted against this outrageous publication, but if I have erred in this respect I wish that you would notify me. Nothing would give me more satisfaction than to hold up further issues that may be as bad as this one—and all of them are bad.[42]

In fact the Post Office Department was ready to take punitive action toward the *Messenger* by refusing to act on its July 6 application for a permanent second-class permit. An exasperated Daly wrote Washington that "we have been informed by the Postmaster, New York Post Office, that so far as he is concerned there is absolutely no reason why the *Messenger*, like any other publication, should not be granted the [permanent] privilege of second-class mailings." Yet the solicitor's office said only that a permit would be granted "as soon as practicable." Daly replied that either the Post Office was discriminating against the magazine or was hopelessly inefficient. Obviously believing the former, he threatened legal redress. The pettiness continued until June 1921, when President Harding's postmaster general acknowledged the excesses of the past and finally restored the permanent second-class permit.[43] But Wilson's postmaster general, Albert Sidney Burleson, remained unrepentant, praising Lamar for trying to suppress "those offensive negro papers which constantly appeal to class and race prejudice." In the end the Post Office and Justice departments, unable to legally suppress the *Messenger,* were reduced instead to harassment.[44]

The Military Intelligence Division likewise maintained a high level of interest in the *Messenger* during the second half of 1919, despite postwar reductions in personnel and narrowed responsibilities. While continuing to collect copies and receive detailed reports from its own officers in New York and Chicago, its principle sources of information were weekly GID summaries, Bureau agents' reports, and British intelligence analyses.

Shortly before returning to the Philippines to resume his pre-war position as director of its military band, Maj. Loving forwarded the July *Messenger* to MID's officer in charge of monitoring black radicalism in mid-1919, Capt. J. E. Cutler. A sociology professor and authority on southern mob violence, Cutler was somewhat more sympathetic to black aspirations than other white officers. Yet the *Messenger* alarmed him: "With the colored population in a state of general unrest and having definite grievances as a foundation for a smoldering resentment against the government, the viciousness of the propaganda in this issue cannot be overstated." Cutler's memorandum to Col. Alexander B. Coxe, MID's acting director, was unusually forthright, blaming the War Department's discriminatory policies for making ex-servicemen ripe for radical propaganda. He was on target in this regard, but lost aim in assessing the motives of Randolph and Owen. Admitting their sincerity, he nonetheless believed the editors were either Bolshevik pawns or hucksters lining their own pockets. This misinformation from one of its most "expert" analysts became incorporated into MID case files and memory.[45]

After Loving's departure MID briefly gained inside information on black militancy from John Lewis Waller, a civilian clerk in the army's New York City quartermaster office. A Spanish-American War veteran, Waller was "intimately acquainted with the situation in Harlem" and had provided Loving with most of his information from New York.[46] One of Waller's reports in early September focused on the enthusiasm of black socialists for street-corner evangelism. Randolph and Owen, as the leading spokesmen, commanded the busiest intersection on Lenox Avenue, while lesser brethren spoke along other Harlem thoroughfares. Every one championed the Soviet form of government. With the influence of the *Messenger,* claimed Waller, the socialist movement had gained a significant hold in Harlem.[47]

MID's most systematic intelligence focus on black militancy in 1919 centered in New York and Chicago. In the latter city, Maj. Thomas B. Crockett enthusiastically continued the wartime practice of using "confidential agents" to spy on civilians. The headquarters of the Industrial Workers of the World was in the Windy City so all intelligence agencies had a presence. There was much to be learned. The *Messenger* could be bought at a new radical bookstore in the Black Belt as well as at two downtown shops. Sales were also actively promoted by the magazine's district agent, William Harvey Tibbs, known to the police and MID as a particularly active black Wobbly. MID found that local "Reds" were especially pleased with the November *Messenger*, predicting it would cause blacks to "raise hell." Spurred by the attorney general's report on the spread of black radicalism, Crockett's agents purchased the *Messenger* at the Radical Book Shop, marked offensive articles, and sent it to Washington.[48]

The *Messenger*'s links to the IWW and its demands that President Wilson be impeached for his hostility toward Soviet Russia seemed particularly significant to MID in the fall of 1919. Its advocacy of "direct action," a general strike, and the formation of paramilitary companies commanded by former black officers, was also alarming. MID hoped that the magazine would be suppressed, announcing that "the District Attorney at New York is continuing the investigation of the most radical of the negro publications, which is viciously inciting the negroes against the whites; . . . the government will institute legal proceedings against the publication." Nothing came of these efforts. Most significant in this commentary, however, was the belief, held by the entire political intelligence community, that the *Messenger* was fostering hatred toward whites. The magazine's outspoken pursuit of justice could not be perceived for what it was; black militancy could be seen only through racially distorted lenses, as black against white.[49]

Army intelligence attention to the *Messenger* waned as the Red Scare faded in 1920. By the end of the year MID summaries only infrequently mentioned the "two notorious negro radicals" who edited the "negro radical paper," and the *Messenger* disappeared from the pages of its weekly surveys entirely by the fall of 1921.[50] But it would be a long time before the Bureau of Investigation lost interest in the *Messenger*, which had become the *bête noire* of the Justice Department by the summer of 1919. It was also a prime example used to seek expanded authority for suppressing radicalism and an asset to Attorney General A. Mitchell Palmer as he sought to ride the Red Scare into the White House.

According to Attorney General Palmer, "the negro is 'seeing red,'" and the *Messenger* was the worst offender, "by all odds the most able and the most dangerous of all the negro publications," an "exponent of open defiance and sedition" in its promotion of Bolshevism, and representing "the fullest flower of negro sedition and flagrant disloyalty." Its editors were men of education, the magazine itself well composed, printed on good paper, and well funded.

Admiration for Washington blacks who killed white rioters and publication of Claude McKay's militant poem "If We Must Die" made the September 1919 issue "more insolently offensive than any other." And Palmer could only gasp in shock at the following month's reply to Rep. Byrnes, which advocated sexual equality and intermarriage.[51]

In anointing the *Messenger* as the most dangerous black publication, the attorney general created an embarrassment for Hoover. Such a pernicious periodical certainly ought to be suppressed, and the GID could appear to be lax if it failed to build a sufficiently strong case. Failure to initiate prosecution in New York was a setback. So the Bureau forged ahead in 1920, gathering still more evidence. Randolph and Owen were well aware of this effort; the meaning of white stenographers at their meetings and rallies was clear. On several occasions the editors gleefully identified federal agents or local police in the audience. Once, after speaking caustically of the Department of Justice, Owen was followed to the rostrum by Richard B. Moore, who denounced federal agents as "skunks," prompting three of them to leave the room. At that point Wilfred A. Domingo rose to express sorrow at the agents' departure, claiming they were looking for him. Such indignities were occupational hazards for white agents and one of the reasons the Bureau began using black informants and agents in 1919.[52]

Because the *Messenger* was headquartered in New York, the fountainhead of much Red Scare radicalism, federal agents there could track its editors, contributors, and financial backers. By late 1919 the Bureau had also learned that blacks could infiltrate organizations which white agents could not penetrate. Three black undercover informants were especially active in investigating the *Messenger*. The first was thirty-five-year-old, Oklahoma-born William A. Bailey.[53]

Like other informants, Bailey had to walk a tightrope since militant groups were often suspicious of one another. Public association with the political radicals would preclude infiltration of Garvey's nationalist movement. Bailey first made the acquaintance of *Messenger* contributing editor Domingo and, while professing to be a socialist, declined to immediately commit himself to "the extreme radical field" so as not to appear too eager to gain acceptance. At the same time he met Cyril Briggs and agreed to promote circulation and solicit advertisements for the *Crusader.* Meanwhile Bailey also began to attend UNIA functions and made himself familiar at Garvey's headquarters. Briggs proved more eager to use Bailey's talents and consequently Bailey provided the Bureau with more information on the *Crusader* than other publications. News dealers, he learned, preferred the *Messenger* although both periodicals were popular among black West Indians. For a while the editors of the *Messenger* and *Crusader* along with Domingo, who was about to launch the short-lived *Emancipator,* planned to form a corporation to operate the magazines jointly. Bailey was given Bureau permission to promote all three and discover the hidden backers who allegedly bankrolled the radical movement, but he never found any damning evidence, and the Bureau terminated his employment after less than three months, at the end of March 1920.[54]

Bailey's replacement, reporter William E. Lucas, first ingratiated himself with Briggs and began, as had Bailey, to distribute the *Crusader.* Acquaintance with Domingo followed, and soon Lucas was also promoting the *Emancipator.* Domingo urged him to become "one of the wide awake Negroes" and join the local socialist club, where he met Owen. Lucas, who was a veteran of the 367th Infantry, simultaneously joined the UNIA, tried to infiltrate its paramilitary African Legion, and helped form a new UNIA branch in Brooklyn. And shortly before his Bureau service ended in June 1920 he was about to be inducted into Briggs's African Blood Brotherhood.

Lucas experienced a dilemma common to undercover operatives: How diligently should he promote radical causes? He assured his Bureau handlers that he did little to increase the *Messenger's* circulation: "To tell the truth I am really trying to prevent too extensive a circulation altho I have to make some kind of a distribution of the copies that are given [to me]." His own opinion of the political radicals was unfavorable: Owen and Domingo were said to be "doing all that is in their power to agitate radicalism and discontent[ment] among their people." Could Lucas infiltrate the *Messenger,* given his background as a reporter? Owen, according to a mutual acquaintance, was "very cautious," having "been fooled by so many of the people of his race that he had to be pretty well acquainted with a person or a person had to be very well endorsed by some intimate friend before he would accept him." Lucas was never able to develop a personal relationship with Owen despite faithful attendance at socialist meetings and distribution of the *Messenger.* The sketchy information he provided on the magazine was probably of little use to the Bureau.[55]

Herbert S. Boulin, a Jamaican-born Harlem businessman, was the most prolific of the early black informants. Although Boulin's major efforts were devoted to infiltrating the Garvey movement, he also investigated the *Messenger* and the black socialist movement, filing reports almost daily from July 1920 through August 1921.[56]

Boulin, like Lucas and Bailey, spent much of each day visiting radical hangouts, joining informal discussions, and attending public meetings. Before long he provided his Bureau handlers with a broad analysis of Harlem's radical factions. Especially pernicious was the *Messenger* circle which, Boulin alleged, preached class hatred, condemned capitalism, praised Bolshevism, and urged blacks to seize control of their destinies as had the Russian workers.[57]

Boulin quickly discovered that news and gossip about the socialist and communist factions could be obtained at their unofficial Harlem rendezvous, Martin Luther Campbell's tailoring shop. It was from that source that the Bureau first learned of Domingo's split with Randolph and Owen. Domingo was a native of Jamaica, and when the *Messenger's* attack on Garvey degenerated into ugly anti–West Indian prejudices, Domingo left the magazine in protest.[58]

The Bureau's undercover informant provided other inside information on the *Messenger,* including the firing of business manager Victor Daly for allegedly misappropriating $2,000. He responded by suing for back wages, winning a judgment of $400. Boulin's lengthy conversation with Owen revealed the paranoia to which radicals who lived beyond political or social respectability were susceptible. Owen charged that Daly had been paid by "capitalists" to discredit the *Messenger.* If the editors hadn't had the foresight to keep confidential documents away from the magazine's office Daly would have revealed their "secret plans" as well. Artfully navigating between the combatants, Boulin got Daly to reveal his role in persuading radical labor unions to withdraw subsidies for the *Messenger.* Somehow remaining on good terms with both sides, Boulin then learned that Owen and Randolph were seeking Daly's arrest for allegedly stealing checks. The black press reveled in these ugly details, prompting Randolph and Owen to file libel suits against the *New York News, Amsterdam News, Negro World,* and *Chicago Defender.*[59]

Boulin spent nearly every Sunday afternoon at the Peoples Educational Forum, which met at Lafayette Hall on West 131st Street, disdainfully calling it "the uptown Negro branch of the Bolshevik free lecture room" where open discussion followed presentations by white and black radicals. The Forum's leading lights included Randolph, Owen, Domingo, Moore, and the tailor Campbell, all of whom frequently differed politically and philosophically. Moore, in Boulin's analysis, was "the most rabid of the Negro radicals," a ceaseless advocate of communism who needled Randolph and Owen for being afraid to embrace openly the Bolshevik cause.[60]

In March 1920, Randolph and Owen founded the Friends of Negro Freedom, an all-black organization to promote civil rights with greater militancy than the NAACP and to organize black workers in radical interracial or independent black unions. Later the FNF devoted itself to opposing Garvey. Boulin gradually gained Owen's confidence, learning organizational details and Owen's conviction that the IWW was still the most viable union.

Naturally this belief guaranteed continued Bureau interest in Owen and the FNF. Although the IWW had been effectively crippled by prosecutions during the war it continued to serve as a convenient bogeyman for the Justice Department.[61]

Boulin had primary responsibility for monitoring Randolph, Owen, and the *Messenger* between July 1920 and August 1921, with white agents covering the magazine from a distance. The New York field office's weekly radical reports typically noted speeches by the magazine's staff and synopsized its most militant articles. Particularly noteworthy were the *Messenger's* criticisms of the army, praise for Russia, and assertion of blacks' right to self-defense. Bureau agents also continued to worry over the magazine's promotion of socialism. Several of the *Messenger* staff ran on the Socialist Party ticket in 1920, Randolph receiving 17 percent of the statewide vote for secretary of state. The editors' activities on behalf of the Friends of Negro Freedom and the National Association for the Promotion of Labor Unionism among Negroes were also analyzed, as well as the magazine's attacks on the NAACP, the National Urban League, and the UNIA. The bloody Tulsa race riot in June 1921 stimulated several predictions from the *Messenger* circle that similar outbreaks were likely in New York and a half dozen other cities. Once again the Bureau noted with dismay the magazine's approval of armed self-defense, with agents branding Owen "an ardent negro radical" and the *Messenger* and FNF "ultra-radical."[62]

While the Bureau's investigations of the *Messenger* circle centered in New York, agents in other cities also monitored its influence. The magazine circulated in every urban center in the northeast and midwest where blacks migrated in the 1910s and 1920s.[63] Chicago was exceeded only by New York as a hotbed of black radicalism. Agent Loula claimed that the black population there was growing at a rate of "40 [railroad] carloads" a day, having doubled in three years to total 125,000 in 1920. The circulation of militant black publications was viewed with apprehension by many whites. Chicago's weekly radical reports labeled the *Messenger* an organ of "socialist propaganda," while the Friends of Negro Freedom was considered "ultra radical." By early 1921 the magazine was still one of two "Negro propaganda publications" circulating in the Chicago district, but a half year later, with radical activities on the wane, Chicago agents ceased their focus on the *Messenger*.[64]

Although Washington was not a center of black radicalism like New York or Chicago, its NAACP chapter included outspoken militants like Archibald and Francis Grimke and schoolteacher Neval H. Thomas. When they invited Randolph and Owen to come fan the flames of racial protest, the Bureau of Investigation was vigilant, given the city's southern racial folkways and the presence of members of congress. The editors were booked to speak in early 1920 at Dunbar High School, the pride of black Washington, but the Department of Justice pressured the city government to prohibit use of the facilities, necessitating a move to a church. Thomas, who taught American history at Dunbar, invited Bureau agents in the audience to take front row seats while he condemned the government's attempts at repression. Thomas did not know that a black informant, Albert Farley, was also in the audience. Meanwhile, another agent combed the city for data on radical publications, finding the *Messenger* and *Crusader* being sold in large numbers. When Randolph and Owen returned three months later Thomas again presided while Farley noted the editors' condemnation of Attorney General Palmer for turning his office into a "Department of Injustice."[65]

The Philadelphia field office also tracked the *Messenger*'s editors in 1920 and 1921, focusing on their efforts to promote radical labor unionism and the Friends of Negro Freedom.[66] Buffalo agents found Owen and especially Randolph attracting sizeable audiences at socialist campaign rallies in the same years.[67] Owen's travels in 1920 took him as far west as St. Louis where 300 Socialist Party faithful and forty black guests heard him damn Postmaster General Burleson, blame capitalism for race riots, and advocate socialism as the only remedy.[68] That same month Randolph's appeal for solidarity between Jewish and black radicals at the annual convention of the *Arbeiter Ring* (Workmen's Circle) in Newark was recorded by a Bureau undercover informant and a Yiddish translator. Delegates responded by voting a $250 subsidy for the *Messenger* as part of its $10,000 benevolence.[69]

In other cities, which Randolph and Owen did not visit, the Bureau nonetheless charted their magazine's distribution. Cleveland agents found that a cigar store, drugstore, and newsstand sold large quantities of the *Messenger* and *Emancipator* in 1920; a year later monthly sales of the former fluctuated between 200 and 1,000 copies.[70] A Boston agent infiltrated the local Communist Party in 1920 and discovered May Day plans for agitation among blacks by distributing large quantities of the *Messenger, Emancipator* and, naively, Garvey's *Negro World*. And in Kansas City, in response to an order from headquarters that all offices investigate the finances and circulation of radical publications, agents found evidence of the *Messenger* but larger sales of Chicago's black newspapers.[71]

White southerners' fear of the *Messenger* dissipated by the end of 1920. Its influence there had always been exaggerated by alarmist newspaper reports, obscuring the fact that its largest circulation was in northern and midwestern cities. As the Red Scare waned so too did southern apprehensions that blacks would be manipulated by socialists or communists into revolt or demands for total equality. The *Messenger* fed white southerners' greatest fear—equal rights and social equality for blacks—in 1919 with its jeering rejoinder to Rep. Byrnes and assertion of the right to sexual equality. But the magazine did not emphasize those themes in 1920, reducing the perceived threat. Thus, only scattered investigations were conducted by the Bureau in the South. Such an effort in Norfolk was understandable, however, since many of its 43,000 black residents (37 percent of the population) were shipyard and navy yard workers. Randolph and Owen placed greater hopes for radical labor unionism there than anywhere else in the South. Special Agent in Charge Ralph H. Daughton reported that the *Messenger* could be purchased at several news-stands and warned that "the dissemination of this printed matter among the colored population in the state would not be at all helpful." He suggested that if the New York field office could uncover the names of subscribers in Virginia, they could be kept under surveillance and any "radical tendencies" stimulated by the magazine could be charted.[72] Fortunately, no such draconian measures occurred.

By the fall of 1921, only New York agents still actively monitored the *Messenger,* continuing to characterize Randolph and Owen as "well known radical agitators with Bolshevik tendencies."[73] There was nothing to spark serious investigation, however, until mid-1922 when the editors breathed new life into the Friends of Negro Freedom. Owen traveled coast-to-coast organizing fourteen new councils and strengthening others. Blacks in Los Angeles greeted his visit with great enthusiasm, reported a Bureau agent, who compiled a list of FNF supporters which included some of Southern California's most outspoken black activists like Attorney E. Burton Ceruti and newspaperwoman Charlotta A. Bass.[74]

When the Friends of Negro Freedom shifted focus to attack Garvey in mid-1922, a heated war of words took place in print and at anti-Garvey rallies, with police often forced to maintain order. On September 5 Randolph received a package in the mail containing a severed human hand with a note, allegedly signed by the KKK. Randolph believed it came from Garveyites, and federal agents were present when he capitalized on this sensational event to step up the attack on his West Indian adversary.[75]

What happened next must have surprised Randolph nearly as much as the gruesome parcel. He and Owen were interviewed by a *black* agent, forty-two-year-old James E. Amos, the second African American agent hired by the Bureau of Investigation but the first to operate publicly. He would serve the Bureau with the high regard of J. Edgar Hoover until 1953. Three years of high school placed Amos among the minority of educated blacks of his day, the erratic spelling on his Bureau application notwithstanding. This had not hindered previous service with the Interior Department, Customs Office, and twelve years as President Theodore Roosevelt's personal attendant, confidential messenger, and bodyguard. Amos's employment as an investigator for the Burns International Detective Agency for seven years was also fortuitous; his old boss, William J. Burns, became director of the Bureau in August 1921, the year Amos was hired. The references Amos listed on his employment application comprise a who's who of American politics: Theodore Roosevelt, Jr.; former Secretary of State Elihu Root; Senator Hiram Johnson; General Leonard Wood; and former Interior Secretary Gifford Pinchot. Few, if any, white applicants could claim such endorsements.[76]

Evincing no bitterness over the prolonged scrutiny they had endured— probably unaware of the full scope of the government's attempts to suppress the *Messenger*—Randolph and Owen agreed to provide Amos with any information that might damage Garvey.[77] The most striking cooperation between the two editors and the Department of Justice was a six-page letter written by Owen in January 1923, co-signed by eight prominent blacks, urging Attorney General Harry M. Daugherty to prosecute Garvey as quickly as possible. Calling Garvey a "menace to harmonious race relationships," Owen charged that the UNIA harbored criminals, some of whom had assassinated a prominent defector, Rev. J. W. H. Eason. Cataloguing many instances of UNIA intimidation, denial of free speech, and attacks on opponents (including Owen), the letter also alleged fraudulent solicitation of money and inept bookkeeping by the Black Star Line. Noting Garvey's collusion with the KKK, the letter urged the Justice Department to disband the "vicious" UNIA and speedily bring Garvey to trial for mail fraud. Before sending the letter to Daugherty and the press, Owen gave a copy to agent Amos. Garvey counterattacked, damning the eight signatories (and Randolph) as traitors to the race.[78] Owen genuinely believed Garvey threatened good racial relations and was leading blacks down a blind alley in pursuit of a misguided African dream, but his cooperation with the Department of Justice was an ironic twist to the racial politics of the early 1920s.

By the time of Owen's letter, even the Bureau's New York field office hardly regarded the *Messenger* as a threat and left monitoring of radical publications largely to postal officials. This prompted a rebuke from Hoover, now assistant director of the Bureau. Why were New York agents so irregular in sending offensive copies to headquarters, he demanded. Special Agent in Charge Edward J. Brennan reminded Hoover that headquarters had never appropriated funds to buy such periodicals and many times, when agents made such purchases, they were not reimbursed. Anyway, most of what they collected was sent to Bowen in the New York post office who was still monitoring the "radical press" under authority of the wartime Espionage Act, more than four years after the Armistice! In any case, concluded Brennan, the *Messenger* was now only occasionally radical.[79]

Six months later, in response to a new directive from Hoover, the New York office filed another report on radical publications. Circulation figures for the *Messenger* were wildly exaggerated. Lacking infiltrators like Bailey, Lucas, or Boulin, the Bureau failed to perceive that the magazine was foundering and had abandoned much of its radicalism by late 1923. Although still a strong voice for racial advocacy, its enthusiasm for Bolshevism had waned. Finally, when the New York office informed headquarters that Owen had renounced socialism and left the city, the Bureau's long crusade against the *Messenger* came to an end.[80]

SIX

❦

"AN UNDESIRABLE, AND INDEED A VERY DANGEROUS, ALIEN"

The Federal Campaign against Marcus Garvey

No black militant drew more investigation and surveillance by the Military Intelligence Division, State Department, and Bureau of Investigation in the Red Scare years than Marcus Garvey, the charismatic founder of the Universal Negro Improvement Association (UNIA). Garvey worried guardians of the racial status quo both in and outside of government for many reasons, but primarily because his flamboyant nationalism and assertions of racial pride drew hundreds of thousands of followers to his movement. While anxious whites watched in dismay, he assured his followers of a destiny in which Africans would again rule Africa and blacks worldwide would exercise power in a new racial equation. A cataclysmic war between the races might be necessary, he said, to bring justice for darker peoples. Even though Garvey did not emphasize protest against racial conditions in America or his native West Indies, his rhetoric seemed no less alarming. Racial power, dignity, and self-respect were ceaselessly proclaimed from the pages of his widely read weekly newspaper, the *Negro World,* and suffused every UNIA program and event. Whites took as much exception to a movement which rejected blacks' absorption into American society as they did to socialist and communist radicals like A. Philip Randolph and Cyril Briggs who demanded inclusion into the American dream with total racial equality, since all repudiated the niche to which black Americans had been consigned for 300 years.

Although Garvey had been in and out of New York City since 1916, a Bureau of Investigation case file was not opened on him until September 1918. In the following weeks, as agents worried that rumors of German atrocities inflicted on African American soldiers in France would erode blacks' patriotism on the home front, they began to watch Harlem's stepladder orators on the street corners of Lenox and 7th avenues between 125th and 138th streets. Garvey was just one of these speakers, but he stood out because of his organizational base and the publicity generated by the *Negro World,* which began publication August 3. Bureau interest in Garvey soon increased when a community coalition including the UNIA named delegates to attend the Versailles peace talks. Although Garvey was not selected, his prediction that the next war would pit white nations against a black-Japanese alliance alarmed federal agents, as did his advocacy of lynching a white person in the North every time a southern black suffered such an abomination.[1]

Garvey excelled in apocalyptic visions, and federal documents repeatedly accused him of preaching "race hatred." Bureau agents in over two dozen cities would report on Garvey's activities between 1918 and 1923, rarely distinguishing between his "race first" chauvinism and genuine racist antipathy. Words were as alarming as actions. Although belligerence sometimes flavored Garvey's language, it does not reveal a deeply grounded hatred of whites but instead a fervent desire to elevate his own race above the wrongs and crimes committed against it by Caucasians. But few whites were capable of making such precise distinctions in an era when a whole new tone of militant black rhetoric was being polished. Even the Communist Party was uncomfortable with the UNIA's racial nationalism and the fact that Garvey was organizing the black masses outside the safe direction of white radicals.

The State Department first took notice of Garvey early in 1919 when officials in British Honduras and Demerara (British Guiana) protested that the *Negro World* was backed by German or communist agents, was antagonistic to whites, and was a source of racial hatred. Colonial authorities suggested that the newspaper might have violated American postal regulations. The State Department contacted the Post Office Department, but it was not yet energized to pursue the *Negro World.*[2]

While the Bureau of Investigation continued to note Garvey's activities through the first half of 1919, it was preoccupied with apprehending alien anarchists and "red" revolutionists. In July, however, it began to take the charismatic Pan-Africanist more seriously when the Post Office's Translation Bureau charged that "the radical movement in the negro press has become remarkably accelerated during the past six months" by spreading racial antagonism and urging direct action to redress grievances. In "Radicalism and

Sedition among the Negroes as Reflected in Their Publications," Translation Bureau head Roger A. Bowen alleged that the *Negro World* intended to counter more conservative black periodicals like the *Crisis* and the *New York News* and *Amsterdam News*.[3]

While copies of his memorandum were being read in the other intelligence bureaucracies, Bowen opened fire on the UNIA, urging postal solicitor William H. Lamar to inform the Justice Department that Garvey's steamship company, the Black Star Line, was a "racket." (Thousands of blacks were purchasing stock, at $5 a share, both to invest in their own economic future and in the race's destiny.) Bowen examined every issue of the *Negro World* for objectionable content that might justify suspension of its second-class mailing permit. Particularly offensive was the July 26 editorial entitled "Race First" which concluded as follows:

> It is true that all races look forward to the time when spears shall be beaten into agricultural implements, but until that time arrives it devolves upon all oppressed peoples to avail themselves of every weapon that may be effective in defeating the fell motives of their oppressors.
>
> In a world of wolves one should go armed, and one of the most powerful defensive weapons within the reach of Negroes is the practice of RACE FIRST in all parts of the world.

According to the Translation Bureau the *Negro World*'s sin was its tendency "to instil into the minds of negroes of this and other countries that they have been greatly wronged and oppressed by the white races and that they can only hope for relief and redress through concerted and aggressive action on their part."[4]

Bowen's efforts soon bore fruit in the Justice Department. Within days of the formation of the General Intelligence Division to coordinate the anti-radical work of the Bureau of Investigation, J. Edgar Hoover outlined the "principal phases of the Negro movement" which the GID would monitor, including the UNIA, Garvey, and the *Negro World*. The citizenship of its staff, sources of funding, and any connections to communism were to be thoroughly probed.[5] Such suspicions reflected the Bureau's conviction that black militancy would never have assumed its present proportions without subversives inciting an otherwise satisfied race. Thus began a course of action which would not be abandoned until Garvey was convicted, imprisoned, and deported.

In order to penetrate the Garvey movement the Bureau needed a black informant, and it reactivated Dr. Arthur Ulysses Craig, who had covered black activities in Washington, D.C., in late 1918.[6] Craig began in August 1919.

Attending two UNIA mass meetings, his middle-class sensibilities were shaken by the fervor of the working-class (and heavily West Indian) crowds which wildly applauded every call for racial change. As a member of the race's educated, upwardly mobile, and assimilationist Talented Tenth, Craig concluded that "the spirit of these meetings is decidedly unAmerican" and was calculated to foster hatred toward whites. Garvey's disclaimer of ties to socialism, communism, or the IWW did not allay Craig's suspicions.[7]

Gaining access to UNIA leadership proved easy for Craig, given his educational and professional background. Volunteer workers were welcome at UNIA headquarters and Garvey was accessible to those seeking an audience. By his fifth day in New York Craig was already a "technical advisor" to the Black Star Line's Capt. Joshua Cockburn, helping him inspect the leaky boilers on an old tramp steamer, the *Yarmouth,* that Garvey envisioned as the first of a fleet linking the black populations of the United States, Caribbean, and Africa. Craig also assisted in mailing the *Negro World.*[8]

Shortly after Craig arrived on assignment, Hoover and Bureau chief Frank Burke decided that the best way to neutralize the growing nationalist movement was to deport Garvey. New York agents were to prepare the case[9] while Craig was to find additional evidence. But after a month he was still mailing newspapers and inspecting boilers. A frustrated Burke repeatedly stressed the need for concrete evidence. Had he been able to substantiate Garvey's suggestion that a white man be lynched every time a black person was the victim of mob violence, or rumors that Garvey's African Legion was a paramilitary organization? Burke emphasized the necessity for a more focused investigation:

> As Marcus Garvey is an alien, it is particularly desirous of establishing sufficient evidence against him to warrant the institution of deportation proceedings. Any advocation by him of opposition to law and order would be ground upon which to have a request for deportation. Therefore, kindly have the informant give particular attention to this phase of the question.[10]

In order to shape up the investigation Burke sent George F. Ruch, Hoover's assistant, to New York.[11] But despite Ruch's efforts to improve efficiency, New York agents continued to have Craig compile background intelligence on the multitude of suspicious black individuals and groups in Harlem. Finally, the New York office, perhaps protecting the reputation of its white agents, concluded that there was no longer a compelling need for Craig's services: "The negro situation has greatly quieted down during the past two or three weeks and it would appear that the contemplated race riots will not take place." When Ruch and Hoover concurred, Craig's services were terminated at the end of September 1919, thus ending his Bureau career.[12]

Craig's discharge was linked to the difficulty in mounting prosecutions against black radicals. The Justice Department was as yet unprepared to make a case for deporting Garvey because it was still operating on a wartime mentality, hoping to halt radical activity by using the Sedition Act. But, as federal attorneys were soon to acknowledge, wartime restrictions on speech and advocacy were nearly useless after the Armistice. A conviction could not be gained solely on the basis of Garvey's flamboyant rhetoric. So the Bureau began to seek evidence of more common criminal conduct.

On the other hand, Craig's short career demonstrated that diligent black informants could often provide better intelligence than white agents on African American cases. An obviously middle-class black had easily infiltrated the UNIA because Garvey, for all his appeal to the black masses and distrust of the Talented Tenth, recognized that educated American-born leadership would give the organization more credibility; this explains his attempts to woo the NAACP's William Pickens and former special assistant to the Secretary of War, Emmett Scott. Craig's performance was, all things considered, encouraging to the Bureau. By the end of 1919 several other black informants were working in New York and James Wormley Jones was appointed as the FBI's first black agent, although he, too, operated undercover and used a coded identity. Four more black agents were appointed in the early 1920s.

The Justice Department's effort to deport Garvey was formally begun on September 15, 1919, when Hoover inquired if the Bureau of Immigration was proceeding against Garvey. Assistant Commissioner General Anthony J. Caminetti replied that his office had no firsthand information on him. This was hardly comforting, given the Bureau's alarm at Garvey's advocacy of retaliatory lynching and the formation of a "well drilled military organization."[13]

Why, given the legion of anarchists and communists seemingly at work in every crossroads of America, did mere rhetorical excesses trigger such responses? Hoover's strategy was to pursue those who could most easily be extirpated: alien radicals and agitators. And, after all, *something* had to be done about the growing ferment in black America. With riots erupting in Washington, Chicago, Harlem, Norfolk, Bisbee, Omaha, and Longview in the summer of 1919, bringing to maturity the militant New Crowd Negro, worried officials decided that whatever could be halted, must be halted. The easiest target seemed the heavily West Indian Universal Negro Improvement Association and its Jamaican leader.

Meanwhile, the Post Office Department also continued to monitor the *Negro World* in the second half of 1919. The ever-alarmed Bowen regularly fed

Solicitor Lamar quotations illustrating the "general mischievous effort of this paper to foster race and class feelings among the negroes." And when Lamar would not approve a postal ban Bowen sent his complaints to the Department of Justice and the Bureau's field office in New York.[14]

The State Department renewed its interest in Marcus Garvey in the fall of 1919, independently of the Post Office and the Bureau. One stimulus was a letter from the United Fruit Company charging the *Negro World* with inciting racial antagonism and fostering black consciousness among its plantation workers in Costa Rica. Simultaneously, the American consulate reported the seizure of the *Negro World* by Costa Rican officials, who charged it with promoting Bolshevism, revolution, and race riots.[15]

At the same time, British authorities in Trinidad were taking their own drastic measures. Learning that thousands of copies of the *Negro World* were being sent to the island and fearing race riots, local postal officials burned as many as they could find, although American consul Henry Baker reported that a large number still reached subscribers. Baker agreed that the weekly promoted "anarchy" and suggested an American mail ban. The State Department forwarded these alarms from Trinidad and Costa Rica to the Post Office, which lamely promised to give attention to the matter.[16] But it could do nothing more than offer agreement that Garvey's paper exerted a pernicious influence.

Fears of violence were confirmed at the end of the year when strikes led to riots in Trinidad and Tobago. Consul Baker believed the *Negro World* was partly responsible for "the rapid growth of class and race feeling, and of anarchistic and Bolshevist ideas among the ignorant population" and again urged that it be banned. His suggestion was forwarded to the Post Office Department. Reporting later on Trinidadian legislation, he noted that both the *Negro World* and the *Crusader* were to be suppressed for "having no other object than to excite racial hatred."[17]

At the same time, the Panama Canal Company, fearing that Garvey would muddy the already troubled racial waters of the Canal Zone, urged the Bureau of Investigation to take more vigorous action. Black laborers, paid lower wages than white workers and excluded from the more lucrative positions, were in ferment. Learning that Garvey planned to visit the Zone, the company requested evidence with which to justify preventing him from landing. The Bureau wanted to cooperate, but had no concrete grounds on which to justify such action.[18]

The British were by now communicating their fears of Garveyism directly to Washington, worried lest the movement, which had initially failed to take root in Jamaica, would reestablish itself in the Caribbean. Their military mission, which investigated militant activities in the United States during World War I, continued to monitor American internal affairs and sent copies of its reports to the Military Intelligence Division. Their most comprehensive analysis was the summary of "Unrest among the Negroes" compiled by Maj. Walter H. Loving of American military intelligence. These reports were not intended simply to inform British policy makers, but to pressure Washington into quarantining the virus of racial discontent. The State Department, eager to cooperate with the British, supplied additional copies to the Justice and Post Office departments.[19]

J. Edgar Hoover needed no foreign encouragement to pursue Garvey in the fall of 1919. Bureau offices were instructed to enlist the help of other federal agencies in covering his every movement. Hoover acknowledged that Garvey was an "exceptionally fine orator" and was clearly disappointed that he had failed to commit criminal acts: "Unfortunately, however, he has not as yet violated any federal law whereby he could be proceeded against on the grounds of being an undesirable alien, from the point of view of deportation." A fruitful tack, Hoover suggested, was to seek evidence of mail fraud in the sale of Black Star Line stock, but for the moment he was still blinded by anti-communism, erroneously concluding that "the Soviet Russian Rule is upheld and there is open advocation [sic] of Bolshevism" in the *Negro World*.[20] He could not have been further from the truth. While Garvey applauded global turmoil as presaging the day when Africa would be liberated, communism was no more trustworthy than any other white-led movement or philosophy. A white communist was a white man first, and as such deserved no confidence.

By early 1920 the Bureau was watching Garvey's influence in the United States and the Caribbean closely, regarding the UNIA and the *Messenger* as the two most dangerous manifestations of black radicalism. According to Chief Burke, Garvey was "the cause of the greater portion of the negro agitation in this country."[21] But if evidence of criminal violation was to be found, the UNIA must again be infiltrated. The Bureau had just the man in early 1920: James Wormley Jones.

Born the son of the lighthouse keeper at Fort Monroe, Virginia, "Jack" Jones attended public schools in Massachusetts and studied one year shy of a degree at prestigious black Virginia Union University. At age twenty-one he joined the Washington, D.C., police department, rising from patrolman and horseman to motorcycle policeman and then detective. His education and experience qualified him for a captain's bars in the 368th Infantry regiment of the 92nd Division during World War I. His first battlefield test was in the Argonne offensive on the French front. Chaotic command coordination; poor planning and provisioning; and the fatigue, hunger, and inexperience of the men led to a retreat, soon labeled a failure, which would haunt black troops for a generation to come. Jones escaped the fate of other black officers who were dismissed, and he continued to command Company F through the last offensive on the Metz front. He left France, as did many black soldiers, aware that his sacrifices on the battlefield were unacknowledged and his fighting mettle questioned.[22]

Soon after resuming employment with the Washington police, he applied to the Department of Justice. Following a background check he was appointed an agent in the Bureau of Investigation in December 1919, beginning a three-and-a-half-year career. The Bureau had chosen its first black agent well. "Failure" was the undeserved reputation of many black officers of the 368th Infantry; it was not to be Jones's at the Department of Justice.

Jones was first posted in Norfolk and instructed to sign reports with the code number "800," as he would be working undercover. During World War I the lower Chesapeake Bay was beset by suspicions of disloyalty, subversion, and draft evasion among blacks. Wartime worries evolved into fears of radicalism after the Armistice, particularly among the thousands of blacks who had swelled the labor force of Newport News shipyards and Norfolk's navy facilities. For months officials of the huge Newport News Shipbuilding and Drydock Company had reported unrest among their laborers, which largely reflected their desires for better wages and benefits from the notoriously anti-union company. But because many labor organizers in the late 1910s were political radicals, and federal agents tended to be biased toward capital and industry, the Bureau was receptive to intelligence supplied by the company. So when it reported UNIA success in recruiting black workers, the Bureau ordered an investigation. Even without the worries of the city's largest employer the Bureau would likely have taken interest, for twice in 1919 Garvey spoke to enthusiastic crowds in Newport News. By late in the year the UNIA had a large chapter in Norfolk and claimed that members had pledged $100,000 to buy ships for the Black Star Line.[23]

Infiltration of the Newport News UNIA by agent Jones proved an easy task. Membership was open to "all persons of Negro blood and African descent" who paid dues of 25 cents monthly.[24] Whether because he was a literate member of the Talented Tenth or on account of his military experience, Jones was soon assigned to help whip the local African Legion into shape. It performed in parades and mass meetings where splendid uniforms and precision drilling attracted potential recruits. Members also guarded the movement's leaders and were promised a role in the liberation of Africa from colonialism. Garvey authorized local chapters to raise companies of sixty-four men and elect noncommissioned officers, although he seems to have reserved the right to name those of higher rank himself. Jones and two others were appointed to revise the U.S. Army drill manual to include a declaration of allegiance to Garvey rather than to the president. Leadership followed: soon Jones was addressing meetings and chaired a committee to audit the books, finding the finances in bad shape, with over $1,500 unaccounted for.[25]

In only two weeks' time Jones not only infiltrated the heart of the UNIA in Tidewater Virginia but also assured the Bureau of his ideological dependability. Summarizing his observations of the local chapter, Jones reported that

> while no definite statements of members showing purely Radical anticipated activities have as yet been noted, Agent has heard sufficient to be certain that the activities of this organization, if allowed to continue, will produce considerable racial antagonism and friction and will very probably lead to trouble. The racial question is always paramount at the meetings of this organization.[26]

Fear that Garveyism would poison racial relations and erode black progress was common among upwardly mobile and assimilationist African Americans. If black agents like Jones did not share exactly the same reverence for the status quo as did most whites they nonetheless believed that further gains depended on interracial cooperation, not confrontation.

Jones quickly proved his capabilities, but Newport News was only a backwater; Harlem was the real center of black militancy, and the Bureau desperately needed a black infiltrator there. He reported for this new assignment a few days after undercover informant William A. Bailey was shifted from Nashville to determine if the UNIA was "drilling with firearms." Bailey served less than two months in New York; thereafter Jones was left with the responsibility for gathering inside intelligence on the Garvey movement. If Hoover's goal of deporting Garvey were to be achieved, credible internal evidence was necessary.

Jones's reputation from Newport News quickly opened doors in New York. Two days after his arrival he addressed a standing-room-only crowd at Liberty Hall, the UNIA's auditorium.[27] Whether he spoke from honest convictions or simply to ingratiate himself with the UNIA leadership is open to conjecture. According to the *Negro World*, "Mr. Jones, who is very light-complexioned, was mistaken by the audience for a white man," necessitating assurances that he was in fact an African American. "'I have no more privileges than the blackest man in the eyes of the white man. He considers me a Negro just as any Negro,'" averred Jones. To the cheers of the audience he condemned the race's own color and class distinctions as its greatest weakness. Continuing, Jones lauded the Black Star Line and Negro Factories Corporation, while acclaiming Garvey a modern Moses. But gains would not come without struggle: the price of racial advancement worldwide was ultimately the shedding of blood. Now was the time for action, "'while the getting was good'"; other groups had already gained from the world war.[28]

Soon thereafter Garvey asked Jones to review the finances of the UNIA's Harlem restaurant. The next Sunday Jones again spoke at Liberty Hall, professing a willingness to lay down his life for Africa. (This speech was reported by informant Bailey, who was unaware Jones was an agent.)[29] How comfortable was the Bureau leadership with Jones's rhetoric? Garvey often spoke of the necessity of bloodshed if the race was to be liberated, and such statements caused shudders in whites with fresh memories of race riots. Jones may have expressed his own sincere hopes; other members of the Talented Tenth, such as W. E. B. DuBois, believed that the postwar months held promise of fundamental change if blacks determined to fight for it. In any case Chief Burke was pleased with his new agent, writing that "he has performed in excellent manner in a very confidential mission. He is very important to us at this time."[30]

Agent Jones's precise activities between March and July 1920 are sketchy as no reports from his hand during this period have been found. Certainly he sought to gain Garvey's confidence, since his primary task was to uncover violations of federal law. Jones was seemingly the first Bureau employee to suggest that Garvey be investigated for violation of the 1910 Mann Act, prohibiting interstate transportation of women for immoral purposes. Suspicions centered on Garvey's extramarital affair with his secretary, Amy Jacques. Hoover was eager to take any path to prosecution, but Jones knew little more than the already widespread gossip concerning Garvey's misbehavior.[31]

By the summer of 1920 Jones was registering incoming mail at UNIA headquarters, informing the Bureau of significant correspondence and the revenue from sale of Black Star Line stock. He also supplied Washington with a list of *Negro World* agents and subscribers.[32] But what the Bureau needed was hard evidence that could support prosecution. Writing in mid-July 1920, as the month-long UNIA international convention approached, Jones was optimistic:

> If I can only hold this job of registering the letters I expect sometime to get some real good information. The hardest thing I have to do now is keeping my name off some kind of a committee. . . . I am trying to keep as much out of the limelight as possible, because I know there are going to be people here from Washington for this convention.[33]

As hundreds of delegates from out of town assembled for the massive gathering, Jones's worst fear was realized. While he was working in Garvey's office, in walked an old acquaintance, Dr. Roscoe Brown of the U.S. Public

Health Service. Relating the incident to George F. Ruch, Hoover's deputy, Jones reported that

> I have known this man for several years and he knows who and what I am, and when he went out of the office he said to a Mr. Thompson, the head book-keeper, "What is [he] doing here? He was a government detective at one time." Now, Mr. Ruch, this man works for the Government and he must have known that I was here on business. I met this same man in Richmond several months ago and told him to keep his mouth shut as to who I was. After he had gone, Thompson came into my office and remained there for several minutes just looking me over. Just what the result will be I do not know as Garvey is in Philadelphia but will return in the morning.[34]

When Jones's background as a policeman was "uncovered," he left New York and returned to Washington. But Garvey never discovered he was an agent for the Bureau of Investigation, and nine months later Jones was again working for the UNIA, this time as circulation manager of the *Negro World*.[35]

With Jones suddenly unable to continue infiltration of the UNIA, the Bureau relied on Herbert S. Boulin, "special confidential informant" P-138, from July 1920 through August 1921. He got as close to Garvey as had Jones, although he did not hold official UNIA positions. Boulin's Bureau service is distinctive for his meticulous attention to detail. No other informant wrote daily reports. (Boulin even filed reports saying that there was nothing worth reporting.) More significantly, Boulin's accounts provide a more intimate picture of the mind and politics of an undercover operative than any of the other black informants or agents. He frequently editorialized on the motives and objectives of his main targets—Garvey, the black socialists, and communists—and commented as well on the alleged gullibility of the Harlem populace in giving serious attention to agitators. A businessman and longtime activist in New York's West Indian community, Boulin disliked left-wing radicalism and racial nationalism. Like Arthur U. Craig, he regarded himself as a patriot and did not hesitate to express alarm to his superiors when he perceived danger brewing.

The Bureau's most urgent need was inside coverage of the upcoming UNIA international convention, and Boulin went undercover on July 30. Like previous informants he soon noted the UNIA's paramilitary aspects, particularly Garvey's armed bodyguard composed of "a number of rough fellows" who were prepared "to either kill or beat up all who are not in sympathy with Garvey." Boulin also began to cultivate his own informants, one of whom alerted him to the presence of Japanese at UNIA meetings,[36] a detail of particular interest to the Justice Department, army, and navy, which were already concerned about links between Garvey and a nation believed to be aggressive, dissatisfied, and anti-American.

Garvey's month-long 1920 convention opened in August with two days of parades. Nightly rallies at Liberty Hall featured speeches which Boulin found bordering on sedition. He was certain that Garvey's bodyguards were armed, and "with the Red speeches and the anti-White talks that they are listening to daily, I would not be at all surprised if some day these teachings would be put to practice." As for the seriousness of the Garvey threat, Boulin had no doubt: "So far as one can judge from the daily talks, etc., Liberty Hall is to-day the greatest hot-bed for the teaching of racial antagonism, racial hatred, and class hatred, and Garvey is the head of the stream." According to Boulin, practically every speaker exhorted the crowds to arm themselves and kill before being killed.[37] The informant's views coincided with those who would soon wage an unremitting "Garvey Must Go" campaign: Not only did Garvey poison relations between the races and foment ill feeling between native and foreign-born blacks, they would allege, his teachings jeopardized the Talented Tenth's opportunity for upward mobility and acceptance in the white world.[38]

On a more objective basis, Boulin detailed the controversies which punctuated the convention. Garvey brooked little dissent, instructed delegates how to vote, and used parliamentary privilege to silence dissenters. When Garvey engineered his election as "Provisional President" of Africa, with an annual salary of $12,000 plus expenses, Boulin met with five disgruntled Africans seeking to block Garvey's influence and discovered they were being encouraged by the British consul general.[39] Despite his obvious dislike for the man and the proceedings, however, Boulin lost no opportunity to flatter Garvey. Meeting the UNIA leader on the street, the informant "warmly congratulated him and praised his work, telling him how wonderful a man he is etc. This gives me an opening to speak further with him."[40]

Thus ended Boulin's first month working undercover. If the Bureau wanted detailed reports on Garvey's activities and one man's assessment of his potential for arousing racial militancy, its investment in Boulin was well spent. P-138 had quickly ingratiated himself with Garvey. But whether that relationship would help bring Garvey to prosecution was not yet demonstrated.

For one who did not actually enter the employ of the UNIA, Boulin was remarkably successful in gaining Garvey's confidence. He had no access to UNIA files, as did Jones. And he did not try to provoke enmity and suspicion between competing movements, as Jones would later do. Rather, Boulin focused on gathering evidence so that the Bureau could assess the radical and nationalist movements in Harlem and respond appropriately. As a monitor of events Boulin served capably, although with definite biases, his interpretations sometimes obscuring rather than clarifying the black radicals' grievances and critiques of American society.[41]

Boulin submitted frequent reports on the UNIA and its leader throughout his entire thirteen-month undercover career. Excluding the six months in 1921 when Garvey was traveling in the Caribbean, he had fifteen conversations with Garvey, full details of which were reported to the Bureau. Boulin was useful to Garvey because of his broad contacts in Harlem and was probably also trusted because he was a fellow Jamaican. And since he was not a UNIA leader Boulin was someone with whom Garvey could vent his own frustrations and disappointments.

Garvey quickly perceived benefit in the relationship. On September 6, he sought Boulin's assistance in resolving a troubling lawsuit before it reached the courts. A year before, Garvey had been indicted for criminally libeling Edgar M. Grey and Richard E. Warner, former Black Star Line directors. An apology in court and published retraction a year later did not satisfy them, and they filed $10,000 civil suits. Garvey hoped that Boulin could halt the proceedings since Grey, while serving as advertising manager of the *Negro World,* had solicited advertising and accepted payment from Boulin under false pretenses. If Boulin threatened to testify to Grey's dishonesty, Garvey believed, Grey would withdraw his suit. But unbeknownst to Garvey, Grey was one of Boulin's chief sources of inside information on the UNIA. Not willing to jeopardize his own "mole," Boulin advised Garvey to seek a compromise settlement.[42] Boulin successfully negotiated this tightrope and continued to receive valuable data from Grey while building a relationship of greater confidence with Garvey.

Boulin gave the Bureau valuable insight on the symbolic importance of Garvey's programs. Soon after the 1920 convention it became apparent that the promised fleet of ships designed to knit the African diaspora in commerce and travel was sailing in troubled waters. Persistent rumors had the Black Star Line sinking literally and financially; without funds to make the overpriced vessels seaworthy or keep up payments, they might be lost. Boulin correctly reported that "the commercial value of these ships is by far a secondary consideration against their moral and racial value." The vessels were visible proof of Garvey's Pan-African ideology. "Hence, if they are lost, Garvey's prestige and power for spreading race hatred will be reduced to a minimum." Boulin recognized that adherents to a dream need to see it materialize; a mass movement cannot exist indefinitely on promises. If the Black Star Line failed, Garvey's credibility would suffer a serious blow.[43]

Black nationalism was not the only concern of the Bureau of Investigation in 1920. Communist and socialist agitation was vibrant. Several of Boulin's reports analyzed the mind and mood of black migrants from the rural South who now faced entrapment in northern cities with little hope for upward mobility. While Garvey promoted racial hatred, warned Boulin, economic radicals preached class hatred. Was it any wonder that "the poor Negro with an undeveloped mind is therefore ready to blame the whites for all his ills." Fortunately, claimed Boulin, this explosive situation was mitigated by "intelligent Negroes, conservative Negro newspapers, and some preachers who are acting as a 'balancing power' to counteract all the other detrimental elements."[44] Boulin was at least partially right; Harlem was in ferment. But there was more than one Harlem. Many of its residents were too preoccupied with cleaning white folks' homes, shining shoes, or running elevators to give much attention to either radical or racial agitation.

That Garvey suffered difficult times in late 1920 is clear from several conversations with Boulin in October. The libel suit remained unsettled. The Black Star Line's financial woes cast a pall over Liberty Hall audiences. Garvey received a letter threatening his life, and Boulin counted eight bodyguards, two more than usual, when he walked home with Garvey one night. Subsequent conversations revealed other lawsuits, filed by disgruntled Black Star Line investors, which were seriously straining the treasury. All enterprises were short of money and Garvey confessed that only radical steps would stave off financial disaster.[45]

Garvey's spirits were even lower in early November when he again bared his burdens to Boulin. He was particular discouraged with Black Star stock salesmen who sold large numbers of shares but turned in expenses exceeding the money they took in. A $10,000 check had just bounced. The Liberian Liberty Loan to finance modernization in that West African country was generating little enthusiasm: "He admitted to me that the general Negro public is a little dubious now about all the African schemes, so many of them being on the market recently."[46]

Boulin was startled the next day when Garvey admitted to having attempted suicide a few months previously after learning that the *Yarmouth* had run aground off Cuba. Now Garvey realized he had been duped by an advisor, Capt. Joshua Cockburn, who brokered the unseaworthy steamship to the Black Star Line, inflated repair costs by 200 percent, and received a kickback from whiskey shippers whose cargo was intentionally jettisoned on one of the ship's comic-opera voyages. Financial pressures, and fear that the membership would learn such details, once more led Garvey to contemplate suicide. Boulin predicted that "if his fanatic hero worshippers should ever get these facts he and his officers would either be killed or chased out of town."[47]

Finances continued to preoccupy Garvey for the remainder of the year, and most of Boulin's reports centered on monetary appeals and UNIA members' trust in their leader's vision and program. In addition, Boulin continued to warn that Garvey's rhetoric could easily provoke racial conflict: "He preaches hate and fear which causes them to give up their last dollar, even after one scheme after another, has completely failed." Thus propagandized, "it would take but little to set the fire of race trouble burning among the Garvey group." Boulin was unable to understand the depth of loyalty to Garvey, seeing his "spellbound" followers as simply brainwashed, rather than co-participants in a vision of rescue and rebirth. The informant could only lament behavior which he found embarrassing: "They still continue to follow blindly, even expecting him to perform some miracle by overthrowing the White race."[48]

Boulin's position as an outsider helped him penetrate the UNIA and gain Garvey's confidence. The double-dealing of Cockburn and conflicts with UNIA leaders led Garvey to distrust many of those around him. He was reputed to be "a very hard man to reach" but because Boulin helped settle Grey's and Warner's libel suits out of court Garvey trusted him more than others. In fact, reported Boulin, "even when his officers want to reach him and are afraid, they will come to me and ask me to put in a good word for them." Despite the popular acclaim he enjoyed, his paranoia isolated him from subordinates: "Garvey is very suspicious and thinks everyone is trying to 'frame him up.'"[49]

But for all his closeness to Garvey, Boulin was unable to uncover evidence for a court case against Garvey. Without a "smoking gun" federal authorities were no closer to their objective. Although the Bureau knew of Garvey's extramarital affair with Amy Jacques and for months sought evidence for a Mann Act prosecution Boulin was not near enough to Garvey on a daily basis to witness any incriminating behavior. And prosecuting Garvey for fraudulent sale and promotion of Black Star stock would have to be based on the sworn testimony of the line's officials, accountants' analyses of its bookkeeping, and proof that misleading advertisements had been transmitted through the mails. Bureau agents ultimately found such evidence; undercover operatives like Boulin did not lay the legal foundation for successful prosecution.

At a Liberty Hall meeting early in January 1921, Garvey made the messianic announcement that "I shall suddenly disappear from you for six or seven weeks." At first Garvey led Boulin to believe he was going to Liberia. In fact a delegation including Cyril Crichlow and Boulin's acquaintance, UNIA Deputy Potentate George O. Marke, was planning to travel secretly to Africa, sailing by way of Spain so as to outwit the British, who were worried about UNIA influence abroad. Boulin arranged a way to maintain contact with Marke by devising "a private code under the pretext of entering into business with him." Rumors that Garvey would go to Africa and that a Black Star ship would offer free passage for emigrants proved a liability when several families, inspired by misleading stories in the *Negro World,* arrived penniless in New York. This information, supplied by Boulin, was of great interest to the Bureau, which was avidly seeking evidence of fraudulent activity, although Garvey was ultimately prosecuted for illegally using the mails in promoting the sale of Black Star Line stock.[50]

Marcus Garvey never set foot on African soil. In fact, his "secret" journey was to the West Indies. Finally revealing his true plans to Boulin, he confided that his subordinates were worried that British authorities might arrest him or American consuls might refuse to visa his passport for a return to the United States. Garvey, though, was confident he could outwit the two governments by traveling as a sailor on one of his own ships. Boulin counseled the Bureau that preventing Garvey's reentry would bring a quick end to the UNIA: "None of his officers would be able to hold the followers together, as they are hero worshippers."[51] But Boulin was wrong; even Garvey's imprisonment four years later did not bring immediate collapse to the movement.

From late February until mid-July 1921, Garvey traveled to Cuba, Jamaica, Costa Rica, Panama, and British Honduras promoting the UNIA, selling Black Star Line stock, and strengthening branches. His absence from the United States, he told Boulin, was deliberate: Liberian president C. D. B. King was soon to arrive seeking badly needed American credits for his impoverished land. Association with the UNIA could sabotage chances for a loan. Once Garvey was out of the country King did meet with UNIA officials in New York and Washington. But despite their hopes no loan was granted at this time.[52]

Garvey's Caribbean tour shows the close relationship that developed between the Bureau of Investigation and the Department of State as the federal intelligence network evolved in the war and Red Scare period. Although State Department personnel were motivated by the same fears that resonated through the Justice Department they were also influenced by a more global concern, the rising tide of nationalism among colonized peoples of color. English fears that the virus of Garveyism was spreading in the Caribbean and Africa found a sympathetic response in Foggy Bottom. American diplomacy in the interwar period rested on three pillars: friendship with Great Britain, friendship with France, and maintenance of the Americas for Americans.[53] Admitting the contradictions inherent in this triad one can nonetheless see how it influenced the State Department. Garveyism threatened British and French possessions in the Caribbean and their hegemony in West Africa. The UNIA similarly posed challenges to American influence in predominantly black regions of the Western Hemisphere.

In the half year preceding Garvey's trip State received many dispatches from the West Indies detailing British fears that its colonial populations were being radicalized by the UNIA. Garvey's election as "provisional president" of Africa led European governments to ban the anti-imperialist *Negro World* in their colonies. No less discomforting was Garvey's prediction that Lenin and Trotsky, along with Chinese, Japanese, and Indian nationalists, would assist in guaranteeing "Africa for the Africans." Assistant Undersecretary of State William L. Hurley and J. Edgar Hoover enjoyed a personal relationship and exchanged consular dispatches for informants' and agents' reports. (Many of these Bureau documents were then passed to the British government through the American embassy in London.) Hoover's weekly GID summaries, plus clippings from the *Negro World,* were also shared with the State Department as part of the Bureau's effort to persuade the Division of Passport Control to deny travel documents to UNIA members destined for Liberia.[54]

The West Indian tour occasioned the Bureau's most sustained effort against Garvey up to that time. Although it was mostly Hoover's show, cooperation from the State Department was essential. In a memorandum to Bureau chief Lewis J. Baley, Hoover wrote that Garvey, still a British subject, intended to travel as a seaman so that he could return without visa complications. The State Department should be persuaded, he argued, to deny reentry.[55]

Garvey left the country on February 28, holding a British passport, and, due mainly to strenuous Bureau efforts to keep it from being visaed, did not return until July. Hoover's office repeatedly cajoled the State Department and the Commissioner General of Immigration to bar his reentry. Throughout an extensive correspondence Garvey was repeatedly referred to as "the notorious negro agitator." No one knew when or where he would attempt to land so the Bureau, fearing that an illegal entry might be made anywhere, alerted agents in every Atlantic and Gulf port to be on alert for such an attempt.[56]

Evidence had to be gathered should Garvey succeed in landing; deportation proceedings could then be initiated. For all the Bureau's prior surveillance this proved no easy task. The Post Office's Translation Bureau was asked for "three bad articles by Marcus Garvey in the *Negro World.*" One, appearing on March 12, implied "the necessity for the use of force in the Negro's aims," according to the government. But this was a thin reed on which to argue denial of entry, and Hoover demanded a "summary memorandum upon the activities of this individual, giving particular attention to utterances either by word, by mouth, or in writing, advocating the overthrow of the Government of the United States by force or violence, or urging the unlawful destruction of property." If necessary, the files of the Military Intelligence Division and the State Department should be combed for evidence.[57]

The most effective way to deal with Garvey was simply to prevent his reentry. Consul C. L. Latham in Kingston, Jamaica, was informed that "in view of the activities of Garvey in political and racial agitation, you are instructed to refuse him a visa" and notify other consuls on Garvey's itinerary of this decision. But where was Garvey? His travels on the Black Star Line's yacht *Kanawha* were extended and detoured by the ship's breakdowns and the need to promote the UNIA. Boulin attempted to keep track of him while the Bureau and State Department also sought the cooperation of MID in monitoring his whereabouts.[58]

Garvey experienced no end of frustration in trying to return to the United States. Latham willingly accepted $1 fees from Garvey, his paramour and secretary, Amy Jacques, and her brother Cleveland. The Jacques's passports were visaed but Garvey was told to return the following day. Anticipating rejection, he and his companions sailed that evening on a commercial steamer for Costa Rica and the Canal Zone. Latham cabled Panama to watch for the trio, and the State Department warned that "his activities while in Kingston indicate that he would arouse considerable racial antagonism among the negroes at the Canal Zone and in the Republic of Panama."[59]

Garvey and his party first reached San Jose, Costa Rica, where he sought a visa to enter the Canal Zone. The State Department's emphatic refusal did not, however, prevent Garvey from going into the Republic of Panama, because he had a visa granted by the Panamanian consul in Boston. The naval intelligence office in the Canal Zone and MID both monitored his activities in Panama City and Colon, the latter notifying the State Department of his return to Jamaica.[60]

When Garvey reappeared in Kingston on May 7 American diplomats learned that their quarry would set sail for the United States as a crew member of the *Kanawha* as soon as that vessel reached Jamaica from Havana. Secretary of State Charles Evans Hughes, in a cable marked "urgent" and "secret," instructed Consul Latham to refuse to visa the *Kanawha's* crew list if Garvey's name was added.[61]

But Garvey was too clever to be stopped. Making his way to Santiago, Cuba, he was signed on as purser by the *Kanawha's* master after the ship had cleared, bypassing the American consul there. Not without his own stratagems, Consul Latham, anticipating the vessel's return to Jamaica before a run to the United States, suggested that it be detained by refusal of a bill of health. Indeed Garvey did return, but not according to his own script: The *Kanawha* limped into Kingston with engine troubles and Garvey appeared at the consulate to charge the captain and other officers with incompetence and drunkenness. Latham, who by this time despised Garvey, was hardly an impartial judge. Regarding Garvey's evidence as inconclusive, exaggerated, or outright false, he ruled that the charges against the master and chief engineer were unfounded. Garvey nonetheless fired the former while the latter voluntarily sought a discharge. Both were awarded extra wages and sufficient funds to return to the United States, over Garvey's protests.[62]

The *Kanawha* set sail on June 18 with Garvey on board, ostensibly for the Canal Zone, but it soon returned to port due to boiler troubles and an insufficient supply of coal and water. A frustrated Garvey cabled Hughes to "please instruct consul here to visa my passport"[63] and in fact that matter was being debated in Washington. Latham had requested a ruling on whether a bill of health could be withheld if Garvey remained a member of the *Kanawha's* crew. But the State Department solicitor's office, while agreeing that Garvey was "an undesirable, and indeed a very dangerous, alien," found no legal reason to refuse a bill of health, unless there was a demonstrable medical condition. And refusing visas to all because of objections to one individual would be similarly high-handed and outside the law.[64]

At the same time Assistant Undersecretary Hurley concluded that further efforts to bar Garvey were counterproductive: "I really think by insisting upon exclusion we would martyrize him." Noting that Garvey was being investigated for violation of federal postal laws and New York state insurance regulations, Hurley suggested that he "be allowed to return and his case will receive the undivided attention of the Department of Justice." Hurley and solicitor Fred K. Nielsen prevailed; the next day Garvey's visa was authorized and he lost no time departing Jamaica.[65]

Hurley was unwilling to manipulate regulations on no stronger evidence than Garvey's flamboyant rhetoric. He did, however, suggest to Hoover that "you may wish to give Garvey a thorough overhauling upon arrival." The same encouragement was given to the Commissioner General of Immigration, whose inspectors subjected Garvey to rigorous questioning when he disembarked in New Orleans. But they, too, found no evidence of seditious, disloyal, or treasonable utterance sufficient to warrant Garvey's exclusion.[66]

Jubilant preparations had been made by the New York UNIA to welcome their leader, but the immigration interrogation forced plans for a reception and parade to be scrapped. Instead, Garvey and his traveling party were met at the train station by only three persons: Black Star Line Secretary Elie Garcia, UNIA High Chancellor Rev. Gabriel E. Stewart, and the Bureau's undercover informant, Herbert S. Boulin![67] How many of the faithful would have sacrificed everything for that privilege?

Garvey's return to the United States only strengthened the Bureau of Investigation's resolve to nail the UNIA's leader. Joined by the State Department, it revived efforts to bring Mann Act charges against him. Such cases were the stock-in-trade of the pre-war Bureau. Although they had separated, Garvey was still legally married to Amy Ashwood Garvey. His affections now lay with Amy Jacques. Could witnesses be found to testify to adulterous behavior? Did Amy

Ashwood Garvey's lawyers have evidence to support her divorce suit? The Bureau and the State Department were confident they could trap Garvey.[68]

Eyewitness testimony to immoral activity was crucial, and several possibilities seemed promising. Garvey and Miss Jacques traveled together on the *Kanawha*, whose master, Capt. Adrian Richardson, was dismissed by Garvey before the end of the voyage, as was Cyrus M. Yarter, the ship's first assistant engineer. Perhaps they had evidence. Cleveland Jacques, Amy's brother, was also on the Caribbean tour and was fired soon thereafter for alleged financial irregularities. Why the Bureau expected him to cooperate in a case involving his sister can best be explained by its conviction that Amy was the "victim" of "white slavery." But in fact she was Garvey's willing paramour. In any case, when Garvey reinstated Cleveland Jacques as his personal chauffeur, the prodigal refused to cooperate with Bureau agents.[69]

Yarter and Richardson, however, had both seen Amy Jacques in Garvey's stateroom on the *Kanawha,* she in her nightclothes and he partially undressed. Capt. Richardson had ordered Garvey to cease all immoral activity and share a cabin with one of the ship's officers, but he refused.[70] Yet despite these witnesses the Bureau's case was sunk simply because the events took place in international waters outside the jurisdiction of American law. Prosecutors would have to prove that Garvey brought Amy Jacques into the country for immoral purposes to even attempt to use such shipboard conduct as evidence. Despite the weakness of its case the Bureau, urged on by Director William J. Burns, doggedly continued its surveillance. By mid-1921 Garvey could not travel without agents or informants observing where he and Amy Jacques were staying.[71]

After Garvey's return to New York, Herbert S. Boulin was also directed to seek Mann Act evidence, counting on the cooperation of Cleveland Jacques and former Black Star captains Cockburn and Richardson. Garvey knew they had reported him to the district attorney but was confident he had enough influence to block their schemes, especially since their friend Edgar Grey, now reconciled to Garvey, would divulge their plans. Garvey was still unaware, however, that Grey was also Boulin's informant. And Amy Jacques was now also confiding in Boulin that her brother submitted inflated expense claims and "lost" records of thousands of dollars of Black Star Line and Liberian Loan contributions he had received. Disciplined by Garvey, he quit the organization. Amy Jacques confessed to being a "nervous wreck" while insisting on her innocence, telling Boulin that when she traveled in Garvey's entourage she was always in the company of Enid Lamos, one of his stenographers.[72]

Attorneys representing Amy Ashwood Garvey were willing to cooperate with the Bureau but had no hard evidence. They heard plenty of rumors, from Pullman porters or disgruntled UNIA employees, that Garvey and Amy

Jacques occupied the same berth on overnight trains. But neither Mrs. Garvey nor her lawyers could confirm these tales. In the end the Bureau was unable to use the Mann Act against Garvey. Hearsay could not be substantiated. Illicit cohabitation on the high seas was beyond the arm of the law. Amy Jacques refused to play the victim. And when, his first marriage at last legally terminated, Garvey married Amy Jacques in July 1922, the government was again checkmated.[73]

The day after Garvey's return from the Caribbean in July 1921, he spoke to a massive crowd in Liberty Hall (despite the 50-cent admission fee) while thousands more stood outside. To Boulin's surprise he waxed patriotic, professing love for America and thanking Secretary of State Hughes for making his reentry possible. He also claimed that critics were mistaken in saying he hated whites; all he asked was an equal chance for blacks. Above all else, Garvey said, his life was devoted to freeing and redeeming Africa.[74] Boulin reported that other officers had also dropped their "anti-white" rhetoric.

As the UNIA's second international convention began in August Garvey's new moderation was still pronounced as he advised blacks to support their individual nations in wartime, so long as such action promoted the interests of humanity. Boulin surmised that Garvey's recent tribulations had wrought a change for the better, and throughout August the convention oratory seemed more "pro-Negro" than "anti-white" and warranted little comment from the informant.[75]

But search for a Mann Act violation, not changes in Garvey's rhetoric, continued to preoccupy the Bureau in mid-1921. Yet the prospect of finding eyewitnesses to Garvey's illicit love life or exploiting Amy Jacques's fears was disregarded when Hoover terminated Boulin's employment at the end of August. No written reasons survive, but it is likely that he was no longer needed when Agent James W. Jones returned to undercover assignment in New York City. Boulin's abrupt discharge should not, however, obscure his skill at infiltration. Preserving his cover for over a year, he gained an extraordinary level of trust with Garvey even though, as a member of the Talented Tenth and an upwardly mobile West Indian, he had no sympathy for Garvey's rejection of an American destiny for blacks. And at the same time Boulin penetrated the African Blood Brotherhood, which was bent on destroying Garvey's movement.

Soon after his Bureau service Boulin founded a private detective agency, advertising the fact that he had been employed by the Department of Justice. Only then did Garvey realize he had been duped, although he lamely declared that he had been suspicious of Boulin. Ironically, Garvey's acknowledgment was made to Agent Jones, whose "cover" was so artful that he was on the UNIA payroll![76]

The bout between the Justice Department and Marcus Garvey was far from over, although he had won the most recent rounds. Federal authorities did not waver from the conviction that Garvey was a threat to race relations, if no longer to national security. Their strategy would henceforth center on identifying illegalities in the sloppy promotional and accounting practices of the Black Star Line. The State Department supplied consular reports on the amount of stock subscriptions from abroad, although this information was ultimately not crucial to successful prosecution. Rather, it was the Black Star Line's own books that proved a prosecutor's gold mine.[77]

When Jack Jones again began submitting reports to the Bureau in August 1921 he was already employed as circulation manager for the *Negro World*. Now he also (secretly) joined the African Blood Brotherhood, which, in a precursor of the communist "united front" strategy of the 1930s, was attempting to ally with the UNIA. Garvey was understandably wary, according to Jones.[78] Although ABB head Cyril Briggs managed to engineer an invitation for white communist Rose Pastor Stokes to address the UNIA convention, where she urged solidarity between the two movements, Garvey kept the ABB at arm's length. Once Briggs saw the futility of getting many UNIA members to defect, he embarked on a campaign to vilify Garvey in the *Crusader,* which Jones assisted in distributing. More significantly, Jones provided Briggs with inside information from the Garvey movement, carefully doled out so that his position of trust in the UNIA would not be compromised. Jones also gave Briggs the names and addresses of UNIA leaders so he could send them issues of the *Crusader* that smeared Garvey.[79]

Jones's most significant role in late 1921 and early 1922 was as an *agent provocateur.* Briggs was aware that Jones was a member of the UNIA and depended on him for confidential inside information. And although Briggs was wary of a "mole" within the ABB, he apparently trusted Jones about as much as he did anyone. Jones fostered the grievances of disaffected UNIA members who held grudges against Garvey or had not been paid promised salaries, steering them toward Briggs. One such defector was Cyril Crichlow, Garvey's stenographic reporter and a member of the UNIA commission sent to Liberia to plan a modernization program for that country. He had access to its confidential report, which condemned the enslavement of native peoples by Liberia's ruling elite. When Crichlow filed suit against Garvey to recover his unpaid salary, Jones encouraged his grievance and believed the Liberian report could be used to discredit Garvey. Twice the black agent rifled Garvey's office in a fruitless attempt to find it.[80] When Crichlow finally located a copy, he gave it to Jones, who passed it on to Briggs for publication in the *Crusader*. Although the document was potentially fatal to UNIA plans to use Liberia as a beachhead for the eventual liberation of all Africa, Briggs decided not to print it, believing it might strengthen Garvey's reputation rather than discredit him. At that point Jones played the role of provocateur masterfully, giving the report back to Garvey, who did not know how it left his office in the first place. Jones led Garvey to believe that Crichlow had stolen it from Briggs and given it to Jones. Garvey apparently accepted this explanation and Jones retained the confidence of the UNIA head.[81]

By the end of 1921 Garvey was feeling the heat of opposition from all sides. His black critics—Briggs and the African Blood Brotherhood, plus A. Philip Randolph and Chandler Owen, editors of the *Messenger* and spark plugs of the anti-Garvey Friends of Negro Freedom—pilloried him unmercifully. Lawsuits continued to pile up. Aware that a federal indictment was imminent, he was ignorant of the fact that it was based in part on evidence supplied to the Post Office Department by Briggs. Yet the likelihood of prosecution did not halt counterattacks. When Briggs organized anti-UNIA meetings in December Garveyites broke them up and forced speakers—some of whom were UNIA defectors—to flee. And despite growing public opposition to Garvey, Jones ruefully noted that most of his followers still trusted him.[82]

On January 12, 1922, Garvey was arrested for using the mails to defraud purchasers of Black Star Line stock. Within days seven members of the UNIA were summoned to give "voluntary statements" to the Post Office inspector compiling evidence for the federal case. One was Capt. James W. Jones, as he was known within the UNIA. The Bureau agent who took stenographic notes was Mortimer J. Davis, with whom Jones often worked; of course, their relationship was not revealed. Here was another delicate situation for the black agent. He was still useful undercover and in fact continued to enjoy Garvey's confidence for another year. As a potential witness, the government needed to keep Jones's true identity secret until Garvey was brought to trial. By interviewing a number of witnesses at the same time the Bureau took the focus off Jones.

Although Jones was questioned regarding fiscal mismanagement of UNIA enterprises the substance of his testimony was already known to the Bureau. He had previously reported several fraudulent activities, which he now spelled out in greater detail. On numerous occasions money subscribed for Black Star stock was used to pay for printing the *Negro World*. Similar fiscal shenanigans left $46,000 missing from the death benefit (insurance) fund. To cover this loss the *Negro World* was "sold" to the UNIA for the identical sum in a strictly paper transaction. Monies collected for Liberian reconstruction were transferred to meet deficits in other UNIA accounts. Finally, Jones testified that the Black Star Line advertised sailings to Africa and accepted payment for passage on a ship—to be named the *Phyllis Wheatley*—that was not yet owned.[83] This was damaging testimony, although not yet the "smoking gun" that was needed for a conviction. Having Jones give a deposition was a calculated risk, but the fact that he was "compelled" to testify did not damn him in Garvey's eyes.

Jones continued to walk the double agent tightrope successfully, enjoying Garvey's confidence while also retaining membership in the African Blood Brotherhood. His next communication to the Bureau contained information that only one close to UNIA leadership could have obtained. Four days after Garvey's arrest Jones phoned J. Edgar Hoover to inform him of a scheme to drop the case in exchange for a bribe. The intended recipient was Postmaster General Will Hays who was allegedly willing to cooperate in order to pay off a political debt. Those representing Garvey were said to be his attorney, Henry Lincoln Johnson, subject of previous bribery rumors; W. S. Burke, Johnson's former private secretary and a member of the UNIA hierarchy; and Perry Howard, leader of the "Black and Tan" Republican Party in Mississippi and a political appointee in the Justice Department. The fact that Burke, who acted as the go-between, revealed these details to Jones attests to his skill as an infiltrator even when his cover was again nearly exposed. Burke recognized Jones but "after some talk I made him believe that it was my brother that he knew."[84]

Hoover took the allegations of a bribe attempt seriously enough to confide them to Bureau Director Burns, who in turn conveyed them to an assistant attorney general. A week later, however, Jones reported that Garvey refused to put up the $20,000 needed to buy off the government, believing he could vindicate himself in court.[85] The absence of documentation on this subject in Justice Department files suggests two possible conclusions: Either federal attorneys judged this to be idle rumor and unworthy of investigation, or they dealt with the matter in-house, perhaps admonishing Perry Howard, in order that nothing impede the effort to prosecute Garvey.

The grand jury investigating Garvey returned a true bill on January 26, 1922. The Justice Department had at last identified charges—mail fraud—that would put him behind bars and then out of the country. While strengthening the case became a high priority, the importance of undercover operations diminished. Nonetheless Jones continued efforts to cripple Garvey and the UNIA. One tack was to urge the Department of Justice to press New York authorities to prosecute Garvey for misuse of death fund contributions. Jones also sought to weaken Garvey on the domestic front. He informed the Bureau that Amy Jacques "told some one in my office that Garvey had beaten her, and that she was tired of his beatings. If there is ever a break between Garvey and Jacques you need never worry about the out come of the case as she knows enough to hang him." Jones added his own intention: "You can rest assure [sic] that anything that I can do to bring about this condition will be done."[86]

With Garvey's future uncertain, speculation arose as to who might succeed him. Jones and others within the UNIA thought that Duse Mohamed Ali, Garvey's old mentor, was the likely candidate. Amy Jacques feared such a prospect, knowing that her influence would disappear if Ali gained power. Worried that Ali would attract "the better class of negro" and make the UNIA "an organization that will really have [to be] reckoned with," Jones sowed seeds of dissension. During one of Garvey's absences, Ali invited John Mitchell, editor of the *Richmond Planet,* to address UNIA members. Mitchell advised them to find a new leader if they were dissatisfied. Jones promised to "see that Garvey gets this information about Mitchell's speech, also the object of the speech." Amy Jacques "will do the informing and you can rest assure [sic] that it will be done well."[87] Jack Jones was indeed an expert *agent provocateur.*

By the spring of 1922 Garvey had been indicted for mail fraud and the Black Star Line was foundering in a sea of financial distress. The government's case was in the hands of accountants and agents who scoured the UNIA's books for evidence. No longer needing infiltration of its headquarters and having a new black agent, James Edward Amos, who operated openly, the Bureau reassigned Jones to other cases. But he went back undercover upon the assassination of Rev. J. W. H. Eason, on New Years Day 1923. Two Garveyites were believed to have murdered the UNIA's former "Leader of American Negroes."

A splendid orator and renowned churchman, Eason had brought luster to the UNIA but he had split with Garvey and was impeached during the 1922 convention. Opposition to Garvey was intensifying: Major critics included UNIA dissidents like Eason; DuBois and other black officials of the NAACP; Robert Abbott of the *Chicago Defender;* and especially the black socialists like Randolph and Owen and communists like Briggs. Under siege by the government, attacked in much of the black press and many public forums, the UNIA became increasingly threatening in response, Garvey predicting a "Waterloo" for his black opponents. UNIA thugs forcibly broke up opposition meetings. After leaving the UNIA Eason attempted to form a rival Universal Negro Alliance. Gunned down while speaking in New Orleans, evidence pointed to two Jamaican members of the local UNIA, Constantine (Fred) Dyer and William Shakespeare, as the killers. Behind them loomed a "hit man" from

UNIA headquarters, Esau Ramus. While Bureau agents in New Orleans investigated the murder, Jones sought links between Garvey, Ramus, and the alleged gunmen. His reports were sent to Director Burns, indicating the level of interest in the murder.

Arriving in New Orleans on January 27, Jones went undercover, meeting first with Sylvester V. Robinson and his wife, the UNIA's local leaders. The couple had visited UNIA headquarters in New York many times during Jones's work on the *Negro World* and accepted him as a loyal member. They confided that Dyer and Shakespeare were indeed the triggermen and had been directed by Ramus, a native of St. Kitts.

Jones began to attend UNIA meetings in hopes of connecting Ramus to the two suspects and discovering where he had fled. Local members, who were raising a defense fund for Dyer and Shakespeare, felt that Eason had gotten his due. Jones next schemed with local authorities to have himself "arrested" and put in the same cell with the two suspects. They denied their guilt and refused to implicate Ramus. But at a preliminary hearing they based their defense on the testimony of Dyer's wife that, shortly before fleeing, Ramus admitted killing Eason. With all local members protesting their innocence and blaming Ramus, Jones returned to New York to search for evidence that Garvey had ordered Ramus to kill Eason.[88]

Remarkably, Garvey talked openly with Jones. He feared implication in Eason's murder but denied any connection. Jones talked with other UNIA officials but could not corroborate reports that Garvey supplied Ramus with instructions and travel funds and that he telegraphed back that he had successfully accomplished his mission.[89] Implicating Garvey in Eason's murder would have ensured his imprisonment and deportation, but too many connecting threads were missing. Dyer and Shakespeare were eventually convicted in New Orleans but the verdicts were reversed on appeal. When Ramus was captured in Detroit, apathetic Louisiana officials refused to authorize extradition funds, even though theirs was the only jurisdiction in which he could be tried for murder. Ramus was already a fugitive from justice, however, and was convicted and sentenced to prison on other charges.[90] Thus ended the Eason murder case. Jones's last UNIA report was dated February 18, 1923, and he resigned from the Bureau two months later.

How significant was the career of the Bureau of Investigation's first black agent? At the very least, Jones's competence encouraged the Bureau to hire four more black agents during his tenure: James Edward Amos and Arthur Lowell Brent in 1921 and Earl E. Titus and Thomas Leon Jefferson the following year. Radical ferment was declining rapidly from its Red Scare peak. No new militant African American movements were founded during this period. Those who followed Jones were not hired because of any emergency, as Jones had been. The Bureau simply recognized the value of having a few black agents to investigate black suspects. (It has been impossible to learn the degree to which they also worked on cases where suspects were white.) Just as clearly, the Bureau did not retain them from a color-blind hiring policy; it was simply a matter of expediency. Jones, Brent, Titus, and Jefferson served only a few years apiece; the Bureau took no special pains to retain its first black agents.[91] Only Amos made a career with the Bureau. Yet it is likely that none of them would have been hired had Jones failed.

On both the Garvey and African Blood Brotherhood cases, Jones frequently gave advice and suggestions to his supervisor in Washington, Agent Ruch, who often endorsed these recommendations to Hoover. Ruch and Jones had a close working relationship, the latter traveling to Washington every few weeks for Sunday conferences. Jones was so well trusted that on one occasion, while conferring with Hoover, he was permitted to rummage through Ruch's files in search of a document.[92] Jones's immediate supervisor in the New York field office was Mortimer J. Davis, a member of the radical squad and the local coordinator of the Garvey case. There is no hint of discord between Jones and the white agents in that office, although there appears to have been some jealousy between Jones and Amos.[93]

Bureau director Burns routinely reviewed a sampling of agents' reports selected for him by Hoover. How many of Jones's reports reached his desk is unknown, but he reacted to one which described conflict between Garvey and the African Blood Brotherhood. His handwritten comment was acerbic: "Here is another case of just giving conversation. He [Jones] states he is trying to find out who is putting up the money [for the *Crusader*]. We want a closer alliance with the subjects."[94] Burns pinpointed the limitation of Jones's undercover work. His usefulness depended upon cultivating intimate relationships with suspects. This necessitated spending many hours working in the *Negro World* office and establishing himself in UNIA and ABB circles. Both the intensity of these relationships and the intricacy of his double agent role defined the opportunities and limitations of Jones's service. He penetrated the UNIA as deeply as any informant or agent. But he had neither the time nor the liberty to ferret out details on the wider connections of the ABB and UNIA. His undercover work was artful, but an informant cannot easily be a detective as well. The Bureau could not have it both ways.

The Bureau's first black agent was an ideal pioneer in ways that the Bureau would have defined: He was well educated, possessed relevant experience, and was politically dependable. His militant speech to the UNIA in 1920 notwithstanding, Jones, like other members of the Talented Tenth, feared that Garvey was poisoning racial relations and believed that progress would only accrue from reasoned civil rights advocacy and appeals to morality. Garvey and the ABB both rejected such equations, although from starkly differing presuppositions: the West Indian Pan-Africanist foresaw no co-existence between different races anywhere on the globe, and thus stressed self-separation and a unifying racial nationalism. While the black communists also rejected the status quo, they anticipated a new interracial brotherhood when the proletarian millennium arrived.

James Wormley Jones left the Bureau of Investigation on April 14, 1923, at the age of forty; he died thirty-five years later in Pittsburgh. His replacement on the Garvey case was James Edward Amos, appointed in August 1921 at $6 per day, the same pay as beginning white agents. His earliest assignments are either shrouded in unreleased case files or were lost in the later intentional destruction of New York field office records. His activities are first traceable in early 1922 when he joined the Bureau team preparing the mail fraud case against Garvey.

Amos's main responsibility for the next seventeen months was to identify and "encourage" witnesses who might testify against Garvey, including over a dozen disaffected UNIA leaders. He worked openly, not undercover, and frequently in partnership with Agent Davis. The two often submitted joint reports and seem to have worked harmoniously. Amos developed a list of potential witnesses after a week's study of the Black Star Line's account books. Many who had sunk hard-earned savings into the hapless ships and now realized their money was irretrievable indicated a willingness to testify. But more useful as witnesses were those who were privy to the Byzantine financial manipulations between the UNIA and the Black Star Line. Several present and past officers willingly spoke with Amos but were reluctant to appear in court. Bishop George A. McGuire, on-again, off-again head of the UNIA's African Orthodox Church, was one such individual, justifiably fearing for his position and reputation if he spoke against Garvey. Gwendolyn Campbell, once head of Garvey's stenographic corps, likewise revealed important financial details but feared for her personal safety should she testify.[95]

Agent Amos's most cooperative witness was Capt. Joshua Cockburn, who had his own axe to grind, having been (justifiably) fired by Garvey after receiving a kickback for promoting the sale of the *Yarmouth* to the Black Star Line and sharing a bribe from an unscrupulous shipper. Capt. Adrian Richardson was also cultivated by Amos, who predicted he would make an excellent witness, given the depth of his bitterness toward Garvey.[96] Amos likewise courted Orlando M. Thompson, one of Garvey's co-defendants. Thompson sought to place the blame for financial irregularities on others and Amos hoped he would turn against his confederates on the witness stand.[97]

The greatest obstacle to maintaining his stable of reliable witnesses was legal delays. Garvey's attorneys gained several postponements, and the trial did not begin until mid-May 1923. Amos's reports repeatedly emphasized "keeping in touch with witnesses."[98] Should they get cold feet or return to Garvey's fold, the case could be jeopardized. The possibility that they might be intimidated into silence became especially serious after the murder of Eason. This was a significant setback for the Bureau, which had counted on his testimony. Apostates were not forgiven in the Garvey movement, and Amos noted pessimistically that "if this case drags along much longer, we will have no witnesses left for the government." In fact, Garvey's loyal followers seemed emboldened to threaten potential witnesses, justifying Amos's concern.[99]

Amos also cultivated those outside the UNIA who might provide evidence. Previous plaintiffs in lawsuits against Garvey were contacted, as were the NAACP's William Pickens and Walter White. Pickens had been courted by the UNIA in an effort to gain legitimacy by appointing well-known American blacks to honorary positions. But he publicly rejected the offer, earning the particular antipathy of UNIA members.[100]

Anti-Garvey politics created strange bedfellows, none more incongruous than the relationship between Amos and co-editors Randolph and Owen. The black agent apparently initiated contact in September 1922 after Randolph received a package in the mail containing the severed hand of a white man. Although an enclosed note was signed "KKK" Randolph believed it came from Garvey's supporters. He and Owen vowed to assist the government in prosecuting Garvey. The following January, shortly after Eason's murder, Owen and seven other well-known blacks including Pickens and Robert W. Bagnall of the NAACP, and newspaper editors Robert Abbott of the *Chicago Defender* and George W. Harris of the *New York News,* wrote an open letter to the attorney general. It called the UNIA a "criminal organization" and detailed numerous examples of intimidation and attack on Garvey's opponents. Owen shared a draft of the letter with Amos prior to making public the final version. Bagnall and Owen did their own investigation of Eason's murder and supplied information on the whereabouts and associates of Ramus.[101] Four years previously the attorney general had labeled Owen's associate Randolph "the most dangerous Negro" and the *Messenger* "the most dangerous Negro publication in America." Now Owen was leagued with his former persecutor.

Marcus Garvey's long-awaited trial began on May 18, 1923. James Amos's year-long effort to "encourage" witnesses was vindicated a month later when the jury found Garvey guilty of mail fraud. For much of his trial Garvey acted as his own attorney. Among his disastrous moves was calling agents Amos and Davis as defense witnesses! Garvey sought to prove that Amos knew a former British ambassador who, he alleged, supplied funds for his prosecution. After the laughter of courtroom spectators subsided, this line of testimony was ruled out of order by the judge. When Garvey next asked Amos if he was connected with the prosecution, he replied, "I should say so. I investigated you!" At this Garvey attempted to have Amos qualified as a hostile witness but the judge denied the motion on the grounds that Garvey himself had summoned Amos for the defense and should have been prepared for his testimony. Ultimately, the agents' testimony was not crucial to convicting Garvey; nevertheless it earned them both death threats.[102]

Garvey was sentenced to a five-year prison term, and Amos represented the Bureau as the courts considered his lengthy appeals. In addition he assisted in preparing income tax fraud charges against Garvey.[103] Before this new issue could be adjudicated, however, the circuit court of appeals sustained the mail fraud conviction on February 3, 1925. Securing a bench warrant, Amos and federal marshals boarded a New York Central Railroad train from Detroit at the 125th Street station and took Garvey into custody. Twenty-four hours later he was on his way to the federal penitentiary in Atlanta.[104]

The Justice Department found Garvey's vulnerability in his chaotic business practices. Ironically, the government's Red Scare zealots never came close to implicating him in any subversive plots or activities. And despite public knowledge of the adulterous disarray of Garvey's personal life, usable evidence could not be garnered. Prosecution for mail fraud, then, was not just the next attempt in a string of actions to get Garvey. It was the only charge with sufficient admissible evidence to offer realistic hopes for conviction. And Garvey was convicted on such terms, although the fact that his co-defendants were acquitted raises the question whether he was unfairly singled out. That is another story, still being debated by historians. What is undeniable is that hundreds of thousands of dollars of Black Star Line stockholders' money were squandered and misappropriated. For this Garvey had to bear major responsibility, and in the end he paid dearly.

It might be argued that Garvey's guilt makes immaterial the long crusade of the Bureau of Investigation and other federal agencies to block his magnetic impact on the black masses. But such a conclusion ignores the repressive weight of federal activity during the Red Scare. Led by Hoover's General Intelligence Division and encouraged by the State Department, the Justice Department was determined to extirpate this alleged menace. Even Garvey's self-destruction through Black Star Line mismanagement cannot hide the

Sum

intention of federal guardians of the racial status quo to "get their man." The Bureau engineered Garvey's arrest, which resulted in conviction, imprisonment in 1925, and deportation three years later. Clearly, zeal to enforce mail fraud statutes was not its primary motivation. Rather, as a self-appointed guardian of the sociocultural consensus on which white hegemony was based, the Justice Department sought to silence Garvey's assertions of racial pride and black self-determination. Neither could be comfortably tolerated by men like Hoover.[105]

With Garvey on his way to prison, Amos ended his final report with a succinct summation: "Closed." Well versed in the art of confidentiality, he performed his duties more discreetly and professionally than many agents, white or black. One searches his reports in vain for personal opinions on Garvey and his movement, which were commonly expressed by Arthur U. Craig, Herbert S. Boulin, and even James Wormley Jones. If Amos believed, as did other blacks who served the Bureau, that Garvey preached anti-white doctrines or poisoned racial relations, he did not freight his reports with such allegations. When New York Division Superintendent Edward J. Brennan catalogued the "heroes" of the long case he gave prominence to two agents:

> A great deal of credit in connection with the investigation of this case is due to our agents Mortimer J. Davis and James Edward Amos; these agents have been busily engaged for months bending every effort in endeavoring to secure the necessary and essential legal evidence to convict [Garvey]. . . .
>
> The United States Attorney and his assistant . . . are very much elated by the work performed by these agents and I will say that I do not think that there is any doubt but that it was the untiring and persistent efforts coupled with the resourcefulness of these agents, Davis and Amos, that was in a great part the cause of the successful prosecution of this case.[106]

Marcus Garvey paid a similar, although backhanded, compliment to the black agent's diligence in an appeal for bail shortly after his conviction:

> Amos has followed me all over New York [for] over a year. He has in many ways tried to interfere with my business activities and to spread disloyalty among my employees. He canvasse[d] stockholders of the Black Star Line and inspired them and dismissed employees of mine to testify against me.

Garvey continued to wrongly insist, however, that black enemies in the NAACP were really responsible for bringing him to trial: "It is my firm belief that he [Amos] is in the employ or in the confidence of a rival Negro organization, which seeks to smash the movement in which I have been engaged for years."[107]

James Edward Amos, having proven himself in his first major case, served the FBI for the next thirty-two years, on several occasions earning the commendation of J. Edgar Hoover. He was not limited to cases involving black suspects. Several mobsters found him on their trail, including the Buchalter Gang and "Dutch" Schultz. Finally retiring because of a heart condition in 1953 at the age of seventy-three, he died soon thereafter. While it is clear that Hoover, who became Director in 1925, was not desirous of hiring black agents, he nonetheless recognized Amos's talent and rewarded him with the Bureau's own loyalty. Hoover responded similarly to "Jack" Jones even though he left the Bureau's employ after only a short career. They maintained a lifelong correspondence, Jones occasionally sending his observations on the state of black militancy, to which Hoover reciprocated warmly. But as a pathfinder Amos has no peer; he, more than any of the other early black agents, "proved" what should never have needed proving: that African Americans could serve the federal government in sensitive positions with objectivity, intelligence, and professionalism.[108]

Early in the Garvey case the Bureau of Investigation mistakenly believed Garvey to be a communist. Disproof of this allegation did not diminish one whit its zeal to eliminate him from America. His real "crime," in the eyes of J. Edgar Hoover and the Justice Department, was in being a *racial* agitator. Garveyism was hardly less threatening than Bolshevism in 1919 and 1920, for his challenge came from within, from the place where white Americans sensed their vulnerability. For all its racial slant Garvey's rhetoric was borrowed from the American Dream, transmuted by the idealism and nationalism and disappointment of World War I into black self-determination. The Bureau and its federal intelligence partners watched Garvey, combed his speeches for seditious utterances, monitored his private life, infiltrated his organization, broke into his office, and brought him to trial, conviction, imprisonment, and deportation. As beneficiaries and promoters of white supremacy they felt compelled to blunt Marcus Garvey's redefinition of the American Dream for blacks, even if that dream was to be apocalyptically achieved on a distant African battlefield. White hegemony demanded black acquiescence to existing racial arrangements.

SEVEN

✹

"THE MOST COLOSSAL CONSPIRACY AGAINST THE UNITED STATES"

Efforts to Thwart the Crusader *and the African Blood Brotherhood*

Skip.

As frightened whites watched the eruption of black militancy in 1919 they focused particularly on the press. Although New Crowd Negro journalism encompassed nearly a dozen explicitly radical periodicals, three of them drew a disproportionate share of the alarm: the socialist *Messenger*, Marcus Garvey's *Negro World*, and the *Crusader*. Forty monthly issues of the *Crusader* were published from the fall of 1918 into the spring of 1922 by Nevis-born Cyril V. Briggs. Emigrating to the United States in 1905 at the age of eighteen, his journalistic career began in 1912 when he joined the *New York Amsterdam News*, rising quickly from staff writer to managing editor. During World War I he used the editorial columns to argue (along the same lines as A. Philip Randolph and Chandler Owen) that blacks stood to gain little from a conflict between imperialist powers. Briggs also shared their view that President Wilson's principle of self-determination should include the destinies of peoples of color. His opposition to jingoistic patriotism was widely quoted in other black papers but brought pressure from military intelligence on the paper's publisher. Briggs refused to moderate his editorials and resigned.[1]

By then the young journalist had found his métier, and soon had a backer. West Indian businessman J. Anthony Crawford recognized Briggs's growing interest in racial pride and black Zionism and offered $200 to help launch a magazine devoted to these goals. The new militant monthly would soon capture the attention of black readers and alarmed federal officials alike.[2]

The first issue of the *Crusader* appeared in September 1918, and minced no words. The cover listed twin objectives, "Onward for Democracy" and "Upward with the Race." The lead article, "Africa for the Africans," outlined the necessity for self-determination: "The settlement of every question, whether of territory, of sovereignty, of economic arrangement, or of political relationship, [rests] upon the basis of the free acceptance of that settlement by the people immediately concerned." The magazine also announced an uncompromising fight against lynching, peonage, segregation, and discrimination. A focus on history would supply the necessary "racial backbone" to enable readers to disregard "the evils of Alien Education—which exalts the white man and debases the negro." The major political parties were condemned, while socialist candidates such as A. Philip Randolph and Chandler Owen were endorsed.[3]

The *Crusader* soon became the publicity organ for the Hamitic League of the World, whose goal was to pressure the Paris peace conference into ensuring "that the full rights of citizenship be granted to all people of Color, that all discrimination because of Color be made illegal, that self-determination be extended to all nations and tribes within the African continent and throughout the World, and that the exploitation of Africa and other countries belonging to people of Color herewith cease."[4] This platform did not stir the interest of federal investigators until the spring of 1919 because they were preoccupied instead with the *Crisis* and the *Messenger.* The first warning concerning Briggs's magazine came from a British intelligence report on "Negro Agitation," which was forwarded to the Military Intelligence Division. After a summary of its editorial positions, the *Crusader* was damned as a "very extreme magazine" for its opposition to imperialism, admiration of Bolshevism, and "abuse of the white man."[5]

This long document fell temporarily on deaf ears, and MID launched no immediate investigation of the *Crusader.* Nor did the other federal intelligence agencies move when the colonial rulers of British Guiana, mindful that whites were heavily outnumbered by blacks, requested that the United States prohibit the export of the *Crusader* and *Negro World.* The American consul there agreed that they were "antagonistic to whites," and the State Department sent copies of the British appeal to the Post Office Department and the Bureau of Investigation,[6] but because they were absorbed with attempting to suppress the *Messenger,* no action was taken.[7]

The first serious investigation of Cyril V. Briggs and the *Crusader* resulted from independent actions by MID and the Bureau in the summer of 1919. In his report, "Unrest among the Negroes," Maj. Walter H. Loving noted Briggs's activities twice, first concerning the Hamitic League and then in an appendix on "Radical Negro Publications." More familiar with the *Messenger* and *Crisis,* Loving deemed the *Crusader* radical but inferior in quality and circulation to the other two.[8] Before seeing this document, J. Edgar Hoover ordered the Bureau's first in-depth probe of Briggs's magazine at the prompting of the Post Office Department, which again forwarded correspondence from colonial authorities in British Guiana complaining of its incendiary influence.[9]

The white agent destined to learn as much about black militancy as any of his colleagues undertook this first serious Bureau investigation. Mortimer J. Davis, a member of the New York field office's radical squad, began by interviewing Robert A. Bowen at the Post Office's Translation Bureau who was already alarmed that the *Crusader* was "entirely radical," pro-black, Pan-African, and sympathetic to Bolshevism. Persistent examination by postal authorities found the magazine "quite bad" but not bad enough to justify its exclusion from the mails. This data was added to that being collected by undercover informant Arthur U. Craig and agents in other cities in the summer of 1919.[10]

A small advertisement on a back page of the *Crusader's* October issue introduced a subject that would alarm federal investigators for the next four years: "Mr. Cyril V. Briggs, Editor of the *Crusader,* announces the organization of the African Blood Brotherhood for African Liberation and Redemption. Membership by enlistment. No dues, fees or assessments. Those only need apply who are willing to go the limit!"[11] In contrast to Marcus Garvey's emphasis on mass participation, the ABB sought a select number who would totally dedicate themselves to freeing peoples of African descent from every form of bondage. "Enlistment" implied a military model and indeed the ABB was organized into "posts." Authorities did not know precisely what was meant by going to "the limit" but frightful scenarios were not difficult to conjure. As one MID analyst put it, "It seems to me that this means only one thing—organization for revolution." MID head Brig. Gen. Marlborough Churchill ordered his New York office to determine what threat the ABB posed.[12]

The reply a week later sought to give reassurance in the midst of doubt. An MID agent discovered "a very definite movement on foot between intelligent Negroes of the United States, the West Indies, and Africa itself" to liberate that continent "from European domination and exploitation." But his inquiry erred in assuming that "this movement has no more relation to our government than the present campaign in this country for the liberation of Ireland . . . it is aimed solely at the European governments."[13] Unlike Garvey's movement, which essentially abandoned a future for blacks in white-dominated America, the ABB simultaneously championed militant self-defense at home and the liberation of Africa.

Contrast

As MID officers tried to digest incendiary rhetoric in the *Crusader* and *Messenger* while also seeking meaning in the summer's riots, a consensus began to emerge: White revolutionaries were stirring the racial pot to a boil. "Agitation among the negroes in the United States leads directly back, through the IWW and the Russian Soviet Bureau, to the machinations of the German government." MID's fantasies took further flight. The German consul in Berne, Switzerland, was said to be leagued with New York bankers who were encouraging racial agitation and storing a cache of arms in Washington. Other reports claimed that black radicals were being trained to carry revolt to the South. Such hysterical rumors were given the legitimacy of "fact" when they were printed in MID's weekly intelligence summaries and distributed through the higher reaches of the federal bureaucracy.[14]

MID analysts believed in late 1919 that radical racial propaganda, chiefly emanating from the *Messenger* and *Crusader,* was forging alliances with other peoples of color to initiate "simultaneous revolutionary activities." This was one of the most troubling scenarios MID could imagine, for it had already greeted peace in Europe by preparing for the next war, either in east Asia or along the Mexican border. By early 1920 MID concluded that the "international phase of negro propaganda" was increasing rapidly. Fueling this fear was news of the formation of the ABB and receipt of a warning that Garvey's paramilitary African Legion was about to be smuggled into the West Indies and Africa.[15]

Despite such omens of worldwide danger, MID suffered sharp cutbacks in 1920 and found itself without sufficient manpower to conduct systematic domestic surveillance. Nor did it have a legal mandate for such intrusions into civilian affairs. But the Bureau of Investigation possessed both. Hoover had already mobilized the General Intelligence Division in mid-1919 to root out black radicalism. It had no hesitation in defining the *Crusader* as a noxious addition to the radical black press. The September issue alone was intolerably bold for claiming that blacks were mentally superior to whites because "the Negro has not had the opportunity to be mean, brutal, cruel and inhuman that the white have [sic] had for several centuries." Inclusion of Claude McKay's poem "If We Must Die," according to the Justice Department, was "calculated" to arouse racial hatred. But the Bureau's greatest difficulty lay in obtaining credible evidence for use in prosecutions. By 1920 the employment of black informants and agents was a necessity.

The first undercover operative to penetrate Briggs's world was William A. Bailey, who began to make contact with Harlem militants in January 1920. Calling on Briggs, Bailey offered to help increase the *Crusader's* circulation.[16] During February and March he volunteered in the magazine's office in Harlem, where Briggs revealed that the greatest number of mailed issues went to the South and the West Indies, with a handful to Africa. Bailey's tasks included distributing copies to newsstands and barbershops, planning prize contests for the best stories and poems and the most new subscriptions sold, and collecting delinquent payments. When out of the office he was supposed to sell subscriptions in Brooklyn, but he found that many blacks regarded the *Crusader* as "too much of a 'knocker'" for the good of the race. The Bureau could have profited from this information and worried less about the radical press. While African Americans applauded the bluntness and iconoclastic style of street-corner speakers and militant publications, they more often trusted mainstream leadership and organizations—the churches, politicians, and the NAACP—to represent their interests and carry their protests.[17]

Bailey had only to walk two doors beyond the *Crusader* office on Seventh Avenue to reach the building where Wilfred A. Domingo put out the short-lived *Emancipator.* Domingo also wrote for the *Messenger* (which was head-quartered in the next block) and since news agents were also asking for that magazine Bailey found it easy to cultivate Domingo. There was talk of forming a corporation to jointly publish all three radical magazines, with Bailey handling promotion. Although they mutually advertised the others and briefly ran a "combination offer" one-year subscription to all three for three dollars, a union of the publications was never consummated.[18]

By March, Bailey's twin goals were to penetrate Garvey's Universal Negro Improvement Association and the African Blood Brotherhood. Briggs was guarded in revealing details but confided that liberation of Africa would necessitate bloodshed, hence only members willing to pay that price were sought. Japan, he believed, was only awaiting an opportune moment to settle its grudges against the United States; if it interfered with attempts to liberate Africa, Japan would support the freedom struggle out of bitterness toward America and jealousy of British supremacy in the Pacific. In reporting this to the Bureau, Bailey added his own warning that "if any International disturbances occur among the Colored People you may be sure that [Briggs, Domingo, and other West Indian radicals] will be the instigators." Yet details of the ABB's plans proved elusive, despite Bailey's diligent efforts to learn Briggs's actual intentions.[19]

In late March, Bailey gathered welcome information for the Bureau concerning a breach in black nationalist circles. Briggs initially supported Garvey's African redemption program but now found himself denounced by the UNIA. In response, Briggs alleged that Garvey was the unscrupulous hireling of whites and offered a $500 reward to anyone who could prove the *Yarmouth* was actually owned by the Black Star Line. Henceforth the *Crusader* devoted much of its energy to attacking Garvey. In return Garvey declared war on all three radical monthlies, urging his followers to drive them out of Harlem.[20]

Bailey concluded his investigations on the last day of March 1920, but his departure did not leave the Bureau shorthanded, for the next day army veteran William E. Lucas began to serve as a "special confidential employee." What is shrouded in still-confidential FBI personnel files are the reasons for Bailey's termination and his relationship with Lucas while both volunteered for the *Crusader* in March. In February Briggs informed Bailey that his name would appear on the masthead the following month, a step which would benefit the magazine because Bailey was well liked in Brooklyn and "people would not doubt the importance and progressiveness of any organization" with which he was associated. But the March issue instead listed Lucas as the only new contributor. Apparently Briggs changed his mind about Bailey shortly before the issue went to press.[21]

How and why Lucas joined the *Crusader* staff in March, and whether he was already a Bureau infiltrator at that time, cannot yet be answered. The thirty-year-old Brooklyn native was a journalist and Briggs may have seen more profit in adding him than making Bailey a member of the staff, although both were undoubtedly unpaid for their services to the radical monthly. In the four months Lucas was listed on the masthead his name never appeared as a byline, although the majority of articles and editorials in any issue were unsigned. Whether Lucas offered his services to the Bureau or was recruited remains unknown.

Lucas's undercover roles were not easily negotiated. Comrades from his old regiment recognized him. While promoting the *Crusader* and *Emancipator* he simultaneously sought to join Garvey's paramilitary African Legion. And he had to convince his Bureau handlers he was not actually contributing to the radical magazines' success. Lucas had good news to report in April when *Crusader* sales plummeted. Still also handling the *Messenger,* he assured headquarters that "I am really trying to prevent too extensive a circulation altho I have to make some kind of a distribution of the copies that are given

[me] for circulation." And like Bailey, he found that many blacks preferred the more moderate *Crisis*.[22]

Undercover work took its toll on Lucas by mid-May: "I have been extremely cautious here of late, . . . Mr. Owens [sic] and Mr. Domingo are curious as to the reasons of my sudden interest in their various publications. They both urge me on encouragingly but other than Briggs I am sure that the others have not absolute confidence in my interest." And there were other frustrations:

> The *Crusader* is becoming very much of a burden upon my hands. The sales of the agents are very small and many of the subscribers are complaining of the radical writings and Socialistic tendency of the publication. I have to pay for a hundred copies each month, at five cents a copy, whether sold or not, to make a creditable showing. I fail to see where my connection with this publication gives me any advantage with my work as Briggs is very careful to leave nothing about the office that would give any information that he would not wish to get out.

At least Lucas was rid of responsibility for the *Emancipator*; it died in April after publishing only seven weekly issues.[23]

Lucas's undercover assignment drew to a close in early June. Sales of the *Crusader* continued to decline and he took responsibility for only fifty copies, even at the risk of alienating Briggs. This did not occur, however, for Briggs approved his membership in the ABB. Whether Lucas actually underwent the secret initiation ritual is doubtful as his federal employment ended on June 14, 1920.[24]

The Bureau learned much new data about the *Crusader* and *Emancipator* from Bailey and Lucas. The personalities, ideologies, and idiosyncracies of key black militants in Harlem were now far better understood. But the Justice Department was no closer to suppressing the publications; it knew, from the abortive efforts to prosecute the *Messenger,* that evidence beyond the editorial content of the magazines was necessary to sustain a court case. As for the ABB, the General Intelligence Division viewed its "propaganda" as especially pernicious, especially a full-page announcement in the *Crusader*'s February issue. Looking like a World War I recruitment poster, it labeled as "yellow" any "slacker"—female or male—who was not "willing to go the limit" and answer the call for "African Liberation and Redemption."[25] If there was hope for muzzling the *Crusader,* it lay in uncovering revolutionary activity on the part of the ABB.

It was not difficult to notice that the *Crusader* became more militant in the spring of 1920. Several themes alarmed the Bureau. Briggs announced that liberation of Africa from the "white race" would require bloodshed. Blacks were urged to put loyalty to race above national allegiance. Briggs's association with Domingo's *Emancipator* was also worrisome, given its advocacy of Bolshevism and attacks on capitalism, imperialism, and the Department of Justice. Briggs picked up Domingo's taunt:

> Naturally, The Crusader is on the list of "dangerous" and "impudent" publications. The Crusader and the Messenger in particular have riled Crackerdom. The editors of The Crusader would not have it otherwise. To have been listed as "well behaved" in the eyes of Crackerdom would have forced us to cease publication and commit suicide since such a misfortune would have convinced us that there was something radically wrong with our radicalism and attitude on the race question. We thank God that we are among those who have been "flayed" by the crackerized Department of Justice.[26]

By mid-1920 the Bureau assessed the *Crusader's* immediate impact with some relief but its long-range influence with considerable apprehension. Circulation had dropped, and New York agents were happily convinced that the ABB had only about fifteen true believers. Yet the character and purposes of the organization were deeply disconcerting, hidden behind secret rituals, passwords, signs, and oaths. Its "Supreme Council," also known as the "War College of Five," encouraged members to link with other oppressed peoples and coordinate blows against "tyranny," study modern chemistry and warfare, and adopt a "race first" attitude. Children were to be protected from "alien education in the white dominated schools" and instructed instead in racial pride and history.[27]

For twelve months following July 1920, the Bureau lacked an infiltrator in the *Crusader* and the ABB. Watch was maintained by the New York field office, however, which condemned the contents of nearly every issue. The December number was more offensive than any in the previous half year, charging America with having "raped" Haiti and St. Domingo, insulted Japan, and exploited Mexico. Believing that the United States would provoke a new war, Briggs wrote that blacks had a duty

> NOT TO FIGHT AGAINST JAPAN OR MEXICO, BUT RATHER TO FILL THE PRISONS AND DUNGEONS OF THE WHITE MAN (OR TO FACE HIS FIRING SQUADS) THAN TO SHOULDER ARMS AGAINST OTHER MEM-BERS OF THE DARKER RACES. The Negro who fights against either Japan or Mexico is fighting for the *white man* against himself, for the *white race* against the darker races and for the perpetuation of *white domination of the colored races,* with its vicious practices of *lynching, jim-crowism, segregation and other forms of oppression.*

Reaction to this editorial was so strong that Hoover sent a copy of the "radical Negro magazine" to the State Department so it could be apprised of the danger.[28]

Relative racial calm was shattered on May 31, 1921, when a bloody race riot erupted in Tulsa following erroneous rumors that a young black man had attacked a white female elevator operator. At nightfall a mob of armed whites, inflamed by provocative press reports, besieged the jail. Determined to prevent a lynching, a smaller number of armed blacks arrived to offer their services to the sheriff. A melee ensued, which precipitated the riot. Whites looted and burned numerous black businesses and over a thousand homes. Hardware stores and pawnshops were ransacked for weapons. Dozens of both races were killed and wounded in hand-to-hand combat, the white death toll considerably higher than publicly admitted. Local authorities blamed the African Blood Brotherhood, which had a post in Tulsa, for fomenting the riot, although recent research has dismissed that claim and instead shown that whites instigated the violence. But accusations against the ABB were repeated nationwide in the white press.[29]

Briggs issued a statement on June 4 denying that ABB members "were in any way the aggressors" but adding that it was "interested in having negroes organized for self-defense against wanton attack." Taking advantage of national news coverage Briggs inflated the ABB's size to 150 posts with 50,000 members and applauded the riot for showing whites that blacks would fight to the death to defend their rights. When the *New York Times* questioned why the ABB did not seek legal redress, Briggs replied that blacks had no confidence in the white-ruled justice system. His press statement was artfully constructed to frighten whites into granting justice as the price of racial peace, and to convince blacks of the legitimacy of militant defense of their rights, a rhetorical combination employed by Malcolm X four decades later:

> Haven't negroes the right to defend their lives and property when these are menaced, or is this an exclusive prerogative of the white man? And were not the negroes who gathered to defend the Tulsa jail against attack by a white mob, and to defend a prisoner confined in that jail against the murderous intents of white hoodlums out for a lynching bee—were not these negroes acting in behalf of "law and order," and in defense of the prisoner's Constitutional right to a legal trial by his peers and with due process of law?

Briggs's logic was unassailable, although hardly persuasive to whites who feared that the ABB was planning a revolution.[30]

With the ABB accused of fomenting the Tulsa riot, infiltration was again a necessity. Fortunately for the Bureau, it already had an experienced undercover man in New York City, Herbert S. Boulin. His Jamaican nativity had gained him entrée to Garvey's UNIA, and now it also facilitated his penetration of the ABB in mid-1921.

Boulin's familiarity with the ABB was slight, but he was already acquainted with both Briggs and Domingo, who was the organization's spokesman since Briggs had a speech impediment and was not an effective orator. Boulin first reported that the ABB was capitalizing on its notoriety, organizing mass meetings in several cities to explain its purposes and reveal the facts about the Tulsa attack. Richard B. Moore was the featured speaker at one such gathering in New York and, in Boulin's words, "I have never heard anyone who spoke so defiantly and disrespectfully of the U.S.A. and the flag." Moore praised the ABB for teaching "self defence by negroes and preparation to fight back" at lynchers and rioters. Boulin concluded that he was "the most pronounced Communist" and had become "the most outspoken, daring and radical among all the other negro 'Reds' in Harlem." No wonder, then, that Bureau agents in New York kept close tabs on Moore and meticulously recorded his views.[31]

The Tulsa riot was a godsend to the ABB; contributions soared as it paraded refugees from Tulsa before sympathetic audiences. Street meetings through the summer attracted large numbers from among the thousands of unemployed persons who crowded Harlem's thoroughfares, often blocking traffic to enjoy the free "entertainment." One such protest gathering drew several hundred people, including Boulin and a New York Times reporter. According to the latter, Domingo justified retaliation: "Our aim is to allow those who attack us to choose the weapons. If it be guns, we will reply with guns. If the attack is made through the white press, the negro press will defend us." Having said that, Domingo and other orators were careful to deny that the ABB caused the riot in Tulsa.[32]

Simultaneous with the Justice Department's revived interest in the ABB was its renewed conviction that white socialists and communists bankrolled black militancy. This dovetailed with the government's longstanding belief that blacks were particularly susceptible to manipulation by outsiders and that agitators of both races were exploiting racial grievances in order to advance the cause of Bolshevism. As he probed deeper into the ABB, Boulin found hearsay evidence that seemed to prove such suspicions. One of Boulin's informants was Edgar M. Grey, a former Garveyite who possessed a talent for walking both sides of an ideological street. In mid-1921 Grey linked up with Hubert H. Harrison's Liberty League, which also sought to organize blacks for self-defense against the expected next wave of race riots. Grey reported that he and Harrison had been invited to supper at the Greenwich Village residence of Rose Pastor Stokes, one of the founding members of the American

Communist Party and the proletarian wife of millionaire philanthropist J. Phelps-Stokes. Also attending were Domingo, Briggs, and Claude McKay.

The purpose of the dinner was straightforward, as Grey told Boulin. Would Harrison's Liberty League help spread communism among blacks? Mrs. Stokes promised plenty of "Russian gold" to any black movement aiding the communist cause. The *Crusader* was already receiving a subsidy, according to Grey, who added that the ABB intended to use every riot as a pretext to start retaliatory killing of whites in the hopes that widespread racial strife would bring on an American Bolshevik revolution. Harrison refused to accept Mrs. Stokes's offer, however, preferring to keep the Liberty League all-black and focused exclusively on the fight for African American rights. As for "Russian gold," the Comintern (the international arm of the Russian communist movement) was in fact subsidizing its infant party in the United States with large quantities of jewels, gold, and silver that would be converted to dollars.[33]

Realizing the importance of this information, Boulin sought confirmation of the details and urged Grey to apply for membership in the ABB. Finding two members to vouch for him, Grey was initiated by Moore, Domingo, and Briggs. Again relying on Grey's information, Boulin excitedly reported that the ABB "has the object of killing white people and to foment and start a massacre of white people whenever there is the slightest sign of race friction." Pictures of Lenin and Trotsky in its meeting room demonstrated the ABB's support for worldwide revolution. The fact that most of its members were not American citizens made matters more ominous, Boulin concluding that "this organization is becoming and will become a serious menace to society."[34]

Mrs. Stokes's offer convinced the Bureau that the ABB was sponsored by the Communist Party. According to New York agents, she was "probably a designated emissary of the Communists to get the cooperation and affiliation of various negro organizations." The Bureau was indeed on the right track. Government repression had shattered much of the Left and forced its declining membership underground. Revival of communism required both open organization and covert infiltration of unions, clubs, and other groups. Stokes represented the wing of the Communist Party that promoted the aboveground Workers Party of America and was assigned by the Comintern to pioneer the recruitment of blacks.[35]

If Boulin's assessment of the ABB's potential was worrisome, news that it was attempting to infiltrate the UNIA was equally disquieting, given that Garvey had hundreds of thousands of followers throughout the black Diaspora. Briggs, Domingo, and the ABB tried to spread their own gospel among the thousands who attended the second annual UNIA convention in August 1921. Four ABB delegates attended and great quantities of the ABB's *Negro Congress Bulletin* were distributed to UNIA members. Garvey, although persuaded to allow Rose Pastor Stokes to address the gathering, disassociated himself from her ideology, having neither love for communism nor faith in any interracial movement, whatever its objectives.[36] Boulin was not the Bureau's only observer at the convention; its first black agent, James Wormley Jones, also attended undercover.

Boulin relied on Grey for much of his information on the ABB and the Liberty League. If only half of what he repeated was accurate, Harlem's radical politics were byzantine. Lifelong friends Grey and Harrison hoped the Liberty League would supplant the UNIA, but Garvey monopolized the attention (and financial contributions) of Harlem, much to his rivals' envy. Garvey and Grey had fallen out years before and engaged in a libel suit, with the latter allegedly still eager to "get even" in 1921. And Harrison, a longtime black nationalist, was supposedly miffed at not being offered a high position in the UNIA. Meanwhile, when the ABB condemned Harrison's refusal to accept Mrs. Stokes's offer, the mercurial Grey joined that organization to try to get even with Domingo.[37]

Boulin never had the chance to follow these maneuvers because the Bureau cut him loose at the end of August. But one of his last reports summarized the dangers he believed the black radicals posed:

> Hubert Harrison is a most dangerous and disturbing faction [sic] among the thousands of idle negroes who walk the streets of Harlem, listening to his militant talk. What makes conditions worse is the rapid growth of the African Blood Brotherhood which tells the negroes that they are the defensive and militant negro organization to fight back at race riots, the doctrine of which is an eye for an [eye] and a tooth for a tooth—kill when you are being killed, etc.[38]

Boulin was an artful double informant, successfully penetrating the communist movement in Harlem at the same time as he infiltrated Garvey's UNIA. Starting with Domingo he ingratiated himself into the radical coterie which met at Martin Luther Campbell's tailor shop and propagandized the public at its weekly Peoples Educational Forum. At the same time he was a sympathetic ear as Garvey unburdened himself concerning his black opponents, particularly Grey. Boulin's contribution to the Bureau was not in developing evidence for prosecutions but in monitoring the heartbeats of the communist and nationalist movements. Working exclusively undercover, he served his masters well but did not, as might have been expected, become an *agent provocateur.*

Bureau personnel often accepted uncritically the "evidence" they or their informants gathered, taking at face value the ABB's announcement that "code experts in its employ are now at work on documents which contain information showing who 'fomented and directed the Tulsa riots.'" And rumors that the ABB was reorganizing to renew attacks on whites stirred agents in Oklahoma in June. Tulsa police reported such tales but had no definite information or even the names of would-be instigators. An attack on whites was supposed to start during a fireworks show on July 3. The police panicked, mobilizing machine guns, volunteer "minute-men," the state guard, and even airplanes, to block all roads into the city. No plot was discovered, nor were ABB literature or organizers. Nonetheless the Bureau instructed local officials to remain vigilant, collect examples of any radical publications, and seek out informants. Nothing came of these efforts.[39]

The New York field office's reading of the July *Crusader* shows how white agents' own racial views often colored their conclusions. They condemned the magazine for being proud of accusations that the ABB started the Tulsa riot and for lionizing those who died fighting back against white aggressors. In fact the magazine's contents were somewhat different. The lead article denounced the "lie" that the ABB started the Tulsa riot. Further, "whether we directed Negroes in their fight in self-defense [which] is certainly no crime in Negro eyes, . . . we neither deny it nor affirm it." Briggs charged state officials with falsely accusing the ABB so as to punish it for teaching "organization and tactics which enabled the attacked Negroes to defend themselves so effectively and eliminate the easy massacre of leaderless Negroes."[40]

It was inevitable that federal intelligence agencies would continue to see the *Crusader* and the ABB as serious threats: their militant rhetoric was as frightening and unacceptable in 1921 as anything in 1919. And their capacity for direct attacks against the racial status quo, or for infiltration of other black groups, seemed even greater. Yet by the end of 1920 the Red Scare was waning. Attorney General A. Mitchell Palmer, the drum major in the anti-radical crusade, had been discredited when predictions of more anarchist attacks had proven groundless. Democrats were repudiated at the polls. The new Harding administration heralded a return to "normalcy." Among the changes was a further shrinking in the number of Bureau agents and a new director, the famed detective William J. Burns. The Bureau's focus had narrowed considerably from the Red Summer of 1919, when every outspoken black publication, organization, meeting, and leader was suspect. Now, in mid-1921, New York agents listed only three "ultra-radical" groups: the African Blood Brotherhood; Marcus Garvey's Universal Negro Improvement Association; and A. Philip Randolph and Chandler Owen's Friends of Negro Freedom. And only two "ultra-radical" black periodicals remained, the *Crusader* and the *Messenger*.[41]

Hoover and the Bureau defined the threat posed by the ABB in unmistakable terms. It was allegedly a branch of the Communist Party. Briggs was hard at work spreading poison "amongst the more ignorant members of his race and . . . taking full advantage of the crowds" attending Garvey's convention to circulate his *Negro Congress Bulletin* filled with "radical and seditious articles." Agents accepted Briggs's claims that the ABB was recruiting many new members out of the UNIA, although in fact no significant number transferred their allegiance. Convinced that the *Crusader* was "financed by the Communist Party," agents described Briggs as one of Rose Pastor Stokes's "able assistants in this work." The Party unquestionably funded the *Negro Congress Bulletin,* hoping to woo Garveyites away from racial nationalism to class-conscious radicalism. Both of Briggs's publications embraced Russia as the only world power sympathetic to peoples of African descent. Blacks and Russians were natural allies because they shared a common enemy: capitalism. So to the Bureau, the ABB was the worst of the black radical groups because it allegedly excelled in inciting racial hatred and promoting Bolshevism.[42]

The Military Intelligence Division also responded to the revitalized ABB and *Crusader* in mid-1921, and likewise concluded, on the basis of Justice Department reports, that the ABB was a branch of the Communist Party, financed through Stokes and McKay, and gaining many converts since the UNIA convention.[43] Only the Bureau, however, was capable of investigating thoroughly the black communist movement. In the wake of the Tulsa riot it quickly resumed infiltration of the ABB, assigning two undercover operatives in New York to part-time surveillance. White informants working on communist cases also reported on the ABB. "Special confidential employees" signed reports only with their code designations, and it has not been possible to discover the identities of P-137 and P-141, although internal evidence indicates they were white. The former tailed Rose Pastor Stokes while P-141 investigated Sinn Fein activities and was present at the headquarters of the Irish American Labor League when Briggs came to have some materials printed. Informants' conversations with Briggs confirmed what the Bureau had long believed, that four of the ABB's seven-member national council were also members of the Communist Party.[44]

The most successful infiltrator into the ABB, more effective even than Boulin, was James Wormley Jones, the first black agent in the Bureau of Investigation. He initially penetrated Garvey's UNIA in 1920, and a year later became a double agent when he also gained entrée to the rival ABB. Both assignments required that he hide his Bureau identity and work undercover.

The Bureau's greatest worry by mid-1921 was the ABB's announced intention to create "paramilitary units to safeguard the [black] community."[45] Capitalizing on his own military background, Jones easily gained ABB mem-

bership and established a "confidential friendship" with Briggs. Tapping
Jones's knowledge of weapons, Briggs revealed his desire to organize the ABB
into squads, platoons, and companies, although other nomenclature would
be used to disguise its military character. Jones's opinion was sought on
various weapons Briggs had seen in a catalogue. When Briggs deposed the
commander of the New York post he offered the position to Jones, although
evidence suggests that he never accepted. Jones also learned that the communists, particularly Stokes, were encouraging Briggs's desire to travel to Moscow. He spoke admiringly of Soviet Russia, leading Jones to conclude that the
ABB leader was a "radical of the worst sort."[46]

When Garvey rebuffed the ABB's attempts to form an alliance, Briggs
opened a campaign of vilification against the UNIA leader. By then aware that
Jones was a UNIA member, he welcomed any intelligence from within the
Garvey camp. At first Jones was hesitant: he had no qualms about harming
Garvey but found Briggs equally repugnant. Soon, however, he began to dole
out inside information from the UNIA in such a way that his position there
would not be compromised. At the same time Briggs stepped up attacks on
Garvey in the *Crusader.* Like Bailey and Lucas before him, Jones assisted in the
magazine's distribution.

Jones reported directly to Washington and sought advice regarding Briggs's
request for the names of UNIA leaders to whom he could send copies of the
Crusader which smeared Garvey. He agonized over the matter, but eventually
furnished the prized address list. Briggs did not underestimate Jones's value
and worried that Garvey might learn of his ABB membership, so Jones could
depend upon Briggs to protect his anonymity. Unbeknownst to Briggs, of
course, Jones sought proof of his links to communists, believing that, as in the
case of Garvey, a felony conviction could provide the mechanism for deporting the ABB's founder. Afraid of jeopardizing his own position, however, he
urged the Bureau to assign someone else to shadow Briggs's daily movements.
Boulin was just being discharged but the Bureau immediately recruited
another black informant, P-134, who maintained on-and-off surveillance for
the next eight months.[47]

The Briggs-Garvey feud heated up still more in October 1921, when the
Negro World accused Briggs of being a white man posing as a "Negro for
convenience."[48] Jones manipulated Briggs's hurt pride, encouraging him to
sue Garvey for libel. When the case came to trial later in the month Jones had
to avoid Briggs so as to keep Garvey from suspecting their association. Despite
both Jones's and Briggs's awareness of the need for secrecy, Jones was now a
"colonel" in the ABB and still under pressure to become New York post
commander. He understandably feared the possibility of exposure through

such a leadership role. Jones believed the suit against Garvey was a golden opportunity to discredit him and urged the Bureau to press the district attorney to prosecute Garvey zealously. Bureau director Burns agreed and Hoover ordered the New York field office to apply pressure.[49] Whether it was effective is unknown, although Garvey was found at fault and ordered to print a retraction in the *Negro World*. This setback hardly had the desired effect, however; Garvey's followers rallied all the more loyally whenever he was beleaguered by the justice system.

Garvey then turned the tables on Briggs, suing him for libelous statements in the October *Crusader* implying that Garvey had abandoned his wife and, years ago, raped a white girl in London. Jones passed Garvey's trial strategy along to Briggs's attorney. To his relief, Jones was not called to testify on Garvey's behalf. Briggs lost the case, convinced that Garvey had "fixed" things with the judge.[50]

Jones played the provocateur's role, encouraging those who held grudges against Garvey or had not been paid promised salaries to abet Briggs. At the same time Jones fed Garvey's fears of internal betrayal. One such defector was Cyril Crichlow, who wrote articles for the *Crusader* exposing the alleged foolhardiness of Garvey's African schemes. Jones took credit for linking Crichlow with Briggs, exulting that "you have got to beat this fellow at his own game, propaganda." Some of Crichlow's own critical reports on Liberia remained in UNIA files and Jones twice searched for them in Garvey's office. He may also have been the one who suggested that Crichlow send the UNIA's Liberia plans to the State Department.[51]

Other disillusioned Garveyites also cooperated with the ABB camp. Briggs persuaded Bishop George Alexander McGuire, the UNIA's former chaplain general, to take out ABB membership, and issued a press release for the occasion. Rev. J. D. Gordon, former assistant president general of the UNIA, and Black Star Line officer Capt. Joshua Cockburn joined Crichlow and McGuire in speaking at anti-Garvey meetings arranged by Briggs. This warfare reached a peak in January 1922, when Briggs alerted New York authorities that the *Negro World* had violated the law by printing advertisements for a cure for venereal disease. As circulation manager of the paper Jones was also named in the complaint.[52]

Meanwhile Jones vainly searched for direct links between Briggs and the communist movement. The militant editor was wary of a "mole" and was often secretive when queried, but he apparently trusted Jones about as much as he did anyone. Briggs claimed he sent 400 free copies of the *Crusader* to Africa and the West Indies, but Jones was unable to discover who might have paid such sizeable postage costs. The Bureau also learned that Briggs attended the convention of the Workers Party, but this data was useless in trying to suppress the magazine or the ABB. Jones did find where Briggs deposited his money, but the *Crusader's* account never exceeded $100, and no large deposits were recorded which might indicate an outside subsidy. A month later evidence of communist funding was finally found through an investigation of the American Federated Russian Relief Committee, a Party front organization; in rifling its files, a Bureau agent found a canceled check for $250 to the *Crusader.* This was the only concrete evidence of outside support the Bureau ever found, but there was nothing illegal about the contribution.[53]

During Jones's penetration of the ABB the Bureau also used an undercover informant from August 1921 to April 1922. No evidence exists to suggest the identity of P-134, although the familiarity he established with Claude McKay and the many hours he spent on stakeout in Harlem suggest he was black. He sought evidence of Briggs's communist connections during the period when Briggs was attempting to forge an ABB-UNIA alliance while simultaneously drawing close to Mrs. Stokes and her communist circle. McKay confided he was a party member and close friend of Stokes, and he also confessed to using narcotics. Visiting McKay's room, P-134 was given communist and ABB literature and learned that the poet hosted communist meetings several days a week. Some months later P-134 attended one of his gatherings to hear about Gandhi's Hindu liberation movement.

The undercover informant also spent entire days tailing Briggs and his contacts, including McKay. During the summer when windows were open he was sometimes able to overhear Briggs's indoor conversations. P-134 discovered that Briggs was popular and well known in Harlem and a frequenter of Campbell's Tailor Shop, already known to the Bureau as a rendezvous for radicals. On other days he staked out a location where Briggs never appeared, or spent ten or twelve hours observing nothing more than Briggs's errands. And he was unable to corroborate rumors that the ABB furnished guns to blacks in Tulsa. For the many hours he waited and watched in Harlem, P-134 uncovered no evidence on which to prosecute Briggs or suppress the *Crusader.*[54]

Bureau coverage of Briggs and the ABB was coordinated directly from Washington in the fall of 1921. Director Burns took a personal interest in the case and ordered "close surveillance" by P-134 to ascertain Briggs's radical associations.[55] Jones was also supervised from headquarters, periodically taking the train to Washington to confer with J. Edgar Hoover's staff. Upon learning of Briggs's efforts to involve the Post Office against Marcus Garvey, Burns ordered New York agents to enlist Briggs's cooperation; he agreed to supply witnesses who received stock solicitations featuring a ship not yet owned by the Black Star Line. Briggs also tried to persuade Rev. McGuire and Crichlow to talk to federal agents, but neither was willing. Briggs's coopera-tion with federal authorities finally became public knowledge in January 1922 after a *New York World* article claimed that the *Crusader* had first spurred the government to investigate Garvey.[56]

Two could play the same game. Even though he knew the Justice Depart-ment was after him, Garvey was not averse to using it to attack his own enemies. One of his attorneys, William C. Matthews, showed Hoover a letter from Briggs inviting Garvey to join the ABB. Hoover agreed with Matthews that language in the letter implied the ABB was responsible for the Tulsa riot. Matthews promised to supply any other information about Briggs's "perni-cious activities."[57] Meanwhile, agents in New York continued to monitor the bitter feud, which peaked in December when UNIA members broke up a large ABB meeting; police reserves had to be summoned to restore order. Unde-terred, the ABB scheduled a repeat meeting for Christmas day! Bureau agents believed Briggs was orchestrating attacks on Garvey primarily to promote the ABB and gain adherents for its communist agenda.[58]

Despite the Garvey-Briggs conflict, the Bureau's interest waned when the *Crusader* expired and the ABB became moribund in 1922. Jones's final report, dated April 12, noted that the magazine, plagued by bad checks from sales agents, had ceased publication. Most ABB members were out of work and unable to pay dues. Historian Robert A. Hill believes that Briggs came to regard the monthly *Crusader* as an imperfect platform for the anti-Garvey movement and concluded that the *Negro World* could only be challenged by an equally vibrant weekly. Briggs laid plans for a publication to be named "The Liberator," but this dream was not fulfilled until 1929. His wife, Bertha Briggs, offered yet another explanation for the *Crusader's* demise: government pres-sure.[59]

To the Bureau, the causes were less important than the fact that the anti-Garvey movement, in which Briggs was prominent, still bore watching. This task fell next to Andrew M. Battle, a forty-five-year-old Tuskegee-educated "special employee" who was a former investigator for the William J. Burns National Detective Agency. Battle had hoped to be hired as a Bureau agent but was turned down. As an undercover operative, he earned $5 per diem, one dollar less than the starting salary for agents. Beginning in May 1922, he served the Bureau for a little over a year.[60]

Battle cultivated a number of Garvey's opponents, including Richard B. Moore, Martin Luther Campbell, Rev. Ethelred E. Brown, and Clarence Carpenter, all friends of Briggs and part of the Harlem communist coterie. Carpenter advocated "overthrowing the Government" and urged Battle to join the Socialist Party. In July when Garvey conferred with the "imperial kleagle" of the Ku Klux Klan, Moore exulted that "the only thing left is for Garvey to sell out his organization to the Klan," which would bring "the entire colored race over" to the communist camp. In fact, Battle learned that ABB meetings were temporarily suspended for fear of mayhem by Garvey's ardent supporters.[61]

From mid-1922 through the spring of 1923 the Bureau of Investigation nearly lost interest in the ABB, Briggs, and other black communists. Battle found little of significance to report. Black radicalism seemed to have almost disappeared. When Hoover rebuked the New York field office for failing to send radical publications to Washington on a regular basis, Special Agent in Charge Edward J. Brennan replied that the *Messenger* was only occasionally radical, the *Crisis* was out of that category altogether, and the *Crusader* had ceased publication.[62]

Federal interest in the ABB experienced one final dramatic renewal in the summer and fall of 1923 when nationwide fears of communism were revived following a raid on a secret Party convention in rural Michigan. As the Bureau redoubled its efforts, at least half a dozen black informants and several white informants, plus both black and white agents, kept Briggs under more intense scrutiny than ever before. The possibility that Moscow might use blacks to subvert American government, institutions, and folkways was a nightmare scenario. Just as during World War I, when it was widely alleged that blacks were easily led into disloyalty, now those same gullible blacks were being manipulated by revolutionaries bent on subverting the nation. Once more, the status quo seemed gravely endangered.

Surveillance of Briggs resumed in August and lasted into December 1923, spearheaded by Earl E. Titus, the fourth of only five black agents employed by the Bureau in the first half of the century. Hired in 1922 at the age of fifty-five, he possessed a high school education and five years' experience on the Indianapolis police force in the early 1900s; thereafter he made his living as a barber. From surviving records it appears he worked exclusively undercover when assigned to black radical cases, including that of Garvey as well as Briggs. Under the jurisdiction of the Bureau's field office in downtown New York, he was supervised by Special Agent in Charge Charles J. Scully and black agent James E. Amos.[63]

The Bureau's fears were also stimulated by the British embassy in Washington, which notified the State Department that ABB member Otto Huiswoud had made contact with Canadian communists to seek their help in breaking down blacks' traditional distrust of labor unions. State wrote Burns that "Negro revolutionists" were cooperating with white communists "by means of the most innocent yet most effective Communist machinery on the North

American continent, the Trade Union Educational League," which was a propaganda arm of the (communist) Workers Party.[64]

Titus easily gained Briggs's confidence the day they met in August 1923, and he began filing almost daily summaries on the activities of Briggs and his associates. Report after report described visits to residences where ABB meetings were held, including Briggs's home and the apartment of ABB and communist activist Grace Campbell, a New York social worker, shelter supervisor, and parole officer. As a member of the *Messenger* circle, she had been a Socialist candidate for the state assembly in 1920, had helped Randolph and Owen found the Friends of Negro Freedom, and spoke frequently on women's issues.[65]

The black agent attended his initial ABB meeting his first night on the job, finding only twelve members present, including Briggs and Huiswoud. He would note more than once that Post Menelek, as the Harlem chapter of the ABB was known, was hardly a beehive of activity when Briggs was absent.[66] Within two weeks Titus was inducted into membership and was soon part of the inner circle of Post Menelek. At the urging of his Bureau supervisors downtown, he paid daily visits to the residences of Briggs and Miss Campbell. Like previous infiltrators he helped distribute ABB publications, particularly the Crusader News Service bulletin, which was mailed twice a week to more than 100 black newspapers. Titus also discovered that Briggs and Huiswoud were trying to persuade the Workers Party to grant the ABB a $100 monthly subsidy, but they found the white communists more interested in organizing the proletariat of their own race. Huiswoud, meanwhile, centered his efforts on establishing an ABB alliance with the Farmer-Labor Party in Chicago.[67]

By mid-September, with Titus volunteering daily to help put out ABB and Crusader News Service mailings, Briggs revealed more about the organization's health. While claiming a membership of 8,722 he admitted that only about 3,000 were "active" and paid up. Approximately 2,000 of the larger total were women. Briggs blamed sparse attendance at meetings on members' summer vacations, the lack of a large facility, and confusion by many people outside New York between the ABB and Garvey's UNIA. At the mid-month ABB meeting Titus and thirty-eight other members heard Grace Campbell announce an invitation to the Workers Party convention. Huiswoud was chosen as delegate, and before long he invited Titus to attend Party meetings too. While the Workers Party did not offer financial assistance the communists did help the Crusader News Service by printing its bulletins at the headquarters of the Trade Union Education League, Titus adding his labor.[68]

The ABB was run by a Supreme Council composed of Briggs, Huiswoud, Domingo, Moore, Grace Campbell, William H. Jones, and Theodore and Ben Burrell. Meetings, to which Titus was not privy, were usually held at the residences of Briggs or Campbell. Briggs confided that he was the mainstay of the organization. Domingo was director of publicity and propaganda and a chief spokesman. General membership meetings were still hard to convene because of the difficulty in renting a suitable hall. Economies in the Crusader News Service were effected, however, when Briggs secured a mimeograph machine.[69]

Titus's daily reports only infrequently recorded Briggs's political views, which put the Bureau at a handicap: With the *Crusader* no longer published, there was no visible barometer with which to chart his ideological emphases. The informant did note, however, Briggs's persistent faith that Bolshevism would overrun Germany, with the rest of Europe then falling to communism. When this happened, should the darker races attempt to right the wrongs done them by Caucasians, Japan would feel free to join the fight against white hegemony.[70]

Most of Briggs's efforts, however, were devoted to domestic issues. On October 19, 1923, informed that he would travel to Washington, New York agents urged colleagues in the capital to cover the man they still deemed one of the most important racial propagandists and communists. Lest they lose him, agents were cautioned that he was a "fast walker." Despite the warning, Briggs eluded his trackers, even with a black undercover informant contacting newspapers and organizations to learn his whereabouts. The Washington office did not believe the ABB had a significant foothold in the city but nonetheless assigned black agent Arthur Lowell Brent to investigate further. He found that Briggs met with Howard University dean Kelly Miller, a well-known moderate leader of the pre–World War I generation. Endeavoring to learn more about the local ABB post, Brent also wrote to Briggs seeking membership information. On returning to New York Briggs told Titus he represented the ABB in planning a black "United Front Conference," which evolved into the "Negro Sanhedrin" in early 1924, a short-lived effort to unite the leadership of all black organizations. Although Miller was a key planner, he was less than forthright in telling Brent his meeting with Briggs was merely a "social call."[71]

In addition to the close relationships with Briggs, Titus also gained the confidence of Grace Campbell, and it was through them that he secured information on Claude McKay, who wrote Campbell from Russia stressing Moscow's interest in American blacks and hope that they would "show some spirit" in getting organized. Party officials obviously wished African Americans had a communist leader possessing the charisma of Marcus Garvey. Although Campbell shared McKay's letter with Titus she was unwilling to reveal his address. Two weeks later Briggs also received a letter from McKay, sent from Germany.[72]

Briggs planned a vigorous ABB membership drive in the fall of 1923, with Titus helping him mail 12,000 announcements, including to the West Indies, Europe, and Africa. Every post got at least ten copies to use in personal evangelism. Others were to be sent to labor unions affiliated with the Workers Party, provided Huiswoud could get their names and addresses. Prospects for a strong ABB post in Philadelphia seemed particularly good following a recruiting trip by Huiswoud and Domingo. The latter related that Huiswoud was a dynamic speaker and an effective organizer, having signed up 300 new members and persuaded them to protest against poor housing.[73]

Titus learned such details easily because, by mid-November, he was part of the ABB's inner leadership, even chairing an executive committee meeting in Huiswoud's absence. That gathering wrestled with the perennial difficulty of securing facilities. The ABB used black churches in other cities but since police in New York always attended meetings and threatened arrests, churches were unwilling to open their doors to the radical organization. Even Post Menelek now had to meet at Grace Campbell's residence.[74]

The relationship between the ABB and the communists was clarified when Miss Campbell told Titus that she and Briggs were still laboring diligently for the Workers Party even though his $50 weekly stipend had ended. Titus interpreted this as a weekly salary, but if that high figure was indeed accurate, it had most probably been a subsidy for the ABB or the Crusader News Service. Despite the drop in income Briggs still counted on party cooperation in renting office space for the ABB. Other members also promoted the Workers Party; a door-to-door salesman told Titus he left ABB and Party literature at every call.[75]

Titus's final week infiltrating the ABB began with a meeting of Post Menelek. A letter from an organizer in Montgomery, West Virginia, reported sixty-two new members in the past six weeks. Huiswoud's recruiting effort in New Jersey was promising. Good relations with the Workers Party had been established, especially since all members of the ABB Supreme Council were also Party members and the ABB had agreed to distribute Party literature. Its Harlem branch seemed willing to rent an office and meeting room jointly with the ABB. The future looked bright to Briggs and his associates at Thanksgiving 1923.[76]

On November 30, 1923, agent Earl E. Titus was summoned to the Bureau office downtown to confer with Bureau director Burns. Two days later he was ordered to report to Washington.[77] Why he was pulled from the ABB case at a time when evidence of its alliance with the communist Workers Party was conclusive cannot be determined from available records. But it clearly was not for lack of diligence or aptitude in infiltrating the ABB. During his nearly four months of daily interaction with Briggs and Campbell he had given the Bureau many leads for further investigation or even prosecution. For example, when Titus learned of Briggs's plan for a sickness and death fund, agents downtown conferred with the state superintendent of insurance to determine if Briggs's scheme was fraudulent. The Bureau gained much new information as a result of his labors.[78]

White agents in the Bureau's New York field office took Titus's reports seriously, particularly information on the communist loyalties of Supreme Council members and the ABB's alliance with the Workers Party. Naively accepting Briggs's highly inflated figure of nearly 9,000 Post Menelek members, agents were especially concerned that this one chapter supposedly included 3,000 "quick action" members. They were also struck by Briggs's intention to organize a "Tiger Scouts" children's auxiliary. And although Titus provided the downtown office with a Crusader News Service bulletin highlighting Leon Trotsky's plea for interracial revolutionary class consciousness, white agents persisted in viewing Briggs as "anti-white."[79]

Titus was reassigned to the Chicago office at the end of 1923. Infiltrating the ABB was not his major assignment, although in working undercover he did gain the confidence of local leader Edward L. Doty. The Chicago post had only about twenty-five members, due in part to an organizational split a year before. Gatherings were held in conjunction with the Workers Party, confirming the alliance between the two. In January 1924, Titus found only 13 people attending an ABB meeting, and by the end of March the post was inactive even though Huiswoud had moved to Chicago.[80]

The abrupt end of Titus's surveillance of Briggs and the ABB reflects several phenomena. The Bureau was still much interested in their operations, but the ABB had for all practical purposes been absorbed into the Workers Party during the fall of 1923 and would be dissolved the next year.[81] Agents continued to monitor the activities of black communists, but the ABB was no longer the focus. Despite Briggs's last-ditch mailing, the ABB gained few new recruits. His claims of several thousand ready and willing ABB members in New York notwithstanding, only a few dozen showed up for meetings. Even given the presence of Huiswoud in Chicago, by early 1924 no viable post existed there. The Bureau's case file on the ABB ended in 1924. Although black communist activities would be continually watched by the Bureau for years to come, a chapter in the history of federal attempts to suppress black radical movements and civil rights activism had closed.

EIGHT

❦

"ULTRA RADICAL NEGRO BOLSHEVIKI"

The Pursuit of Black Wobblies

No group of radicals excited more alarm during World War I than the "Wobblies," the Industrial Workers of the World. Socialists in various ideological camps were also feared, but the radical syndicalists of the IWW, many of whose leaders were not American citizens, appeared to pose the greatest danger to established government and institutions. (There was no American communist party until after the war.) The IWW's goal was to organize all workers, irrespective of race or nationality, into "One Big Union" and bring dramatic changes in society and the economy through the use of general strikes. The union opposed World War I as a power struggle between capitalists and plutocrats, fought with the lives and blood of the oppressed working masses, but which would bring them no benefit. This combination of economic radicalism, militant unionism, and opposition to war guaranteed the hostility of all levels of government toward the IWW and made it certain that the war would be used as a pretext to smash the union, a goal that conservatives in and out of government had long sought. The IWW was successful in Philadelphia and several Gulf ports in organizing strong interracial locals, a fact that was troublesome to white officials who stereotyped blacks as easily manipulated by subversive whites. The realization that at least a few disaffected blacks were uniting with the most radicalized segment of the white proletariat—a population that included significant numbers of unnaturalized aliens—was especially disturbing to defenders of capitalist hegemony.

One hundred one Wobbly leaders were convicted in June 1918 on violations of the Selective Service and Espionage acts. One of the defendants was Ben Fletcher, a black longshoreman. The trial, coming months after the Armistice, made it clear that the IWW could expect continuing persecution in the Red Scare, persecution fueled in part by widespread suspicions that white and black Wobblies were engaged in what the Justice Department called "Negro subversion."

During the war the overtaxed Bureau of Investigation devoted most of its manpower to enforcing the draft and suppressing alleged enemy subversion. Yet its agents also investigated and compiled evidence against the Wobblies. Their task was made more difficult by private detectives hired by corporations to spy on workers, infiltrate their organizations, and discredit them through promoting violent incidents. While he was convinced that the IWW would be troublesome in any case, wartime Bureau chief A. Bruce Bielaski was also convinced that company detectives were often provocateurs who justified their employment "through exaggeration and misrepresentation."[1]

The Bureau's own agents were likewise compromised by their support for employers in struggles between capital and labor. In addition, the demand for total patriotism during the war encouraged agents, in concert with United States attorneys, to disregard the niceties of due process. The Post Office, given license by its solicitor, William H. Lamar, was intent on halting the distribution of IWW publications and incoming mail containing financial contributions for legal appeals. Bielaski and special wartime assistant attorney general John Lord O'Brian had reservations about the legality of interdicting the IWW leaders' mail, but Lamar was not interested in their advice, only in whether such procedures would interfere with the Justice Department's prosecutions.[2] Thus strong curbs on the IWW's civil liberties developed during the war and continued afterward. And black Wobblies would enjoy no more tolerance for their radicalism than did their white brethren.

Benjamin Harrison Fletcher was the first black Wobbly to feel the scrutiny of the federal political intelligence network. Born and raised in Philadelphia, he worked as a longshoreman and while still a young man helped organize the Marine Transport Workers Local 3 of the IWW. Local 3 conducted a number of strikes between 1913 and 1916 which resulted in concrete gains for dock workers and, for the moment, a strong union. The local was also noteworthy for a monthly rotation of the chairmanship between black and white workers, an extraordinary example of racial solidarity in that era. Fletcher was a zealous propagandist for the union and became a paid organizer. (The Military

Intelligence Division would later offer him a grudging compliment, calling him an "eloquent agitator.") It was inevitable, then, that his distribution of anti-conscription leaflets in Boston, two months after America entered the war, would draw the attention of the Bureau and local police. The latter found incriminating IWW leaflets during a warrantless search of his rented rooms, although the Post Office Translation Bureau's Robert Adger Bowen naively concluded that the suspect was "the real type of 'Southern Nigger Agitator' with no education [and] poor grammar," incapable of posing a threat to the draft or the government.[3]

But the IWW itself certainly seemed threatening; in a letter to his attorney general, president Woodrow Wilson expressed the view that "the I.W.W.s . . . certainly are worthy of being suppressed." The Justice Department hardly needed the chief executive's encouragement, having already determined to destroy the despised Wobblies. Ultimately 166 leaders were charged with a conspiracy to sabotage and obstruct the war effort, Fletcher being the lone black defendant. Refusing to surrender voluntarily, he was tracked down in Philadelphia, working for the Pennsylvania Railroad. Two Bureau agents and a railroad policeman took Fletcher into custody, gaining entrance to his apartment by claiming to be charity solicitors. Held under $10,000 bail, he languished in the city jail for over a month before that sum was raised.[4]

Fletcher, along with his co-defendants, was brought to trial in April 1918, remarking to IWW leader "Big Bill" Haywood that "if it wasn't for me, there'd be no color in this trial at all." The Wobbly defendants needed all the humor they could muster, for after two months of testimony it took the jury only one hour to convict all 101 defendants. As Fletcher received a ten-year sentence, he observed that the judge "is using poor English today. His sentences are too long." Although they filed appeals, the convicted Wobblies were sent to the federal penitentiary at Leavenworth, Kansas, where they proceeded to recruit other prisoners into the IWW, hold classes, sympathize with their underpaid and non-unionized guards, and carry on a wide correspondence with other radicals and sympathizers.[5]

During his initial incarceration Bureau agents in Kansas City opened Fletcher's mail, with important contents relayed to other offices. J. Edgar Hoover, head of the Bureau's anti-radical General Intelligence Division, hoped that Fletcher's letters would reveal details about the broader current of "negro agitation." In that he was disappointed. Although the imprisoned Wobbly's correspondents included prominent white socialist Elizabeth Gurley Flynn and A. Philip Randolph, most mail was to or from individuals who played no major role in radical circles. His own letters expressed confidence that momentous changes were occurring: Capitalism appeared to be on the wane, and blacks were abandoning allegiance to that system. But despite his optimism, Leavenworth prison, even in the company of fellow Wobblies, was "a hell of a place."[6]

One regular correspondent was black Wobbly Joseph J. Jones. The two had met in Leavenworth, and Fletcher helped convert Jones to labor radicalism. When Jones emerged from prison in March 1919, he was a zealous disciple of the "One Big Union." His mentor, facing the possibility of lengthy incarceration, undoubtedly hoped that Jones would continue his work. Although Randolph and Chandler Owen were avid supporters of the IWW, they were committed to the Socialist Party, not day-to-day Wobbly agitation among blacks. In fact Jones had considerable potential; on leaving prison he plunged into radical activism in New York and Boston, undeterred by arrests and harassment.[7]

All across the country Wobblies and their sympathizers raised funds to liberate their jailed comrades. Eventually enough cash and collateral was assembled to free forty-six of them, including Fletcher, who was released on $40,000 bond in early February 1920, after serving a year and a half of his sentence. He maintained an active correspondence with Wobblies still in Leavenworth which Bureau agents continued to read, warning that Fletcher was again engaged in "radical IWW work," including raising funds to secure the freedom of those still in prison. Undercover informants and agents spotted him at IWW meetings and offices in New York, Baltimore, and Philadelphia. Fletcher's involvement in Local 3 activities, particularly a strike in mid-1920, was also watched. All was not harmonious within the IWW, however. Members in New York sought the expulsion of Local 3 for loading munitions on ships bound for Poland, believing the arms were destined for Russia and use against the Bolsheviks. Fletcher and other Philadelphians, they claimed, had violated the principle of working-class solidarity. In November Bureau agents found Fletcher organizing Pullman porters and railroad dining car workers in the South. By 1921 he was promoting the IWW in Butte, Montana, scene of bitter conflicts between the union and federal and local authorities, urging listeners to demand that the government free imprisoned socialist leader Eugene V. Debs as well as the IWW prisoners still at Leavenworth. From there he went to Duluth, Minneapolis, and Superior, Wisconsin, to preach the One Big Union gospel.[8]

The Seventh Circuit Court of Appeals in Chicago upheld the Wobblies' convictions, and when the Supreme Court refused to review that ruling, thirty-eight of those free on bond, including Fletcher, surrendered on April 25, 1921, to finish their terms at Leavenworth; the other eight, including Haywood, fled to Russia. Once again Bureau agents monitored Fletcher's mail.

One correspondent was Owen, who while reporting the *Messenger's* efforts to free the IWW prisoners revealed his disenchantment with "abstract ideological principles" and the doctrinaire politics of the communists, socialists, and the IWW. Fletcher was moving in the same direction. When president Warren G. Harding commuted his sentence a year later, Fletcher returned to Philadelphia but became disillusioned with the IWW, eventually leading local longshoremen into the previously despised American Federation of Labor in 1924.[9]

Ben Fletcher continued to promote working-class unity up to his death in 1949, but after leaving prison he was of no further interest to the Bureau. By then the IWW had been fatally wounded by wartime and Red Scare persecutions. But during its heyday, Fletcher was not only the most prominent black Wobbly, he was a potent symbol to those who feared the radical interracial organization of the proletariat. To the vast majority of whites, Fletcher and other black Wobblies advocated unthinkable changes in America's racial status quo. They would have agreed that the government was fully justified in imprisoning him and suppressing the movement he espoused.

Soon after the Armistice the Bureau accelerated its probe of ties between the Wobblies and African Americans. Several targets besides Fletcher soon came into focus. One was the *Messenger.* It encouraged blacks to join the IWW as the only union which both promoted their interests and did not discriminate against them as did the American Federation of Labor. Numerous articles between 1919 and 1921 praised the union, especially Fletcher's Philadelphia local. The Bureau accused the *Messenger* of promoting the IWW, Bolshevism, socialism, and anarchism. Agents' reports made little distinction between these movements, falsely assuming that a single radical movement in America was poised to overthrow the government and white supremacy.[10]

Other black Wobblies also became Bureau targets in the postwar months. Joseph J. Jones drew particularly close scrutiny when it appeared that he had become Fletcher's protégé. Interception of Fletcher's mail revealed pleas for Jones to link up with leading racial radicals like Randolph and Owen. And Jones's willingness to work street-corner crowds was the kind of activism Fletcher recognized as necessary if ordinary blacks were to be reached with the Wobbly gospel. Because Jones operated publicly, Bureau agents could keep him under surveillance.

Jones's life was characterized by a desperate search for racial identity and personal significance. Born in Boston in 1880, he never knew his black father and was given the surname of his Irish-American mother. Orphaned at age five, he was apprenticed to New England farm families but escaped rural Vermont by volunteering to fight in the Spanish-American War. Soon afterwards he joined an all-black regiment destined for the Philippines and the suppression of Emilio Aguinaldo's dark-skinned guerrilla fighters. Returning to the United States, he enlisted in a black regular army regiment, serving first at isolated western frontier posts and then back in the Philippines. Jones frequently ran afoul of military regulations, as did other soldiers, but the attempted rape of a Filipino soldier's wife earned him a dishonorable discharge and a five-year sentence to Leavenworth federal penitentiary. Incarceration became a course in radical politics. Entering prison a disgraced soldier, Jones graduated a Wobbly. Fletcher and the other imprisoned IWWs, regarding themselves as political prisoners, lost no opportunity to organize political and educational activities, circulate books and pamphlets, deliver speeches, recite original poetry and stories, and convert other prisoners. The will to dominate their surroundings triumphed in an intellectual life and political activism that was not quenched even by solitary confinement.[11]

Jones had never attended a school like this. Several Wobbly prisoners were leading theoreticians of radical ideologies. It was at Leavenworth, Jones later admitted with pride, that he became an IWW and a Bolshevik. The world opened to him as he read the *Nation, New Republic, Liberator, Class Struggle,* and *Rebel Worker,* which Wobbly prisoners were permitted to receive. Jones was befriended by Fletcher and Bulgarian-born George Andreytchine, who would later be the only "American" member of the Soviet Comintern. Two Russian-born Wobblies taught him mathematics and their native language. A new breed of political prisoners entered Jones's world when convicted conscientious objectors arrived. The Bureau concluded, rightly, that Jones had no radical inclinations prior to his incarceration, but that "he became infected with the Bolshevist principles through his acquaintance with the Russian and Jew IWW prisoners."[12]

Nothing had ever changed Jones as much as his forty months at Leavenworth. His "diploma" from the "university of radicalism" included a new self-image and membership in the oppressed working class, an identity in which the politics of race was subordinated to the radicalization of the proletariat. This broader cause, according to its ideology, would erase racial inequality as it eliminated political and economic exploitation. Jones did not shed all racial identity, working, upon his own release, for Fletcher's freedom, but he never found time to cultivate the race radicals as he instead quickly linked up with Russian Jewish Wobblies in New York.[13]

Jones left Leavenworth on March 15, 1919, carrying a letter of introduction to the wife of Andreytchine, with whom he stayed in Chicago. Receiving small amounts of money from relatives of other prisoners, Jones arrived in New York on March 25 and soon made his way to the famed Rand School, a "workers' college" where radicals offered a wide variety of courses on contemporary issues. Jones enrolled in a class on the "Negro problem" taught by Chandler Owen and found work selling propaganda literature for the Friends of Freedom for India at a 30 percent commission. He rented lodgings from Mrs. Theresa Klein, a widowed Jewish Wobbly who lived with her children and mother in a crowded immigrant tenement on East 17th Street, a location described by a probation officer as "a single room in a dirty, poor neighborhood." Distributing radical literature to soldiers, Jones soon gained the attention of the local police as well as the Bureau.[14]

Association with Mrs. Klein placed Jones at the center of New York IWW activism. The $10 a month she charged him for room and board supplemented her earnings as a dressmaker, but she also devoted much time to the cause. The Bureau, which had several undercover informants in the movement, recognized her as one of the Wobblies who had thrown sulfur "stink balls" in a Chinese restaurant to protest white waiters scabbing against the striking Chinese. (They ate first, and left without paying.) The Bureau also noted that she was secretary for the *Industrialist,* the organ of the Russian section of the IWW, and held a similar position with *Klassen Kampf* (Class Struggle), the official New York IWW Yiddish publication.[15]

Three weeks after arriving in New York, Jones was arrested for distributing "Bolshevik propaganda" to wounded veterans at a debarkation hospital. A pamphlet entitled "Are You For Or Against?" claimed that 65 percent of the country's wealth was owned by 5 percent of the people, including 30,000 millionaires who were to blame for starvation wages, child labor, prostitution, and war profits. But Bolshevism would guarantee jobs for all, abolish rent and interest, and end bosses' profits. Jones tried to give this pamphlet to a sergeant outside the hospital, who told him to leave. Hauled before the hospital adjutant, he offered him the same leaflet, argued in favor of Bolshevism, and claimed that "America is no good." This incident was sufficient to secure his conviction in district court.[16]

The Bureau assigned agent J. F. Kropidlowski to probe Jones's associations and activities, an inquiry requiring circumspection so as not to arouse the suspicions of Civil Liberties Bureau (ACLU) attorney Albert de Silver, who unsuccessfully appealed Jones's thirty-day sentence to the Blackwell's Island workhouse. Mrs. Klein appeared in court for his sentencing, displaying considerable interest in the case. Kropidlowski employed a ruse to gain Jones's trust and the unsuspecting Wobbly related his tragic early life, military service, and radicalization at Leavenworth. He denied spreading Bolshevik propaganda or holding IWW membership, however, claiming that he had simply been distributing leaflets promoting India's freedom on a hot day, holding a few Bolshevik pamphlets in his hand to keep perspiration from damaging those concerning India. Kropidlowski did not believe his explanation.[17]

The Bureau also benefited from documents obtained when Jones's probation officer interviewed Mrs. Klein. She first denied knowledge of any papers belonging to her boarder but subsequently produced considerable evidence which was passed to Kropidlowski without the knowledge of attorney de Silver. In addition the Bureau secured Jones's notebook containing the addresses of Randolph and Owen, IWW members in Boston, and several white radicals. On the basis of his conversation with Jones and examination of his papers, Kropidlowski concluded that "he speaks English correctly and seems to be of more than average intelligence but it may be possible that he does not realize the full significance and danger of the Bolshevik propaganda which he came in contact through the Rand School and the Friends of Freedom for India." There was no doubt, however, that Jones's case illustrated a serious lapse in security. The New York field office immediately sent Kropidlowski's report to headquarters, emphasizing Jones's conversion to radicalism at Leavenworth, where "unwholesome" literature was freely available to inmates. Acting Chief John T. Suter concurred that IWW influence had indeed poisoned Jones.[18]

Jones's activities for the next five months are clouded. After thirty days in the workhouse he remained in New York into August, if not later. Aside from intercepting mail from Fletcher in Leavenworth, the Bureau gained nothing of significance on Jones until he again engaged in propaganda leafleting, this time in Boston.[19]

To both the Justice and Post Office Departments, one of the most pernicious IWW leaflets was "Justice for the Negro—How He Can Get It." A gruesome photograph of a lynching graced its cover, and the contents urged revolutionary action by the working masses of all races. Its four pages also included a picture of the burned body of James Washington, who was lynched in Waco, Texas, on May 15, 1916. The text blamed capitalism for the wrongs done to black Americans and urged them to join the IWW. It was precisely such propaganda that Massachusetts legislators had in mind when they enacted an anti-anarchy bill in mid-1919 which drastically curbed free speech. Jones was arrested on September 26 in predominantly black Roxbury for distributing "Justice for the Negro" without a permit. The arresting officer procured evidence of considerable interest to the Bureau. In Jones's possession were copies of the *Messenger, Rebel Worker,* and *Klassen Kampf,* plus an IWW circular in Russian. He also carried a certificate authorizing him to collect dues and initiate members into the IWW; his own membership card was dated

September 1918, and issued at Leavenworth Penitentiary. At the time of his arrest, according to police, Jones shared a boarding house with other Wobblies, communists, and violators of the Espionage Act. The Boston press reported that he was arraigned for "exhibiting, distributing, and promulgating a paper . . . advocating, advising, counseling, and inciting the overthrow of the Government." This was the first test case of the state's new anti-anarchy statute.[20] In addition to observing court hearings and searching Jones's room in Boston, the Bureau continued to intercept letters from Fletcher, who urged Jones to continue working for his release and cooperate with Owen and Randolph on radical projects. Jones's reply related that he was supporting himself as a concrete worker. Apparently Fletcher knew about Mrs. Klein, for Jones wrote of her ill health and desire to come to Boston. Meanwhile, a Boston agent translated the issue of *Klassen Kampf* and the Russian pamphlet seized at Jones's arrest; both were found to advocate revolutionary action.[21]

Jones gained a continuance and was released on bond in mid-October. By this time the Military Intelligence Division had taken interest in the case, either because of Jones's attempts to propagandize soldiers, or because the Bureau sent MID copies of reports likely to concern the army. While MID followed the case in Boston, its operatives in New York researched Jones's IWW activities on the assumption he was responsible for inciting disorder among blacks.[22]

Despite the fact he faced the possibility of a three-year sentence and $1,000 fine, Jones was undeterred.[23] His tutelage by indomitable political prisoners at Leavenworth had robbed imprisonment of its terror. Jones was busy selling the *Rebel Worker* at a communist rally on Boston Common five days before a Suffolk County grand jury deliberated without decision, allowing him to remain free on $3,000 bond. He returned to New York, and when the city's bomb squad raided IWW headquarters the night of November 15, Jones was searched and questioned.[24]

Then tragedy struck. In a fetid immigrant tenement on Wednesday night, November 19, 1919, Theresa Klein lay dead from two bullet wounds. Jones had killed himself with a single shot to his head. In his pockets the police found "anarchist literature," noting wryly that Klein, too, was a "radical." Most of the metropolitan newspapers ignored the grisly scene; there was, after all, little newsworthy in murder and suicide among the city's huddled masses. New York's dailies were preoccupied instead with Senate rejection of the League of Nations and the visit of the Prince of Wales to Gotham. Only the *Evening Telegram,* a "yellow journal," supplied a motive: unrequited love. Jones had returned to the flat, ostensibly to retrieve a satchel, and roused the sleeping occupants. He argued with the twice-wedded Mrs. Klein for several minutes, finally shouting "if you don't marry me you won't marry anybody else." Then three shots echoed through the awakened halls.[25]

Race and color had seemed irrelevant in the IWW, that is, until Jones's relationship with Theresa Klein put the movement's egalitarianism to the ultimate test. Perhaps her refusal was based on age, or an unwillingness to venture marriage after previous unhappy experiences, or any other "logical" explanation. But to Jones the loss was inextricably linked to the racial dilemma of his life.

The tragic death of Joseph J. Jones robbed the IWW of one of its most promising black activists, perhaps a successor to the imprisoned Ben Fletcher. Wobbly propaganda continued in the pages of the *Messenger*, and a handful of other blacks crisscrossed the country as organizers among their race. But their number was not large, and the union must have felt the loss. How the Bureau reacted to Jones's death is unrecorded, but there must have been some relief, if not satisfaction, that one of the more fearless radicals was no longer troubling the waters. The IWW's work went on, minus one of its bright black converts.

Although the Department of Justice had the greatest role in monitoring and suppressing the IWW, the military services also took alarm at its activities. During the war the Office of Naval Intelligence investigated IWW locals in seaports from which military supplies or soldiers were shipped and was particularly worried about the interracial character and leadership of Fletcher's local in Philadelphia.[26] The army's vision was wider: Since the Wobblies sought to organize workers in mines, industries, transportation, and on farms, they might cause "unrest" in any part of the country and require the use of troops to suppress civil disorder. Beyond that, MID was worried that soldiers would be wooed by the IWW's attacks on capitalism and conventional politics. Thus its watch on the Wobblies lasted well into the Red Scare.

The Bureau of Investigation's attention to Wobbly influence among blacks quickened in the winter and spring of 1919, in part because radicalism in general seemed on the increase, but also because of fears that the IWW, Bolsheviks, and anarchists were promoting "black rule." In February southern white businessmen and professionals, including the chairman of the board of the Federal Reserve Bank in New Orleans, received a circular entitled "Negro Domination" which included the following text:

> Bolshevism would mean for the Southern States NEGRO DOMINATION. If you wish Negro Domination then encourage President Wilson to in his turn encourage the Russian Bolsheviki and our own Bolsheviki, IWW, Anarchists, Sinn Feiners and Other Reds who have all joined in a get-together movement

for rule by the LOWEST social strata through the medium of AUTOCRATIC MOB LEADERS.

The pamphlet was mailed from Philadelphia, and agents there attempted unsuccessfully to discover its origins.[27] This incident helped foster the conviction that communists and Wobblies were using racial issues to undermine America. In the spring of 1919, an agent in Boston erroneously accused outspoken editor William Monroe Trotter of advocating Bolshevik and Wobbly methods to halt lynching. Indeed, any black leader who counseled militant measures to increase black political power or secure greater civil rights was likely to be linked to a radical group, as was future House of Representatives member Oscar DePriest in Chicago. But what convinced the Bureau more than anything else that revolutionary forces were propagandizing blacks was support for the IWW and the Bolshevik revolution in the pages of the *Messenger.*[28]

The Bureau's fear of IWW subversion peaked in the "Red Summer" of 1919. Additional "evidence" came from the New York legislature's Lusk Committee, which carried out its own extensive investigation, concluding that Wobblies and Bolsheviks were converting blacks to radicalism. J. Edgar Hoover ordered agents in New York to investigate the individuals, organizations, and publications named by the Lusk staff. The white press amplified fears: A *New York Times* headline claimed that "Reds try to stir Negroes to revolt" by urging them to join the IWW and left-wing socialist movements. The *New York Tribune* concluded that the "IWW and other agitators" were "financed from Russia" and "spreading propaganda aimed to breed race hatred." What seemed to validate these suspicions was the violence which erupted in Chicago in the last days of July, the worst race riot of the era. Bureau agents and local police (with MID watching anxiously) combed Chicago and the nation for evidence to prove their suspicion that socialist, communist, or IWW propaganda was responsible for inciting the violence, ignoring the fact that all of the radical movements, especially the Wobblies, gave at least verbal support to interracial working-class unity. In the end federal investigators were disappointed to learn that even Chicago's white authorities believed that local tensions were primarily responsible for sparking the violence.[29]

This conclusion did not, however, dissuade Hoover from the conviction that radicals were arming and inciting blacks. Instructing the St. Louis office to investigate whether blacks were purchasing guns, he stressed that "special attention should be given toward the Negro agitation which seems to be prevalent throughout the industrial centers of the country and every effort should be made to ascertain whether or not this agitation is due to the influence of the radical elements such as the IWW and Bolsheviks." Recognizing that the Justice Department could not abrogate the Second Amendment, Hoover nonetheless suggested that local ordinances preventing the sale of guns to persons who would not use them responsibly should be used to keep blacks from arming themselves. He also demanded that the Chicago office make "an immediate and vigorous investigation" to determine whether radical black publications "are being solely supported through the income received from the advertisements contained in them and the subscriptions to the same" or whether "the IWW organization or other radical elements are lending funds to the encouragement of the negro agitation." In fact, it was the race's own growing sense of empowerment and articulation of grievances that were being seen and heard.[30]

Historians have searched in vain for evidence that the IWW or other radical groups instigated the riots in mid-1919. In fact, Wobbly success in inspiring blacks to militant action was much exaggerated, not only by fear-mongering federal officials, but by *agents provocateurs* paid by private detective agencies. In Philadelphia, Bureau agents were alerted that a black man was active in IWW affairs. He proved to be Adolphus Hall, a clerk in the downtown post office who served as an undercover informant during the war. When the American Protective League was disbanded after the Armistice, individual units lived on, funded by local industrialists, to pursue radicals and union activists with as much zeal as they had "slackers" during the war. Such was the Philadelphia Protective League, for which Hall now worked. Local Bureau agents believed that probably twenty black men like Hall were employed by government agencies, private detective services, and "patriotic" anti-radical groups.[31]

The line between informant and instigator was blurred when Hall became a leader in the IWW's stevedore local, helping plan a general strike. The fact that he was a federal employee made the situation unacceptable to United States attorney Francis Fisher Kane, who sent a blunt warning to Attorney General Palmer in mid-1919. Investigation of Bolshevism in Philadelphia was in the capable hands of Bureau agents who used informers to good effect. But the Secret Service, ONI, and the Emergency Fleet Corporation also employed informants, with no coordination guiding their efforts. Worse, several corporations paid private detective agencies to send infiltrators into radical groups, and a dozen of these, including Hall, were bona fide provocateurs, fomenting trouble where it did not exist because their pay depended on "egging on" the radicals. They even had the gall to try to sell their information to federal agents or seek federal employment.

Kane was not opposed to receiving intelligence from private agencies, but he balked at their demand that the government reciprocate with access to Bureau reports. He also correctly guessed that the Post Office and State departments, army intelligence, local and state police, state attorneys, and most large corporations also had their fingers on the pulse of radicalism. His letter ended with a startling assessment, coming from an employee of the Justice Department: "If the Philadelphia situation is a sample of what exists in other large cities, it would certainly indicate that the danger from Bolshevism in America is not as great as the newspapers would have us believe it to be."[32] Nor as great a danger as the attorney general and the Bureau of Investigation would have the nation believe.

In mid-summer 1919, the Bureau was confident it had evidence that the IWW was stepping up efforts to propagandize and recruit blacks. One example was the broad distribution of "Justice for the Negro," the pamphlet circulated by Jones in Boston. Police in Baltimore also discovered it when a black informant told them of a white man who was allegedly passing out revolvers along with the pamphlet. Baltimore's Bureau office employed the common practice of recruiting black employees in the federal building—probably janitors and elevator operators—to scour the local community for information. But they found nothing about the circular, nor did agents conducting their own investigations. The mysterious white man was never identified either. But the New York field office was notified so that it could investigate IWW headquarters there.[33]

A second pamphlet appeared about the same time, an IWW recruiting leaflet entitled "To Colored Workingmen and Women." Both publications were found in localities across the country. Even where there was no evidence that the IWW was putting specific effort into recruiting blacks, Red Scare logic magnified the danger. Agents in Norfolk, for example, could find only one person who acknowledged receiving "Justice for the Negro" but concluded that others probably would not admit it because of the current "unrest." Bureau agents undoubtedly took their cues from Hoover. Not satisfied with the investigation in Baltimore, he directed informant Arthur U. Craig to determine how widely radicalism was spreading in that city and whether the *Baltimore Afro-American* was printing radical leaflets. But Craig found that the man Bureau agents identified as the chief black Wobbly, Ollis Brown, was in fact a longshoreman opposed to the IWW![34]

There was no dearth of suspected Wobbly activity among blacks elsewhere, however. Besides the cities mentioned above, Bureau agents (and in some cases MID officers) reported incidents in Chicago and Rockford, Illinois, San

Francisco, New York, St. Louis, Houston, Boston, Toledo, Seattle, El Paso, and Indianapolis in the summer of 1919.[35] Much of the focus was on the *Messenger's* view that the IWW was the only logical labor organization for blacks. Strenuous efforts were made to find grounds on which to prosecute its editors, but they escaped indictment when the United States attorney in New York argued that no jury would convict them on Espionage Act charges. Even the *Crisis* was accused of promoting the IWW. Postal solicitor Lamar wanted to ban it from the mails too but confessed that its alleged sins were not flagrant enough to make a case stick.[36]

If Bureau headquarters had read reports from the field with dispassion in the fall of 1919, it should have concluded that IWW activity was on the wane. An informant in Philadelphia noted that individual black Wobblies remained, but no active movement existed. Omaha agents attributed the riot there to local conditions, not the IWW. Rumors in Detroit that the radical union was about to provoke a race riot proved false, as were fears that it was fomenting a strike in Wilmington, North Carolina, and organizing a local in Jacksonville. True, pro-IWW speakers like Owen and Chicago Wobbly Roscoe T. Sims were still finding audiences and distributing "Justice to the Negro." That pamphlet also turned up in Bisbee, Arizona, where the IWW had long been active in the copper mines. MID worried that black soldiers guarding the border with Mexico were being radicalized by the IWW. Two black troopers were employed to discover the source of the circular while the army also prepared a counter-propaganda leaflet to sow dissension between black and white Wobblies. But anticipated violence failed to occur. In fact the IWW was unsuccessful in recruiting any significant numbers of blacks during the postwar radical season.[37]

One reason for the lack of widespread IWW success is found in the story of Lovett Fort-Whiteman. Born in Dallas, he studied the machinist trade at Tuskegee Institute and medicine at Meharry Medical College in Nashville. Making his way to New York, he enrolled at City College, only to be expelled, he later claimed, on account of his radicalism. A friendlier reception awaited him at the Rand School. By 1919 he had joined the IWW and was a contributor to the *Messenger*; he would later write for the communist-leaning *Crusader.*[38]

Fort-Whiteman first came to the Bureau's notice in August 1919, when an informant found him fishing for converts at a socialist picnic in Philadelphia. In ensuing weeks other undercover sources learned that he claimed to be acquainted with Ludwig C. A. K. Martens, the Russian communist government's unrecognized "ambassador" to the United States. Fort-Whiteman was an itinerant organizer whose schedule that fall took him from New York to

Philadelphia, Pittsburgh, and nearby Braddock and New Castle, then on to Youngstown, Cleveland, Toledo, and finally St. Louis. He distributed thousands of copies of "Justice for the Negro" and a flier promoting left-wing socialism. Like other radical evangelists, he hardly got rich on the hustings. Philadelphia socialists paid him $20, but he got only $5 a day plus expenses in Pittsburgh and Toledo and a small collection and a meal after speaking in a church in New Castle.[39]

St. Louis workers had proven resistant to the IWW, hence the arrival of Fort-Whiteman in early October to help organize a local. But the Bureau was determined to cripple the movement. Spearheading this effort was agent Louis Loebl, working undercover, who convinced radicals that he was one of them. Loebl was "anxious to prevent" the Wobbly organizer from speaking to black audiences, and, acting on an informant's tip that such an event would occur on October 11, arranged for local police to arrest Fort-Whiteman and a group of eleven whites as they began an IWW meeting on the night of October 10. According to the police, their rhetoric emphasized "placing the negroes upon an equal footing with the whites," engineering the "overthrow of capitalism and the present form of government" and promoting "Soviet control and dictatorship of the proletariat."[40]

The next day's newspapers called it an "IWW raid" and quoted government agents in describing Fort-Whiteman as a "dangerous radical" trying to start a race riot. But even enemies of the IWW knew that it was an interracial working-class movement trying to bridge the gulf between black and white workers. Nonetheless, the press, intent on generating hostility to the radical movement, printed extensive excerpts from IWW propaganda, particularly the leaflet against lynching. A letter from Rose Pastor Stokes was also reproduced along with Fort-Whiteman's admission that he was a disciple of Karl Marx and received financial support from the left-wing (communist) branch of the Socialist Party. The press further noted, with satisfaction, that a delegation of St. Louis blacks, headed by a city detective, went to the jail and condemned Fort-Whiteman for "stir[ring] up trouble" between the races: "We don't want you here and can assure you that if you were turned over to the negroes of St. Louis for a few hours we would teach you a lesson you wouldn't forget."[41]

The fear of interracial radicalism, nurtured by the Red Scare, was clearly evident in the confused reporting of the *St. Louis Daily Globe-Democrat,* which first reassured whites that "race riots and a general uprising among the negroes . . . are believed to have been nipped in their inception." White Wobblies were as responsible for trying to provoke violence as were blacks. But the newspaper also stressed a contradictory theme. Employing a subhead stating "Negro

Dominates Whites," the paper editorialized that the black organizer "appeared to be dominating the work of the eleven white men." "Negro domination" was a powerful southern expression, conjuring up Reconstruction-era fears of social equality between the races. So the IWW was accused of both fomenting violence between blacks and whites, and simultaneously promoting interracial intimacy. Meanwhile, the *Post-Dispatch,* St. Louis's highest-circulation newspaper, reflected another ancient southern fear, warning that black Wobblies were "more menacing than the original IWW because of the credulity and ignorance of large masses of the negroes."[42]

Fort-Whiteman and his white confederates were interrogated by Bureau agents and immigration inspectors, reflecting the government's strategy of identifying aliens who could be deported. Insufficient evidence was found against the whites, but the assistant United States attorney held Fort-Whiteman on a pretext until Espionage Act charges could be presented to a federal grand jury. Bureau agents noted with satisfaction that local blacks had not bailed him out and that the raid had dampened considerably the IWW's activities.[43]

The black organizer remained in jail twelve more days until his preliminary hearing and release on bond, raised by local Wobblies and the Workers Defense Union. He denied witnesses' claims that he had praised the Soviet form of government at the aborted IWW meeting, saying that he only had time to extend greetings before the raid took place. Disbelieving this statement, federal officials planned to add the charge of perjury. He was questioned about individuals listed in his address book, and their names were sent to Bureau field offices in the cities where they resided. The eleven arrested whites were compelled to testify against their comrade. But his own defiant statement was regarded as sufficient proof of criminal intentions: "We must organize the negroes under the banner of the IWW if the negro is to be emancipated. We may overthrow capitalism, even though by so doing it becomes necessary for us to overthrow our present form of government and to establish Soviet control and dictatorship of the proletariat."[44]

Such rhetoric was truly frightening to anxious whites during the Red Scare. A United States senator requested the Judiciary Committee to investigate recent race riots, believing Fort-Whiteman and the IWW might be instigators. MID leapt to the same conclusions, based solely on a Bureau informant's claim that Fort-Whiteman "assisted in the preparations for race riots in New York City and stated that they were prepared to resist the police" with enough pistols and machine guns to make the Chicago riot appear tame.[45]

Deeply desirous of suppressing IWW activism, Bureau agents and federal attorneys in St. Louis nonetheless had no case against Fort-Whiteman. His perjury indictment was worthless. But the government's key weakness was the Espionage Act. Although technically still enforceable since the war was simply suspended by the Armistice but not yet formally ended, juries across the country refused to convict suspects under that law, unconvinced that radical speech would impair the nation's ability to wage war since the draft was suspended and the army demobilized. Sometime after the last recorded hearing on October 28, 1919, Fort-Whiteman's case was suspended.[46]

Thus ended a scenario that was all too common during the Red Scare, as zealous and vindictive Bureau agents and United States attorneys persecuted radicals—both black and white—by employing raids, arrests, interrogations, and untriable Espionage Act charges. They could deter socialist, communist, and IWW activism through intimidation, threats of punishment, and the monetary costs of mounting a defense. In the short run, the government's strategy against Fort-Whiteman was successful; no further Bureau reports linked him to Wobbly activism. But its effort to extinguish his radicalism ultimately failed. Fort-Whiteman soon became one of the first African American communists, joined the African Blood Brotherhood, and when the Party ordered the ABB replaced by the new American Negro Labor Congress in 1925, he became its national organizer.[47]

As 1920 began the Department of Justice sought to strengthen its attack on the IWW, seeking legislation declaring it to be anarchistic and making membership by noncitizens grounds for deportation. At the same time, determined to keep the Bureau's anti-radical work under his personal direction, J. Edgar Hoover argued against plans to give the Chicago field office independent jurisdiction over IWW cases west of the Mississippi. But he had a bigger problem: The public had lost patience with dragnet raids against suspected radicals which snared citizen and alien, leader and casual member alike. So Hoover planned to focus the GID's "IWW division" on 500 "leading alien agitators" to seek evidence warranting their deportation. Wobbly publications would not be ignored, however; agents were to obtain their mailing lists on the assumption that 90 percent of subscribers were probably Wobblies. And headquarters would scour their contents for "pernicious" utterances.[48]

In practical terms this meant a diminished focus on the black-IWW nexus. But individual agents in the field continued to report frequently on the activities of local Wobblies. As the communist-leaning *Crusader* came to the Bureau's attention, it was erroneously believed to be a tool of either the IWW or the Socialist Party. Agents reached other faulty conclusions. One was certain that *Crisis* editor W. E. B. DuBois was promoting the Wobblies, simply because he urged blacks to organize industrially. Another labeled NAACP executive secretary James Weldon Johnson "an advocate of IWWism." And others persisted in maintaining that IWW leaflets like "To Colored Working-men and Women" and "Colored Workers of America—Why You Should Join the IWW" were "dedicated to race hatred."[49]

Another black Wobbly who drew the Bureau's focus was Roscoe T. Sims, a Chicago organizer and co-founder of the National Brotherhood Workers of America, an effort to federate all black labor unions and provide an opportunity for workers who as yet had none. It galled the Bureau that Sims, described by a Chicago agent as an "ultra radical negro Bolsheviki propagandist and IWW," was on the payroll as a janitor at city hall. Sims was a fearless and riveting orator. Speaking in Pittsburgh, he noted the presence of plainclothes policemen in the audience and declared that the only way the capitalist "bulls" would prevent the Wobblies from their mission was to stand them up against the wall and shoot them. At a gathering in Chicago he delivered a "fiery speech" on the topic "To Hell with the Law." The Bureau report dourly noted that this was followed by a collection of $70, a tidy sum for a radical meeting with 200 in attendance. And at a May Day assembly, his plea for funds to hire lawyers for indicted Wobblies garnered over $400! Sims himself was such a defendant, charged under Illinois's criminal syndicalism statute. The disposition of his case is unknown, but legal difficulties did not slow Sims's promotion of the One Big Union.[50]

By 1920 the Bureau was well organized to pursue the Industrial Workers of the World. In addition to staff and files in Washington, the Chicago office had its own "IWW Room" with six agents to monitor the "unlawful association." Over 20,000 names were recorded in half a dozen separate lists in Chicago alone, the vast majority simply subscribers to Wobbly publications.[51] But the IWW was only a skeleton of its former self. Weekly radical reports continued to mention the occasional black Wobbly speaker or circulation of a leaflet in New York or Chicago, but agents elsewhere found no significant activity. Despite the fact the IWW placed a full-page ad in the December 1920 *Messenger,* the union's influence within black America, which had never been decisive, was negligible.[52] When conflict erupted in 1921 on the Philadelphia waterfront as the AFL-affiliated International Longshoremen's Association challenged the IWW's Marine Transport Workers Union, some black Wobblies abandoned their local and affiliated with the ILA. Black interest elsewhere was slight. The average individual, noted a Chicago agent, had little time for radicalism, with unemployment being his primary concern. Neither socialists nor IWW "soap-boxers" had a significant following; their capacity to cause unrest was nil.[53]

The IWW enjoyed its greatest success among blacks in organizing the docks in Philadelphia and several Gulf ports prior to 1917. World War I brought intense persecution and the imprisonment of its top leadership, including Ben Fletcher, the most prominent black Wobbly. As radicalism peaked during the Red Scare, the IWW gained a dynamic advocate in the *Messenger*. But despite its support for the only national union that sought to organize all workers, irrespective of race or craft, the majority of black laborers held the One Big Union at arm's length. Many were influenced by a powerful anti-union heritage whose origins went back to Booker T. Washington and the black churches, a tradition which stressed that white employers, not white workers, were the race's only friends. There was logic behind this anti-union bias, for the dominant workers movement in the early twentieth century, the American Federation of Labor, permitted its affiliated unions to bar blacks entirely or restrict them to membership in powerless Jim Crow locals. The IWW offered a positive alternative, but it was so tainted with the hue of radicalism that most black workers felt they had enough obstacles in life being black, without being red as well. And even when they may have been willing to experiment with radicalism, the IWW was being eclipsed by communism.

The federal government's fear that the Wobblies were subverting African Americans was exaggerated far out of proportion to the union's actual influence in the postwar years. But, as was the case with other social movements, the Bureau of Investigation, Military Intelligence Division, and other agencies engaged in domestic counter-espionage were motivated as much by what the Wobblies stood for as by their actual membership and influence. Their goal was a proletariat united against capital, an *interracial* proletariat. Not only would IWW success end class exploitation, it would revolutionize racial relations. Both scenarios were nightmares to the worried guardians of the status quo in the Justice Department. The IWW must be crushed if the wealth, privilege, and power of America's elite were to be preserved. And there was no less doubt that the Wobblies' plan for interracial equality, at least within the ranks of labor, must also be challenged. The United States government, fortified with support from business and commerce, the press, churches, and the middle class, declared war on the IWW. And won.

EPILOGUE

"The Force of the Law"

The State Department, Military Intelligence Division, Office of Naval Intelligence, Post Office Department, and Bureau of Investigation continued to gather and share political intelligence data despite the waning of the Red Scare. Although the communist movement had been driven underground, it had not disappeared. And even though radical activism among blacks had abated, it had not ceased. Thus it is not surprising that Red-baiting of left-wing organizations and individuals also persisted. But changes came to the Justice Department in 1924 which, in theory, should have curtailed the gathering of domestic political intelligence. Plagued by scandals, incompetence, and criminal activity, the "Department of Easy Virtue" underwent a much-needed housecleaning by new Attorney General Harlan Fiske Stone. His predecessor, Harry M. Daugherty, implicated in the Teapot Dome affair, was twice tried, although acquitted, for conspiring to defraud the government. Bureau director William J. Burns was fired soon after Daugherty but escaped indictment. Both men had turned the Bureau into "a dumping ground for political hacks." Even when no more positions on the payroll were available for would-be agents pushed by influential congressional sponsors, political appointees served as dollar-a-year men, some nonetheless garnering up to $2,000 a month while working on prohibition cases. Several agents were ultimately convicted of jury tampering, larceny, and conspiracy, although no black employees were implicated in such scandals.[1]

Attorney General Stone, a former dean of the Columbia University Law School, was determined not only to weed out rot and corruption, but also to strictly limit the scope of the Bureau of Investigation. The day after firing "Billy" Burns, Stone issued a statement announcing his intentions:

> There is always the possibility that a secret police may become a menace to free governments and free institutions because it carries with it the possibility of abuses of power which are not always quickly apprehended or understood.

The enormous expansion of Federal legislation, both civil and criminal, in recent years, however, has made a Bureau of Investigation a necessary instrument of law enforcement. But it is important that its activities be strictly limited to the performance of those functions for which it was created and that its agents themselves be not above the law or beyond its reach.

The Bureau of Investigation is not concerned with political or other opinions of individuals. It is concerned only with their conduct and then only with such conduct as is forbidden by the laws of the United States. When a police system passes beyond these limits, it is dangerous to the proper administration of justice and to human liberty, which it should be our first concern to cherish.

Although he had opposed the Red Scare–era Palmer raids, which J. Edgar Hoover orchestrated, Stone perceived in Hoover a straight-arrow bureaucrat who would welcome removing the Bureau from politics, and on May 10, 1924, offered to make him acting director. Hoover readily (and seemingly genuinely) agreed with Stone's philosophy, vowing to accept the position only if the Bureau was "divorced from politics" and agents were appointed solely on merit. He gave assurances that the Bureau would curtail, if not halt, political intelligence, writing disingenuously that

> It is, of course, to be remembered that the activities of Communists and other ultra-radicals have not up to the present time constituted a violation of the federal statutes, and consequently, the Department of Justice, theoretically, has no right to investigate such activities as there has been no violation of the federal laws.[2]

Quickly passing Stone's scrutiny, Hoover was appointed Director of the Bureau of Investigation at the end of the year.[3]

Until recently historians of the Bureau and biographers of Hoover have taken at face value his seeming eagerness to get the Bureau out of political intelligence and assumed that this role was not revived until 1936 when President Franklin D. Roosevelt directed the FBI to investigate communism and fascism. But, to use Hoover's own carefully chosen word, the Bureau was only "theoretically" unconcerned with suspects' political ideas. In fact, Hoover was well prepared for large-scale political intelligence operations in the mid-thirties because the FBI already had substantial information at hand—much gathered since 1924—and had never halted coordinated intelligence efforts with the State Department, ONI, and MID. The collection of political intelligence, and the interagency partnership born in World War I, did not cease in 1924. For the next twelve years, Hoover used the Bureau "to gather information on activities of the Bureau's critics, and on labor and radical political organizations" and activists.[4]

Those who witnessed Stone's cleansing of the Justice Department put faith in Hoover's vow to keep the Bureau uninterested in individuals' beliefs and opinions. Even Roger Baldwin, head of the American Civil Liberties Union, was convinced that Hoover was an ally. Yet it had been subject to intense surveillance ever since the Red Scare and, Hoover's assurances notwithstanding, agents continued to monitor it after 1924. Years later, Baldwin admitted that "we never knew . . . about the way that Hoover's FBI kept track of us after the 1924 reform announcements. They never stopped watching us."[5] Perhaps contemporaries were misled by the dismantling of the General Intelligence Division, which had led the pursuit of radicals ever since 1919. But for at least a year after Hoover became director, if not longer, the Bureau continued to compile reports on "Negro Activities" and the radical press, paying particular attention to the *Daily Worker*'s promotion of communism among blacks. Covert political investigations of those who had violated no federal statues, the use of paid informants, and liaison with local "red squads" had not stopped. Surely Stone and others knew of these activities, if only through the Bureau's monthly bulletins, which continued to be distributed within the executive branch and military intelligence circles. He seems not to have objected. Despite his intentions, political intelligence hardly missed a beat.[6]

Left-wing radicalism and labor unionism characterized many suspects investigated by the Bureau and its intelligence partners between 1924 and 1936. Recent studies identify at least four dozen well-known writers and artists on whom Bureau files were opened during that period, including black poet Langston Hughes. All were suspected of harboring unconventional or subversive beliefs.[7] But those African Americans who were most frequently monitored were communist activists and fellow travelers. Although many of the new cases in the later twenties were initiated by the State Department, it found a willing ally in Hoover's Bureau, whose agents and informants possessed far greater investigative capability. This, too, violated Stone's 1924 order: He intended that the Bureau would not furnish intelligence on lawful political activities to the State Department or any other agency without the approval of the attorney general. And the continued investigation of left-wing radicals ignored the Justice Department's own opinion that no federal statute made mere Communist Party membership and activity unlawful.[8]

After the African Blood Brotherhood's failure to woo the black masses away from Marcus Garvey, communist leadership in Russia ordered the establishment of a black workers' front organization, the American Negro Labor Congress, under the leadership of Lovett Fort-Whiteman. The Bureau maintained separate case files on the ANLC and its leader after 1924, employing agents as well as informants to gather information, but eventually handed the cases over to the State Department. Harry Haywood, a veteran of the African Blood Brotherhood and a communist youth league, joined the Party in 1925. His Bureau case was likewise transferred to the State Department when he was sent to Moscow for training in 1926. A year later, with cooperation from the State and Post Office departments, the Bureau opened a file on James W. Ford, who became the Communist Party's vice presidential candidate in 1932.[9]

Agent James E. Amos and a white colleague maintained surveillance of a suspect whose "offenses" included taking photographs of an airplane demonstration and military drill in Central Park and being acquainted with Claude McKay. Association with the black poet was the pretext for having Bureau "confidential sources" investigate another individual, this time at the request of the British government. The Bureau, State Department, and the ONI similarly shared information on William L. Patterson, a black communist who spent time in Russia in the late twenties. Another subject of federal investigations at the same time was George Padmore, although his initial interest in communism and the American Negro Labor Congress was supplanted by anti-colonialism. When the British embassy alerted American authorities to his promotion of an International Anti-Imperialist Youth League at Howard University, Hoover ordered an investigation of Padmore and his associates on the campus.[10]

The Bureau also continued to monitor the activities of the (communist) Workers Party after Attorney General Stone's edict in 1924. The State Department's own sources asserted that the Communist International had appropriated over seven million gold rubles for propaganda work among blacks. Hoover's agents claimed to have uncovered a much more modest sum, $60,000, being funneled to the party for this purpose. What worried the Bureau most was not the amount of money but Moscow's insistence that the best hope for a Bolshevik revolution in America lay in an uprising of blacks and foreign-born workers.[11]

Clearly, the Bureau did not limit itself to being a "fact-gathering organization," ignoring the private or political opinions of individuals. Investigations of blacks whose only "crime" was advocacy of political and economic radicalism continued, albeit with less frequency. And by the end of the twenties, Bureau critics suspected that Hoover's agents were monitoring them. In the first two years of Roosevelt's presidency the Bureau began investigating fascist and pro-Nazi organizations, and in 1936 the net was expanded to include all other "subversives." And soon after World War II began the president authorized the FBI (it assumed its modern name in 1935) to recreate the General Intelligence Division, employ "warrantless wiretaps and bugs," and open the mail of those "suspected of subversive activities against the government." The FBI and MID kept the black press under special scrutiny in the two years before Pearl Harbor. When involvement in World War II became inevitable the FBI, MID, and their compatriots reacted as if it were still 1919 when America stood at Armageddon. Viewing the world through perceptions embedded in their organizational memories twenty years earlier, they again defined black activists and the black press as subversive.

During World War II at least seven federal agencies—including the FBI, MID, and the Post Office Department—heavy-handedly investigated black publications. Encouraged by the White House, they sought draconian suppression which was only averted by the strong opposition of Attorney General Francis Biddle. Prominent African Americans were also subjected to thorough investigations because of their beliefs and advocacy, including labor and civil rights leader A. Philip Randolph, militant scholar-activist W. E. B. DuBois, communist leader Richard B. Moore, and West Indian nationalist Wilfred A. Domingo. Investigations of all but Domingo continued into the 1960s. The federal domestic intelligence network duplicated its efforts of World War I, monitoring nearly anyone in the first half of the forties who seemed to threaten the racial status quo.[12]

Political intelligence efforts against a wide spectrum of Americans from the 1940s on into the 1970s have been widely documented. Particularly newsworthy were revelations of FBI surveillance of civil rights leaders, especially Martin Luther King, Jr., as well as the COINTELPRO "counter-intelligence program" to crush the Black Panther Party and other allegedly subversive organizations. When Hoover fixated on King's alleged communist ties and sympathies, he replayed a forty-year-old scenario. Recent reports highlight as well long-standing army intelligence probes of African American activists, including three generations of the King family.[13]

Why did the FBI and its domestic intelligence partners remain so consistently hostile to African American aspirations and advocates up through the 1960s? Those who have looked no earlier than the civil rights era have missed an essential point. It was during World War I and the postwar Red Scare that their response to black militancy for the next fifty years took shape. In 1917 and 1918 the federal government conducted wholesale investigations of "subversives" and domestic "enemies," including many black suspects. The Justice, State, Navy, War, and Post Office departments coordinated these efforts to ensure a thorough crackdown on dissent and suspected treason, subversion, and sedition. Blacks were stereotyped as easily duped by enemy agents. Black disloyalty was assumed to be widespread. No sooner did the war end than fears of German intrigue were transformed into an even greater specter: Bolshevism would sweep across the world and engulf even America. Once again blacks were believed to be especially receptive to the diabolical manipulation of communists, socialists, or other radicals.

J. Edgar Hoover's first major assignment with the Bureau of Investigation was to establish and systematize its anti-radical efforts. Immersing himself in the radicals' own literature, he embraced its apocalyptic visions and became convinced that America was imperiled not only by white Bolsheviks and anarchists, but by black militancy as well. In his mind there was little difference between civil rights activism, Pan-Africanism, and promotion of communism or socialism; all threatened to unhinge the racial status quo and unleash internal dissension that would leave the nation vulnerable to attack from within or without. Conservative army and navy officers who staffed their intelligence services shared similar apprehensions. So too did career bureaucrats in the State Department, including diplomats who witnessed firsthand the march of communism in Europe and learned of its intent to use blacks' unmet aspirations to provoke domestic unrest. By 1920 these assumptions had become fixed in the minds of those responsible for national security. Any qualms about the propriety of domestic espionage and political surveillance were put aside when an enemy or communist (often synonymous) threat appeared.

During the Red Scare following World War I, the *Crisis* advocated full civil rights with the *Messenger* going even further, demanding complete social equality. Neither goal was acceptable to Hoover in 1919, because each would destroy the assumptions and power relationships on which white Americans organized their present and planned their future. Both, he believed, would also weaken the nation and leave it vulnerable to foreign ideologies and subversion. Nothing seemed fundamentally different to Hoover in the 1960s as King and others posed the most militant threat ever to white supremacy, even though their weapon was nonviolence. Full civic and social equality for African Americans was as unthinkable then as it had been two generations before. The Bureau's response to legitimate black aspirations changed little if at all in fifty years; the federal intelligence community's hostility to black freedom had been engraved in stone in 1919 and 1920.

Two questions remain: Did federal intelligence agencies respond to genuine threats to national security when they took the offensive against black militancy during the Red Scare? And how much damage was done to black advocacy and activism during that period? Recent research in former Soviet archives demonstrates that the Communist International (Comintern), Lenin's effort to control Bolshevik-inspired revolutionary movements and new communist parties all over the world, indeed supplied funds and gave orders to

American communists. More than $1 million was funneled through journalist John Reed in 1920. Both the Communist Party of America and the Communist Labor Party, which merged in 1921, "proclaimed themselves dedicated to the violent overthrow of the American state and issued terrifying threats."[14] American communists spied for the Soviet Union's foreign intelligence agency, and a number—including several blacks—went to Russia for training or conferences. These were reasonable grounds for monitoring their activities. Information that Cyril Briggs received a personal stipend and subsidies for the *Crusader* from the Workers Party was probably accurate. On that account the Bureau had justification for monitoring the African Blood Brotherhood and its leadership.

right

But numerous others, who had no ties to the Communist International, Soviet Russia, or American communists, endured federal surveillance. Many of those labeled Bolsheviks by federal agents were in fact socialists and never members of a communist party or active promoters of a communist agenda. The *Messenger* received financial support from socialist sources, not from communists. While it admired the fruits of the Bolshevik revolution and gave rhetorical support to revolutionary methods, it was not formally linked to any group actually trying to start a revolution in America. As for Marcus Garvey's UNIA and nondoctrinaire periodicals like the *Crisis* and *Chicago Defender*, there was never any reasonable cause to believe that their ideas or agendas endangered national security. Members of the Industrial Workers of the World tended toward anarcho-syndicalism, an ideology emphasizing the abolition of both private property and formal government, but by 1919 the Wobblies were decimated as an organization, and most of their black members and supporters were ideological socialists with few if any real ties to communists or their parties.

wrong

But protecting national (or military) security was not the only justification used by the Bureau, MID, and the Post Office and State departments in seeking to blunt African American militancy. They were equally intent on preserving the racial status quo. Here is clear evidence of federal injustice. Whites, as individuals, had the political freedom (as distinguished from a moral right) to try to preserve their racial privilege. But government did not possess that liberty. The political intelligence partners exceeded their authority when they sought to delegitimize blacks' political expression, aspirations for full citizenship, and right to personal security.

If domestic political intelligence is justified in a democratic state, it must be limited by strictly defined parameters, with threats to national security being clearly demonstrated. Such standards were often ignored in the Red Scare years. The *political* agenda of many white Americans—white supremacy—

political agenda became security agenda

became the *security* agenda of powerful arms of the national government. That this abuse of federal authority did not cease in 1924 is all the more serious because it helped perpetuate broad interference in First Amendment freedoms in subsequent times. Hoover and the Bureau defined civil rights militancy and demands for full equality as communist- or radical-inspired following World War I. As late as the 1960s, Hoover's FBI frequently charged that communists were manipulating the civil rights movement. Thus he justified widespread surveillance as it had been justified forty years before.

Finally, how much damage did federal political intelligence efforts do to black movements from 1919 to 1925? Red-baiting is a powerful weapon for delegitimizing political advocacy, and every prominent black dissenter felt such attacks. Militants knew they were being watched, their words recorded, their mail opened and copied, their office files rifled. Many also recognized that their plans and purposes were being distorted. The *Messenger* was denied a second-class mailing rate for many months, and thus had to pay much more to disseminate its views. Other periodicals knew they were being watched when individual issues were delayed for examination by the postal solicitor's office. Every editor of a militant publication had to fear losing his second-class permit. It is also likely that Randolph and Owen were aware that the Justice Department would use the Espionage and Sedition acts to silence them if it could.

Many leaders also suspected that their organizations were being infiltrated, and particularly in the case of the UNIA and the ABB, fears of betrayal were successfully fueled by Bureau agents and informants. Any organization is weakened if it becomes paranoid about the loyalty of its members. Furthermore, every outspoken critic of the political and racial status quo who was not an American citizen also had to fear the prospect of deportation; the expulsion of "anarchists" in 1919 was a lesson that could not have been lost on Garvey as well as the largely unnaturalized leadership of the ABB. Garvey was relentlessly pursued by a federal intelligence network which probed every corner of his public actions and private affairs. Certainly he was guilty of misleading investors in the Black Star Line. The government's main objective, however, was not to prosecute a mail fraud case, but to silence a leader whose influence over the black masses was deemed dangerous. Randolph could have spoken for Garvey, Briggs, and many others when he remembered that "I felt the force of the law and the force of public opinion . . . and I had no peace anywhere."[15]

How much, if any, of this federal intrusion was warranted? Ben Fletcher was imprisoned as a result of wartime hysteria, his "offenses" including opposition to the war and leadership in an organization (the IWW) which the

government was determined to crush, no matter the constitutional consequences. This case is most accurately located within the context of extreme
intolerance toward dissent during World War I. After the armistice, did any
black organization put in motion concrete steps for a revolution? No arms
cache or act of violence was ever linked to the ABB, the *Messenger* circle, or the
NAACP. Garvey's African Legion possessed guns which were only for show or
the protection of UNIA leadership. Promotion of armed defense against
rioters and lynchers by the ABB/*Crusader* group, the *Messenger,* and Marcus
Garvey was clearly lawful, as federal attorneys knew. So too was the militant
advocacy, in speech and print, of racial pride, social equality, civil rights, and
even communism and socialism.

Given the intensity of investigation, surveillance, and infiltration, if pros-
ecutable offenses had been committed by Randolph, Briggs, or other black
radicals, the Justice Department would have acted with vigor and dispatch.
The conclusion is inescapable: The federal intelligence partners, led by the
Justice Department's Bureau of Investigation, knew that even strident racial
advocacy and self-defense were lawful. But their distaste for black militancy
was so profound that they persisted in harassing individuals engaged in legal,
if unpopular, activities. The even-handed administration of justice was sacrificed. Federal injustice prevailed. And it established a pattern of hostility to
racial and civil rights progress that persisted for the next fifty years, until after
the death of J. Edgar Hoover in 1972.

NOTES

Prologue

1. *New York Evening Telegram,* 20 Nov. 1919.
2. Robert A. Bowen, "Radicalism and Sedition among the Negroes as Reflected in Their Publications," 2 July 1919, "Old German" case file 359561, Record Group 65, Investigative Case Files of the Bureau of Investigation, 1908–1922, Records of the Federal Bureau of Investigation, National Archives.
3. William Cohen, "Riots, Racism, and Hysteria: The Response of Federal Investigative Officials to the Race Riots of 1919," *Massachusetts Review* 13 (1972), p. 373.
4. Theodore Kornweibel, Jr., ed., *Federal Surveillance of Afro-Americans (1917–1925): The First World War, the Red Scare, and the Garvey Movement* (Frederick, Md., 1986), 25 reels of microfilm.
5. Robert A. Hill, ed., *The Marcus Garvey and Universal Negro Improvement Association Papers* (Berkeley, Calif., 1983-).
6. See the descriptive brochure "Investigative Case Files of the Bureau of Investigation, 1908–1922," Washington: National Archives and Records Service, 1983.
7. U.S. Senate, *Investigation Activities of the Department of Justice,* 66th Cong., 1st Sess., Sen. Doc. 153 (Washington, 1919), pp. 13, 162.

1. "Unrest and Radicalism Are Rife"

1. An excellent discussion of the nature of political intelligence, and its dangers to an open society, is Frank J. Donner, *The Age of Surveillance: The Aims and Methods of America's Political Intelligence System* (New York, 1980), chap. 1.
2. Donner, pp. 30–32.
3. Donner, *Age of Surveillance,* p. 32; Frank Donner, *Protectors of Privilege: Red Squads and Police Repression in Urban America* (Berkeley, Calif., 1990); Sidney L. Harring, *Policing a Class Society: The Experience of American Cities, 1865–1915* (New Brunswick, N.J., 1983); Gerda W. Ray, "Activists Rescue Detroit Red Squad Files," *Organization of American Historians Newsletter* 21 (August 1993), pp. 3–4.
4. Robert Justin Goldstein, *Political Repression in Modern America, from 1870 to the Present* (Cambridge, Mass., 1978), pp. 24–33.
5. William Preston, Jr., *Aliens and Dissenters: Federal Suppression of Radicals, 1903–1933* (New York, 1966), pp. 3–4; Goldstein, p. 41.
6. Goldstein, pp. 54–63.
7. Goldstein, pp. 63–70; Preston, p. 4.
8. Quoted in Goldstein, pp. 72–73.
9. Preston, pp. 5–6.
10. Max Lowenthal, *The Federal Bureau of Investigation* (New York, 1950), pp. 12–13; Don Whitehead, *The FBI Story: A Report to the People* (New York, 1956), pp. 23, 27–31, 330n7; Joan M. Jensen, *The Price of Vigilance* (Chicago, 1968), pp. 10–16, 21, 23, 29–30; Edward M. House Diary, 3 Mar. 1917, in Arthur M. Link, ed., *The Papers of Woodrow Wilson,* vol. 41 (Princeton, N.J., 1966–), p. 318 [hereafter *Wilson Papers*]; Thomas Watt Gregory to William Gibbs McAdoo, 12 June 1917, *Wilson Papers,* vol. 42, pp. 510–11. At

the beginning of World War I naval intelligence, like its army counterpart, was "a tiny, insignificant organization." Jeffery M. Dorwart, *Conflict of Duty: The U.S. Navy's Intelligence Dilemma, 1919–1945* (Annapolis, Md., 1983), p. 7.

11. House Diary, 14 Dec. 1916, *Wilson Papers,* vol. 40, pp. 238–41; Robert Lansing to Woodrow Wilson, 8 Apr. 1917, *Wilson Papers,* vol. 42, pp. 16–17, McAdoo to Wilson, 16 Apr. 1917, Woodrow Wilson Papers, Manuscript Division, Library of Congress [hereafter Wilson Papers, LC]; Jensen, pp. 40–41; Col. Claud E. Stadtman and Capt. Carmelo J. Bernardo, *History of the War Department Military Intelligence Activities 1885–1920* (Washington: Office of the Chief of Military History, Department of the Army, n.d.), pp. 2–4.

12. Stadtman and Bernardo, chap. 6, p. 6; McAdoo to Wilson, 15 May 1917, Wilson Papers, LC; Gregory to McAdoo, 12 June 1917, Gregory to Wilson, 14 June 1917, McAdoo to Wilson, 2 June 1917, Wilson to Gregory, 4 June 1917, *Wilson Papers,* vol. 42, pp. 440–43, 446, 509–19; Wilson to Gregory, 12 July 1917, *Wilson Papers,* vol. 43, pp. 154–55; Gregory to Wilson, 16 Apr. 1917, 14 June 1917, Gregory to McAdoo, 17 Apr. 1917, Quartermaster General to Secretary of War, 28 June 1917, Secret Service Operative Thomas J. Callaghan to Chief William J. Flynn, 29 June 1917, McAdoo to Wilson, 5 July 1917, Wilson Papers, LC; Jensen, pp. 43, 54–55; Stadtman and Bernardo, chap. 6, pp. 16–17.

13. McAdoo to Newton D. Baker, 9 July 1917, McAdoo to Wilson, 9 July 1917, Thomas Callaghan to W. J. Flynn, 29 June 1917, Wilson Papers, LC; Stadtman and Bernardo, chap. 6, pp. 14–17. At the same time the Post Office Department, in investigating alleged disloyalty of one of its employees, utilized Bureau of Investigation agents to assist its own inspectors; Second Assistant Postmaster General Otto Praeger to Albert Sidney Burleson, July 16, July 17, 1917, Wilson Papers, LC; House diary, 7 Aug. 1917, *Wilson Papers,* vol. 43, pp. 390–91; Josephus Daniels diary, 31 Aug. 1917, *Wilson Papers,* vol. 44, p. 107.

14. Harry N. Scheiber, *The Wilson Administration and Civil Liberties, 1917–1921* (Ithaca, N.Y., 1960), pp. 13–26.

15. Scheiber, pp. 17, 22, 26–28; Zechariah Chafee, Jr., *Free Speech in the United States* (Cambridge, Mass., 1941), p. 214; Roy Talbert, Jr., *Negative Intelligence: The Army and the American Left, 1917–1941* (Jackson, Miss., 1991), p. 66.

16. *Annual Report of the Attorney General of the United States for the Year 1919,* p. 12.

17. Whitehead, pp. 39–47.

18. Whitehead, p. 50.

19. Samuel J. Graham to Joseph P. Tumulty, 6 June 1917, Wilson Papers, LC; *Congressional Record,* 56th Cong., 2nd. Sess., vol. LVI, 22 June 1918, pp. 8138–39; Jensen, p. 155; *Annual Report of the Attorney General of the United States for the Year 1917* (Washington, 1917), pp. 82–84; *Annual Report of the Attorney General of the United States for the Year 1918* (Washington, 1918), pp. 14–16, 104–105; *Attorney General Annual Report 1919* (Washington, 1919), p. 12; John Whiteclay Chambers II, *To Raise an Army: The Draft Comes to Modern America* (New York, 1987), pp. 211–12.

20. *Attorney General Annual Report 1919* (Washington, 1919), p. 12.

21. Contemporary writers usually did not capitalize "negro," and their usage has been retained in quotations.

22. Hoover to Bureau, 10 Oct. 1919, Hoover, "Memorandum upon Work of Radical Division," 18 Oct. 1919, OG374217, RG65, BI, NA. *New York Times,* 17 July 1919, p. 5, col. 1; Scully to Bureau, 9 Oct. 1919, OG258421, RG65, BI, NA.

23. Lowenthal, pp. 48–50.

24. U.S. Senate, *Investigation Activities of the Department of Justice,* 66th Cong., 1st Sess., Sen. Doc. 153 (Washington, 1919), pp. 172–73, 179, 181–82, 184.

25. Marc Powe, *The Emergence of the War Department Intelligence Agency: 1885–1918* (Manhattan, Kan., 1975), pp. 76–102; Bruce Bidwell, *History of the Military Intelligence Division, Department of the Army General Staff: 1775–1941* (Frederick, Md., 1986), pp. 95–99, 105, 109–11, 113–15, 117–18; Stadtman and Bernardo, chap. 14, pp. 1–2; Talbert, pp. 8–9.

26. Bidwell, pp. 110–12, 122–26, 203; Powe, pp. 94–95; Stadtman and Bernardo, chap. 6, pp. 14–15, chap. 14, pp. 38–39; Talbert, p. 9.

27. Marlborough Churchill, "The Military Intelligence Division, General Staff," *Journal of the United States Artillery* 3 (Apr. 1920), p. 294.

28. Bidwell, pp. 190–91.

29. Bidwell, pp. 236–37; Stadtman and Bernardo, chap. 10, pp. 1–2, chap. 14, p. 31.

30. Stadtman and Bernardo, chap. 14, pp. 32–33.

31. Talbert, pp. 135–43; *New York Times*, 26 Jan. 1919.

32. Talbert, pp. 145–50, 156–64.

33. Talbert, pp. 170–74; Robert K. Murray, *Red Scare: A Study in National Hysteria, 1919–1920* (New York, 1964), pp. 68–78, 167.

34. Bidwell, pp. 277–78; Stadtman and Bernardo, chap. 15, pp. 1–3, 10–11; Talbert, pp. 183–90.

35. Stadtman and Bernardo, chap. 15, pp. 1–3, 10–11; Bidwell, pp. 275–78; Talbert, pp. 192–206.

36. Talbert, pp. 206–207, 221.

37. Talbert, p. 206.

38. J. B. S. to Lamar, 2 Mar. 1918, unarranged file, Amendments to [Espionage and Trading with the Enemy] Acts, 1917–21, Horton [?] to Lamar, 10 Feb. 1919, case file 51378A, "War Activities of Post Office Department, Office of Solicitor," RG28, PO, NA; Lamar, "Open letter to Taft," Albert Sidney Burleson Papers, University of Texas [hereafter Burleson Papers, UT].

39. *Annual Report of the Postmaster General for the Fiscal Year Ended June 30, 1919* (Washington, 1919), pp. 112–13; Scheiber, p. 35; *Annual Report of the Postmaster General for the Fiscal Year Ended June 30, 1920* (Washington, 1920), pp. 125–26.

40. Lansing, Baker, and Daniels to Wilson, 13 Apr. 1917, Gregory to Wilson, 20 Feb. 1918, Lansing to Wilson, 20 Feb. 1918, John Lord O'Brian to Gregory, 18 Apr. 1918, Lansing to Wilson, 25 July 1918, J. M. Host to Tumulty, 14 Oct. 1920, Sec. of State Bainbridge Colby to Tumulty, 26 Oct. 1920, Wilson Papers, LC; Frank Lyon Polk to American Commissioners, 27 Jan. 1919, *Wilson Papers*, vol. 54, p. 126; Charles Flint Kellogg, *NAACP: A History of the National Association for the Advancement of Colored People, Volume I, 1909–1920* (Baltimore, 1967), pp. 278–82; Stephen R. Fox, *The Guardian of Boston: William Monroe Trotter* (New York, 1970), pp. 224–30.

41. Bertram D. Hulen, *Inside the Department of State* (New York, 1939), pp. 59–63; *Register of the Department of State, 1918* (Washington, 1919); *Register of the Department of State, 1922* (Washington, 1922); Rachael West, *The Department of State on the Eve of the First World War* (Athens, Ga., 1978), pp. 56, 58.

42. Hulen, pp. 262–63, 269–75.

43. Dorwart, pp. 5–13.

44. Arthur E. Barbeau and Florette Henri, *The Unknown Soldiers: Black American Troops in World War I* (Philadelphia, 1974), pp. 36–37; Theodore Kornweibel, Jr., "Apathy and Dissent: Black America's Negative Responses to World War I," *South Atlantic Quarterly* 80 (Summer 1981), 322–38.

45. Richard Gid Powers, *Secrecy and Power: The Life of J. Edgar Hoover* (New York, 1987), chap. 1, evokes the world of middle-class federal employees in Washington's segregated neighborhoods.

46. Even with the return of a Republican administration in 1921, black federal employees were overwhelmingly elevator operators, chauffeurs, and laborers. See statistics in case file 93, "Negro Matters," Warren G. Harding Papers, Ohio Historical Society.

47. Hulen, pp. 9–10.

48. See, for example, Robert Russa Moton to Wilson, 8 Aug. 1919, Wilson to Moton, 12 Aug. 1919, Wilson Papers, LC.

49. See, for example, Wilson to Colby, 29 Sept. 1920, Wilson Papers, LC; diary of Raymond Blaine Fosdick, 8 Dec. 1918, *Wilson Papers,* vol. 53, pp. 340–41; diary of Dr. Grayson, 5 Mar. 1919, *Wilson Papers,* vol. 55, p. 442; Joe P. Byrne to Burleson, 24 June 1919, Burleson Papers, UT; "Address of Hon. Thomas W. Gregory at the Meeting of the New York Southern Society, December 9th, 1914," "Reconstruction and the Ku Klux Klan," paper read before the Arkansas and Texas Bar Associates, 10 July 1906, Thomas Watt Gregory Papers, University of Texas; "Human Interest Stories about Albert S. Burleson," n.d., Burleson Papers, UT; Gregory, "How the Rear of Our Armies Was Guarded during the World War." Burleson was accused of using convict labor on his large Texas plantation, and defended himself by saying that he had no control over the labor used thereon when the state government leased his land; besides, the convicts were white, he claimed. See House to Burleson, 24 Apr. 1918, press release from Burleson's office, 26 Apr. 1919, Burleson Papers, UT.

2. "Dangerous Influences at Work upon the Negro"

1. A good summary of these Byzantine developments and events is in Robert K. Murray, *Red Scare: A Study of National Hysteria, 1919–1920* (c. 1955; New York, 1964), pp. 41–52.

2. Agent R. W. Finch to Bureau, 13 Nov. 1918, "Old German" case file 208369 [hereafter OG], Finch to Bureau, 11 Feb. 1919, 12 Feb. 1919, 20 Feb. 1919, 10 Mar. 1919, 20 Mar. 1919, OG258421, Record Group 65, Investigative Case Files of the Bureau of Investigation, 1908–1922, Records of the Federal Bureau of Investigation, National Archives [hereafter RG65, BI, NA].

3. Theodore Kornweibel, Jr., *No Crystal Stair: Black Life and the Messenger, 1917–1928* (Westport, Conn., 1975), pp. 75–80; see also the Bureau's futile efforts, discussed in chapter 7, to discover the source of the circular entitled "Negro Domination" which stated that the triumph of Bolshevism would guarantee black rule over white in the South.

4. Agent J. F. Kropidlowski to Bureau, 29 Apr. 1919, OG36727, agent H. A. Lewis to Bureau, 8 Apr. 1919, OG49899, 22 May 1919, OG366523, Counselor L. Lanier Winslow to Acting Chief W. E. Allen, 26 Feb. 1919, agent W. H. Poling to Bureau, 15 Apr. 1919 (2 documents), OG185161, RG65, BI, NA.

5. "What Is Attorney General Palmer Doing," *Nation* 110 (14 Feb. 1920), pp. 190–91 (6 Mar. 1920), pp. 285, 299, Arthur Wallace Dunn, "The 'Reds' in America from the Standpoint of the Department of Justice," *American Review of Reviews* 61 (Feb. 1920), p. 166, *Providence Journal,* 1 June 1919, *New York Times,* 28 July 1919.

6. *New York Times,* 27 Aug. 1919.

7. Robert A. Bowen, "Radicalism and Sedition among the Negroes as Reflected in Their Publications," OG359561, RG65, BI, NA.

8. Agent Roy C. McHenry to Bureau, 11 June 1919, OG136944, agent J. A. Brann to Bureau, 13 June 1919, agent Mortimer J. Davis to Bureau, 12 Aug. 1919, agent Joseph G. Tucker to Bureau, 12 Aug. 1919, special confidential informant S–500 to Bureau, 20 Aug. 1919, OG258421, agent F. C. Haggarly to Bureau, 23 July 1919, OG369936, agent Mills Kitchin to Bureau, 7 Aug. 1919 (2 documents), OG369914, Assistant Director and Chief Frank Burke (initialed J. Edgar Hoover) to Division Superintendent William M. Offley, 23

July 1919, OG370965, H. A. Lewis to Bureau, 25 July 1919, OG336880, Gov. W. P. Hobby to Attorney General A. Mitchell Palmer, 29 July 1919, Hobby to Div. Supt. C. E. Breniman, 29 July 1919, agent Claude McCaleb to Bureau, 31 July 1919, Breniman to Burke, 31 July 1919, Breniman to Hobby, 31 July 1919, Burke to Breniman, 6 Aug. 1919, OG369955, "Special News of the Day in Brief," 3 Aug. 1919, OG129548, RG65, BI, NA; agent Frank L. Turner to Bureau, "Bureau Section" case file [hereafter BS] 215365, RG65, BI, NA.

9. Burke (initialed Hoover) to Acting Special Agent in Charge J. J. McLaughlin, 9 Aug. 1919, OG161973, McLaughlin to Burke, 12 Aug. 1919, agent William C. Sausele to Bureau, 18 Oct. 1919 (2 documents), OG375446, agent Louis Loebl to Bureau, 8 Oct. 1919, OG373512, Davis to Bureau, 29 Aug. 1919, OG387162, Davis to Bureau, 22 Aug. 1919, OG185161, Act. Div. Supt. J. A. Baker to Burke, 21 Aug. 1919, OG3057, agent C. J. Scully to Bureau, 23 Aug. 1919, OG208369, special confidential informant C-C [Arthur U. Craig] to Bureau, 30 Aug. 1919, OG258421, agent Gus T. Hall, 16 Sept. 1919, OG371751, Rear Adm. A. P. Niblack to Burke, 14 Oct. 1919, OG376475, RG65, BI, NA.

10. Hoover to Burke, 12 Aug. 1919, OG258421, Hoover to Mr. Ridgely, 11 Oct. 1919, OG329359, consolidated with BS198940, RG65, BI, NA.

11. McHenry to Bureau, 4 Feb. 1920, OG97671, Special Assistant to the Attorney General Alfred Bettman to Chief A. Bruce Bielaski, 10 Sept. 1918, Special Agent in Charge Bliss Morton to Bielaski, 11 Sept., 18 Sept. 1918, OG234939, RG65, BI, NA; Philip S. Foner, *American Socialism and Black Americans from the Age of Jackson to World War II* (Westport, Conn., 1977), p. 255.

12. Special confidential informant P–138 [Herbert S. Boulin] to Bureau, 14 Oct. 1920, OG258421, agent J. S. Apelman to Bureau, 2 Sept. 1919, OG31462, agent Claude P. Light to Bureau, 26 Aug. 1919, SAC Charles P. Tighe to Burke, 22 Sept. 1919, Burke to agent Barkey, 3 Oct. 1919, Burke to Tighe, 14 Oct. 1919, OG97671, RG65, BI, NA.

13. McHenry to Bureau, 4 Feb. 1920, OG97671, agent Walter O. Lewis to Bureau, 30 Apr. 1920, OG370818, "Weekly Bulletin of Radical Activities" no. 17, 15 May 1920, OG374217, Apelman to Bureau, 12 June 1920, OG248775, special confidential informant P–135 to Bureau, 18 May 1920, P–138 to Bureau, 14 Oct. 1920, OG258421, agent T. C. Wilcox to Bureau, 10 July 1920, agent Emil A. Solanka to Bureau, 24 July, 4 Sept. 1920, OG229849, agent August H. Loula to Bureau, 5 June 1920, BS202600–14, agent W. L. Buchanan to Bureau, 27 Sept. 1920, BS202600–1613, RG65, BI, NA.

14. Apelman to Bureau, 14 Feb. 1921, BS202600–23–20x, Solanka to Bureau, 23 Mar. 1921, BS202600–26–25, agent Jacob Spolansky to Bureau, 2 May 1921, BS202600–1778–22, Loula to Bureau, 16 May 1921, BS202600–1778–13, Loula to Bureau (attn. Hoover), 23 May 1921, BS202600–14–65, Buchanan to Bureau, 8 Aug. 1921, BS202600–1613–23, 15 Aug. 1921, BS202600–33–304, agent Henry J. Lenon to Bureau, 12 Sept. 1921, BS202600–1768–22, RG65, BI, NA.

15. W. Burghardt Turner and Joyce Moore Turner, eds. *Richard B. Moore, Caribbean Militant in Harlem: Collected Writings, 1920–1972* (Bloomington, Ind., 1988), pp. 165–66.

16. MID weekly reports, weeks ending 7 Jan. 1920, 13 Jan. 1920, 21 Jan. 1920, 4 Feb. 1920, 11 Feb. 1920, 24 Mar. 1920, 31 Mar. 1920, 21 July 1920, 25 Aug. 1920, OG377098, Colvin to MILSTAFF, 17 July 1920, Col. John M. Dunn to Burke, 23 July 1920, OG3057, RG65, BI, NA.

17. Agent R. W. Tinsley to Bureau, 12 Jan. 1920, Acting Chief to Breniman, 24 Feb. 1920, OG105390, SAC J. V. Bell to Deputy Sheriff R. A. Hagen, 15 Jan. 1920, Bell to Breniman, 20 Jan. 1920, OG369955, Breniman to Bell, 16 Jan. 1920, 23 Jan. 1920, Breniman to Texas Atty. Gen. C. N. Carsten, 16 Jan. 1920, OG386064, RG65, BI, NA.

18. Informant Albert Farley to Bureau, 21 Jan. 1920, 19 Apr. 1920, agent M. A. Joyce to Bureau, 22 Jan. 1920, OG369936, special confidential informant WW (William A. Bailey) to Bureau, 30 Jan. 1920, 6 Feb. 1920, 20 Mar. 1920, OG258421, RG65, BI, NA.

19. P–138 to Bureau, 21 Aug. 1920, 30 Aug. 1920, OG329359, consolidated with BS198940, 4 Sept. 1920, 7 Sept. 1920, 9 Sept. 1920, 27 Sept. 1920 (2 documents), OG329359, consolidated with BS198940, 15 Sept. 1920, 22 Sept. 1920, 27 Oct. 1920, 29 Oct. 1920, OG258421, RG65, BI, NA.

20. P–138 to Bureau, 14 Oct. 1920, 18 Oct. 1920, 19 Oct. 1920, OG258421, 28 Nov. 1920, BS198940–35, 7 Dec. 1920, BS202600–667–3, 31 May 1921, BS202600–1628–66, 2 June 1921, BS202600–2155, 7 June 1921, BS202600–1628, 29 June 1921, BS202600–667–59, RG65, BI, NA; 22 June 1921, 9–12–725–11, RG60, DJ, NA.

21. Weekly radical reports, Div. Supt. George F. Lamb to Burke (attn. Hoover), 21 Aug. 1920, 11 Sept. 1920, 18 Sept. 1920, agent T. M. Reddy to Burke (attn. Hoover), 16 Oct. 1920, OG208369, 4 Dec. 1920, BS202600–33–111, RG65, BI, NA.

22. Weekly radical report, Loula to Bureau (attn. Hoover), 27 Mar. 1920, 21 May 1920, BS202600–14, General Intelligence Bulletin, Loula to Bureau, 18 Apr. 1921, BS202600–14–53, RG65, BI, NA.

23. Agent H. M. Zorian to Bureau, 19 Mar. 1920, OG17969, agent William M. Doyas to Bureau, 9 June 1920, OG174344, agent H. S. Hubbard to Bureau, 31 Jan. 1921, BS202600–40–1, agent William J. Gaffney to Bureau, 21 Jan. 1921, BS202600–667–22, SAC Walter C. Foster to Chief (attn. Hoover), 24 Mar. 1921, BS202600–1338–2, agent J. F. McDevitt to Bureau, 20 May 1921, BS202600–1617–16, agent Edward P. Morse to Bureau, 28 May 1921, BS202600–1687–2, agent Adrian L. Potter to Bureau, 21 Feb. 1921, BS202600–22–54x, 10 Apr. 1921, BS202600–22–65, 2 May 1921, BS202600–22–84, 30 May 1921, BS202600–22–95, RG65, BI, NA; Buchanan to Bureau, 7 Mar. 1921, 202600–33–182x, RG60, DJ, NA.

24. Monthly Report on Radical Publications, Scully to Bureau, 16 July 1921, BS202600–33–285, RG65, BI, NA. For more information on the Tulsa riot, see chapter 7, pp. 140ff.

25. Div. Supt. R. B. Spencer to Chief (attn. Hoover), 1 July 1921, BS202600–1768–8, SAC Clarence D. McKean to Chief (attn. Hoover), 6 July 1921, BS202600–1768–10, RG65, BI, NA.

26. Apelman to Bureau, 2 Aug. 1921, BS202600–23–41, Weekly radical report, Foster to Chief (attn. Hoover), 2 July 1921, BS202600–1617–27, General Intelligence Bulletin, agent W. J. West to Bureau, 11 July 1921, BS202600–1622–12, Col. Matthew C. Smith to Chief Lewis J. Baley, 7 July 1921, BS202600–1628–100, Baley to agent Frank X. O'Donnell, 11 July 1921, BS202600–1628–103, agent W. C. Treadwell to Bureau, 20 Aug. 1921, BS202600–1687–5, Weekly radical reports, Wilcox to Bureau, 26 July 1921, BS202600–1689, 18 July 1921, BS202600–1689–24, Monthly reports on radical publications, Wilcox to Bureau, 15 July 1921, BS202600–1689–23, Apelman to Bureau, 16 Aug. 1921, BS202600–1689–29, Spencer to Chief (attn. Hoover), 1 July 1921, BS-202600–1768–8, agent F. M. Ames to Bureau, 7 July 1921, BS202600–1768–9, McKean to Chief (attn. Hoover), 6 July 1921, BS202600–1768–10, Weekly radical reports, Lenon to Bureau, 11 July 1921, BS202600–1768–11, 18 July 1921, BS202600–1768–12, Weekly radical reports, Potter to Bureau, 11 July 1921, BS202600–1804–5, 18 July 1921, BS202600–1804–6, 29 Aug. 1921, BS202600–1804–10, SAC William P. Hazen to Dir. William J. Flynn, 12 July 1921, Flynn to Sen. Frank B. Brandegee, 13 July 1921, Baley to Hazen, 12 Aug. 1921, agent William T. Lynch to Bureau, 19 Aug. 1921, [illegible private citizen] to Attorney General, 22 Aug. 1921, agent [illegible] to Bureau, 13 Sept. 1921, BS202600–2253, Hoover to District of Columbia Commissioner James F. Oyster, 7 July 1921, BS202600–2253–1, Lewis to Baley, 11 July 1921, BS202600–2253–3, Harold P. Wilder to Secret Service, 15 July 1921, Secret Service to Bureau, 15 July 1921, BS202600–2253–6, agent J. P. Rooney to Bureau, 14 July 1921, BS202600–2253–7, Baley (initialed Hoover) to Rooney, 19 July 1921, BS202600–2253–8, agent Edwin C. Shanahan

to Bureau, 26 July 1921, BS202600–2253–14, RG65, BI, NA; Morse to Bureau, 3 Sept. 1921, case file 186701–226–10, Record Group 60, Department of Justice, National Archives [hereafter RG60, DJ, NA].

27. Lenon to Bureau, 18 July 1921, BS202600–1768–12, RG65, BI, NA.

28. General Intelligence Bulletins no. 46, 16 Apr. 1921, no. 49, 7 May 1921, no. 57, 2 July 1921, OG374217, RG65, BI, NA.

29. Turner and Turner, pp. 19–44.

30. WW to Bureau, 1 Mar. 1920, 6 Mar. 1920, OG185161, 26 Mar. 1920, OG258421, Weekly radical reports, Lamb to Director (attn. Hoover), 6 Mar. 1920, 20 Mar. 1920, 27 Mar. 1920, OG208369, General Intelligence Report, no. 7, 6 Mar. 1920, Weekly Bulletin of Radical Activities, no. 9, 20 Mar. 1920, OG374217, MID weekly report, 3 Apr. 1920, OG377098, RG65, BI, NA.

31. P–135 to Bureau, 11 May 1920, 18 May 1920, 11 June 1920, OG258421, RG65, BI, NA.

32. P–138 to Bureau, 20 Sept. 1920, OG329359, consolidated with BS198940, 21 Dec. 1920, BS202600–667–9x, 3 Mar. 1921, BS202600–667–30x, 29 Mar. 1921, BS202600–667–32, 4 Apr. 1921, BS202600–667–33x, 6 May 1921, BS202600–667–44, 31 May 1921, BS198940–145, 3 June 1921, BS202600–2015, Weekly radical reports, Reddy to Chief (attn. Hoover), 25 Dec. 1920, BS202600–33–130, 21 May 1921, BS202600–1628–40, 4 June 1921, BS202600–1628–76, RG65, BI, 9 Apr. 1921, straight numerical file 202600–33–209, RG60, DJ, NA.

33. P–138 to Bureau, 14 June 1921, BS202600–2031–3, Weekly radical reports, Reddy to Bureau, 11 June 1921, BS202600–1628–84, Scully to Bureau, 18 June 1921, RG65, BI, NA.

34. P–138 to Bureau, 17 June 1921, BS198940–164, 2 July 1921, BS202600–667–62, 30 July 1921, BS202600–667–75, 6 Aug. 1921, BS202600–667–76, 10 Aug. 1921, BS202600–2031–7, 15 Aug. 1921, BS202600–667–78, 22 Aug. 1921, BS202600–2031–8, 22 Aug. 1921, BS202600–667–81, 30 Aug. 1921, BS202600–667–84, Weekly radical reports, Scully to Baley, attn. Hoover, 16 July 1921, BS202600–1628–107, Div. Supt. Edward J. Brennan to Director William J. Burns, BS202600–1628–138, RG65, BI, NA.

35. Agent Andrew M. Battle to Bureau, 8 July 1922, 19 July 1922, 26 July 1922, 4 Aug. 1922, 2 Oct. 1922, Bureau of Investigation case files 61–826, 61–50, obtained by author from the FBI through the Freedom of Information Act (hereafter FBI-FOIA).

36. Agent Earl E. Titus to Bureau, 27 Aug. 1923, 24 Sept. 1923, 11 Nov. 1923, 61–826, 61–50, FBI-FOIA.

37. Turner and Turner, pp. 45–51, 67ff.

38. Cooperation between State, Justice, and MID in sharing summaries of investigations and lists of suspects and subversive publications can be traced through Office of Counselor 504–69, 504–177, 800.9–226, 800.9–240, 811.01–27, 861.0–2213, 861.0–2417, Record Group 59, Department of State, National Archives [hereafter RG59, DS, NA]; correspondence from William L. Hurley and Winslow to the Bureau is in OG3057, OG374217, and OG377098, plus Hoover to Mrs. Bartley, 4 Jan. 1921, OG374217, RG65, BI, NA.

39. E. Bell to Winslow, 15 Apr. 1919, Winslow to Bell, 5 May 1919, Office of the Counselor case file 861.0–358, RG59, DS, NA; *Register of the Department of State: 1918* (Washington, 1918), pp. 13, 29; *Register of the Department of State: 1922* (Washington, 1922), pp. 8, 22; Bertram D. Hulen, *Inside the Department of State* (New York, 1939), pp. 59–63.

40. Robert A. Hill, ed., *The Marcus Garvey and Universal Negro Improvement Association Papers* I (Berkeley, 1983), p. 314, a biography of Jonas is on pp. 531–32; Claud E. Stadtman and Carmelo J. Bernardo, *History of the War Department Military Intelligence Activities 1885–1920* (Washington: Office of the Chief of Military History, Department of the Army, n.d.), chap. 6, p. 12, Bruce W. Bidwell, "History of the Military Intelligence Division, Depart-

ment of the Army General Staff," Office of the Chief of Military History, Department of the Army, n.d., chap. 6, p. 2, both in Record Group 319, National Archives. See also Herbert O. Yardley, *America's Black Chamber* (New York, 1931) on British cooperation with American cryptologists. British fears for its Caribbean colonies is in W. F. Elkins, "'Unrest among the Negroes': A British Document of 1919," *Science and Society* 32 (Winter 1968). For a summary of British fears, prepared by the MID office in New York, see Capt. J. B. Trevor to Brig. Gen. Marlborough Churchill, 5 Apr. 1919, case file 10218–324/1 273X(50), Record Group 165, Military Intelligence Division, National Archives [hereafter RG165, MID, NA]. British reports on black radicalism are in W. Phillips to J. W. Davis, 14 Nov. 1919, Phillips to Postmaster General Albert S. Burleson, 17 Nov. 1919, Burleson to Secretary of State Robert Lansing, 20 Dec. 1919, Central Decimal File 811.4016, RG59, DS, NA; Baker to Burke, 21 Aug. 1919, J. B. Wright to Lansing, 10 Oct. 1919, Division of Western European Affairs to Department of Justice, 5 Nov. 1919, OG3057, RG65, BI, NA.

41. Young to Secretary of State, 23 Aug. 1920, Office of Counselor 000–612, Hurley to Winslow, 18 Oct. 1920, Winslow to Hurley, 1 Nov. 1920, Office of Counselor 504–64, Hurley to Hoover, 20 Dec. 1920, Hurley to Brig. Gen. Dennis Nolan, 20 Dec. 1920, Office of Counselor 811.01–48, RG59, DS, NA.

42. Claude McKay, *A Long Way from Home* (c. 1937; New York, 1969), pp. 108–109.

43. Winslow to Hurley, 11 Mar. 1921, Hurley to Hoover, 30 Mar. 1921, Burns to Hurley, 21 July 1922, Hurley to S. Whitehouse, American Embassy, Paris, 28 July 1922, B. A. Beals, American Embassy, London, to Hurley, 18 Oct. 1922, Hurley to Burns, 1 Nov. 1922, 811.01–48, P–134 to Bureau, 23 Mar. 1922, in 811.01–273, Beals to Hurley, 10 Mar. 1922, 800.11–396, Minister F. W. B. Coleman, Riga, to Secretary of State, 5 Dec. 1922, Burns to Hurley, 13 Dec. 1922, Hurley to Burns, 11 Jan., 29 Jan. 1923 (2 documents), Hurley to Coleman, 12 Jan. 1923, Beals to Hurley, 7 Feb. 1923, Coleman to Hurley, 19 Feb., 5 Mar. 1923, Consul Prince, Copenhagen, to Secretary of State, 8 Mar. 1923, State Department to Burns, 17 Mar. 1923, 861.0–1906, Office of Counselor, RG59, DS, NA.

44. Burns to Hurley, 10 Feb. 1923, Hurley to Consul Stokeley W. Morgan, 28 Feb. 1923, Morgan to Hurley, 14 Apr., 30 Apr. 1923, 14 May 1923, Hurley to Burns, 12 May 1923, 861.0–1914, Office of Counselor, RG59, DS, NA.

45. Unidentified informant (New York) to Bureau, 16 Dec. 1921, Burns to Hurley, 12 Dec. 1922, Brennan to Burns, 13 Dec. 1922, 12 Mar. 1923, Burns to Brennan, 24 Mar. 1923, Burns to Hurley, 9 Apr. 1923, Bureau of Investigation case file 61–3497, obtained by the author from the FBI through the Freedom of Information Act. This same case file has instructions to Bureau agents in Seattle, Los Angeles, San Francisco, Portland, Chicago, Milwaukee, Sault St. Marie, Cleveland, Boston, New York, Baltimore, Galveston, New Orleans, Wilmington, North Carolina, and Charleston to be on the alert for McKay. False reports that McKay had returned to New York are also in this case file. It was not until January 1924 that black agent James E. Amos found authoritative evidence that McKay was in France: Amos to Bureau, 31 Jan. 1924, FBI 61–3497. Coleman to Secretary of State, 7 Dec., 11 Dec. 1922 (2 documents), Hurley to Burns, 11 Jan. 1923, Bureau of Investigation case file 61–826, obtained by the author from the FBI through Freedom of Information Act. Although it does not use State Department or Bureau of Investigation files, Wayne F. Cooper's *Claude McKay: Rebel Sojourner in the Harlem Renaissance* (Baton Rouge, La., 1987) is a well-detailed study which gives a more balanced treatment than McKay's autobiography, *A Long Way from Home,* although the latter is still helpful for this time period.

46. Coleman to Secretary of State, 30 Apr. 1923, C. Burnett, Military Attache, Tokyo, to Acting Chief of Staff, G–2, 19 June 1923, Coleman to Hurley, 30 Apr. 1923, Hurley to Gen. H. K. Bethell, Military Attache, British Embassy, 5 May 1923, Bethell to Norman Armour, 18 June 1923, Bethell to Hurley, 23 Apr. 1923, 861.0–1906, Office of Counselor, RG59, DS, NA.

47. Armour to Burns, 2 July 1923, Bureau of Investigation case file 61–50–401, obtained by the author from the FBI through the Freedom of Information Act; Beals to Armour, 11 Mar. 1924, 861.0–1906, Coleman to Secretary of State, 7 Jan. 1924, Armour to Burns, 9 Jan. 30 Jan. 1924, Burns to Armour, 2 Jan., 4 Jan. 1924, 861.0–2014, Wheeler (for Beals) to Armour (for Secretary of State, 2 Jan. 1924, 861.0–2020, Office of Counselor, RG59, DS, NA. McKay's residence in France is described in Cooper, chaps. 7–9. Continuing red-baiting of race militants in the 1920s is discussed in Kornweibel, *No Crystal Stair,* 94–99. Failure of the American communist party to win substantial black adherents in the 1920s is analyzed in Theodore Draper, *American Communism and Soviet Russia* (New York, 1960), chap. 15; Mark Naison, *Communists in Harlem during the Depression* (Urbana, 1983), chap. 1; and Earl Ofari Hutchinson, *Blacks and Reds: Race and Class in Conflict, 1919–1990* (East Lansing, 1995), chaps. 1–3.

3. "They Are Viciously Edited with a View of Creating Racial Hatred"

1. Thomas W. Gregory to Woodrow Wilson, 9 Jan. 1919, Woodrow Wilson Papers, Manuscript Division, Library of Congress.

2. Wilson to Attorney General Albert Sidney Burleson, 27 Nov. 1918, 2 Dec. 1918, Burleson to Wilson, 30 Nov. 1918, Arthur M. Link, ed., *The Papers of Woodrow Wilson,* vol. 53 (Princeton, N.J., 1966-), pp. 214, 260, 289 [hereafter *Wilson Papers*]; Gregory to Wilson, 17 Jan. 1919, *Wilson Papers,* vol. 54; Wilson to Burleson, 28 Feb. 1919, Dudley Field Malone to Wilson, 28 Feb. 1919, Gregory to Wilson, 1 Mar. 1919, Joseph P. Tumulty to Wilson, 1 Mar. 1919, *Wilson Papers,* vol. 55, pp. 327, 337–38, 344–48; Tumulty to Wilson, 4 Apr. 1919, *Wilson Papers,* vol. 56, pp. 618–19.

3. Diary of Dr. Grayson, 10 Mar. 1919, *Wilson Papers,* vol. 55, p. 471.

4. Theodore Kornweibel, Jr., *No Crystal Stair: Black Life and the Messenger, 1917–1928* (Westport, Conn., 1975), chaps. 1–2.

5. Special Agent in Charge Forrest C. Pendleton to Bureau, 9 Apr. 1917, agent Edward S. Chastain to Bureau, 24 Apr. 1917, "Old German Files" [hereafter OG] 5911; agent A. W. Davis to Bureau, 16 Apr. 1917, agent R. S. Phifer to Bureau, 30 Apr. 1917, OG3057, Investigative Case Files of the Bureau of Investigation, 1908–1922, Record Group 65, Records of the Federal Bureau of Investigation, National Archives [hereafter RG65, BI, NA].

6. Chief A. Bruce Bielaski to Division Superintendent Hinton G. Clabaugh, 9 Apr. 1917, agent J. E. Hawkins to Bureau, 16 Apr. 1917, Hawkins to Bureau, 16 Apr. 1917, agent P. E. Hilliard to Bureau, 17 Apr. 1917, D. Whipple to A. M. Briggs, 3 July 1917, Acting Div. Supt. Furbershaw to Bielaski, 10 July 1917, Bielaski to Clabaugh, 17 Aug. 1917, SAC Robert L. Barnes to Clabaugh, 19 Sept. 1917, agent H. B. Mock to Bureau, 20 Dec. 1917, agent B. D. Adsit to Bureau, 22 Dec. 1917, agent E. J. Kerwin to Bielaski, 2 May 1918, 9 May 1918, Adsit to Bureau, 24 May 1918, Bielaski to R. E. Baily, 3 July 1918, American Protective League operative 36 to Headquarters, 24 Sept. 1918, APL National Director C. F. Lorenzen to Bielaski, 1 Oct. 1918, 3 Oct. 1918, OG5911; Clabaugh to Bielaski, 16 Apr. 1917, "Mexican Files" [hereafter MEX] 1651; R. L. D. to Phifer, 8 May 1917, OG3057, RG65, BI, NA.

7. Operative Leo Spitz to Col. Carl Reichmann, 25 Apr. 1918, case file 10218–133–1, Reichmann to Col. Ralph Van Deman, Chief, Military Intelligence Branch, 29 Apr. 1918, 10218–133–3, Van Deman to Maj. Walter H. Loving, 3 May 1918, 10218–133–4, Loving to Van Deman, 10 May 1918, 10218–133–5, Robert S. Abbott to Loving, 11 May 1918, 10218–133–6, Loving to Van Deman, 20 May 1918, 10218–133–7, Col. Marlborough Churchill, Chief, MIB, to Maj. Joel E. Spingarn, 22 June 1918, 10218–154–14, Churchill to Chief of Staff, 2 July 1918, 10218–154–15, Record Group 165, Records of the Military Intelligence Division, National Archives [hereafter RG165, MID, NA].

8. Charles E. Boles to postal solicitor William H. Lamar, 13 June 1918, Lamar to Abbott, 13 June 1918, Postmaster M. E. Nash to Lamar, 22 June 1918, Sen. John Sharp Williams to Postmaster General Albert Sidney Burleson, 22 June 1918, Burleson to Williams, 11 July 1918, memorandum, Translation Bureau, 6 July 1918, L. How to U.S. Assistant District Attorney, 26 July 1918, 16 Aug. 1918, 26 Aug. 1918, 2 Sept. 1918, Robert A. Bowen to U.S. Assistant District Attorney, 26 July 1918, case file B–47522, Record Group 28, Espionage Act cases, Post Office Department, National Archives [hereafter RG28, PO, NA].

9. Lamar to Postmaster R. W. B. Sewell, 7 May 1920, B–349, RG28, PO, NA.

10. For the full story of the newspaper's wartime travails, see Theodore Kornweibel, Jr., "'The most dangerous of all Negro journals': Federal Efforts to Suppress the *Chicago Defender* during World War I," *American Journalism* 11 (Spring 1994), 154–68.

11. Maj. Thomas B. Crockett to Director, MID, 10 Mar. 1919, 10218–133–10, Col. J. M. Dunn, Acting Director, MID, to Crockett, 15 Mar. 1919, 10218–133–11, Dunn to W. E. Allen, Acting Chief, Bureau of Investigation, 15 Mar. 1919, 10218–133–12, RG165, MID, NA; Allen to agent P. H. Berry, 20 Mar. 1919, agent P. P. Niedak to Bureau, 28 Mar. 1919, OG5911, RG65, BI, NA.

12. Crockett to Churchill, 27 Mar. 1919, 10218–133–14, operative Charles Furthmann to Department Intelligence Office, 3 June 1919, 10218–133–19, Crockett to Churchill, 11 Aug. 1919, 10218–133–16, RG165, MID, NA.

13. Crockett to Churchill, 6 June 1919, 10218–133–20, RG165, MID, NA.

14. Rear Adm. A. P. Niblack to Allen, 20 June 1919, OG3057, RG65, BI, NA.

15. Kerwin to Bureau, 12 Mar. 1919, OG185161, RG65, BI, NA.

16. Charles Flint Kellogg, *NAACP: A History of the National Association for the Advancement of Colored People* (Baltimore, 1967), p. 236; Rep. William D. Upshaw to 1st Assistant Postmaster General J. C. Koons, 2 July 1919, sheriff T. R. Hughes to Sen. Joseph E. Ransdell, 21 July 1919, 16 Aug. 1919, Ransdell to Burleson, 21 Aug. 1919, B–349, RG28, PO, NA; W. H. Rossman to Lamar, 28 June 1919, Lamar to Rossman, 8 July 1919, Lamar to W. F. Keohan, 8 July 1919, B–47522, RG28, PO, NA.

17. Postmaster H. C. Blalock to Acting 3rd Assistant Postmaster General H. J. Barron, 17 July 1919, B–349, RG 28, PO, NA; SAC W. E. McElveen to Bielaski, 14 July 1919, OG5911, RG65, BI, NA.

18. Sewell to Inspector in charge C. B. Anderson, 6 Aug. 1919 (3 documents), Anderson to Chief Inspector R. S., 9 Aug. 1919, R. S. to Lamar, 13 Aug. 1919, B–398, RG28, PO, NA; Postmaster T. I. Celoshe to Sen. Pat Harrison, 7 Aug. 1919, memorandum, Post Office Department, 26 Aug. 1919, B–349, RG28, PO, NA.

19. Agent M. Kitchen to Bureau, 2 Aug. 1919, agent A. H. Loula to Bureau, 2 Aug. 1919, OG369914, RG65, BI, NA.

20. Agent C. G. Outlaw to Bureau, 7 Aug. 1919, OG374245, Outlaw to Assistant Director and Chief Frank Burke, 6 Aug. 1919, Special Assistant to the Attorney General J. Edgar Hoover to Outlaw, 10 Aug. 1919, OG5911, RG65, BI, NA.

21. Div. Supt. Charles E. Breniman to Bureau, 28 Aug. 1919, OG105390, RG65, BI, NA; Steven A. Reich, "Soldiers of Democracy: Black Texans and the Fight for Citizenship, 1917–1921," *Journal of American History* 82 (March 1996), pp. 1499–1500.

22. Agent R. W. Tinsley to Bureau, 5 Sept. 1919, 27 Sept. 1919, OG379422, RG65, BI, NA.

23. Gov. Charles E. Brough to Burleson, 17 Oct. 1919, Brough to Acting Solicitor H. L. Donnelly, 4 Nov. 1919, B–349, RG28, PO, NA. For background on the "riot" see Kellogg, pp. 241–45; Richard C. Cortner, *A Mob Intent on Death: The NAACP and the Arkansas Riot Cases* (Middletown, Conn., 1988); Nan Elizabeth Woodruff, "African-American Struggles for Citizenship in the Arkansas and Mississippi Deltas in the Age of Jim Crow," *Radical History Review* 55 (1993), pp. 41–44.

24. Acting Solicitor H. L. Donnelly to Chief Postal Inspector, 10 Oct. 1919, Koons to James A. Horton, 10 Oct. 1919, Donnelly to Jarman, 18 Oct. 1919, Donnelly to Brough, 27 Oct. 1919, Lamar to Brough, 26 Nov. 1919, B–349, RG28, PO, NA.

25. C. G. Wharton to 3rd Assistant Postmaster General, 5 Jan. 1920, Lamar to Wharton, 20 Jan. 1920, A. Smith to Burleson, 23 Feb. 1920, Lamar to Smith, 4 Mar. 1920, B–398; unidentified clipping, "Enjoins Incendiary Negro Publication," 16 Feb. 1920, Upshaw to Koons, 5 Apr. 1920, Acting 3rd Assistant Postmaster General H. J. Barron to Lamar, 8 Apr. 1920, Sewell to Chief Clerk, Post Office Department, 27 Apr. 1920, Lamar to Upshaw, 29 Apr. 1920, Lamar to Sewell, 7 May 1920, B–349; George McDowell to "Dear Sir," 25 May 1920, McDowell and G. G. Kilgore to "Dear Sir," 27 May 1920, B–398, RG28, PO, NA; Neil McMillen, *Dark Journey: Black Mississippians in the Age of Jim Crow* (Urbana, Ill., 1990), p. 174.

26. Bulletin of Radical Activities, No. 1, 17 Jan. 1920, OG374217, RG65, BI, NA.

27. Bulletin of Radical Activities, 27 Feb. 1920, OG374217, RG65, BI, NA.

28. See, for example, Loula to Bureau, 27 Mar. 1920, "Bureau Section" case file 202600–14 [hereafter BS], 20 Nov. 1920, BS202600–14–20, Loula to Hoover, 20 Dec. 1920, BS202600–14–24x, 31 Jan. 1921, BS202600–14–28x, Loula to Bureau, 21 Feb. 1921, BS202600–14–31x, agent M. F. Burger to Bureau, 25 Aug. 1921, BS202600–1778–56, RG65, BI, NA. Other Chicago office reports on the *Defender* are in case files OG154434 and OG369914.

29. Agent J. O. Peyronnin to Bureau, 3 Oct. 1919, 5 Oct. 1919, 6 Oct. 1919, 8 Oct. 1919, 29 June 1920, OG329359, RG65, BI, NA; agent James E. Amos to Bureau, 6 Feb. 1923, 61–50–211, agent T. L. Jefferson to Bureau, 20 Feb. 1923, 61–50–239, Bureau of Investigation case files obtained from the FBI through the Freedom of Information Act (hereafter FBI-FOIA).

30. Churchill to Burke, 27 Dec. 1919, W. L. Hurley, State Department, to Burke, 10 Dec. 1919, 23 Jan. 1920, Maj. Wrisley Brown to Hoover, 21 Feb. 1920, Lt. Col. Alexander B. Coxe to Hoover, 29 May 1920, 10 July 1920, OG377098, RG65, BI, NA.

31. P. Adams, Division of Passport Control, to "U–2," State Department, Record Group 59, Office of the Counselor, Central File 1918–1927, case file 800.9–226, National Archives. MID case file 10110–1520 contains numerous communications from intelligence officers submitting publications to headquarters.

32. See Roi Ottley, *The Lonely Warrior: The Life and Times of Robert S. Abbott* (Chicago, 1955).

33. Loula to Bureau, 2 Aug. 1919, Kitchin to Bureau, 2 Aug. 1919, OG369914, Loula to Bureau, 6 Aug. 1919, OG373051, RG65, BI, NA.

34. Crockett to Churchill, 13 Dec. 1919, 10218–384–2, RG165, MID, NA; MID weekly report, 21 Feb. 1920, OG377098, RG65, BI, NA. The practice of IOs in Chicago regularly sending copies of the *Whip* and other "radical" black papers to Washington persisted at least through the end of 1920; see Lt. Col. Gordon Johnston to Churchill, 13 Dec. 1920, 10218–384–3, RG165, MID, NA.

35. Weekly radical reports, Loula to Bureau, 27 Feb. 1920, 27 Mar. 1920, 10 Apr. 1920, 17 Apr. 1920, 24 Apr. 1920, 22 May 1920, 19 June 1920, BS202600–14, Bulletin of Radical Activities, no. 7, 27 Feb. 1920, no. 13, 17 Apr. 1920, no. 14, 1 May 1920, no. 18, 29 May 1920, OG374217, memorandum, "Negro Agitation," agent George F. Ruch to Bureau, 14 May 1920, OG3057, RG65, BI, NA.

36. Weekly radical reports, Loula to Bureau, ? July 1920, 25 Sept. 1920, BS202600–14, 13 Nov. 1920, BS202600–14–17x, 20 Nov. 1920, BS202600–14–20, 20 Dec. 1920, BS202600–14–24x, 27 Dec. 1920, BS202600–14–26x, General Intelligence Bulletin, no. 30, 25 Sept. 1920, OG374217, RG65, BI, NA.

37. General intelligence reports, Loula to Bureau, 3 Jan. 1921, BS202600–14–27, 10 Jan. 1921, 17 Jan. 1920, BS202600–14–27x, 24 Jan. 1921, BS202600–22–50, 31 Jan.

1921, BS202600–14–28x, 14 Feb. 1921, BS202600–14–30x, 21 Feb. 1921, BS202600–14–31x, 28 Feb. 1921, BS202600–14–33x, 7 Mar. 1921, BS202600–14–36x, 14 Mar. 1921, BS202600–14–39, 21 Mar. 1921, BS202600–14–41, monthly radical publications reports, Loula to Bureau, attn. Hoover, 16 May 1921, BS202600–1778–11, 16 June 1921, BS202600–1778–29, 15 Aug. 1921, BS202600–14–77, 15 Sept. 1921, BS202600–1778–64, agent Max F. Burger to Bureau, 4 Feb. 1921, BS202600–1778-x, 25 Aug. 1921, BS202600–1778–56, RG65, BI, NA.

38. For the *Age,* see case file 50827, RG28, PO, NA; case file 10218–120, RG165, MID, NA; OG271659, RG65, BI, NA. For the *News,* see case file 50829, RG28, PO, NA; case file 10218–120, RG165, MID, NA.

39. Bowen to J. Bond Smith, 2 Jan. 1919, Bowen to New York City Postmaster, 20 Mar. 1919, 50829, NYC Postmaster to Lamar, 13 Mar. 1919, 18 Mar. 1919, Lamar to NYC Postmaster, 20 May 1919, B–236, RG28, PO, NA.

40. Bowen, "Radicalism and Sedition among the Negroes as Reflected in their Publications," 2 July 1919, OG359561, RG65, BI, NA, also in B–240, RG28, PO, NA; Bowen to Lamar, 25 July 1919, B–240, 10 Sept. 1919, B–398, RG28, PO, NA.

41. Agent Mortimer J. Davis to Bureau, 29 Aug. 1919, OG387162, RG65, BI, NA; Bowen to Lamar, 28 Aug. 1919, B–398, RG28, PO, NA.

42. Weekly radical reports, Lamb to Director, attn. Hoover, 6 Mar. 1920, 13 Mar. 1920, 3 Apr. 1920, 3 May 1920, 19 June 1920, 3 July 1920, OG208369, General intelligence report, no. 7, 6 Mar. 1920, Bulletin of radical activities, 3 July 1920, OG374217, special confidential informant P–138 [Herbert S. Boulin] to Bureau, 7 Sept. 1920, OG258421, RG65, BI, NA.

43. Niblack to Allen, 20 June 1919, Niblack to Act. Chief J. T. Suter, 30 June 1919, Baker to Burke, 21 Aug. 1919, 29 Oct. 1919, Directorate of Intelligence, Home Office, special report no. 10, "Unrest among the Negroes," 7 Oct. 1919, OG3057, agent James G. C. Corcoran to Bureau, 3 Dec. 1918, OG17011, agent H. A. Lewis to Bureau, 8 Apr. 1919, 21 Apr. 1919, 28 Apr. 1919, 3 May 1919, 18 June 1919, 25 July 1919, 18 Sept. 1919, OG49899, FEH to Hoover, 29 Dec. 1919, OG185161, special confidential informant C-C [Arthur U. Craig] to Bureau, 30 Aug. 1919 (3 documents), 5 Sept. 1919, 9 Sept. 1919 (2 documents), 11 Sept. 1919, 13 Sept. 1919, 17 Sept. 1919, 20 Sept. 1919, OG258421, agent R. W. Finch to Bureau, 10 May 1919, Lewis to Bureau, 22 May 1919, OG366523, Corcoran to Bureau, 23 Dec. 1918, unidentified agent or informant to Bureau, ? Sept. 1919, C-C to Bureau, 25 Sept. 1919, 26 Sept. 1919, OG369936, RG65, BI, NA. An excellent biography of Trotter is Stephen R. Fox, *The Guardian of Boston: William Monroe Trotter* (New York, 1970).

4. "The Existence of This Organization May Be for No Good Purpose"

1. DuBois's role in challenging the leadership and strategy of Booker T. Washington is addressed in several biographies; the most recent and comprehensive is David Levering Lewis, *W. E. B. DuBois: Biography of a Race, 1868–1919* (New York, 1993).

2. For the wartime travails of the *Crisis,* see Mark Ellis, "'Closing Ranks' and 'Seeking Honors': W. E. B. DuBois in World War I," *Journal of American History* 79 (June 1992), pp. 96–124; William Jordan, "'The Damnable Dilemma': African-American Accommodation and Protest during World War I," *Journal of American History* 81 (March 1995), pp. 1562–83; Mark Ellis, "W. E. B. DuBois and the Formation of Black Opinion in World War I: A Commentary on 'The Damnable Dilemma,'" *Journal of American History* 81 (March 1995), pp. 1584–90; Lewis, pp. 552–60.

3. Agent James G. C. Corcoran to illegible [Chief A. Bruce Bielaski? or Special Assistant to the Attorney General Alfred Bettman?], 3 Dec. 1918, "Old German" case files [hereafter OG] 17011, Record Group 65, Investigative Case Files of the Bureau of Investigation,

1908–1922, Records of the Federal Bureau of Investigation, National Archives [hereafter RG65, BI, NA]; Lewis, pp. 561–78.

4. Agent R. W. Finch to Bureau, 20 Mar. 1919, OG258421, RG65, BI, NA; Acting Director Col. John M. Dunn to Special Assistant to the Secretary of War Emmett J. Scott, 27 Feb. 1919, case file 10218–296–7, Record Group 165, Military Intelligence Division, National Archives [hereafter RG165, MID, NA]. By the war's end the New York office of the Bureau was taking special interest in the NAACP and the *Crisis*; see, e.g., Finch to Bureau, 12 Nov. 1918, 7 Jan. 1919, OG208369, RG65, BI, NA.

5. Jerome Kidder to MID, 12 Feb. 1919, 10218–312–1, Maj. John W. Geary to Dunn, 24 Feb. 1919, 10218–312–2, RG165, MID, NA.

6. See entire MID case file 10218–279, especially Maj. Walter H. Loving to Brig. Gen. Marlborough Churchill, 6 May 1919, 10218–279–14, Capt. J. E. Cutler to Churchill, 9 May 1919, 10218–279–15, Churchill to Chief of Staff, 9 May 1919, 10218–279–16, RG165, MID, NA; Robert A. Hill, ed., *The Marcus Garvey and Universal Negro Improvement Association Papers* I (Berkeley, 1983), p. 329n3.

7. *Crisis,* May 1919, pp. 13–14.

8. Hill, *Garvey Papers* I, pp. 453–54n1.

9. W. G. R., Translation Bureau, to Postmaster T. G. Patten, 24 Apr. 1919, Robert A. Bowen to Patten, 25 Apr. 1919, Patten to Solicitor William H. Lamar, 26 Apr. 1919, memorandum, W. W. B., 1 May 1919, Lamar to Patten, 2 May 1919, case file 47732, Record Group 28, Espionage Act Cases, Post Office Department, National Archives [hereafter RG28, PO, NA]; *New York Tribune,* 2 May 1919.

10. The protests are all in case file 47732, RG28, PO, NA.

11. Bowen to Churchill, 25 Apr. 1919, Churchill to Bowen, 3 May 1919, 10218–139, Bowen to Churchill, 24 May 1919, 10218–139–34, Bowen to Churchill, 25 June 1919, 10218–139–35, RG165, MID, NA; agent Mortimer J. Davis to Bureau, 29 Aug. 1919, OG387162, RG65, BI, NA.

12. Bowen, "Radicalism and Sedition among the Negroes as Reflected in their Publications," 2 July 1919, OG359561, RG65, BI, NA.

13. Assistant Director and Chief Frank Burke to Lamar, 18 Sept. 1919, Lamar to Burke, 23 Sept. 1919, OG17011, RG65, BI, NA.

14. Capt. George R. Ford to Churchill, 1 May 1919, Churchill to Ford, 9 May 1919, 10218–158–17, Ford to Churchill, 17 May 1919, 10218–158–19, Maj. John Kennard to Churchill, 9 May 1919, 10218–139–30, Churchill to Kennard, 12 May 1919, 10218–139–?, Brig. Gen. W. D. Beach to Col. Fulton Q. C. Gardner, 19 Aug. 1919, Gardner to Beach, 22 Aug. 1919, 10218, RG165, MID, NA.

15. Maj. J. B. Pate to Churchill, 20 Aug. 1919, 10218–139–39; Maj. John P. Smith to Churchill, 3 Dec. 1920, 10218–158–27, RG165, MID, NA; James Weldon Johnson, *Along This Way* (New York, 1933), p. 341.

16. Rear Adm. A. P. Niblack to Acting Chief William E. Allen, 24 May 1919, Allen to Special Agent in Charge William M. Offley, 25 May 1919, Offley to Allen, 10 June 1919, agent A. W. Willett to Bureau, 3 July 1919, OG17011, RG65, BI, NA.

17. Niblack to Allen, 20 June 1919, OG3057, RG65, BI, NA; Capt. John B. Trevor to Churchill, 5 Apr. 1919, 10218–324–1, RG165, MID, NA.

18. J. Edgar Hoover to Burke, 12 Aug. 1919, OG258421, RG65, BI, NA.

19. Theodore Kornweibel, Jr., *No Crystal Stair: Black Life and the Messenger, 1917–1928* (Westport, Conn., 1975), pp. 85–87.

20. Attorney General A. Mitchell Palmer (by Assistant Attorney General Frank K. Nebeker) to U.S. Attorney Francis G. Caffey, 12 Sept. 1919, 9–12–725–1, Caffey to Palmer, 17 Sept. 1919, 9–12–725, RG60, DJ, NA; agent C. J. Scully to Bureau, 23 Sept. 1919, agent Edward Anderson to Bureau, 3 Oct. 1919, OG258421, RG65, BI, NA.

21. Palmer to Caffey, 20 Oct. 1919, 9–12–725–3, Caffey to Palmer, 3 Nov. 1919, 9–12–

725, Asst. Attny. Gen. Robert P. Stewart to Caffey, 12 Nov. 1919, 9–12–725–4, RG60, DJ, NA.

22. For additional information on Craig and other blacks who served the Bureau, see Theodore Kornweibel, Jr., "Black on Black: The FBI's First Negro Informants and Agents and the Investigation of Black Radicalism during the Red Scare," *Criminal Justice History* 8 (1987), pp. 123–24.

23. C-C [Arthur U. Craig] to Bureau, 6 Sept. 1919, 9 Sept. 1919, 16 Sept. 1919, 17 Sept. 1919, 18 Sept. 1919, 20 Sept. 1919 (2 documents), 26 Sept. 1919, OG258421, RG65, BI, NA.

24. Scully to Bureau, 23 Sept. 1919, "Bureau Section" [hereafter BS] case file 198940, agent Samuel R. Stone to Burke, 19 Sept. 1919, OG17011, agent William T. Lynch to Bureau, 26 Sept. 1919, 1 Oct. 1919, 6 Oct. 1919, agent William P. Hazen to Bureau, 1 Oct. 1919, agent Charles Noble to Bureau, 21 Oct. 1919, OG901, RG65, BI, NA.

25. Division Superintendent George F. Lamb to Burke, 28 Oct. 1919, OG258421, RG65, BI, NA.

26. WW [William A. Bailey] to Bureau, 30 Jan. 1920, 6 Feb. 1920, 28 Feb. 1920, P–135 [William E. Lucas] to Bureau, 11 May 1919, OG258421, RG65, BI, NA.

27. P–138 [Herbert S. Boulin] to Bureau, 4 Oct. 1920, OG259421, 28 Dec. 1920, BS198940–46, 28 Dec. 1920, BS298940–47, 31 Dec. 1920, BS202600–667–9X, 10 Jan. 1921, BS202600–667–16X, 29 Mar. 1921, BS202600–667–32, 10 May 1921, BS202600–667–71, 17 May 1921, BS198940–136, 17 May 1921, BS202600–33–262, 17 May 1921, BS202600–667–45, RG65, BI, NA; 12 May 1921, 202600–33–253, RG60, DJ, NA. Walter White's autobiography is *A Man Called White* (New York, 1948). Johnson engineered the arrest of pickets so as to bring pressure on the mayor to ban the film. The protesters were convicted but given suspended sentences.

28. A good history of the first ten years of the NAACP is Charles Flint Kellogg, *NAACP: A History of the National Association for the Advancement of Colored People, 1909–1920* (Baltimore, 1967), which discusses the two legal victories: the grandfather clause was struck down in *Guinn* v. *United States,* 238 U.S. 347 (1915); enforced residential segregation was barred, in a case from Louisville, in *Buchanan* v. *Warley,* 245 U.S. 60 (1917).

29. The New Crowd Negroes' rejection of DuBois is discussed in Kornweibel, *No Crystal Stair,* pp. 245–49.

30. Agent M. A. Joyce to Bureau, 4 Sept. 1919, OG 360036, RG65, BI, NA; Loving to Churchill, 17 Mar. 1919, 10218; Cutler to Chief, Negative Branch, 15 Mar. 1919, 10218–158–14, RG165, MID, NA; agent Walter O. Lewis to Bureau, 11 Sept. 1919, OG17011, agent L. Herman to Bureau, 26 Feb. 1920, OG383474, special confidential informant K–500 to Bureau, 1 Aug. 1919, Special Agent in Charge Bliss Morton to Assistant Director and Chief Frank Burke, 5 Aug. 1919, OG370678, agent H. A. Lewis to Bureau, 18 Sept. 1919, OG49899, RG65, BI, NA.

31. Burke to Division Superintendent H. B. Pierce, 14 Apr. 1920, agent George F. Ruch to Bureau, 26 Apr. 1920, OG382224, agent N. H. Castle to Bureau, 30 Aug. 1919, 17 Jan. 1920, OG371936, SAC E. Blanford to Bureau, 29 Aug. 1919, Blanford to Burke, 31 Aug. 1919, OG17011, RG65, BI, NA.

32. Breniman to Burke, 18 Aug. 1919, OG3057, RG65, BI, NA. The travails of Texas NAACP branches in this period are admirably detailed in Steven A. Reich, "Soldiers of Democracy: Black Texans and the Fight for Citizenship, 1917–1921," *Journal of American History* 82 (March 1996), pp. 1478–1503.

33. Special confidential informant WW [William A. Bailey] to Bureau, 19 Dec. 1919, 5 Jan. 19[20], 16 Jan. 19[20], OG267600, SAC J. M. Towler to Bureau, 24 Jan. 1920, WW to Bureau, 27 Jan. 1920, OG245295, 28 Feb. 1920, OG384671, RG65, BI, NA.

34. Div. Supt. George F. Lamb to Acting Chief John T. Suter, 28 Feb. 1920, Lamb to Burke, 17 Apr. 1920, OG208369, RG65, BI, NA.

35. Lamb to Burke, 19 Aug. 1920, 21 Aug. 1920, 25 Sept. 1920, 2 Oct. 1920, SAC T. M. Reddy to Burke, 9 Oct. 1920, 16 Oct. 1920, OG208369, 11 Dec. 1920, BS202600–33–115, 8 Jan. 1921, BS202600–33–140, RG65, BI, NA; 26 Mar. 1921, case file 202600–33–194, RG60, DJ, NA. Johnson's autobiography gives no hint he was aware the Bureau was monitoring his activities.

36. Acting Div. Supt. Reddy to Chief, 19 Mar. 1921, 202600–33–186, 2 Apr. 1921, 202600–33–203, 9 Apr. 1921, 202600–33–209, RG60, DJ, NA; 23 Apr. 1921, BS-202600–1628–2, 30 Apr. 1921, BS202600–1628–12, agent J. G. Tucker to Bureau, 7 May 1921, BS202600–1628–20, RG65, BI, NA; Reddy to Chief, 14 May 1921, 202600–33–260, RG60, DJ, NA; 16 May 1921, BS202600–1628–28, 4 June 1921, BS202600–1628–76, agent Mortimer J. Davis to Chief Lewis J. Baley, 9 July 1921, BS202600–1628–101, Act. Div. Supt. C. J. Scully to Baley, 23 July 1921, BS202600–1628–110, Div. Supt. Edward J. Brennan to Baley, 3 Sept. 1921, BS202600–1628–145, 16 Oct. 1921, BS-202600–1628–182, RG65, BI NA.

37. Brennan to Chief William J. Burns, 19 June 1922, case file 61–23–161, obtained from the Federal Bureau of Investigation through the Freedom of Information Act [hereafter FBI-FOIA]; Tucker to Burns, 29 July 1922, 12 Aug. 1922, 61–826, Brennan to Burns, 26 Feb. 1923, 61–349–156, FBI-FOIA.

38. Tucker to Bureau, 17 Sept. 1923, 61–349–218, FBI-FOIA.

39. Burns to Norman Armour, 27 Mar. 1924, case file 861.0–2113, Record Group 59, Office of Counselor Central File, Department of State, National Archives [hereafter RG59, DS, NA].

40. Capt. John B. Trevor to Churchill, 15 May 1919, 10218–139–32, Bowen to Churchill, 24 May 1919, 10218–139–34, 25 June 1919, 10218–139–35, Maj. H. A. Strauss to Churchill, 31 July 1919, 102180139–37, Maj. J. B. Pate to Churchill, 20 Aug. 1919, 10218–139–39, Capt. George R. Ford to Churchill, 1 May 1919, 10218–158–17; extensive correspondence regarding "radical" publications from MID offices throughout the country, which included the Crisis, are in case files 10110–1520–149 through 151, 10110–1520–165, and 10110–1522–129 through 141; MID's collection of the Crisis is in the front of case file 10218 and scattered throughout 10218–139. All citations in this note from RG165, MID, NA.

41. For information on MID's system of reports and summaries see "General Introduction" to vol. 1 and "Introduction" to vol. 27, Richard D. Challener, ed., United States Military Intelligence (New York, 1978–); circulation of the reports through the various cabinet departments can be charted in 5–4–69, Off. of Counsel. Cent. File, RG59, DS, NA.

42. Challener, Military Intelligence 9, p. 1621.

43. Challener, Military Intelligence 9, pp. 1723–24, 1864; 10, p. 2100.

44. Robert L. Zangrando, The NAACP Crusade Against Lynching, 1909–1950 (Philadelphia, 1980), p. 85.

45. Challener, Military Intelligence 10, pp. 2175, 2380, 2425–26; 11, pp. 2652, 2785; 12, p. 2969.

46. Attorney General A. Mitchell Palmer to Joseph Tumulty, 26 Dec. 1919, Woodrow Wilson Papers, Manuscript Division, Library of Congress.

47. In the printed version of this MID weekly report the "negro radical" was not identified by name, but in the manuscript version, circulated to the Bureau of Investigation, that individual was identified as W. E. B. DuBois; it was not uncommon, in the printed summaries, to mask the identity of suspects. Challener, Military Intelligence 11, p. 2852; 12, p. 3026; W. L. Hurley to Burke, 23 Jan. 1920, OG377098, RG65, BI, NA; Kornweibel, No Crystal Stair, p. 88.

48. Churchill to J. Edgar Hoover, 3 Apr. 1920, OG377098, RG65, BI, NA.

49. Acting Director Alexander B. Coxe to Hoover, 10 Apr. 1920, 24 Apr. 1920, 1 May 1920, OG377098, RG65, BI, NA.

50. Coxe to Hoover, 5 June 1920, 19 June 1920, 30 June 1920, OG377098, RG65, BI, NA.

51. Edward Bell to L. Lanier Winslow, 29 July 1919, 504–64, Off. of Counsel. Cent. File, RG59, DS, NA.

52. Bell to Winslow, 2 May 1919, 861.0–358, Maj. J. S. Moon to Winslow, 20 Sept. 1919, 812.0–727 [Thwaites], Maj. Gen. H. K. Bethell to Capt. D. E. Wallace, 29 Sept. 1919, 841.57, Off. of Counsel. Cent. File, RG59, DS, NA.

53. Scully to Bureau, 17 Sept. 1919, OG3057, RG65, BI, NA; Maj. H. A. Strauss to Churchill, 27 Sept. 1919, 10218–364–7, RG165, MID, NA.

54. Special Report No. 10, "Unrest among the Negroes," Directorate of Intelligence, Home Office, 7 Oct. 1919, OG3057, RG65, BI, NA.

55. Strauss to Churchill, 13 Jan. 1920, 10218–364–19X, 10 Feb. 1920, 10218–364–21, RG165, MID, NA.

56. Winslow to W. L. Hurley, 4 Mar. 1920, Hurley to Winslow, 5 Mar. 1920 (2 documents), Winslow to Hurley, 5 Mar. 1920, memo, Office of the Undersecretary, 16 Mar. 1920, Winslow to Hurley, 19 Mar. 1920, 19 Aug. 1920, Hurley to Winslow, 3 Sept. 1920, 841–107, Winslow to Hurley, 22 Sept. 1920, 504–64, Off. of Counsel. Cent. File, RG59, DS, NA.

57. Hurley to Hoover, 2 June 1921, 800.9–181, Off. of Counsel. Cent. File, RG59, DS, NA (same document in 158260–1–26, RG60, DJ, NA); various other examples are in 811.4016, Central Decimal File, RG59, DS, NA;

58. Agent James E. Amos to Bureau, 9 Aug. 1922, 61–50–129X, 23 Aug. 1922, 61–50–137, 20 Sept. 1922, 61–50–150, 19 Oct. 1922, 61–50–155, Brennan to Burns, 26 Oct. 1922, 61–50–156, Chandler Owen to Attorney General Harry M. Daugherty, 15 Jan. 1923, 198940–282, RG60, DJ, NA; Amos to Bureau, 17 Jan. 1923, 61–50–186, Amos and Davis to Bureau, 13 Feb. 1923, 61–50–219, Brennan to Burns, 30 June 1923, 61–50–394, Davis to Bureau, 2 July 1923, 61–50–402, FBI-FOIA. The informant is known only as "Williams."

59. This activity is revealed in 800.9–226 and 800.9–240, Off. of Counsel. Cent. File, RG59, DS, NA.

60. Lt. Col. W. T. Faulkner to Lt. Col. J. A. Moss, 27 Nov. 1925, 10218–158–29, Moss to Faulkner, 28 Dec. 1925, 10218–158–29, Moss to Acting Chief of Staff, G–2, 28 Dec. 1925, 10218–158–29, Acting Chief of Staff, G–2, to Moss, 5 Jan. 1926, 10218–158–30, MID, NA.

61. Patrick S. Washburn, A Question of Sedition: The Federal Government's Investigation of the Black Press during World War II (New York, 1986), pp. 178–80.

5. "The Most Dangerous of All the Negro Publications"

1. James Weldon Johnson, Black Manhattan (New York, 1969), p. 247.

2. Theodore Kornweibel, Jr., No Crystal Stair: Black Life and the Messenger, 1917–1928 (Westport, Conn., 1975), p. 21.

3. Agent J. F. Sawken to Bureau, 4 Aug. 1918, "Old German Files" (hereafter OG) 234939, Investigation Case Files of the Bureau of Investigation, 1908–1922, Record Group 65, Records of the Federal Bureau of Investigation, National Archives (hereafter RG65, BI, NA); Luther A. Huston, The Department of Justice (New York, 1967), p. 221.

4. Messenger, July 1928, p. 13. A. Philip Randolph and/or Chandler Owen to Frederick G. Detweiler, 19 Mar. 1921, in Detweiler, The Negro Press in the United States (Chicago, 1922), p. 171.

5. Sawken to Bureau, 10 Aug. 1918, OG239339, 10 Aug. 1918, OG265716, RG65, BI, NA; Kornweibel, pp. 3–4, 33.

6. Detweiler, p. 171; *Messenger,* July 1928, p. 13. For the zeal of federal authorities to suppress militant utterances see Harry N. Scheiber, *The Wilson Administration and Civil Liberties, 1917–1921* (Ithaca, N.Y., 1960), pp. 32–34; William Hard, "Mr. Burleson, Espionagent," *New Republic,* 10 May 1919, pp. 42–43; "'The Nation' and the Post Office," *Nation,* 28 Sept. 1918, pp. 336–37.

7. Agent R. W. Finch to Bureau, 9 Nov. 1918, 12 Nov. 1918, 13 Nov. 1918, OG208369, agent D. Davidson to Bureau, 6 Dec. 1918, "Bureau Section" case files [hereafter BS] 198940, RG65, BI, NA; Kornweibel, p. 134.

8. Maj. Walter H. Loving to Director, Military Intelligence Division, 23 Dec. 1918, case file 10218–274–2, Record Group 165, Military Intelligence Division, National Archives [hereafter RG165, MID, NA].

9. Loving to Col. John Dunn, Acting Director, MID, 15 Jan. 1919, 10218–296–2, Dunn to Capt. John B. Trevor, 27 Jan. 1919, 10218–296–3, meeting announcement, International League of Darker Peoples, ? Jan. 1919, 10218–296–26, RG165, MID, NA.

10. Robert A. Hill, ed., *The Marcus Garvey and Universal Negro Improvement Association Papers* I (Berkeley, 1983), pp. 531–32.

11. Finch to Bureau, 12 Feb. 1919, 20 Feb. 1919, 10 Mar. 1919, OG258421, RG65, BI, NA.

12. Finch to Bureau, 18 Mar. 1919, OG265716, RG65, BI, NA; Randolph to Adolph Germer, 11 Mar. 1919, 10218–296–10, Trevor to Director, 18 Mar. 1919, 10218–296–11, RG165, MID, NA.

13. Finch to Bureau, 20 Mar. 1919, OG258421, agent August H. Loula to Bureau, 26 Mar. 1919, OG368678, RG65, BI, NA.

14. Trevor to Dunn, 20 Feb. 1919, 10218–296–6, Dunn to Special Assistant to the Secretary of War Emmett J. Scott, 27 Feb. 1919, 10218–296–7, Brig. Gen. Marlborough Churchill to Trevor, 22 Apr. 1919, 10218–296–1, RG165, MID, NA; Finch to Bureau, 10 Mar. 1919, OG258421, RG65, BI, NA; Hill, p. 405n1.

15. Trevor to Churchill, 5 Apr. 1919, 10218–324–1, RG165, MID, NA.

16. Robert A. Bowen to Solicitor William H. Lamar, 15 May 1919, unnumbered file, box 2, "Messenger," Record Group 28, Espionage Act cases, Post Office Department, National Archives [hereafter RG28, PO, NA]; Churchill to Bowen, 31 May 1919, 10218–139, Trevor to Churchill, 22 May 1919, 10218–296–15, agent Jacob Spolansky to Maj. T. B. Crockett, 10110–853–370, RG165, MID, NA; marked issue of May-June 1919 *Messenger* in OG3057, Rear Adm. A. P. Niblack to Acting Chief W. E. Allen, 26 May 1919, OG258421, RG65, BI, NA.

17. Capt. Henry A. Frothingham to Churchill, 6 June 1919, 10218–296–18, *Providence Journal,* 1 June 1919, in 10218–296–17, RG165, MID, NA, also in case file 9–12–725, Record Group 60, Department of Justice, National Archives [hereafter RG60, DJ, NA]. During the war the *Providence Journal* was the "most notorious of the concoctors of spy stories" according to historian Joan M. Jensen, *The Price of Vigilance* (Chicago, 1968), p. 99.

18. Loving to Churchill, 1 June 1919, 10218–296–1, H. B. Arnold to Maj. Henry G. Pratt, 18 June 1919, 10218–296–19, Loving to Churchill, 26 June 1919, 10218–296–21, Churchill to Chief, Bureau of Investigation, 23 June 1919, 10218–296–19, RG165, MID, NA; agent Roy C. McHenry to Bureau, 11 June 1919, OG136944, agent J. A. Brann to Bureau, 13 June 1919, OG258421, Niblack to Allen, 20 June 1919, OG3057, RG65, BI, NA.

19. Bowen to Lamar, 30 June 1919, "Messenger" case file, RG28, PO, NA; Bowen to Churchill, 30 June 1919, 10218–341–1, RG165, MID, NA.

20. New York Postmaster to Lamar, 1 July 1919, Victor Daly to Postmaster General Albert S. Burleson, 3 July 1919, *Harlem Home News,* 6 July 1919, "Messenger" case file, W. T. Hornaday to Lamar, 10 July 1919, F. E. Williamson to Lamar, 11 July 1919, John Riley to Burleson, 16 July 1919, J. V. Esom to Lamar, 19 July 1923, case file B–240, RG28, PO,

NA. For details on the Lusk Committee see Julian F. Jaffe, *Crusade Against Radicalism: New York during the Red Scare, 1914–1924* (Port Washington, N.Y., 1972)

21. Unsigned memorandum, Post Office Department, New York, 8 July 1919, Lamar to Postmaster, New York, 3 July 1919, "Messenger" case file, RG28, PO, NA. The release date is recorded on a *Chicago Defender* clipping, "Burleson Places Ban on Messenger Magazine," 12 July 1919, in 10218, RG165, MID, NA. Bowen's spleen was handwritten on the *Harlem Home News* clipping referred to in note 22 below.

22. Bowen to Justice Department, 2 July 1919, OG359561, RG65, BI, NA; another copy is in B–240, RG28, PO, NA.

23. Finch to Bureau, 18 Mar. 1919, OG265716, RG65, BI, NA; Kornweibel, pp. 54, 63n13. The 33,000 figure was supplied by office manager Victor Daly to a Bureau agent operating undercover in late July. The *Crisis,* not nearly so radical but still worrisome, deposited 119,000 copies in the New York post office in July, a fact noted with concern by Bowen.

24. Bowen to James A. Horton, 28 July 1919, B–240, RG28, PO, NA; Bowen to Churchill, 28 July 1919, 10218–341–6, Bowen to Maj. Strauss, 28 July 1919, 10218–341–7, Strauss to Churchill, 29 July 1919, 10218–341–8, RG165, MID, NA; Postmaster June Hickman to Lamar, 9 Aug. 1919, Lamar to Hickman, 22 Aug. 1919, B–240, RG28, PO, NA.

25. Kornweibel, p. 135; agent Mortimer J. Davis to Bureau, 10 July 1919, BS198940, RG65, BI, NA.

26. New York state Special Deputy Attorney General John B. Trevor to Div. Supt. William A. Offley, 7 Aug. 1919, Trevor to Assistant Director and Chief Frank Burke, 11 Aug. 1919, agent C. J. Scully to Bureau, 20 Aug. 1919, OG265716, Davis to Bureau, 31 July 1919, 12 Aug. 1919, special confidential informant S–500 to Radical Division, New York, 20 Aug. 1919, OG258421, RG65, BI, NA.

27. *New York Tribune,* 29 July 1919, in OG3057, agent Miles Kitchin to Bureau, 2 Aug. 1919, OG369914, RG65, BI, NA.

28. J. Edgar Hoover to Burke, 12 Aug. 1919, OG258421, RG65, BI, NA.

29. Div. Supt. George F. Lamb to Burke, 25 Sept. 1919, BS198940, Hoover to Burke, 12 Aug. 1919, Hoover to Act. Div. Supt. J. A. Baker, 11 Aug. 1919, OG258421, Scully to Bureau, 23 Aug. 1919, OG208369, RG65, BI, NA.

30. Special confidential informant C-C [Arthur U. Craig] to Bureau, 27 Aug. 1919, 28 Aug. 1919, 30 Aug. 1919 (2 documents), OG258421, Scully to Bureau, 23 Aug. 1919, OG208369, Burke to Lamb, 15 Sept. 1919 (3 documents), 25 Sept. 1919, BS198940, Hoover, "Confidential Report of the Radical Section," 3 Oct. 1919, OG374217, RG65, BI, NA.

31. Baker to Burke, 21 Aug. 1919, OG3057, RG65, BI, NA. See also Davis to Bureau, 29 Aug. 1919, OG387162, RG65, BI, NA.

32. Rep. James F. Byrnes to Attorney General A. Mitchell Palmer, 25 Aug. 1919, 9–12–725, RG60, DJ, NA; *Congressional Record,* 66th Cong. 1st Sess., LVIII (Washington, D.C., 1919), pp. 4303–4305.

33. Hoover to Rep. H. F. Fisher, 10 Sept. 1919, Assistant Attorney General Robert P. Stewart to Byrnes, 12 Sept. 1919, 9–12–725, RG60, DJ, NA.

34. Assistant Attorney General Frank K. Nebeker to U.S. Attorney Francis G. Caffey, 12 Sept. 1919, Caffey to Palmer, 17 Sept. 1919, 11 Oct. 1919, Stewart to Caffey, 30 Sept. 1919, 9–12–725, RG60, DJ, NA.

35. Bowen to William F. Keohan, 1 Oct. 1919, Burke to Lamb, 4 Oct. 1919, Scully to Bureau, 9 Oct. 1919, OG258421, RG65, BI, NA; Palmer to Caffey, 20 Oct. 1919, 12 Nov. 1919, Caffey to Palmer, 3 Nov. 1919, 9–12–725, RG60, DJ, NA; Hoover, "Memorandum upon Work of the Radical Division," 18 Oct. 1919, OG374217, RG65, BI, NA.

36. Caffey to Palmer, 3 Nov. 1919, 9–12–725, RG60, DJ, NA.

37. Hoover to Assistant U.S. Attorney Ben A. Matthews, 3 Dec. 1919, Matthews to Hoover, 5 Dec. 1919, OG258421, RG65, BI, NA; Caffey to Palmer, 10 Dec. 1919, 9–12–725, RG60, DJ, NA.

38. Assistant Attorney General to Byrnes, 14 Nov. 1919, 9–12–725, RG60, DJ, NA; Stewart to Burleson, 24 Sept. 1919, B–240, RG28, PO, NA.

39. Detweiler, p. 171; Kornweibel, pp. 51–52.

40. Bowen to Lamar, 16 Aug. 1919, B–240, Lamar to Third Assistant Postmaster General A. M. Dockery, 22 Aug. 1919, 3 Nov. 1919, Dockery to Lamar, 5 Sept. 1919, 20 Sept. 1919, "Messenger" case file, RG28, PO, NA.

41. Daly to Lamar, 30 Sept. 1919, Bowen to Lamar, 1 Oct. 1919, B–240, RG28, PO, NA; Bowen to Keohan, 1 Oct. 1919, OG258421, RG65, BI, NA.

42. Bowen to Lamar, 1 Oct. 1919, B–240, RG28, PO, NA.

43. Daly to Superintendent Second Class Mail, 10 Dec. 1919, Dockery to Lamar, 16 Dec. 1919, "Messenger" case file, Acting Third Assistant Postmaster General H. J. Barrow to Solicitor John H. Edwards, 27 Apr. 1921, Edwards to Third Assistant Postmaster General, 3 June 1921, B–240, RG28, PO, NA.

44. Burleson to Lamar, 25 June, 1921, quoted in Maryland War Service Record of William Harmong Lamar, Office of the Solicitor, Official Records of William H. Lamar, RG28, PO, NA.

45. Capt. J. E. Cutler to Col. Alexander B. Coxe, 1 Sept. 1919, case file 10218–295–6, RG165, MID, NA.

46. Hill, Garvey Papers II, p. 630 n1.

47. John Lewis Waller to Maj. Henry Strauss, 6 Sept. 1919, 10218–367–1, Strauss to Churchill, 8 Sept. 1919, 10218–367–2, RG165, MID, NA.

48. Agent no. 7 to Crockett, 18 Oct. 1919, 10110–1241–21, Crockett to Churchill, 21 Oct. 1919, 10110–1241–102, Crockett to Churchill, 7 Nov. 1919, 10218–296–24, 10218–296–25, Chicago Daily News, 5 Nov. 1919, in 10218–296–23, RG165, MID, NA; MID agent Bowens to Crockett, 1 Dec. 1919, 10110–1460–18, Crockett to States Attorney Maclay Hoyne, 1 Dec. 1919, 10110–1460–19, agent no. 9 to Crockett, 13 Dec. 1919, 10110–1460–32, Crockett to Churchill, 15 Dec. 1919, 10110–1460–34, agent no. 20 to Crockett, 23 Dec. 1919, 10110–1460–36, Crockett to Churchill, 26 Dec. 1919, 10110–1460–37, RG165, MID, NA.

49. Weekly Intelligence Summary no. 128, 8 Nov. 1919, no. 130, 22 Nov. 1919, no. 131, 29 Nov. 1919, no. 132, 6 Dec. 1919, in Richard D. Challener, ed., United States Military Intelligence, X (New York: 1978–).

50. MID Weekly Situation Survey 10 Dec. 1919, 17 Dec. 1919, 24 Jan. 1920, 13 Mar. 1920, 20 Mar. 1920, 3 Apr. 1920, 10 Apr. 1920, 24 Apr. 1920, 28 Aug. 1920, 4 Sept. 1920, OG377098, RG65, BI, NA; Weekly Situation Survey, 14 Aug. 1920, 29 Jan. 1921, 19 Feb. 1921, 26 Feb. 1921, 7 May 1921, 4 June 1921, 23 Aug. 1921, case file 504–69, Record Group 59, Department of State, Office of the Counselor, Central File 1918–1927, National Archives.

51. U.S. Senate, Investigation Activities of the Department of Justice, 66th Cong., 1st Sess., Sen. Doc. 153 (Washington, 1919), pp. 172–73, 179, 181–82, 184.

52. Assistant Attorney General William L. Frierson to Stewart, 2 Jan. 1920, OG369936, special confidential informant WW [William A. Bailey] to Bureau, 26 Mar. 1920, OG258421, RG65, BI, NA. For the history of the Bureau's first black personnel see Theodore Kornweibel, Jr., "Black on Black: The FBI's First Negro Informants and Agents and the Investigation of Black Radicalism during the Red Scare," Criminal Justice History 8 (1987), pp. 121–36.

53. Kornweibel, "Black on Black," pp. 124–27; Hill, Garvey Papers II, p. 170n1.

54. WW to Bureau, 30 Jan. 1920, 6 Feb. 1920, 28 Feb. 1920, 11 Mar. 1920, 20 Mar. 1920, 26 Mar. 1920, 3 Apr. 1920, OG258421, RG65, BI, NA.

55. Special confidential informant P–135 [William E. Lucas] to Bureau, 22 Apr. 1920, 29 Apr. 1920, 11 May 1920, 18 May 1920, 27 May 1920 (2 documents), 14 June 1920 (3 documents), OG258421, RG65, BI, NA.

56. Kornweibel, "Black on Black," pp. 127–29.

57. Special confidential informant P–138 (Herbert S. Boulin) to Bureau, 27 Sept. 1920, BS198940, RG65, BI, NA.

58. Kornweibel, *No Crystal Stair,* pp. 143–44.

59. P–138 to Bureau, 30 Sept. 1920, BS198940, 8 Oct. 1920, 14 Oct. 1920, 17 Oct. 1920, 2 Nov. 1920, 5 Nov. 1920, OG258421, 6 Nov. 1920, BS198940–39, 22 Dec. 1920, BS202600–667–9X, 12 Jan. 1921, BS202600–667–20, 28 Jan. 1921, BS202600–33–158, RG65, BI, NA.

60. P–138 to Bureau, 2 Nov. 1920, OG258421, 7 Dec. 1920, BS202600–667–3, 2 Mar. 1921, BS202600–667–30X, 6 May 1921, BS202600–667–44, 31 May 1921, BS198940–145, RG65, BI, NA, 22 Mar. 1921, BS202600–33–198X, 22 June 1921, 9–12–725–11, RG60, DJ, NA.

61. P–138 to Bureau, 22 Mar. 1921, 202600–33–198X, 11 Apr. 1921, 9–12–725–9, 8 June 1921, 9–12–725, RG60, DJ, NA, 19 Apr. 1921, BS202600–667–35, RG65, BI, NA. For a history of the Friends of Negro Freedom see Kornweibel, *No Crystal Stair,* pp. 256–61.

62. Lamb to Act. Chief J. T. Suter, 28 Feb. 1920, Lamb to Director, 30 Mar. 1920, 31 July 1920, 28 Aug. 1920, 2 Oct. 1920, SAC T. M. Reddy to Director, 23 Oct. 1920, 30 Oct. 1920, OG208369, agent J. G. Tucker to Bureau, 30 Oct. 1920, 1 Jan. 1921, OG3057, Reddy to Chief, 1 Jan. 1921, BS202600–33–133, 12 Feb. 1921, BS202600–33–165, Scully to Bureau, 16 July 1921, BS202600–33–285, Scully to Chief Lewis J. Baley, 10 Aug. 1921, BS202600–33–296, Reddy to Bureau, 29 Jan. 1921, BS202600–51–9, Reddy to Chief, 4 June 1921, BS202600–1628–76, 11 June 1921, BS202600–1628–84, Scully to Chief, 2 July 1921, BS202600–1628–99, RG65, BI, NA; Reddy to Chief, 26 Mar. 1921, 202600–33–194, 16 Apr. 1921, 202600–33–218, RG60, DJ, NA. For Randolph's electoral activities see Kornweibel, *No Crystal Stair,* p. 224; *New York Times,* 30 Nov. 1920, p. 21, col. 5.

63. For economic currents effecting African Americans during this period see Theodore Kornweibel, Jr., "An Economic Profile of Black Life in the Twenties," *Journal of Black Studies* 6 (1976), pp. 307–20.

64. Loula to Hoover, 10 Apr. 1920, 8 May 1920, Loula to Bureau, 22 May 1920, 10 July 1920, 31 July 1920, BS202600–14, 13 Nov. 1920, BS202600–14–17X, 1 June 1921, BS202600–1771–3X, agent Max F. Burger to Bureau, 4 Feb. 1921, BS202600–1778-X, RG65, BI, NA.

65. Informant Albert Farley to Bureau, 21 Jan. 1920, 19 Apr. 1920, agent M. A. Joyce to Bureau, 22 Jan. 1920, Acting Chief to Ahern, 12 Feb. 1920, OG369936, agent W. W. Grimes to Bureau, 24 Jan. 1920, OG387162, agent J. O. Wynn to Bureau, 31 Jan. 1921, BS202600–48–10X, RG65, BI, NA. For information on Thomas see Marshall Hyatt, "Neval H. Thomas and Federal Segregation," *Negro History Bulletin* 42 (1979), pp. 96–97, 100–102.

66. Div. Supt. H. B. Pierce to Burke, 3 July 1920, OG317834, agent Oscar Schmitz to Chief, 16 June 1921, BS4–2–3–14–194, agent Walter Foster to Director, 24 Sept. 1921, BS202600–1617–55, agent J. F. McDevitt to Bureau, 1 Oct. 1921, BS202600–1617–57, RG65, BI, NA.

67. Agent M. F. Blackmon to Bureau, 27 Mar. 1920, agent W. L. Buchanan to Bureau, 27 Sept. 1920, 4 Oct. 1920, 1 Nov. 1920, BS202600–1613, 25 Oct. 1920, BS202600–1615, RG65, BI, NA, 28 Feb. 1921, 202600–33–175X, 14 Mar. 1921, 202600–33–182X, 21 Mar. 1921, 202600–33–189X, RG60, DJ, NA.

68. Agent Emil A. Solanka to Bureau, 18 May 1920, OG295364, 22 May 1920, OG229849, RG65, BI, NA.

69. Special confidential informant N–121 and translator Nathan A. Serber to Bureau, 12 May 1920, BS202600–1771, RG65, BI, NA.

70. SAC Bliss Morton to Bureau, 27 Mar. 1920, OG234939, 3 Apr. 1920, OG196605, Div. Supt. Calvin S. Weakley to Director, 15 Sept. 1921, BS202600–1717–6, Morton to Weakley, 12 Aug. 1921, BS202600–36–93, agent E. B. Sisk to Bureau, 13 Aug. 1921, Div. Supt. C. E. Breniman to Chief, 11 Aug. 1921, BS202600–2126, RG65, BI, NA.

71. Agent H. M. Zorian to Bureau, 13 Mar. 1920, OG17969, agent William C. Sausele to Bureau, 19 July 1921, BS202600–1646–12, Schmitz to Bureau, 15 Oct. 1921, BS4–2–3–14–215, RG65, BI, NA.

72. SAC Ralph H. Daughton to Bureau, 3 Jan. 1920, OG258421, RG65, BI, NA.

73. SAC E. J. Brennan to Director, 15 Oct. 1921, BS202600–1628–184, 16 Oct. 1921, BS202600–1628–182, RG65, BI, NA.

74. Tucker to Bureau, 17 June 1922, case file 61–826, obtained by the author from the Federal Bureau of Investigation through the Freedom of Information Act [hereafter FBI-FOIA]; agent A. A. Hopkins to Bureau, 9 Mar. 1922, 61–1284, FBI-FOIA; agent (censored) to Bureau, 6 June 1922, 61–1397, FBI-FOIA; undated *California Eagle* clipping describing Owen's second visit to Los Angeles in 1922, in 61–1284, FBI-FOIA.

75. Brennan to Director, 19 June 1922, 61–23–161, FBI-FOIA, 9 Aug. 1922, 61–1397, FBI-FOIA, Tucker to Bureau, 29 July 1922, 12 Aug. 1922, 19 Aug. 1922, 26 Aug. 1922, 2 Sept. 1922, 9 Sept. 1922, 16 Sept. 1922, 61–826, FBI-FOIA.

76. Personnel File, agent James Edward Amos, FBI-FOIA; *New York Times,* 9 June 1923.

77. Agent James E. Amos to Bureau, 28 Sept. 1922, 61–50–151, FBI-FOIA.

78. Chandler Owen et al to Attorney General Harry M. Daugherty, 15 Jan. 1923, 198940–282, RG60, DJ, NA; Amos to Bureau, 17 Jan. 1923, 61–50–186, 26 Jan. 1923, 61–50–198, 6 Feb. 1923, 61–50–211, special employee Andrew M. Battle to Bureau, 1 Mar. 1923, 61–50–275, 1 Mar. 1923, 61–50–284, FBI-FOIA.

79. Brennan to Director, 26 Feb. 1923, 61–349–156, FBI-FOIA.

80. Tucker to Bureau, 8 Sept. 1923, 61–826, 17 Sept. 1923, 61–349–218, FBI-FOIA. For the *Messenger's* evolution away from political and economic radicalism see Kornweibel, *No Crystal Stair,* esp. chaps. 6–7.

6. "An Undesirable, and Indeed a Very Dangerous, Alien"

1. Agent S. B. Pfeifer to Bureau, 18 Sept. 1918, Agent R. W. Finch to Bureau, 12 Nov. 1918, 21 Nov. 1918, "Old German" case file [hereafter OG] 258421, Agent D. Davidson to Bureau, 12 Nov. 1918 (three documents), 5 Dec. 1918 (two documents), Finch to Bureau, 3 Dec. 1918 (two documents), OG329359, Davidson to Bureau, 5 Dec. 1918, Record Group 65, Investigative Case Files of the Bureau of Investigation, 1908–1922, Records of the Federal Bureau of Investigation, National Archives [hereafter RG65, BI, NA]. A brief account of Garvey's travails is in Emory J. Tolbert, "Federal Surveillance of Marcus Garvey and the U.N.I.A.," *Journal of Ethnic Studies* 14 (Winter 1987), pp. 25–46.

2. L. Lanier Winslow to Acting Chief W. E. Allen, 26 Feb. 1919, Allen to Winslow, 18 Mar. 1919, Winslow to Colville Barclay, 21 Mar. 1919, Barclay to William Phillips, 24 Feb. 1919, case file 800.9–71, Record Group 59, Office of the Counselor Central File, 1918–1927, Department of State, National Archives [hereafter RG59, DS, NA]; the first two documents are also in OG185161, RG65, BI, NA; Acting Colonial Secretary George Ball-Greene to Consul G. E. Chamberlain, 3 May 1919, Chamberlain to Secretary of State Robert Lansing, 9 May 1919, case file B–398, Record Group 28, Espionage Act Cases, Post Office Department, National Archives [hereafter RG28, PO, NA].

3. Robert Adger Bowen, "Radicalism and Sedition among the Negroes as Reflected in Their Publications," 2 July 1919, B–240, RG28, PO, NA.

4. Bowen to Postal Solicitor William H. Lamar, 10 July 1919, 18 July 1919, memorandum, Translation Bureau, 16 Aug. 1919, B–240, Third Assistant Postmaster General A. M. Dockery to Lamar, 11 July 1919, Bowen to Lamar, 24 July 1919, memorandum, Translation Bureau, 22 Aug. 1919, B–500, Lamar to Acting Chief John T. Suter, 22 July 1919, Lamar to Assistant Director and Chief Frank Burke, 1 Aug. 1919, B–398, RG28, PO, NA.

5. J. Edgar Hoover to Burke, 12 Aug. 1919, OG258421, RG65, BI, NA.

6. Hoover to Burke, 12 Aug. 1919, OG258421, agent Charles J. Scully to Bureau, 23 Aug. 1919, OG208369, RG65, BI, NA.

7. C-C [Arthur U. Craig] to Bureau, 30 Aug. 1919, OG258421, RG65, BI, NA.

8. C-C to Bureau, 27 Aug. 1919, 28 Aug. 1919, 30 Aug. 1919, OG258421, RG65, BI, NA.

9. Burke to Acting Division Superintendent J. A. Baker, 15 Aug. 1919, OG185161, RG65, BI, NA.

10. Burke to Div. Supt. George F. Lamb, 15 Sept. 1919 (3 documents), "Bureau Section" case file [hereafter BS] 198940, Record Group 65, Investigative Case Files of the Bureau of Investigation, 1908–1922, Records of the Federal Bureau of Investigation, National Archives [hereafter RG65, BI, NA].

11. Scully to Bureau, 23 Sept. 1919, BS198940, RG65, BI, NA.

12. Lamb to Burke, 25 Sept. 1919, BS198940, Hoover, Confidential report of the Radical Section, 3 Oct. 1919, OG374217, RG65, BI, NA.

13. Special Assistant to the Attorney General John W. Creighton to Assistant Commissioner General of Immigration Anthony Caminetti, 13 Aug. 1919, OG185161, 16 Aug. 1919, BS198940, Burke to Lamb, 15 Sept. 1919 (3 documents), OG329359, RG65, BI, NA. The African Legion was conspicuous for its uniforms and pomp, but its members were rarely armed, and they posed a threat only to hecklers at meetings.

14. Bowen to Lamar, 11 Sept. 1919, 22 Sept. 1919, 25 Sept. 1919, 9 Oct. 1919, 31 Oct. 1919, Lamar to Third Assistant Postmaster General, Division of Classification, H. J. Barron, 8 Oct. 1919, B–500, RG28, PO, NA.

15. American Vice Consul in Charge, Port Limon, to Lansing, 24 Aug. 1919, Lansing to Postmaster General Albert S. Burleson, 20 Sept. 1919, Walter S. Penfield to Lansing, 25 Sept. 1919, Burleson to Lansing, 8 Oct. 1919, Phillips to Burleson, 27 Oct. 1919, Acting Solicitor H. J. Donnelly to Penfield, 3 Nov. 1919, B–500, RG28, PO, NA.

16. Consul Henry D. Baker to Lansing, 5 Oct. 1919, Acting Postmaster General Otto Praeger to Lansing, 30 Oct. 1919, B–500, RG28, PO, NA.

17. H. D. Baker to Lansing, 8 May 1919, 8 Dec. 1919, 5 Mar. 1920, Central Decimal File 844g.5045/2, H. D. Baker to Lansing, 5 Dec. 1919, Cent. Dec. File 844g.5045/3, Hurley to Burke, 20 Feb. 1920, Off. of Counsel. 000–612, RG59, DS, NA; H. D. Baker to Lansing, 7 Feb. 1920, BS198940, RG65, BI, NA.

18. A. L. Flint to Burke, 22 Sept. 1919, Burke to Flint, 23 Sept. 1919, BS198940, RG65, BI, NA.

19. J. A. Baker to Burke, 21 Aug. 1919, Scully to Bureau, 17 Sept. 1919, Directorate of Intelligence, Home Office, "Unrest among the Negroes," 7 Oct. 1919, OG3057, RG65, BI, NA; Phillips to Burleson, 17 Nov. 1919, Lamar to Burke, 26 Nov. 1919, Burleson to Lansing, 20 Dec. 1919, B–398, RG28, PO, NA.

20. Hoover to Mr. Ridgely, 11 Oct. 1919, BS198940, RG65, BI, NA; Attorney General A. Mitchell Palmer to Secretary of Labor William B. Wilson, 15 Oct. 1919, case file 198940–4, Record Group 60, Department of Justice, National Archives [hereafter RG60, DJ, NA].

21. Agent George F. Ruch to Bureau, 14 May 1920, OG3057, Burke to Acting Chief, Passport Division, C. B. Welsh, 7 May 1920, OG272751, RG65, BI, NA.

22. Personnel file, agent James Wormley Jones, obtained from the Federal Bureau of Investigation through the Freedom of Information Act [hereafter FBI-FOIA]; Arthur E. Barbeau and Florette Henri, *The Unknown Soldiers: Black American Troops in World War I* (Philadelphia, 1974), pp. 88, 149–57, 159, 161, 162, 173.

23. Robert A. Hill, ed., *The Marcus Garvey and Universal Negro Improvement Association Papers* I (Berkeley, Calif., 1983-), p. 438; II, pp. 112–20.

24. Universal Negro Improvement Association Constitution and Book of Laws, Hill, *Garvey Papers* I, pp. 256–81.

25. Agent James Wormley Jones to Bureau, 9 Feb. 1920 (2 documents), OG185161, RG65, BI, NA.

26. Jones to Bureau, 9 Feb. 1920, OG185161, RG65, BI, NA.

27. 800 [James W. Jones] to Bureau, 12 Mar. 1920, OG185161, RG65, BI, NA.

28. *Negro World,* 13 Mar. 1920, in Hill, *Garvey Papers* II, pp. 245–46.

29. WW [William A. Bailey] to Bureau, 20 Mar. 1920, OG258421, RG65, BI, NA. Informants were recruited and paid locally, with the approval of Bureau headquarters. Agents, on the other hand, submitted formal applications to the Department of Justice, listing references, and upon appointment became federal employees.

30. Burke to Maj. L. H. Cassford, 24 Apr. 1920, OG374217, RG65, BI, NA.

31. Ruch to Hoover, 3 June 1920, Hoover to Ruch, 8 June 1920, BS198940, RG65, BI, NA.

32. 800 to Bureau, 14 July 1920, 21 July 1920, OG258421, 16 July 1920, OG185161, RG65, BI, NA.

33. 800 to Bureau, 16 July 1920, OG185161, 14 July 1920, OG258421, RG65, BI, NA.

34. 800 to Bureau, 21 July 1920, OG258421, RG65, BI, NA.

35. Agent J. W. Bales to Bureau, 24 Sept. 1920, BS198940, RG65, BI, NA; statement of Capt. J. W. Jones to agent Mortimer J. Davis, 13 Jan. 1922, case file 61–50–31, obtained from the Federal Bureau of Investigation through Freedom of Information Act.

36. P–138 [Herbert S. Boulin] to Bureau, 5 Aug. 1920, BS198940, RG65, BI, NA.

37. P–138 to Bureau, 5 Aug. 1920, 6 Aug. 1920, 11 Aug. 1920, BS198940, RG65, BI, NA.

38. For details on the "Garvey Must Go" campaign see Theodore Kornweibel, Jr., *No Crystal Stair: Black Life and the Messenger, 1917–1928* (Westport, Conn., 1975), chap. 5.

39. P–138 to Bureau, 11 Aug. 1920, 12 Aug. 1920, 14 Aug. 1920, 17 Aug. 1920 (2 documents), 18 Aug. 1920, 19 Aug. 1920, 21 Aug. 1920, 25 Aug. 1920, BS198940, RG65, BI, NA.

40. P–138 to Bureau, 19 Aug. 1920, 23 Aug. 1920, BS198940, RG65, BI, NA.

41. P–138 to Bureau, 5 Nov. 1920, OG258421, RG65, BI, NA.

42. P–138 to Bureau, 7 Sept. 1920, BS198940, RG65, BI, NA.

43. P–138 to Bureau, 24 Sept. 1920, 8 Oct. 1920, 19 Oct. 1920, BS198940, RG65, BI, NA.

44. P–138 to Bureau, 27 Sept. 1920, 19 Oct. 1920, BS198940, 4 Oct. 1920, OG258421, RG65, BI, NA.

45. P–138 to Bureau, 8 Oct. 1920, 14 Oct. 1920, BS198940, 22 Oct. 1920, BS198940–5, RG65, BI, NA.

46. P–138 to Bureau, 5 Nov. 1920, BS198940–41, RG65, BI, NA.

47. P–138 to Bureau, 6 Nov. 1920, BS198940–40, RG65, BI, NA.

48. P–138 to Bureau, 17 Dec. 1920, BS202600–667–7, 20 Dec. 1920, BS202600–667–8, RG65, BI, NA.

49. P–138 to Bureau, 4 Jan. 1921, BS202600–667–15, RG65, BI, NA.

50. P–138 to Bureau, 4 Jan. 1921, BS202600–667–10, 4 Jan. 1921, BS202600–667–13, 7 Jan. 1921, BS202600–667–16x, 31 Jan. 1921, BS198940–58, 28 Jan. 1921, BS198940–71x, 3 Feb. 1921, BS202600–33–159, RG65, BI, NA.

51. P–138 to Bureau, 31 Jan. 1921, BS202600–667–26, 11 Feb. 1921, BS202600–667–29, RG65, BI, NA.

52. P–138 to Bureau, 7 Mar. 1921, BS198940–78x, 18 Mar. 1921, BS198940–112, 23 Mar. 1921, BS198940–95x, RG65, BI, NA; 7 Mar. 1921, 10 Mar. 1921, 11 Mar. 1921, 202600–33–182x, 14 Mar. 1921, 16 Mar. 1921, 202600–33–185x, RG60, DJ, NA.

53. Bertram D. Hulen, *Inside the Department of State* (New York, 1939), p. 13.

54. Radical Division, Weekly Bulletin of Radical Activities, undated fragments, Aug. 1920, OG374217, Hoover to William L. Hurley, 10 Aug. 1920, OG388439, 6 Aug. 1920, 18 Aug. 1920, OG185161, 22 Aug. 1920, BS198940, 10 Jan. 1921, BS198940–53, Hurley to Hoover, 25 Sept. 1920, BS198940, RG65, BI, NA; Hoover to Hurley, 21 Aug. 1920, Winslow to Secretary of State Bainbridge Colby, 4 Aug. 1920, Hurley to Winslow, 11 Aug. 1920, 000–612, Winslow to Hurley, 7 Aug. 1920, 000–1386, Hurley to Winslow, 800.9–71, Off. of Counsel. Cent. File, Winslow to Colby, 4 Aug. 1920, Colby to Winslow, 7 Aug. 1920, 811.108 G 191/26, Central Decimal File, RG59, DS, NA.

55. Hoover to Chief Lewis J. Baley, 11 Feb. 1921, BS198940–72, 18 Feb. 1921, BS198940–72x, RG65, BI, NA.

56. Hoover to Commissioner General of Immigration Caminetti, 24 Feb. 1921, BS198940–76, Division Superintendent T. M. Reddy to Baley, 9 Mar. 1921, BS198940–79, Special Agent in Charge Howard P. Wright to Baley, 11 Mar. 1921, BS198940–81, RG65, BI, NA; Hoover to Hurley, 24 Feb. 1921, 000–612, Off. of Counsel. Cent. File, RG59, DS, NA.

57. Assistant Commissioner General of Immigration Alfred Hampton to Hoover, 11 Mar. 1921, BS198940–80, Bowen to Hoover, 17 Mar. 1921, BS198940–81x, Hoover to Ruch, 18 Mar. 1921, BS198940–80, RG65, BI, NA; this request provides some insight into the workings of the Bureau of Translation. Formerly, its director wrote, the *Negro World* had been on "list III," rather on the more dangerous "list II" containing "present day outright radical papers." Having viewed the March 12 issue, however, "I am not so sure that we should be amiss in including the *Negro World* as an ultra-radical paper of the moment" by upgrading its status to "list I." Bowen to Hoover, 17 Mar. 1921, BS198940–81x, RG65, BI, NA.

58. Consul C. L. Latham to Secretary of State Charles Evans Hughes, 1 Mar. 1921, Hoover to Hurley, 21 Mar. 1921, 25 Mar. 1921, 30 Mar. 1921, Hurley to Brig. Gen. Dennis E. Nolan, 22 Mar. 1921, Hurley to Hoover, 22 Mar. 1921, 000–612, Off. of Counsel. Cent. File, RG59, DS, NA.

59. Latham to Hughes, 12 Apr. 1921, Hurley to Hoover, 13 Apr. 1921, First Secretary Walter C. Thurston to Hughes, 15 Apr. 1921, 000–612, Off. of Counsel. Cent. File, RG59, DS, NA.

60. Hurley to Hoover, 20 Apr. 1921, Hurley to Nolan, 20 Apr. 1921, Hurley to Winslow, 20 Apr. 1921, Lt. Comdr. C. M. Hall to Rear Adm. M. Johnston, 30 Apr. 1921, Thurston to Hughes, 2 May 1921, Latham to Hughes, 7 May 1921, Col. Matthew C. Smith to Hurley, 7 May 1921, 000–612, Off. of Counsel. Cent. File, Thurston to Hughes, 14 Apr. 1921, 811.108 G 191/1, 19 Apr. 1921, 811.108 G 191/9, Hughes to American Legation, San Jose, 23 May 1921, 811.108 G 191/9, Cent. Dec. File, RG59. DS, NA; Marcus Garvey to Hughes, 14 July 1921, BS198940–201, RG65, BI, NA.

61. Hoover to Hurley, 11 May 1921, Latham to Hughes, 11 June 1921, Hurley to Hoover, 16 May 1921, 23 May 1921, 7 June 1921, Consul W. Domingo Price to Hughes, 18 May 1921, Hurley to Nolan, 16 May 1921, Hurley to Winslow, 16 May 1921, 000–612, Off. of Counsel. Cent. File, Hughes to Latham, 10 May 1921, 811.108 G 191/10, Latham to Hughes, 7 May 1921, 811.108 G 191/13, Price to Hughes, 18 May 1918, 811.108 G 191/16, J. Preston Doughten to Hurley, 18 June 1921, 811.108 G 191, Cent. Dec. File, RG59, DS, NA; George C. Van Dusen to Hoover, 19 Mar. 1921, BS198940–107, Bowen to Hoover, 17 Mar. 1921, BS198940–81x, RG65, BI, NA.

62. Latham to Hughes, 1 June 1921, Hughes to Latham, 4 June 1921, 195.7/3347 [Kanawha], Latham to Hughes, 9 June 1921, Hughes to Latham, 10 June 1921, 195.7/

3363 [Kanawha], Latham to Hughes, 11 June 1921, 195.7/3379 [Kanawha], Latham to Hughes, 14 June 1921, 17 June 1921, 195.7/3370 [Kanawha], Latham to Hughes, 18 June 1921, 195.7/3402 [Kanawha], Cent. Dec. File; Latham to Hughes, 4 June 1921, Garvey to Latham, 1 June 1921, Latham to Garvey, 1 June 1921, 000–612, Off. of Counsel. Cent. File; Latham to Hughes, 18 May 1921, Hughes to Latham, 20 May 1921, Hughes to Consul Stewart E. McMillin, Hughes to Secretary of Commerce Herbert Hoover, 811.108 G 191/12, Latham to Hughes, 30 May 1921, 811.108 G 191/14, Cent. Dec. File, RG59, DS, NA.

63. Latham to Hughes, 18 June 1921, 195.7/3377 [Kanawha], Vice-consul William W. Heard to Hughes, 22 June 1921, 195.7/3386, Garvey to Hughes, 22 June 1921, 811.108 G 191/30, Cent. Dec. File; Heard to Hughes, 24 June 1921, 000–612, Off. of Counsel. Cent. File, RG59, DS, NA.

64. Doughten to Richard W. Flournoy, Jr., 18 June 1921, 811.108 G 191, Flournoy to Doughten, 21 June 1921, 811.108 G 191/31, Solicitor Fred K. Nielsen to Flournoy, 23 June 1921, 811.108 G 191/14, Cent. Dec. File, RG59, DS, NA.

65. Hurley to Harry A. McBride, 24 June 1921, Heard to Hughes, 28 June 1921, 000–612, Off. of Counsel. Cent. File; Acting Secretary of State Henry P. Fletcher to Latham, 25 June 1921, 811.108 G 191/19a, Cent. Dec. File, RG59, DS, NA. There is evidence that the secretary of state tired of the petty maneuvers to deny Garvey a visa. During this last flurry of events, Hughes sent to president Harding, for his signature, an executive order requiring that "masters of vessels entering ports of the United States must submit crew lists containing the names of all alien seamen on such vessels, visaed, *if possible,* by consular officers of the United States" (emphasis added); Secretary of State Charles E. Hughes to Warren G. Harding, 24 June 1921, Secretary to the President to Hughes, June 27, 1921, Reel 143, Secretary of State, Warren G. Harding Papers, Ohio Historical Society, Columbus.

66. Hurley to Hoover, 30 June 1921, Hurley to Commissioner General of Immigration W. W. Husband, 30 June 1921, 000–612, Off. of Counsel. Cent. File, RG59, DS, NA.

67. P–138 to Bureau, 19 July 1921, BS198940–205, RG65, BI, NA. Months before, Boulin had been instructed by Charles J. Scully, his immediate superior in the New York office of the Bureau, to arrange to meet Garvey upon his arrival and learn whatever plans he had for the future. Scully to Baley, 15 Apr. 1921, BS198940–195, RG65, BI, NA. Whether Boulin merely showed up at the railroad station or coordinated plans with Stewart and Garcia is unknown, although both UNIA officials must have known the confidence Garvey innocently placed in the undercover operative.

68. Hurley to Counselor Sheldon Whitehouse, 6 Sept. 1921, 000–612, Off. of Counsel. Cent. File, RG59, DS, NA; Director William J. Burns to Brennan, 6 Sept. 1921, BS198940–250, RG65, BI, NA.

69. Faulhaber to Bureau, 30 Aug. 1921, BS198940–249, Brennan to Burns, 30 Aug. 1921, BS198940–249, 31 Aug. 1921, BS198940–250, RG65, BI, NA.

70. Brennan to Bureau, 31 Aug. 1921, BS198940–251, Faulhaber to Bureau, 31 Aug. 1921, BS198940–250x, RG65, BI, NA.

71. Burns to SAC W. B. Matthews, 1 Sept. 1921, BS198940–255, RG65, BI, NA.

72. P–138 to Bureau, 11 Aug. 1921, BS198940–232, 22 Aug. 1921, BS198940–239, RG65, BI, NA.

73. Reddy to Baley, 9 Apr. 1921, BS198940–113, Baley to Reddy, 15 June 1921, BS198940–163, Baley to O'Donnell, 8 Aug. 1921, BS198940–229, Scully to Baley, 9 Aug. 1921, BS198940–231, Brennan to Burns, 30 Aug. 1921, BS198940–249, 31 Aug. 1921, BS198940–250, 31 Aug. 1921, BS198940–251, 7 Sept. 1921, BS198940–261, Burns to Matthews, 1 Sept. 1921, BS198940–255, Hoover to Hurley, 2 Sept. 1921, BS198940–259, Burns to Brennan, 6 Sept. 1921, BS198940–249, Anderson to Bureau, 7 Sept. 1921, BS198940–262, Ruch to Hoover, 15 Sept. 1921, BS198940–268, RG65, BI, NA.

74. P–138 to Bureau, 25 July 1921, BS198940–209, RG65, BI, NA.

75. P–138 to Bureau, 30 July 1921, BS198940–217, 31 July 1921, BS198940–218, 3 Aug. 1921, BS198940–225, P–138 to Bureau, 30 Aug. 1921, BS198940–247, RG65, BI, NA.

76. 800 to Bureau, 6 Dec. 1921, case file 61–286-x10, obtained from Federal Bureau of Investigation through the Freedom of Information Act [hereafter FBI-FOIA].

77. Consul A. C. Frost to Hughes, 9 Mar. 1922, Hurley to Burns, 29 Mar. 1922, Burns to Hurley, 31 Mar. 1922, 10 May 1922, 000–612, Off. of Counsel. Cent. File, RG59, DS, NA; Burns to Hurley, 7 Mar. 1922, 61–50–54, Burns to T. P. Merrilees, 7 Mar. 1922, 61–50–55, FBI-FOIA.

78. Statement of Jones to Davis, 13 Jan. 1922, 61–50–31; 800 to Ruch, 10 Aug. 1921, 61–826, FBI-FOIA; Amy Jacques-Garvey, ed., *Philosophy and Opinions of Marcus Garvey* II (c. 1923; New York, 1968), pp. 69–71.

79. 800 to Ruch, 23 Sept. 1921, 29 Sept. 1921, 61–826, FBI-FOIA.

80. 800 to Ruch, 23 Sept. 1921, 29 Sept. 1921, 7 Oct. 1921, 61–826, 18 Nov. 1921, 61–826-x7, 26 Nov. 1921, 61–50–14x, Davis to Bureau, 21 Jan. 1922, 61–826, FBI-FOIA.

81. 800 to Ruch, 16 Dec. 1921, 61–826-x13, 7 Jan. 1922, 61–826-x23, FBI-FOIA.

82. 800 to Ruch, 4 Dec. 1921, 61–826-x9, 16 Dec. 1921, 61–826-x13, 19 Dec. 1921, 61–826-x14, 20 Dec. 1921, 61–826-x15, 7 Jan. 1922, 61–826-x23, FBI-FOIA.

83. 800 to Ruch, 14 Dec. 1921, 61–826-x12, Davis to Bureau, enclosing statement of Jones, 13 Jan. 1922, 61–50–31, FBI-FOIA.

84. 800 to Ruch, 7 Jan. 1922, 61–826-x23, 17 Jan. 1922, 61–826-x24, Ruch to Hoover, 17 Jan. 1922, 61–826-x25, Hoover to Burns, 16 Jan. 1922, Burns to Assistant Attorney General John W. H. Crim, 19 Jan. 1922, 61–50–356, FBI-FOIA.

85. Hoover to Burns, 16 Jan. 1922, Burns to Crim, 19 Jan. 1922, 61–50–356, 800 to Ruch, 22 Jan. 1922, 61–826-x26, FBI-FOIA.

86. 800 to Ruch, 9 Mar. 1922, 61–826–1, 21 Mar. 1922, 61–826–3, FBI-FOIA.

87. 800 to Ruch, 9 Mar. 1922, 61–826–1, 21 Mar. 1922, 61–826–3, 8 May 1922, 61–826–9, FBI-FOIA.

88. Jones to Burns, 27 Jan. 1923, 61–50–202, 29 Jan. 1923, 61–50–204, 4 Feb. 1923, 61–50–209, 7 Feb. 1923, 61–50–224, FBI-FOIA.

89. Jones to Burns, 14 Feb. 1923, 61–50–258, 18 Feb. 1923, 61–50–254, FBI-FOIA.

90. Further details on the trials of Dyer, Shakespeare, and Ramus are in Hill, *Garvey Papers* V.

91. Jones served for three and a half years, Brent and Titus for less than three years, and Jefferson slightly more than seven years, according to brief biographical information supplied by the FBI's Research Unit, Office of Congressional and Public Affairs.

92. Ruch to Hoover, 10 Oct. 1921, 5 Nov. 1921, 800 to Ruch, 18 Oct. 1921, 800's expense accounts, May-Sept. 1921, 61–826, 800 to Ruch, 14 Dec. 1921, 61–826-x12, 2 Jan. 1922, 61–826-x22, Hoover to Burns, 16 Jan. 1922, 61–50–356, FBI-FOIA.

93. 800 to Ruch, 8 May 1922, 61–826–9, agent James E. Amos to Brennan, 15 May 1922, 61–826, Brennan to Burns, 16 May 1922, 61–826–11, FBI-FOIA.

94. Hoover to Burns, 18 Nov. 1921, 61–826-x6, FBI-FOIA.

95. Amos and Davis to Bureau, 6 Mar. 1922 (2 documents), 61–50–59, Amos to Bureau, 28 Mar. 1922, 61–50–75. 14 Apr. 1922, 61–50–80, FBI-FOIA.

96. Tony Martin, *Race First: The Ideological and Organizational Struggles of Marcus Garvey and the Universal Negro Improvement Association* (Westport, Conn., 1976), p. 166. For Cockburn, see Amos to Bureau, 21 Mar. 1922, 61–50–69, 28 Mar. 1922, 61–50–75, 7 Apr. 1922, 61–50–79, 14 Apr. 1922, 61–50–80, 24 Apr. 1922, 61–50–84. 29 May 1922, 61–50–97, 28 June 1922, 61–50–105, 26 July 1922, 61–50–123, 2 Aug. 1922, 61–50–127, 23 Aug. 1922, 61–50–137, 13 Sept. 1922, 61–50–146, Amos and Davis to Bureau,

23 Jan. 1923, 61–50–189; for Richardson, see Amos to Bureau, 6 July 1922, 61–50–111, 12 July 1922, 61–50–126, FBI-FOIA.

97. Amos to Bureau, 21 Feb. 1922, 61–50–48, 24 Apr. 1922, 61–50–84, 9 May 1922, 61–50–89, 29 May 1922, 61–50–97, 28 June 1922, 61–50–105, 21 July 1922, 61–50–118, 26 July 1922, 61–50–123, FBI-FOIA.

98. Amos to Bureau, 9 May 1922, 61–50–89, 29 May 1922, 61–50–97, 21 Apr. 1923, 61–50–349, 19 June 1923, 61–50–375, 19 June 1923, 61–50–377, 19 June 1923, 61–50–378, FBI-FOIA.

99. Amos to Bureau, 6 Jan. 1923, 61–50–175, Amos and Davis to Bureau, 23 Jan. 1923, 61–50–189, FBI-FOIA.

100. Amos to Bureau, 9 Aug. 1922, 61–50–129x, 23 Aug. 1922, 61–50–137, 20 Sept. 1922, 61–50–150, 19 Oct. 1922, 61–50–155, FBI-FOIA.

101. Amos to Bureau, 28 Sept. 1922, 61–50–151, 17 Jan. 1923, 61–50–186, 26 Jan. 1923, 61–50–198, 6 Feb. 1923, 61–50–211, Amos and Davis to Bureau, 13 Feb. 1923, 61–50–219, FBI-FOIA.

102. *New York Times,* 9 June 1923, *New York Herald,* 9 June 1923, clippings in 61–50–370; special employee Andrew M. Battle to Bureau, 17 June 1923, 61–50–387, 3 July 1923, 61–50–399, FBI-FOIA.

103. Amos to Bureau, 26 June 1923, 61–50–391, 25 Oct. 1923, 61–50–455, 24 Nov. 1923, 61–50–488, 24 Nov. 1923, 61–50–490, 28 Nov. 1923, 61–50–498, 3 Dec. 1923, 61–50–499, 19 Dec. 1923, 61–50–504, 1 Apr. 1924, 61–50–509, 24 May 1924, 61–50–510, 9 Aug. 1924, 61–50–516, 7 Aug. 1924, 61–50–522, 24 Oct. 1924, 61–50–521, 19 Nov. 1924, 61–50–523, 5 Jan. 1925, 61–50–525, 20 Jan. 1925, 61–50–526, 4 Feb. 1925, 61–50–529, FBI-FOIA.

104. Amos to Bureau, 6 Feb. 1925, 61–826, FBI-FOIA.

105. The influence of Hoover's upbringing in "southern" Washington is stressed in three very useful biographies: Richard Gid Powers, *Secrecy and Power: The Life of J. Edgar Hoover* (New York, 1987); Curt Gentry, *J. Edgar Hoover: The Man and the Secrets* (New York, 1991); and Athan G. Theoharis and John Stuart Cox, *The Boss: J. Edgar Hoover and the Great American Inquisition* (Philadelphia, 1988).

106. Brennan to Burns, 21 June 1923, 61–50–383, FBI-FOIA.

107. Affidavit of Marcus Garvey, plaintiff-in-error, against United States of America, defendant-in-error, 19 July 1923, quoted in Hill, *Garvey Papers* V, p. 409.

108. Personnel files of Jones and Amos, FBI-FOIA; "Special Agent James Amos," Office of Congressional and Public Affairs, FBI [1984].

7. "The Most Colossal Conspiracy against the United States"

1. Good background on Briggs is in Robert A. Hill, ed., *The Marcus Garvey and Universal Negro Improvement Association Papers* I (Berkeley, 1983), pp. 521–27; *Crusader,* facsimile edition, Robert A. Hill, ed., I (New York, 1987), pp. v–lxx.

2. *Crusader,* Sept. 1918, pp. 22–23.

3. *Crusader,* Sept. 1918, pp. 1–5, 8.

4. *Crusader,* Nov. 1918, p. 1, Dec. 1918, p. 3.

5. Capt. John B. Trevor to Brig. Gen. Marlborough Churchill, 5 Apr. 1919, case file 10218–324–1, Record Group 165, Records of the Military Intelligence Division, National Archives [hereafter RG165, MID, NA].

6. Consul G. E. Chamberlain to Secretary of State Robert Lansing, 9 May 1919, "Old German" case files [hereafter OG] 359561, Record Group 65, Investigative Case Files of the Bureau of Investigation, 1908–1922, Records of the Federal Bureau of Investigation, National Archives [hereafter RG65, BI, NA]; Post Office Solicitor William H. Lamar to Bureau of Investigation Acting Chief John T. Suter, 22 July 1919, Postmaster General

Albert S. Burleson to Lansing, 28 July 1919, Lamar to Bureau of Investigation Assistant Director and Chief Frank Burke, 1 Aug. 1919, case file B–398, Record Group 28, Espionage Act cases, Post Office Department, National Archives [hereafter RG28, PO, NA].

7. Agent J. A. Brann to Bureau, 13 June 1919, OG 258421, RG65, BI, NA; Robert A. Bowen, "Radicalism and Sedition among the Negroes as Reflected in their Publications," 2 July 1919, Bowen to Lamar, 18 July 1919, B–240, RG28, PO, NA. Bowen's lengthy document was also composed for the Bureau of Investigation and became part of a special report by the Attorney General: OG359561, RG65, BI, NA.

8. Directorate of Intelligence, Home Office, "Unrest among the Negroes," 7 Oct. 1919, OG3057, RG65, BI, NA.

9. Lamar to Burke, 1 Aug. 1919, Burke to Acting Division Superintendent J. A. Baker, 18 Aug. 1919, OG359561, RG65, BI, NA.

10. Agent Mortimer J. Davis to Bureau, 20 Aug. 1919, OG387162, C-C [Arthur U. Craig] to Bureau, 6 Sept. 1919, 9 Sept. 1919, 22 Sept. 1919, OG258421, Baker to Burke, 21 Aug. 1919, agent Charles J. Scully to Bureau, 17 Sept. 1919, OG3057, agent M. A. Joyce to Bureau, 4 Sept. 1919, OG360036, RG65, BI, NA.

11. *Crusader,* Oct. 1919, p. 27.

12. Richardson to Col. Alexander B. Coxe, ? Oct. 1919, 10218, Churchill to Maj. H. A. Strauss, 13 Oct. 1919, 10218–349–7, RG165, MID, NA.

13. Unidentified MID operative, New York, to ?, 20 Oct. 1919, 10218–349–5, Strauss to Churchill, 22 Oct. 1919, 10218–349–6, RG165, MID, NA.

14. Weekly Intelligence Summary no. 126, 25 Oct. 1919, no. 127, 1 Nov. 1919, in Richard D. Challener, ed., *United States Military Intelligence* X (New York, 1978); MID agent W. E. Rowens to ?, 13 Nov. 1919, 10218–349–8, Maj. Thomas B. Crockett to Churchill, 18 Nov. 1918, 10218–349–9, RG165, MID, NA.

15. Weekly Intelligence Summary no. 132, 6 Dec. 1919, in Challener, *Military Intelligence* XI; Maj. Wrisley Brown to Special Assistant to the Attorney General J. Edgar Hoover, 31 Jan. 1920, OG377098, RG65, BI, NA.

16. WW [William A. Bailey] to Bureau, 30 Jan. 1920, 6 Feb. 1920, OG258421, RG65, BI, NA.

17. WW to Bureau, 28 Feb. 1920, 11 Mar. 1920, OG258421, RG65, BI, NA.

18. WW to Bureau, 11 Mar. 1920, 20 Mar. 1920, 26 Mar. 1920, OG258421, RG65, BI, NA.

19. WW to Bureau, 6 Mar. 1920, OG185161, 26 Mar. 1920, OG258421, RG65, BI, NA.

20. WW to Bureau, 3 Apr. 1920, OG258421, RG65, BI, NA.

21. WW to Bureau, 6 Mar. 1920, OG185161, 11 Mar. 1920, OG 258421, RG65, BI, NA.

22. P–135 to Bureau, 29 Apr. 1920, OG258421, RG65, BI, NA.

23. P–135 to Bureau, 18 May 1920, 27 May 1920 (2 documents), OG258421, RG65, BI, NA.

24. P–135 to Bureau, 10 June 1920 (2 documents), 11 June 1920, 14 June 1920, OG258421, RG65, BI, NA.

25. Radical Division (General Intelligence Division), "Bulletin of Radical Activities" no. 7, 27 Feb. 1920, OG374217, RG65, BI, NA; *Crusader,* Feb. 1920, p. 29.

26. "Bulletin of Radical Activities," no. 9, 20 Mar. 1920, no. ?, ? Mar. 1920, OG374217, agent George F. Lamb to Director, 6 Mar. 1920, 13 Mar. 1920, 20 Mar. 1920, OG208369, RG65, BI, NA; *Crusader,* May 1920, pp. 5–6.

27. Agent J. G. Tucker to Bureau, 29 May 1920, 19 June 1920, OG258421, RG65, BI, NA.

28. *Crusader,* Dec. 1920, pp. 11–12; Lamb to Director, 17 July 1920, 7 Aug. 1920, 25 Sept. 1920, agent T. M. Reddy to Director, 20 Oct. 1920, OG208369, Reddy to Chief, 11 Dec. 1920, "Bureau Section" case files [hereafter BS] 202600–33–115, 8 Jan. 1921,

BS202600–33–140, RG65, BI, NA; Hoover to William L. Hurley, 15 Dec. 1920, case file 800.9–151, Record Group 59, Office of the Counselor Central File 1918–1927, Department of State, National Archives [hereafter RG59, DS, NA]; MID "Weekly Situation Survey" no. 164, 23 Feb. 1921, Off. of Counsel. Cent. File 504–69, RG59, DS, NA; Reddy to Chief, 12 Mar. 1921, Case file BS202600–33–183, Record Group 60, Department of Justice, National Archives [hereafter RG60, DJ, NA].

29. For a thorough discussion of the riot, its background causes, and its results, see Scott Ellsworth, *Death in a Promised Land: The Tulsa Race Riot of 1921* (Baton Rouge, 1982).

30. *New York Times,* 4 June 1921, p. 1, 14, 5 June 1921, p. 21; Hill, *Crusader,* pp. xxxiii–xxxv.

31. P–138 to Bureau, 14 June 1921, BS202600–2031–3, Weekly radical reports, Reddy to Bureau, 11 June 1921, BS202600–1628–84, Scully to Bureau, 18 June 1921, RG65, BI, NA. For more information on Richard B. Moore, see chapter 2, pp. 65–69.

32. *New York Times,* 21 June 1921, p. 8, col. 3; P–138 to Bureau, 22 June 1921, BS202600–2031–4, 22 June 1921, BS202600–2031–5, 29 June 1921, BS202600–667–60, RG65, BI, NA.

33. Harvey Klehr, John Earl Haynes, and Fridrikh Igorevich Firsov, *The Secret World of American Communism* (New Haven, Conn., 1995), pp. 20–25.

34. P–138 to Bureau, 13 July 1921, BS202600–2031–6, 6 Aug. 1921, BS202600–667–76, RG65, BI, NA.

35. Scully to Baley, 16 July 1921, BS202600–1628–107, RG65, BI, NA; Hill, *Crusader,* xxxvii–xli.

36. P–138 to Bureau, 15 Aug. 1921, BS202600–667–78, RG65, BI, NA.

37. P–138 to Bureau, 22 Aug. 1921, BS202600–667–81, 31 Aug. 1921, BS202600–667–86, RG65, BI, NA.

38. P–138 to Bureau, 22 Aug. 1921, BS202600–667–81, RG65, BI, NA.

39. Scully to Baley, 16 July 1921, BS202600–1628–107, RG65, BI, NA; agent T. F. Weiss to Bureau, 5 July 1921, 158260–8–17, RG60, DJ, NA.

40. Scully to Baley, 16 July 1921, BS202600–33–285, RG65, BI, NA; *Crusader,* July 1921, pp. 5–6, 10–11.

41. Act. Div. Supt. Scully to Baley, 10 Aug. 1921, BS202600–33–296, RG65, BI, NA.

42. Scully to Baley, 20 Aug. 1921, BS202600–1628–127, Div. Supt. Edward J. Brennan to Director William J. Burns, 27 Aug. 1921, BS202600–1628–138, Brennan to Burns, 3 Sept. 1921, BS202600–1628–145, Brennan to Burns, 15 Sept. 1921, BS202600–1628–156, "General Intelligence Bulletin" no. 64, 13 Aug. 1921, OG374217, agent Henry J. Lenon to Bureau, 12 Sept. 1921, BS202600–1768–22, RG65, BI, NA; Hill, *Crusader* I, pp. xli–xliii.

43. MID "Weekly Situation Survey" no. 179, 8 June 1921, no. 182, 2 July 1921, no. 184, 16 July 1921, no. 191, 3 Sept. 1921, no. 192, 10 Sept. 1921, Off. Counsel. Cent. File 504–69, RG59, DS, NA.

44. Richard Gid Powers, *Secrecy and Power: The Life of J. Edgar Hoover* (New York, 1987), p. 131; P–137 to Bureau, 30 Aug. 1921, BS202600–2031–12, P–141 to Bureau, 28 Sept. 1921, BS202600–2031–14, RG65, BI, NA.

45. Quoted in Ellsworth, p. 24.

46. 800 [James Wormley Jones] to agent George F. Ruch, 10 Aug. 1921, 4 Sept. 1921, Ruch to agent W. W. Grimes, 23 Sept. 1921, case file 61–826, obtained from the Federal Bureau of Information through the Freedom of Information Act.

47. 800 to Ruch, ? Sept. 1921, 23 Sept. 1921, 29 Sept. 1921, 7 Oct. 1921, Ruch to Hoover, 10 Oct. 1921, 61–826, FBI-FOIA.

48. *Negro World,* 8 Oct. 1921, in Hill, *Garvey Papers* IV, p. 107.

49. 800 to Ruch, 18 Oct. 1921, 25 Oct. 1921, agent Edward Anderson to Bureau, 21 Oct. 1921, Burns to Brennan, 20 Oct. 1921, 61–826, FBI-FOIA; Burns to Brennan, 13 Oct. 1921, BS202600–2674, RG65, BI, NA.

50. 800 to Ruch, 18 Nov. 1921, 61–826-X7, 4 Dec. 1921, 61–826-X9, 26 Nov. 1921, 61–50–14X, 25 Nov. 1921, 61–50–14X1, FBI-FOIA.

51. 800 to Ruch, 23 Sept. 1921, 29 Sept. 1921, 7 Oct. 1921, 61–826, 16 Nov. 1921, 61–826-X5, 18 Nov. 1921, 61–826-X7, 4 Dec. 1921, 61–826-X9, 16 Dec. 1921, 61–826-X13, 20 Dec. 1921, 61–826-X15, 7 Jan. 1922, 61–826-X23, Ruch to Hoover, 5 Nov. 1921, Davis to Bureau, 8 Dec. 1921, 61–826, 800 to Ruch, 26 Nov. 1921, 61–50–14X, FBI-FOIA.

52. Ruch to Hoover, 17 Nov. 1921, 61–826-X6, 800 to Ruch, 4 Dec. 1921, 61–826-X9, 16 Dec. 1921, 61–826-X13, 19 Dec. 1921, 61–826-X14, 25 Jan. 1922, 61–826-X27, FBI-FOIA.

53. Burns to Brennan, 21 Oct. 1921, Davis to Bureau, 31 Oct. 1921, Tucker to Bureau, 31 Dec. 1921, 61–826, Ruch to Hoover, 4 Nov. 1921, 61–826-X2, 5 Nov. 1921, 61–826, 800 to Ruch, 18 Nov. 1921, 61–826-X7, 6 Dec. 1921, 61–826-X10, 24 Dec. 1921, 61–826-X16, 24 Dec. 1921, 61–826-X17, 25 Dec. 1921, 61–826-X18, 26 Dec. 1921, 61–826-X19, Davis to Bureau, 8 Nov. 1921, 61–57–80, Brennan to Burns, 9 Jan. 1922, 61–167–119, FBI-FOIA.

54. P–134 to Bureau, 28 Aug. 1921, BS202600–2131–10, 30 Aug. 1921, BS202600–2131–11, 15 Sept. 1921, BS202600–2265–80, 17 Oct. 1921 (2 documents), BS202600–2674, RG65, BI, NA; P–134 to Bureau, 19 Oct. 1921, 61–44–1, 20 Oct. 1921, 61–44–2, 20 Oct. 1921, 61–44–4, 20 Oct. 1921, 61–44–5, ? Oct. 1921, 61–826, 4 Jan. 1922, 61–50–24, FBI-FOIA; P–134 to Bureau, 23 Mar. 1922, Off. Counsel. Cent. File 811.01–273, RG59, DS, NA.

55. Burns to Brennan, 13 Oct. 1921, BS202600–2674, RG65, BI, NA.

56. Burns to Brennan, 9 Nov. 1921, Davis to Bureau, 18 Nov. 1921, 61–286, 8 Dec. 1921, 61–50–15, 8 Dec. 1921, 61–50–28, FBI-FOIA; *New York World,* 13 Jan. 1922.

57. Hoover to Ruch, 17 Nov. 1921, 61–826, FBI-FOIA.

58. Tucker to Bureau, 10 Dec. 1921, 24 Dec. 1921, 25 Feb. 1922, 61–826, FBI-FOIA.

59. 800 to Ruch, 12 Apr. 1922, 61–826–5, special employee Andrew M. Battle to Bureau, 2 Oct. 1922, 61–50–152, FBI-FOIA; Hill, *Crusader,* p. xlvii.

60. "Special Employee Andrew M. Battle," biographical sketch, Office of Congressional and Public Affairs, FBI [1984].

61. Battle to Bureau, 8 July 1922, 61–50–112, 26 July 1922, 61–50–122, 2 Oct. 1922, 61–50–152, FBI-FOIA.

62. Brennan to Burns, 26 Feb. 1923, 61–349–156, FBI-FOIA.

63. "Special Agent Earl E. Titus," biographical sketch, Office of Congressional and Public Affairs, FBI [1984].

64. Military Attache, British Embassy, to Norman Armour, 22 June 1923, 880-L–2, Office of the Counselor, RG59, DS, NA; Armour to Burns, 2 July 1923, 61–50–401, FBI-FOIA.

65. Hill, *Garvey Papers* IV, p. 688n1; Philip S. Foner, *American Socialism and Black Americans: From the Age of Jackson to World War II* (Westport, Conn., 1977), p. 314.

66. Agent Earl E. Titus to Bureau, 16 Aug. 1923, 61–50–410, 16 Aug. 1923, 61–50–411, 16 Aug. 1923, 61–50–412, 16 Aug. 1923, 61–50–413, 15 Aug. 1923, 61–50–414, 21 Aug. 1923, 61–50–416, 21 Aug. 1923, 61–50–417, 24 Aug. 1923, 61–50–418, 23 Aug. 1923, 61–50–419, FBI-FOIA.

67. Titus to Bureau, 28 Aug. 1923, 61–50–420, 27 Aug. 1923, 61–50–422, 24 Aug. 1923, 61–50–423, 30 Aug. 1923, 61–50–425, 31 Aug. 1923, 61–50–426, 4 Sept. 1923, 61–50–427, 4 Sept. 1923, 61–50–428, 7 Sept. 1923, 61–50–429, 10 Sept. 1923, 61–50–432, 13 Sept. 1923, 61–50–433, 13 Sept. 1923, 61–50–434, FBI-FOIA.

68. Titus to Bureau, 18 Sept. 1923, 19 Sept. 1923, 22 Sept. 1923, 24 Sept. 1923 (2 documents), 61–826, 18 Sept. 1923, 61–50–435, 19 Sept. 1923, 61–50–436, 10 Oct. 1923, 61–50–443, FBI-FOIA.

69. Titus to Bureau, 29 Sept. 1923, 1 Oct. 1923, 61–826, 27 Sept. 1923, 61–50–437, 5 Oct. 1923, 61–50–440, 8 Oct. 1923, 61–50–441, 9 Oct. 1923, 61–50–442, 10 Oct. 1923, 61–50–443, FBI-FOIA.

70. Titus to Bureau, 17 Oct. 1923, 61–50–448, FBI-FOIA.

71. Brennan to E. P. Bohner, 19 Oct. 1923, Titus to Bureau, 19 Oct. 1923, 22 Oct. 1923, 23 Oct. 1923 (2 documents), 26 Oct. 1923, 31 Oct. 1923, 3 Nov. 1923, agent John T. Flourney to Bureau, 26 Oct. 1923, agent A. L. Brent to Bureau, 7 Nov. 1923, 61–826, Brent to Bureau, 7 Dec. 1923, 61–50–502, FBI-FOIA; Hill, *Crusader* I, pp. xlii–xliii. Discussion of the Sanhedrin's failure is in Earl Ofari Hutchinson, *Blacks and Reds: Race and Class in Conflict, 1919–1990* (East Lansing, 1995), pp. 16–20.

72. Titus to Bureau, 22 Oct. 1923, 61–50–451, 16 Nov. 1923, 61–50–475, FBI-FOIA.

73. Titus to Bureau, 29 Oct. 1923, 61–50–459, 3 Nov. 1923, 61–50–461, 31 Oct. 1923, 61–50–463, 2 Nov. 1923, 61–50–465, 8 Nov. 1923, 61–50–469, 6 Nov. 1923, 61–50–470, 12 Nov. 1923, 61–50–471, 13 Nov. 1923, 61–50–472, 12 Nov. 1923, 61–50–473, 16 Nov. 1934, 61–50–475, 16 Nov. 1923, 61–50–476, 19 Nov. 1934, 61–50–477, FBI-FOIA.

74. Titus to Bureau, 19 Nov. 1923, 61–50–477, 21 Nov. 1923, 61–50–486, FBI-FOIA.

75. Titus to Bureau, 21 Nov. 1923, 61–50–484, 27 Nov. 1923, 61–50–491, 27 Nov. 1923, 61–50–492, FBI-FOIA.

76. Titus to Bureau, 27 Nov. 1923, 61–50–493, 27 Nov. 1923, 61–50–494, 30 Nov. 1923, 61–50–495, 30 Nov. 1923, 61–50–496, 30 Nov. 1923, 61–50–497, FBI-FOIA.

77. Titus to Bureau, 1 Dec. 1923, 61–50–500, FBI-FOIA.

78. Titus to Bureau, 18 Sept. 1923, 6 Nov. 1923, Burns to Special Agent in Charge L. E. Sawyer, 29 Oct. 1923, Burns to SAC J. J. McLaughlin, 29 Oct. 1923, Burns to SAC E. L. Osborne, 16 Nov. 1923, Burns to SAC Walter C. Foster, 20 Nov. 1923, 61–826, FBI-FOIA.

79. Tucker to Bureau, 18 Aug. 1923, 8 Sept. 1923, 15 Sept. 1923, 22 Sept. 1923, 29 Sept. 1923, 17 Nov. 1923, 1 Dec. 1923, 15 Dec. 1923, 61–826, FBI-FOIA.

80. Titus to Bureau, 19 Dec. 1923, 61–50–505, 18 Jan. 1924, 61–50–507, 28 Mar. 1924, 61–50–508, FBI-FOIA.

81. Hill, *Garvey Papers* I, p. 525.

8. "Ultra Radical Negro Bolsheviki"

1. CW to Chief A. Bruce Bielaski, 13 July 1917, case file 186701–49, Record Group 60, Department of Justice, National Archives [hereafter RG60, DJ, NA], Bielaski to Assistant Attorney General W. E. Fitts, 23 Aug. 1917, 186701–22, RG60, DJ, NA.

2. Bielaski to Fitts, 2 Feb. 1918, 186701–60–1, Bielaski to Special Assistant to the Attorney General John Lord O'Brian, 18 Sept. 1918, 188032–303, RG60, DJ, NA.

3. Agent Henry M. Bowen to Bureau, 11 June, 4 July 1917, "Old German" [hereafter OG] case file 29434, Record Group 65, Investigative Case Files of the Bureau of Investigation, Records of the Federal Bureau of Investigation, 1908–1922, National Archives [hereafter RG65, BI, NA], W. L. Hurley to Assistant Director and Chief Frank Burke, 7 Jan. 1920 [enclosing MID report of 31 Dec. 1919], OG377098, RG65, BI, NA; Irwin M. Marcus, "Benjamin Harrison Fletcher," *Dictionary of American Negro Biography,* Rayford W. Logan and Michael R. Winston, eds. (New York, 1982), pp. 225–26.

4. Woodrow Wilson to Thomas W. Gregory, 3 Apr. 1918, Woodrow Wilson Papers, Library of Congress; agent Robert Evans to Bureau, 30 Jan. 1918, agent J. F. McDevitt to Bureau, 30 Jan., 14 Feb., 15 Feb. 1918 [2 documents], agent P. T. Schmid to Bureau, 11 Feb. 1918, agent Roy C. McHenry to Bureau, 23 Feb. 1918, Special Agent in Charge F. L. Garbarino to Bureau, 27 Mar. 1918, OG29434, RG65, BI, NA.

5. Melvyn Dubofsky, *We Shall Be All: A History of the Industrial Workers of the World* (Chicago, 1969), pp. 324–25; Patrick Renshaw, *The Wobblies: The Story of Syndicalism in the United States* (Garden City, N.Y., 1967), pp. 233–34.

6. Acting Chief (by J. Edgar Hoover) to agent Argabright, 23 Aug. 1919, Division Superintendent A. T. Bagley to Burke, 2 Sept. 1919, Bagley to agent K. H. Stroud, 1 Jan. 1920, Bagley to Div. Supt. Edward J. Brennan, 16 Jan. 1920, Bagley to SAC T. E. Campbell, 24 Jan. 1920, Bagley to Div. Supt. Todd Daniel, 29 Jan., 4 Feb. 1920, OG29434, agent William J. West to Bureau, 7 Oct. 1919, OG36727, agent Edward Portley to Bureau, 14 Oct. 1919, OG377477, RG65, BI, NA.

7. Bagley to Burke, 2 Sept. 1919, OG29434, West to Bureau, 7 Oct. 1919, OG36727, Portley to Bureau, 14 Oct. 1919, OG377477, RG65, BI, NA. For the full story of Jones's life, including his stay in Leavenworth, conversion to the IWW, and brief and tragic career as a Wobbly, see Theodore Kornweibel, Jr., "Race, Radicalism, and Rage: The Life of Joseph J. Jones," *Afro-Americans in New York Life and History* 13 (Jan. 1989), pp. 19–38.

8. Bagley to agent R. B. Spencer, 14 Feb. 1920, OG384231, Bagley to Daniel, 23 Feb. 1920, agent R. D. Clark to Bureau, 19 Apr., 29 Apr. 1920, agent William M. Doyas to Bureau, 30 Apr. 1920, OG29434, special confidential informant S-S to Bureau, 28 Feb. 1920, Act. Div. Supt. T. M. Reddy to Director, 16 Aug. 1920, OG208369, McDevitt to Bureau, 20 Mar. 1920, OG105842, agent C. K. Bigg to Bureau, 7 Apr. 1920, OG186646, "Bulletin of Radical Activities" no. 12, 10 Apr. 1920, "General Intelligence Bulletin" no. 29, 18 Sept. 1920, OG374217, Bagley to Doyas, 12 May 1920, Bagley to agent Billups Harris, 4 June 1920, Bagley to agent H. B. Pierce, 9 June 1920, OG369127, Doyas to Bureau, 22 May 1920, 12 June 1920, OG275205, Bagley to Pierce, 1 July 1920, OG23179, Spencer to Burke, 2 Feb. 1920, "Bureau Section" case file [hereafter BS] 202600–1768-x, agent Louis Loebl to Bureau, 22 Nov. 1920, BS202600–14, agent F. W. Kelly to Bureau, 21 Mar. 1921, BS202600–27–66, 22 Mar. 1921, BS202600–27–67, Div. Supt. Oscar Schmitz to Chief, 11 Feb. 1921, BS4–2–3–14–101, agent Roger B. Skelly to Chief, 4 Apr. 1921, BS202600–24–16x, 11 Apr. 1921, BS202600–24–17, RG65, BI, NA; Cleveland office to Bureau, 1 Nov. 1920, 9–12–738–5, Kelly to Bureau, 28 Mar. 1921, 186701–27, RG60, DJ, NA.

9. Dubofsky, pp. 448, 459; *Messenger,* June 1923, pp. 740–41; SAC Walter C. Foster to Chief William J. Burns, 9 May 1921, BS202600–1617–9, Schmitz to Burns, 4 May 1921, BS4–2–3–14–159, 10 May 1921, BS4–2–3–14–162, 15 June 1921, BS4–2–3–14–192, 16 June 1921, BS4–2–3–14–194, 6 July 1921, BS4–2–3–14–202, 15 Oct. 1921, BS4–2–3–14–215, RG65, BI, NA; Loebl to Bureau, 6 Nov. 1922, case file 61–1225, obtained through the Freedom of Information Act from the Federal Bureau of Investigation.

10. Theodore Kornweibel, Jr., *No Crystal Stair: Black Life and the Messenger, 1917–1928* (Westport, Conn., 1975), chap. 6.

11. Agent J. F. Kropidlowski to Bureau, 29 April 1919, Joseph J. Jones's New York City probation report, 24 Apr. 1919, OG36727, Portley to Bureau, 14 Oct. 1919, OG377477, RG65, BI, NA; Military service records, Company G. 1st Vermont Infantry, muster rolls, Company A, 48th U.S. Volunteer Infantry, sick and wounded reports, Co. A, 48th U.S. Vol. Inf., RG94, Adjutant General's Office, NA; General Court Martial Orders No. 476, Headquarters, Philippine Department, case file 10110–1719–6, Record Group 165, War Department, Military Intelligence Division, National Archives [hereafter RG165, MID, NA]; Military Service Branch, NA, to author, 20 Aug. 1982; Willard B. Gatewood, *Black Americans and the White Man's Burden, 1898–1903* (Urbana, Ill., 1975), pp. 214–17; Jack D. Foner, *Blacks and the Military in American History* (New York, 1974), pp. 89–91; Willard B. Gatewood, *"Smoked Yankees" and the Struggle for Empire: Letters from Negro Soldiers, 1898–1902* (Urbana, 1971), pp. 12–15; William G. Muller, *The Twenty Fourth Infantry Past and Present* (c. 1923; Fort Collins, Colo., 1972), pp. 48–56; David R. Sturtevant, *Popular Uprisings in the Philippines: 1840–1940* (Ithaca, N.Y., 1976), pp. 129–31; Marvin Fletcher, *The Black Soldier and Officer in the United States Army, 1891–1917* (Columbia, Missouri, 1974), pp. 71–72.

12. Kropidlowski to Bureau, 29 Apr. 1919, Acting Chief J. T. Suter, memorandum for files, 2 May 1919, OG36727, BI, NA.

13. Kropidlowski to Bureau, 29 Apr. 1919, West to Bureau, 7 Oct. 1919, OG36727, Portley to Bureau, 14 Oct. 1919, OG377477, RG65, BI, NA.

14. Kropidlowski to Bureau, 29 Apr. 1919, Jones's probation report, 24 Apr. 1919, OG36727, RG65, BI, NA.

15. Special confidential informant D–60 to Bureau, 2 Jan. 1919, OG208369, L. L. Winslow to Acting Chief William E. Allen, 4 Mar. 1919, OG349921, Act. Chief to Div. Supt. W. M. Offley, 3 May 1919, OG364001, RG65, BI, NA.

16. Kropidlowski to Bureau, 29 Apr. 1919, OG36727, RG65, BI, NA.

17. Kropidlowski to Bureau, 29 Apr. 1919, OG36727, RG65, BI, NA.

18. Kropidlowski to Bureau, 29 Apr. 1919, Jones's probation report, 29 Apr. 1919, Offley to Allen, 1 May 1919, Suter, memorandum for files, 2 May 1919, OG36727, RG65, BI, NA.

19. Bagley to Burke, 2 Sept. 1919, OG29434, RG65, BI, NA.

20. West to Bureau, 7 Oct. 1919, OG36727, RG65, BI, NA; *Boston Evening Transcript,* 3 Oct. 1919, p. 27; *Boston Herald,* 4 Oct. 1919, p. 3.

21. West to Bureau, 7 Oct. 1919, agent F. F. Weiss to Bureau, 30 Oct. 1919, agent C. M. Robinton to Bureau, 23 Oct., 24 Oct., 28 Oct. 1919, OG36727, Portley to Bureau, 14 Oct. 1919, OG377477, West to Bureau, 18 Oct. 1919, BS202600–22, RG65, BI, NA.

22. Intelligence Officer, Northeastern Department, to Director, 20 Oct. 1919, 10110–913–304 Inspector H. C. Jessup to Maj. H. A. Strauss, 22 Oct. 1919, 10110–920, Director to Intelligence Officer, U.S. Disciplinary Barracks, Ft. Leavenworth, 28 Oct. 1919, Post Intelligence Officer and Warden, Ft. Leavenworth, to MID, 6 Nov. 1919, Director to Judge Advocate General of the Army, 12 Nov. 1919, 10110–1719, RG165, MID, NA.

23. This law was closely drawn to penalize "the advocacy of killing, destruction of property, or violent revolution," without "legislating against anarchy and opinion." Zechariah Chafee, Jr., *Freedom of Speech* (New York, 1920), pp. 198, 402.

24. Agent R. M. Valkenburgh to Bureau, 7 Nov. 1919, West to Bureau, 5 Dec. 1919, OG161047; agent J. B. Hanrahan to Bureau, 8 Nov. 1919, BS202600–22, RG65, BI, NA; *New York Sun,* 21 Nov. 1919, p. 20. There is no extant record of who posted bail for Jones in Boston; liberal sympathizers of the IWW, or persons wishing to test the anti-anarchy law, may have raised the funds.

25. *New York Evening Telegram,* 20 Nov. 1919, p. 24; *New York Sun,* 21 Nov. 1919, p. 20; *New York News,* 21 Nov. 1919, p. 2; death certificates, Joseph J. Jones and Theresa Arico [Klein], Municipal Archives, New York City.

26. Rear Adm. Roger Welles to Bielaski, ? Sept. 1918, 4 Nov. 1918, OG366145, RG65, BI, NA.

27. W. C. Perry to agent Robert C. Newman, 24 Feb. 1919, E. J. Perry to Newman, 24 Feb. 1919, James E. Zunts to U.S. Attorney Joseph W. Montgomery, 25 Feb. 1919, Sen. F. M. Simmons to Bureau, 28 Feb. 1919, Allen to Daniel, 20 Feb. 1919, 25 Feb. 1919, Allen to U.S. Attorney John L. Neely, 1 Mar. 1919, Allen to Div. Supt. Forrest C. Pendleton, 1 Mar. 1919, Allen to Newman, 3 Mar. 1919, Allen to Simmons, 11 Mar. 1919, Neely to Allen, 25 Feb. 1919, Newman to Allen, 26 Feb. 1919, McDevitt to Bureau, 27 Feb. 1919, agent E. J. Geehan to Bureau, 6 Mar. 1919, Pendleton to Allen, 6 Mar. 1919, Div. Supt. C. E. Breniman to Daniel, 20 Feb. 1919, Aide for Information, 8th Naval District, to Director of Naval Intelligence, 28 Feb. 1919, Act. Dir. Naval Intell. Capt. George W. Williams to Allen, 4 Mar. 1919, OG348540, RG65, BI, NA.

28. Agent H. A. Lewis to Bureau, 8 Apr. 1919, OG49899, agent R. W. Finch to Bureau, 12 May 1919, OG295314, agent J. A. Brann to Bureau, 13 June 1919, agent A. H. Loula to Bureau, 7 July 1919, agent N. H. Castle to Bureau, 14 July 1919, OG258421, Castle to Bureau, 5 July 1919, OG3435429, RG65, BI, NA.

29. Burke (initialed Hoover) to Offley, 23 July 1919, OG370965, Loula to Bureau, 31 July 1919 (3 documents), agent Mills Kitchen to Bureau, 2 Aug. 1919, 7 Aug. 1919, agent J. P. Folsom to Bureau, 4 Aug. 1919 (2 documents), 7 Aug. 1919, OG369914, RG65, BI,

NA; *New York Times,* 28 July 1919, *New York Tribune,* 29 July 1919, both in OG3057, RG65, BI, NA.

30. Burke (initialed Hoover) to acting special agent in charge J. J. McLaughlin, 9 Aug. 1919, McLaughlin to Burke, 12 Aug. 1919, OG375446, Burke (initialed Hoover) to Brennan, 13 Aug. 1919, OG369914, RG65, BI, NA.

31. McDevitt to Bureau, 12 June 1919, 17 June 1919, OG366012, RG65, BI, NA.

32. U.S. Attorney Francis Fisher Kane to Attorney General A. Mitchell Palmer, 16 July 1919, 202600–39–2, RG60, DJ, NA.

33. Agent J. E. Elliott, 2 Aug. 1919, 6 Aug. 1919 (2 documents), 7 Aug. 1919, Doyas to Bureau, 7 Aug. 1919, 27 Aug. 1919, Harris to Bureau, 9 Aug. 1919, agent C. J. Scully to Bureau, 1 Aug. 1919, Hoover to Harris, 13 Aug. 1919, OG186646, RG65, BI, NA.

34. Secret Service agent in charge Thomas B. Foster to Chief H. W. Moran, U.S. Secret Service, 3 Aug. 1919, OG372158, SAC Ralph H. Daughton to Burke, 13 Aug. 1919, OG372661, Doyas to Bureau, 5 Sept. 1919, 6 Sept. 1919 (2 documents), special confidential informant C-C [Arthur U. Craig] to Bureau, 3 Sept. 1919 (6 documents), OG186646, RG65, BI, NA.

35. Brann to Bureau, 13 June 1919, Loula to Bureau, 7 July 1919, Castle to Bureau, 14 July 1919, agent Mortimer J. Davis to Bureau, 12 Aug. 1919, C-C to Bureau, 11 Sept. 1919, 20 Sept. 1919, OG258421, informant Julian W. Bowes to Chief, Secret Service, 30 June 1919, OG208369, Castle to Bureau, 5 July 1919, OG345429, Foster to Moran, 3 Aug. 1919, OG372158, agent F. F. Weiss to Bureau, 30 Aug. 1919, OG342203, agent Jacob Spolansky to Bureau, 29 Aug. 1919, OG369914, agent Harold L. Scott to Burke, 4 Sept. 1919, OG224877, agent Gus T. Jones, 16 Sept. 1919, OG371751, agent W. W. Green to Bureau, 17 Sept. 1919, OG382476, Lewis to Bureau, 18 Sept. 1919, OG49899, Loula to Bureau, 16 Sept. 1919, OG374877, RG65, BI, NA.

36. Hoover to Mr. Fisher, 10 Sept. 1919, Palmer (by Asst. Attny. Gen. Frank K. Nebeker) to U.S. Attorney Francis G. Caffey, 12 Sept. 1919, Caffey to Palmer, 17 Sept. 1919, 11 Oct. 1919, 3 Nov. 1919, 10 Dec. 1919, Palmer (by Asst. Attny. Gen. Robert P. Stewart) to Caffey, 30 Sept. 1919, Hoover to Asst. U.S. Attny. Ben A. Matthews, 3 Dec. 1919, 9–12–725, RG60, DJ, NA; postal solicitor William H. Lamar to Burke, 23 Sept. 1919, OG17011, RG65, BI, NA.

37. Daniel to Burke, 2 Oct. 1919, OG329359 (consolidated with BS198940), Loula to Bureau, 11 Oct. 1919, BS202600–1778-x, agent P. M. Ames to Bureau, 13 Oct. 1919, agent W. W. Wright to Bureau, 19 Oct. 1919, OG295364, Loula to Bureau, 18 Oct. 1919, BS202600–14, agent John A. Dowd to Bureau, 28 Oct. 1919, OG376429, agent O. L. Tinklepaugh to Bureau, 25 Nov. 1919, 8 Dec. 1919, Tinklepaugh to Breniman, 8 Dec. 1919, OG356667, agent A. A. Nelms to Bureau, 30 Nov. 1919, 15 Dec. 1919, OG250518, agent Thomas R. L. Carter to Bureau, 15 Dec. 1919, OG138463, MID weekly reports, 3 Dec. 1919, 10 Dec. 1919, OG377098, RG65, BI, NA; Maj. H. C. Dagley to Intelligence Officer R. B. Woodruff, 15 Dec. 1919, 10218–386, RG165, MID, NA.

38. Philip S. Foner and James S. Allen, eds., *American Communism and Black Americans: A Documentary History, 1919–1929* (Philadelphia, 1987), p. 41; Geehan to Bureau, 14 Oct. 1919, OG373512, RG65, BI, NA.

39. TBF, memorandum for files, 3 Nov. 1919, agent William C. Sausele to Bureau, 23 Oct. 1919, OG373512, RG65, BI, NA.

40. Loebl to Bureau, 8 Oct. 1919, 13 Oct. 1919, OG229848, 16 Oct. 1919, OG373512, RG65, BI, NA.

41. *St. Louis Star,* 11 Oct. 1919, *St. Louis Times,* 11 Oct. 1919, *St. Louis Post Dispatch,* 11 Oct. 1919, 12 Oct. 1919.

42. *St. Louis Daily Globe-Democrat,* 12 Oct. 1919; *St. Louis Post-Dispatch,* 12 Oct. 1919.

43. Loebl to Bureau, 17 Oct., 18 Oct. 1919, OG229849, Burke (by Hoover) to McLaughlin, 20 Oct. 1919, TFB, memorandum for files, 3 Nov. 1919, OG373512, RG65, BI, NA.

44. Loebl to Bureau, 25 Oct. 1919, OG229849, Loebl to Bureau, 27 Oct. 1919, 29 Oct. 1919, Sausele to Bureau, 23 Oct., 28 Oct., 30 Oct., 4 Nov. 1919, OG373512, Davis to Bureau, 23 June 1921, BS202600–2126–19, RG65, BI, NA.

45. Sen. Charles Curtis to Burke, 27 Oct. 1919, OG3057, MID to Burke, MID weekly report, 17 Dec. 1919, OG377098, Morton to Bureau, 8 Dec. 1919, OG373512, RG65, BI, NA.

46. A check of federal district court and United States attorneys records at the National Archives branch (Federal Records Center) at Kansas City, Missouri, found nothing on the Fort-Whiteman case, which indicates that the grand jury failed to bring an indictment; phone calls, Liza Rognas to the author, 3 June, 7 June 1993. This conclusion is supported by a perusal of the *St. Louis Post-Dispatch* and *St. Louis Daily Globe-Democrat* for the end of June; no mention of grand jury action was found, which again supports the conclusion that it was not persuaded there was sufficient evidence to charge Fort-Whiteman and bring him to trial.

47. Hutchinson, *Blacks and Reds,* chap. 2.

48. Hoover to Burke, 16 Jan. 1920, 21 Feb. 1920, Suter to Hoover, 18 Feb. 1920, 186701–14, Hoover to Thomas J. Howe, 1 Mar. 1920, 186701–17, Hoover to Mr. Fisher, 23 Apr. 1920, 186701–19, RG60, DJ, NA.

49. Agent W. W. Grimes to Bureau, 24 Jan. 1920, OG387162, agent L. Herman to Bureau, 26 Feb. 1920, OG383474, unattributed report, 17 Feb. 1920, OG208369, agent Thomas J. Howe to Bureau, 7 Feb. 1920, OG154434, consolidated with BS202600–14, Acting Chief to Pendleton, 8 Apr. 1920, OG382182, RG65, BI, NA.

50. Kornweibel, *No Crystal Stair,* p. 185; Howe to Bureau, 7 Feb. 1920, Loula to Bureau, 27 Mar. 1920, agent R. A. Carter to Bureau, 14 Apr. 1920, BS202600–14, agent H. J. Lenon to Bureau, 5 Apr. 1920, OG215915, Loebl to Bureau, 26 Apr. 1920, OG391665, agent E. C. Shanahan to Bureau, 3 May 1920, OG384234, RG65, BI, NA.

51. Brennan to Burke (attn. Hoover), 3 Aug. 1920, OG154434, consol. with BS202600–14, RG65, BI, NA.

52. Agent George F. Lamb to Burke, 19 Aug. 1920, OG208369, Loebl to Bureau, 12 Sept. 1920, 8 Nov. 1920, BS202600–14, agent A. A. Hopkins to Bureau, 1 Nov. 1920, BS202600–5–13, agent J. G. Tucker to Bureau, 1 Jan. 1921, OG3057, RG65, BI, NA.

53. Special confidential informant P–138 [Herbert S. Boulin] to Bureau, 9–12–725–9, Agent W. L. Buchanan to Bureau, 7 Mar. 1921, Straight Numerical Files 202600–33–182x, RG60, DJ, NA; agent E. M. Blanford to Bureau, 15 Jan. 1921, BS202600–5–22x, SAC Vincent W. Hughes to Bureau, 21 Feb. 1921, BS202600–11–11, P–134 to Bureau, 11 July 1921, BS186701–247–52, McDevitt to Bureau, 15 June 1921, BS202600–1617, 21 Mar. 1921, BS202600–1617-x, Foster to Burns, 16 July 1921, BS202600–1617, 6 Sept. 1921, BS202600–1617–40, SAC Adrian L. Potter to Bureau, 20 June 1921, BS202600–1804–2x, 27 June 1921, BS202600–22–102, Loula to Bureau, 12 Sept. 1921, BS202600–1778–63, RG65, BI, NA.

Epilogue

1. Curt Gentry, *J. Edgar Hoover: The Man and the Secrets* (New York, 1992), pp. 116–23; Richard Gid Powers, *Secrecy and Power: The Life of J. Edgar Hoover* (New York, 1987), pp. 140–43; Athan G. Theoharis and John Stuart Cox, *The Boss: J. Edgar Hoover and the Great American Inquisition* (Philadelphia, 1988), pp. 76–80. The Justice Department, and indeed all cabinet agencies, had very few black employees above the janitorial and subclerical grades; for lists of such employees see correspondence addressed to presidential secretary Charles E. Hard, October 1921 and the spring of 1922, reel 174, case file 93, "Negro Matters," Warren G. Harding Papers, Ohio Historical Society, Columbus. For an example of an appointment of a (white) agent on the basis of political rather than

professional qualifications, see Director William J. Burns to Hard, 28 Oct. 1921, reel 256, Harding Papers.

2. Quoted in Homer Cummings and Carl McFarland, *Federal Justice: Chapters in the History of Justice and the Federal Executive* (New York, 1937), pp. 430–31.

3. *New York Times*, 10 May, 1924; Don Whitehead, *The FBI Story: A Report to the People* (New York, 1956), p. 67.

4. David Williams, "'They Never Stopped Watching Us': FBI Political Surveillance, 1924–1936," *UCLA Historical Journal* 2 (1981), pp. 5–6.

5. Quoted in Williams, p. 5.

6. Gentry, pp. 138–42; Williams, pp. 9–17. A copy of the Bureau's report on the radical press for October and November 1925 is in J. Edgar Hoover to Alexander C. Kirk, 12 Jan. 1926, Office of Counselor central file 861.0–2417, Record Group 59, Department of State, National Archives [hereafter RG59, DS, NA].

7. Natalie Robins, *Alien Ink: The FBI's War on Freedom of Expression* (New York, 1992); Herbert Mitgang, *Dangerous Dossiers: Exposing the Secret War Against America's Greatest Authors* (New York, 1988).

8. Williams, pp. 8–9, 17.

9. Many of these files were obtained by the author from the FBI through the Freedom of Information Act: American Negro Labor Congress, case file 61–5941; Fort-Whiteman, case file 61–4960; Haywood, case file 100–14017; Ford, case file 100–14632; and the NAACP, case file 61–3176. Some of the same documents are also in Department of State case files: Office of Counselor, central files 811.01–565, 811.01–693, Office of Counselor, confidential files of the Chief Special Agent, file 142 (on Fort-Whiteman); Office of Counselor, central file 811.01–548 (on Haywood), RG59, DS, NA. Rogers's case file is Office of Counselor, central file 811.01–598, RG59, DS, NA. Background on the ANLC and individual communists is in Theodore Draper, *American Communism and Soviet Russia* (New York, 1960); Wilson Record, *The Negro and the Communist Party* (c. 1951; New York, 1971); and Mark Naison, *Communists in Harlem during the Depression* (Urbana, 1983). Many events and personalities connected with black communist activities in this period are described in Harry Haywood, *Black Bolshevik: Autobiography of an Afro-American Communist* (Chicago, 1978).

10. Central Decimal File 800.00B-Crouch, Paul, 800.00B-Patterson, W. L., 800.00B-Bradley, William A., 800.00B Sobrian, R. K., 800.00B-Padmore, George, 800.00B-Nurse, Malcolm, RG59, DS. NA. For details on Patterson see William L. Patterson, *The Man Who Cried Genocide: An Autobiography* (New York, 1971).

11. Secretary of State Frank B. Kellogg to Calvin Coolidge, 3 Apr. 1925, Arthur Bliss Lane to Hoover, 18 July 1925, Hoover to Kirk, 11 Jan. 1926, Office of Counselor, confidential files of the Chief Special Agent, file 155, RG59, DS, NA.

12. Background on investigations of blacks during the Thirties and the pre-war months is in Patrick S. Washburn, *A Question of Sedition: The Federal Government's Investigation of the Black Press during World War II* (New York, 1986), pp. 7–9, 30–31. Several World War II–era FBI files (which frequently include army and navy intelligence documents as well) have been obtained by the author through the Freedom of Information Act: for Randolph, "internal security" case files 100–19194, 100–15348, 100–20233, 100–20237, 100–9973, 100–8644, 100–1192, 100–11906, 100–1524, 100–9314, 100–8458, 100–1520, 100–20237, 100–20307; for DuBois, case file 100–99729; for Moore, case file 100–10911; for Domingo, case file 100–58250.

13. David J. Garrow, *The FBI and Martin Luther King, Jr.* (New York, 1983); Kenneth O'Reilly, *Racial Matters: The FBI's Secret File on Black America, 1960–1972* (New York, 1989); Memphis *Commercial Appeal*, 21 Mar. 1993; *San Diego Union-Tribune*, 23 Mar. 1993.

14. Harvey Klehr, John Earl Haynes, and Fridrikh Igorevich Firsov, *The Secret World of*

American Communism (New Haven, 1995), pp. 3–7, 20–25; "One Book on Communism That Should Shake the World," *Wall Street Journal,* 11 Apr. 1995; "Book: American Communist Party Spied," *Washington Post,* 12 Apr. 1995.

15. Interview, A. Philip Randolph, 13 July 1972.

INDEX

THEODORE KORNWEIBEL, Jr., Professor of African American history in the Africana Studies Department at San Diego State University, is author of *No Crystal Stair* and *In Search of the Promised Land*.